Jesus
and the
Reign
of
God

" … and dwelt among us … "

—JOHN 1:14

Jesus
and the
Reign
of
God

C. S. SONG

Fortress Press   Minneapolis

Interior design: ediType
Cover design: Keith McCormick

Library of Congress Cataloging-in-Publication Data

Song, Choan-Seng
    Jesus and the reign of God / C. S. Song.
      p.   cm.
    Includes bibliographical references and index.
    ISBN 0-8006-2671-0 (alk. paper)
    1. Jesus Christ—Person and offices.   2. Kingdom of God.
  I. Title.
  BT202.S65   1993
  231.7'2—dc20   92-30936
                                        CIP

Manufactured in the U.S.A.   AF 1-2671

97   96   95   94   93   1   2   3   4   5   6   7   8   9   10

To the Pacific School of Religion, Berkeley,
a theological community that seeks to tell the Jesus-story
in our cross-cultural world

Contents

PREFACE

Jesus has been an "object" of intense interest for the past two thousand years. One can safely predict that he will continue to engage human minds intensely for the next two thousand years. The fragile moral fiber of our world will not disintegrate as long as the name of Jesus is remembered in the hearts of people, mentioned on their lips, and celebrated in their struggle for a life richer in meaning and more fertile in hope.

Jesus holds the central place in Christian devotion. Theologians do not spare efforts to penetrate the mystery surrounding his person and to decipher the meaning of the signs evoked by his ministry. Artists through the ages, inspired by the beauty and tragedy of the noble figure of Jesus, pour out their genius to recast him in portrait, in plastic image, or in oratorios. And in the world of injustice, oppression, and greed, Jesus is held as a liberator who brings God's justice, love, and freedom to the suffering multitudes.

What, then, did Jesus actually look like? How did he sound? What was his gait like? No camera, no television, no video existed in those days, so one has no choice but to leave such questions to one's own imagination. Still, one wonders why no portrait of him, not even a simple drawing of him, was done by his contemporaries. At least we are not aware of its existence. But would such a portrait or drawing make a difference to our faith in him? Perhaps not. Preoccupation with his person would, in fact, have jeopardized the message he preached. It might have diverted the attention of the writers of the Synoptic Gospels from the challenge of his message to the cult of his person.

The heart of Jesus' message is the reign of God (*basileia tou theou*). In all he said and did he was at pains to make clear that God's reign is primarily concerned with the people victimized by a class-conscious society and a tradition-bound religious establishment. God's reign, in light of what Jesus said and did, inaugurates an era of people. It sets a new stage for their life and history. It marks a fresh beginning of the divine-human drama of salvation. Indeed, the reign of God has become flesh "and dwelt among us," to use the words of John, the author of the Fourth Gospel. It is this extraordinary message of God's reign that we will now set out to explore in this second part of the trilogy of the Jesus-story.

Our study of "Jesus, the Crucified People" in the first book in this series concluded with these words: "The reign of God! This will be the next station of our 'christological' journey in the second volume."[1] The task we set out to accomplish here is to explore the contemporary meaning of God's reign. The word "contemporary" needs to be emphasized. All too often Christians understand the reign of God to be a kingdom, a territory, a domain, in which God will rule with justice and peace and God's elect will live in happiness and enjoy an eternal life. For Jesus God's reign is neither a kingdom nor a territory. Above all, it is not something to be realized only in the future. This will become evident in the course of our discussion.

As we proceed to explore what Jesus meant by the reign of God and what challenges it poses for us today, we may gain a further glimpse of who Jesus is. This shows us a different approach to come to grips with this most extraordinary life the world has ever known. To put it another way, we may be able to know Jesus more deeply as we grapple with how he practiced the reign of God in his life and ministry. This must be so because the reign of God is central to his message and pivotal to his mission.

In emphasizing the relationship between Jesus and his message of God's reign, I am saying that our approach to Jesus has to be historical and theological. Let me explain. Traditional Christian theology has, roughly speaking, approached Jesus in two ways, and it so happens that these two ways have taken exactly the opposite directions. One approach is to begin with an attempt to construct a "biography" of Jesus even though the "biographical" data in the Gospels of the New Testament are meager and of legendary character in some instances. These data can be regarded as historical only in a very qualified sense. In the end it has to be admitted that it is futile to attempt a "life of Jesus" or to write a biography of Jesus. The problem with this approach, among other things, is that having begun with faulty "biographical" information it leads to a faulty construction of christology.

The other approach is what I call the "philosophical" approach. It comes to Jesus with a set of theological presuppositions derived not so much from biblical witnesses as from philosophical norms and concepts of particular traditions and backgrounds. We all know how much traditional Christian theology has been shaped by Greek ideas and concepts, especially by those of Plato and Aristotle. Greek philosophy has so dominated Christian theology that it becomes almost impossible to study theology

---

1. See C. S. Song, *Jesus, the Crucified People* (New York: Crossroad/Meyer-Stone, 1989), 232.

without first studying the history of Greek philosophy. The result, when it comes to Jesus, is that he is detached from his historical roots and molded into a philosophical construct disguised as christology. This is one of the reasons why christological controversy has always revolved around the divine nature and the human nature of Jesus. It ends mostly in the victory of his divine nature over his human nature. This has been considered "orthodox" from the early centuries of the history of Christianity on to the present time. But "orthodox" in relation to what? To the traditions of the church? To the prevailing doctrines? To official teachings? Or to the Bible?

These are important theological questions. Theologians in the Third World, black theologians, and feminist theologians in the West have been grappling with them with encouraging and rewarding results. These contemporary efforts prove extremely important—contemporary in the sense of interactions between the impact of Jesus' message in his day and the impact of his message today. Theology that ceases to be contemporary becomes historically irrelevant. It neither speaks out of the situations of Jesus' day nor speaks into our situations today. Its primary concern is timeless doctrine. Its chief interest consists in transmission of the teachings of the church with as little change as possible. New directions in theology in recent years have successfully challenged the pretension of traditional theology to be the sole guardian of God's truth and the only spokesperson of that truth.

If both the "biographical" approach and the "philosophical" approach fail to help us penetrate the mystery surrounding the life and ministry of Jesus, is there a different approach that may give us deeper insights into it? Our answer is yes. This is an approach that moves from the message of Jesus to his life and ministry, or, if you like, to his person and work. Message communicates. This is self-evident. Needless to say, the message that does not communicate is not message. The question is what it communicates. It, of course, communicates the contents, intention, and purpose of what the communicator envisions, advocates, and affirms. That is why we study the thought of a philosopher, a scientist, an artist, a politician, a theologian. Our study is part of what is called the intellectual history of humankind.

But is this all we have to do? Does the message only disclose its "intellectual" content? Does it only tell us how it has influenced and shaped the intellectual history of humankind? There must be something more in the message. It must also be able to tell us something about the bearer of the message himself or herself. The message reveals not only the thought but the person behind the thought. It discloses something not only external to the bearer of the message but something internal to the bearer of the message. This is not all. Since the bearer of the message is not an isolated individual but someone who lives in a community of relations, the message can also tell us what that community is like in its historical, social-political, and cultural-religious settings. I have always felt that this is not quite understood in theological training. In dogmatic theology, for instance, attention is focused on the contents of the Christian faith as eternal truths with no vital relationships with human situations.

It is immensely important for us to recognize this dynamic relationship between the message and the bearer of the message. In the case of christology this approach provides an invaluable inroad into the mind of Jesus. The deeper we go into the message of Jesus, the closer a glimpse we should be able to gain of Jesus. And this closer glimpse of Jesus in turn enables us to deepen even more our understanding of the message he communicated. This is an ongoing process. There is always something new both about his message and his person. Christology, just as theology, is an open inquiry.

If this is true, we must then ask what is central to the message of Jesus. The heart of Jesus' message, as we will discuss presently, is the reign of God. Is it not, then, necessary to focus our attention on Jesus' message of God's reign? This is what we propose to do in this second volume of our study on Jesus. The reign of God must offer us clues as to why Jesus said and did certain things. Further, it must also enable us to come into closer contact with the person who bears the message of God's reign in words and in action. From his message of God's reign we do not arrive at a biography of Jesus. We know this is a futile enterprise. This does not mean, however, that we are to engage in a philosophical study of Jesus with no reference either to his person or to his situations. The result of our approach to Jesus from his message of God's reign is a historical-theological description of the life and mission of Jesus born two thousand years ago. Furthermore, our approach compels us to grapple with the meaning of Jesus and his message of God's reign for us in the present-day world.

This book is dedicated to the Pacific School of Religion in Berkeley, where I have been Professor of Theology and Asian Cultures since 1985. I am glad to be among the colleagues who, regardless of their fields and disciplines, constantly raise questions such as: What makes us a community of theological learning that is distinct from other theological schools in this country? What should be the vision that guides and inspires us as a graduate school of theology located on the Pacific Rim? Although there are no ready answers to these questions and our search continues, it is good to be in the company of theologians open to new theological developments not anticipated in the Atlantic-oriented theological traditions.

Over the years quite a number of students from the Pacific School of Religion and from the Graduate Theological Union, a consortium of nine theological schools including the Pacific School of Religion, have attended the courses I have offered and wrestled with me over how to do Christian theology in our cross-cultural world. It is my hope that in these classes, in which I shared with them reflections on Jesus and the reign of God, they have learned to be messengers of God's reign in the church today—a church in which the message of God's reign is all too prone to be replaced by the message of spiritual comfort and worldly success.

The first chapters of the book were delivered as the G. Peter Kaye Lectures at Vancouver School of Theology, Vancouver, Canada, on March 4 and 5, 1991, in a series of four lectures entitled "The Way, the Truth, and the Life of Jesus," "The Banquet of God's Reign," "Not a Homogeneous God," and "Epiphanies of God in the *Oikumenē*." I must take this opportunity to thank Dr. Arthur Van Seters, principal of Vancouver School of Theology, and his colleagues for extending to me the honor of occupying this prestigious lectureship. For the warm hospitality they showed me and for the lively exchanges with pastors, faculty, and students in the lecture hall and at small seminars I am very grateful.

It is my great pleasure once again to extend my warm thanks to John Eagleson, who undertook the editing of my manuscript. He has been my editor for almost all my books published in this country. He is ever so patient with me whose mother tongue is not English. To Michael West, senior editor of Fortress Press, and to Lois Torvik I also owe many thanks for the final appearance of this book. Michael West's support and encouragement throughout lightened the pressures under which I had to work toward publication.

And to my family who continue to travel with me on my theological journey I am eternally grateful. It is a journey of worry and joy, tension and hope, toward the reign of God to be fulfilled not in human time but in God's time. Even to catch some fleeting glimpses of that reign in our life and world here and now gives me more than encouragement to continue my journey. It gives me faith in the future of God—a future whose puzzling reflections we can see only in a mirror (1 Cor. 13:12). And so the journey goes on . . .

ACKNOWLEDGMENTS

The excerpt from *Through Peasant Eyes: More Lukan Parables, Their Culture and Style* by Kenneth Bailey (Grand Rapids, MI: William B. Eerdmans Publishing Co., 1980) is used by permission of the publisher.

"The People's Creed" by Canaan Banana is from *The Gospel According to the Ghetto* (Geneva: World Council of Churches, 1974), and is used by permission of WCC Publications, Box 2100, CH-1211 Geneva 2, Switzerland.

"Stones" by Aruna Gnanadason is from *Stree: An Occasional Newsletter*, No. 18, August 1988 (Madras: All India Council of Christian Women, a unit of the National Council of Churches in India, 1988), and is used by permission of Aruna Gnanadason.

The story by Hsu T'in is from *Short Stories*, ed. Ch'i and Lin Ye Mu (Hong Kong: Ta Tao Book Co., 1981).

The poem by Harvey L. Parkins is from *Root for Vision: Reflections on the Gospel and the Churches, Task in Re-opening the De-peopled* (Singapore: Christian Conference of Asia, 1985), and is used by permission of Christian Conference of Asia.

The excerpt from *The Bhagavad Gita*, tr. Juan Mascaró (Penguin Classics, 1962), copyright © 1962 Juan Mascaró, is used by permission of Penguin Books, Ltd.

The poem "My Mother's Name Is Worry" is reprinted from *My Mother's Name Is Worry: A Preliminary Report of the Study on Poor Women in Korea* (Seoul: Christian Institute for the Study of Justice and Development, 1983).

The poem by Arun Kamble, tr. Cauri Deshpaude, is from *No Place in the Inn: Voices of Minority Peoples of Asia* (Christian Conference of Asia – Urban Rural Mission, 1979), and is used by permission of Christian Conference of Asia.

The poem by Sherina Niles is from *Urban Rural Action*, No. 5, September 1985 (Christian Conference of Asia – Urban Rural Mission News & Notes, 1985), and is used by permission of Christian Conference of Asia.

The excerpt from *Mao's Revolution and the Chinese Political Culture* by Richard H. Solomon, copyright © 1971 Center for Chinese Studies, University of Michigan, is used by permission of the University of California Press.

The poem by Max Ediger is from *Life for the People: Peace with Justice in Asia,* Vol. 1, No. 2, March–June 1988 (Hong Kong: Christian Conference of Asia – International Affairs, 1988), and is used by permission of Christian Conference of Asia.

The memorial by Ku Ch'en and Yang Lien is from *The Nineties,* Special Issue, June 16, 1989.

The poems "For Nelia" and "My Daughters" are from *Pintig: Poems and Letters from Philippine Prisoners* (Hong Kong: Research Centre for Philippine Concerns, 1979).

The excerpt from *On the Trial of Jesus* by Paul Winter (Berlin: Walter de Gruyter & Co., 1961) is used by permission of the publisher.

The excerpt from *Theology in a New Key: Responding to Liberation Themes* by Robert McAfee Brown, copyright © 1978 The Westminster Press, is used by permission of Westminster/John Knox Press.

The poem by Ranjani Mendis is from *Life for the People: Ecumenical Peace Program in Asia,* Vol. 1, No. 3, September–December 1988 (Hong Kong: Christian Conference of Asia – International Affairs, 1988), and is used by permission of Christian Conference of Asia.

The poem by Ranjini Rebera is from *In God's Image,* October 19–25, 1985 (Singapore: Christian Conference of Asia, 1985), and is used by permission of Christian Conference of Asia.

The story by Mariakutty Thoman is from *Stree: An Occasional Newsletter,* No. 14, March 1984 (Madras: All India Council of Christian Women, a unit of the National Council of Churches in India, 1984), and is used by permission of Aruna Gnanadason.

The passage by Cho Hai is from *Life for the People: Peace with Justice in Asia,* Vol. 1, No. 3, September–December 1988 (Hong Kong: Christian Conference of Asia – International Affairs, 1988), and is used by permission of Christian Conference of Asia.

The poem from *Life for the People: Peace with Justice in Asia,* Vol. 1, No. 3, September–December 1988 (Hong Kong: Christian Conference of Asia – International Affairs, 1988), is used by permission of Christian Conference of Asia.

The prayer by Jeffrey Abayasekera is from *Tradition and Innovation: A Search for a Relevant Ecclesiology in Asia* (Christian Conference of Asia – Commission on Theological Concerns, 1983), and is used by permission of Christian Conference of Asia.

The cover art, "Christ and St. John from the Last Supper," is from *The Faces of Jesus* by Frederick Buechner with photographs by Lee Boltin, published by Harper & Row, copyright © 1989, and is used by permission of Stearn Publishers, Ltd., New York.

Part I

VISION

Things begin with visions. We are familiar with those stirring words of Joel the prophet in ancient Israel: "Then afterward I will pour out my spirit on all flesh; your sons and daughters shall prophesy, your old people shall dream dreams, and your people shall see visions" (Joel 2:28, NRSV). Prophecy kept the religious conscience of the people alive, dreams enabled them to face the hardships of life with hope, and visions empowered them to look to the future in the midst of ruins and captivity.

Having inherited this tradition of his people, Jesus was a prophet, dreamer, and visionary par excellence in his time. No one can dispute the fact that Jesus was a prophet. His close association with John the Baptist must have enhanced his credibility as a prophet sent by God. The appearance of John the Baptist on the scene must have caused a great stir. The Gospel writers have left us a vivid account of the great impact John's fiery preaching on repentance made on the people. "When he saw many of the Pharisees and Sadducees coming for baptism," Matthew tells us, "he said to them: 'Viper's brood! Who warned you to escape from the wrath that is to come? Prove your repentance by the fruit you bear'" (Matt. 3:7-8; par. Luke 3:7-8). Do we not hear echoes of this in what Jesus said to his religious opponents: "Snakes! Viper's brood! How can you escape being condemned to hell?" (Matt. 23:33)? Jesus was the prophet. He made the voice of God resound once again in the Jewish community.

Jesus was also a dreamer. To be able to dream is a capacity to transcend the conditions of life and to overcome the limitations of history. It liberates human beings from enslavement to the status quo and empowers them to strive for something different and new. In one of his last discourses Jesus, according to John's Gospel, said to his disciples: "In the world you face persecution. But take courage! I have conquered the world" (16:33). For a true dreamer, unlike daydreamers, the world of trouble is real, but the power not to succumb to it and even to change it is also real. To be able to dream about a world of peace within the world of conflicts and to dedicate one's life to its realization is one of the forces that change the course of

1

human history. Without that capacity to dream, how could Jesus have faced the suffering of the cross?

And Jesus was a visionary. A vision has to be something that grows out of the awareness of the incomplete nature of life and history. Life is not the sum-total of our everyday experiences. And history is not just the accumulation of what happened in the past. There is always something yet to come, something unknown that beckons us to move forward, something that challenges us to envision a future from within the present. This something is what we call "vision." It is the recognition of the fact that life and history are not self-explanatory. It is also an anticipation of a full disclosure of their meaning in the days to come. A vision such as this enables us to live in the tension between the present and the future, to face the hard realities of the world, and to turn anxiety and despair into the creative energy that defies the power of decay and gives birth to a new life. Without vision such as this, how can there be creative arts, social transformations, or religious reforms?

Jesus is no exception. The vision that inspired him to say what he said and compelled him to do what he did was the reign of God. This vision of God's reign is the *hermeneutical* principle of the life and ministry of Jesus. It is the *ethical* standard of his lifeview and worldview. It is the *theological* foundation of his relation to God and to his fellow human beings. And it is the *eschatological* vantage-point from which he relates the present time and the end of time. In short, the vision of God's reign is like a magnifying lens that gives us an enlarged picture of life and the world as Jesus sees them and of life and the world as we must also see them. If we remove that vision from the pages of the Gospels, then all we see is a man engaged in a futile attempt at social and religious reform. Take that vision from him, then we are left with a helpless victim of the caprice of historical forces. And with that vision suppressed, Jesus is just one of many persons who live and die in their illusion. As to ourselves, we lose the basis, the standard, and the vantage-point to come to grips with the ministry of Jesus, the life behind that ministry, and the person who lived that life and was engaged in that ministry.

The reign of God was Jesus' vision. It is a vision that has inspired countless men and women after him to live not just for themselves, but for their community and for God. From the standpoint of the Christian faith, that vision is the heart of life, both individual and communal. That vision is also the power that moves people, people wronged and oppressed, to challenge the history imposed on them and to create a history in which they earn the right to decide their future and destiny. What is, then, the content of Jesus' vision of God's reign? What is it like? Who are entitled to it? These are some of the questions that engage us here.

CHAPTER 1

A GREAT BANQUET

A man was giving a big dinner party and had sent out many invitations. At dinnertime he sent his servant to tell his guests, "Come please, everything is now ready." One after another they all sent excuses. The first said, "I have bought a piece of land, and I must go and inspect; please accept my apologies." The second said, "I have bought five yoke of oxen, and I am on my way to try them out; please accept my apologies." The next said, "I cannot come; I have just got married." When the servant came back he reported this to his master. The master of the house was furious and said to him, "Go out quickly into the streets and alleys of the town, and bring in the poor, the crippled, the blind, and the lame." When the servant informed him that his order had been carried out and there was still room, his master replied, "Go out on the highways and along the hedgerows and make them come in: I want my house full. I tell you not one of those who were invited shall taste my banquet." (Luke 14:16-24)

The Time Has Come!

It must have been a moving sight—the sight of Jesus surrounded by crowds of people. It must have been an awe-inspiring experience, too. It did not take long for Jesus to realize that he had become a center of attraction to the people, especially those persons in need—persons with physical needs and persons with spiritual needs. There was, for example, that unforgettable scene in the town of Capernaum in Galilee. Men, women, and children in great numbers came to him in the house where he was staying. It became so crowded that "it is impossible even for water to seep through" (*schwei shieh pu thong*), as the Chinese would say. Most of them must have been simple folks—village folks and town folks who eked out their living by the sweat of their brow. As they were hanging onto the words Jesus was saying to them, there was a sudden commotion. Four men carrying a paralyzed man, unable to get near Jesus because of the crowd, "made an opening in the roof over the place where Jesus was, and when they had broken through they lowered the bed on which the paralysed man was lying" (Mark 2:1-5; pars. Matt. 9:1-3; Luke 5:17-20). Deeply moved by their faith, Jesus healed him.

The life of Jesus was to be a life with the crowds. His ministry was to be a ministry among the multitudes. Life with the crowds is an intense life. And ministry among the masses of people has no end. To be with people must have overwhelmed Jesus as well as inspired him. To minister to them must have both invigorated him and exhausted him. From time to time he sought a place where he could be alone (Mark 6:32; par. Matt. 14:13) and pray (Mark 6:46; par. Matt. 14:23). But it was his communion with people that must have given him the vision of God's reign. It was a communion of despair and hope, suffering and healing. Above all, it was a communion in which God was experienced as the God of saving love.

How that vision of God's reign unfolded in the life and ministry of Jesus! According to the Gospel of Mark, that vision marked the beginning of his public ministry. "The time has arrived," he declared, "the reign of God is upon you. Repent, and believe the gospel" (1:14-15; par. Matt. 4:17). The words are few but the note is urgent. The speech is short, but the tone is resolute. The sermon is rhythmed with staccatos, and the invitation offered is compelling. In words and in deeds Jesus lived that vision with people and among people throughout his ministry. He was to die on account of that vision. But that vision did not remain in the tomb. It rose with him from the dead and continues to be the source of faith, love, and hope for Christians. And one also perceives in that vision a reflection of visions of many a woman and man in every age and in all parts of the world struggling to live a life of peace and bliss. His deep communion with God and with people enabled him to announce the exciting news of the presence of God's reign here and now. It was a news that was to make a radical difference to the life of people.

The reign of God, then, "sums up the whole message of Jesus."[1] It is more than that. All Jesus said and did has to do with the reign of God. "Jesus appeared as one who proclaimed the Kingdom," it is further pointed out. "All else in his message and ministry serves a function in relation to that proclamation and derives meaning from it."[2] This "all else" must mean literally all else, including Jesus' own person. Jesus did a lot of healing. But

---

1. Günther Bornkamm, *Jesus of Nazareth*, trans. Irene and Fraser McLuskey with James M. Robinson (London: Hodder & Stoughton, 1960), 64.
2. Norman Perrin, *Rediscovering the Teaching of Jesus* (New York: Harper & Row, Publishers, 1967), 54.

he was not a physician, nor was he a medicine man. How is one, then, to understand the meaning of his healing activity? It has to be understood in relation to the healing power of God's reign. This must be how Jesus himself understood it as he testified in that "Beelzebub controversy" (Luke 11:14-23; par. Matt. 12:22-30). Hearing the dumb speak and witnessing the blind see in the presence of Jesus, people were truly astonished. But his opponents were not amused. They contended that Jesus was in league with devils to defeat devils. "It is by Beelzebub prince of demons," they charged, "that he drives the demons out." The charge was entirely groundless. This was Jesus' answer: "If it is by the finger of God ["Spirit of God" in Matthew] that I drive out the demons, then be sure the reign of God has already come upon you." Healing is a sign that God's reign is a present reality.

Jesus was also engaged in heated controversies with the religious leaders of his time. Essentially he was not a polemical person. Why, then, did he not avoid confrontation with them? The reason has got to be found in the stance he took with regard to God's reign. What is at stake is not his personal likes or dislikes but the reign of God. In his view the religious authorities have completely misrepresented God's reign to people. They have made the reign of God into the traditions they represent, the teachings they have accumulated, the privileges and interests with which they surround themselves. This contradicts totally what Jesus means by the reign of God. What he has encountered in the religion of his day is not the reign of God but the reign of the religious hierarchy, not the power of God, but the power of religious leaders, not the saving love of God but the fear with which people are taught to view God. Jesus had no alternative but to engage his opponents in argument about what he deemed the reign of God must be.

Further, Jesus could have been persuaded to take up the political cause of his nation and lead his people in one more attempt at revolt against Roman rule. But he rejected political messianism. What is the ground of his rejection? It must have been closely related to what he believed to be God's reign. Since the reign of God for him does not signify a kingdom, it is not to be realized in military confrontation with the Roman empire. Since it is not defined in terms of a territory, it is not to be achieved through restoration of a lost principality. And since it is not identified with a political entity, it is not to be realized in an effort to reestablish a nation-state. Jesus has no choice but to reject the temptation to turn the reign of God into an ideology of political struggle for national independence. His famous but somewhat cryptic reply to the question about paying taxes to the Roman emperor, "Render to Caesar the things that are Caesar's, and to God the things that are God's" (Mark

12:17, RSV), can perhaps be understood in light of his message of God's reign.

There is, moreover, that death on the cross. He could have avoided falling victim to it, but he seemed to walk right into it. Why? One should be able to derive the meaning of his death from his ministry of God's reign. The people who he said belong to God's reign are religious outcasts. The men and women he encouraged and empowered to regain their human dignity are socially and politically marginalized. Jesus cannot be so naive not to know that these people, when mobilized, could constitute a religious and political force against the ruling religious and political powers. Nor can he be so innocent not to realize that his opponents would not view his ministry of God's reign as a threat to their authority and privileges. To avoid the cross he would have to modify his message of God's reign. To shun it he would have to align himself not with the poor and the oppressed but with the rich and the powerful. In other words, he would have to be other than what he claims to be and what he professes to do. He would have to betray himself as the reign of God, betray men and women who belong to the reign of God, and thus betray the very reign of God.

And there is mystery surrounding the person of Jesus. Among his contemporaries John the Baptist should have known who he must be. As soon as he spotted Jesus among the people who had come out to him to be baptized in the river Jordan, he was reported to have exclaimed: "Behold, the Lamb of God, who takes away the sin of the world!" (John 1:29, RSV). But even this John grew uncertain about who Jesus was as time went by. His doubt and uncertainty must have reached its acutest when he was arrested and imprisoned by Herod Antipas. In his lonely prison cell uncertain about his own fate, the image of that man from Nazareth he had baptized must have come back to haunt him. Who is he after all? Is he that coming one? Or are we to wait for someone else?[3] It was precisely these questions that he sent his disciples to ask Jesus.

This is a serious "christological" question. It is serious because it was asked by someone in prison, someone who might be facing death. It is not an academic question asked in the comfort of a book-lined study. It is not a polemical question posed by an opponent in the heat of a debate. Nor is it a question of a skeptic who has nothing to lose whether the person in question is "the Coming One" or not. John had staked his mission on that man. This is how his namesake, the author of the Fourth Gospel, understands it. Did he not say, according to the latter's report, when that man came to him for baptism: "After me there comes a man who ranks ahead

---

3. Floyd V. Filson, *A Commentary on the Gospel according to St. Matthew*, Harper's New Testament Commentaries (New York: Harper & Brothers, Publishers, 1960), 136.

of me; before I was born, he already was. I did not know who he was; but the reason why I came, baptizing in water, was that he might be revealed to Israel" (John 1:30-31)? This is a very high christology indeed, perhaps reflecting more the theology of the early church than that of John the Baptist himself. But high christology or not, John must have decided that he wanted a direct answer from that man himself. Consequently, he sent his disciples to Jesus with the question that must have troubled him for some time (Matt. 11:2-3; par. Luke 7:18-20).

Jesus must have realized that this was a serious question that required a serious answer. He must have perceived that it was a question from the heart that must be reciprocated with an answer from the heart. The question posed to him must be answered, not with a theological argument, not with a metaphysical theory, not with an ontological proof, *but* with witness, with testimony, with acts of faith. This is the answer Jesus sent back to John: "The blind recover their sight, the lame walk, lepers are made clean, the deaf hear, the dead are raised to life, the poor are brought good news—and blessed are those who do not find me an obstacle to faith" (Matt. 11:5-6; par. Luke 7:22-23). One cannot but wonder how John reacted to Jesus' answer. Unfortunately, we are not told. We may surmise that John understood what Jesus meant and went to his death certain that he had done his part in preparing for the coming of God's reign.

Jesus alluded to God's reign in his answer to John. The sick are healed and the physically disabled have their health restored. Above all, "the poor are brought good news." This must have made a deep impression on John, for "the emphasis on the greatest blessing brought by Jesus, the proclamation of joy to the poor is unprecedented."[4] The poor are to loom very large in Jesus' message of God's reign. John could not have missed the point. Did he not himself earlier reply to the people who asked him what they were to do: "Whoever has two shirts must share with anyone who has none, and whoever has food must do the same"(Luke 3:10)? Without knowing it, John was also preaching the reign of God. And it must have dawned on him that to know Jesus as the coming one, it is necessary first to know what Jesus meant by the reign of God.

From God's reign to Jesus. From the witness of God's reign to the witness of Jesus. From the experience of God's reign to the experience of Jesus. And from what God's reign is to who Jesus is. The reign of God is the key. Jesus without it is a disincarnated person—a person without a body. Jesus separated from it is a theological construct that does not correspond to the reality. Jesus only loosely connected with it is a phantom that

---

4. Eduard Schweizer, *The Good News according to Matthew*, trans. David E. Green (Atlanta: John Knox Press, 1975), 256.

preoccupies the doctrinal interest of the religious authorities but haunts the hearts of people in the street. Jesus without the reign of God is an incomplete Jesus. Jesus whose life and mission are not shaped by it is not the way, the truth, and the life (John 14:6), to use that profound expression in John's Gospel. Jesus is the way because his is the way of God's reign. Jesus is the truth because his is the truth revealed by it. Jesus is the life because his is the life empowered by it.

The Way of Jesus

The way of Jesus is closely related to the way of God's reign. The former is derived from the latter. Jesus had no way independent from that of God's reign. He came to announce it in a manner reminiscent of the prophets of ancient Israel but remarkably different from the religious leaders of his day. He identified it with the people—men, women, and children who were marginalized from society and from the religious community because they were poor, because they were engaged in professions shunned by those in good standing with the religious community, or because they were simply Gentiles who had no share in the religious privileges enjoyed only by the insiders of the religious tradition. Without hesitation Jesus declared that he belonged to them because the reign of God belonged to them. He did not hesitate to be associated with them because God's reign was in the midst of them.

The way of Jesus derived from the way of God's reign tells us many things. First and foremost, it tells us who God is and how God carries out God's saving activity in the world. The God illuminated by Jesus' way with people is the God who does not discriminate against them on account of creed, color, or sex. God is a classless God, too. And this is a God who has no patience with those believers who wish to turn God into a national God and make God stand for their national cause. This was the way of Christians and Christian churches in the West in the heyday of Western domination of the world. Their God was not able to rise above the cultural and political limits consciously or unconsciously imposed by them. But this is not the way of Jesus simply because it is not the way of God's reign.

The way of Jesus that manifests the way of God's reign points us to the God of the nations and peoples. It opens our eyes to how the Spirit of that God is at work in creation and in human community. It shows us what a Christian church must be in order to give witness to the presence of God's reign in the world. It reveals the fact that it has no mission other than the mission of God's reign. The Christian church does not define its relation to the world independently. That relation must be shaped by the relation of God's reign to the world. In short, what church is and what it must do is derived from the way of Jesus, which in turn is derived from God's reign. There is no need for the Christian church to spend its time and energy trying to explain itself to the world. God's reign explains what it must be. The Christian church authenticates itself when it allows itself to be shaped by the demands of God's reign in its life, mission, and structure. "Set your mind on God's reign and God's justice before everything else," says Jesus, "and all the rest will come to you as well" (Matt. 6:33). This applies not only to individual men and women who follow Jesus, but also to the Christian church.

The way of Jesus informed by the way of God's reign opens God's saving love to the people beyond the immediate confine of his religious tradition. It challenges the religion that sets conditions and limits to the accessibility of that love. It demolishes the barriers that exclude the majority of people in the world solely on the ground of their religious allegiance. It envisions a human community in which the practice of love is more important than adherence to creeds and observation of religious laws. And it inspires people to live not just for oneself but for one's neighbor. It is, therefore, a way of suffering. The reign of God preached and practiced by Jesus has little to do with the power and glory that have come to be closely associated with the traditional Christian belief in "the kingdom of God." What is expressed in such language of the Christian church has misled Christians to identify the Christian church with the power and glory of a secular state. This is not how Jesus understood God's reign to be. This must be one of the reasons why he was not able to be a part of the national movement to restore the Davidic kingdom. To the disciples seeking power and glory in such a "kingdom" Jesus had to say: "Can you drink the cup that I drink, or be baptized with the baptism I am baptized with?" (Mark 10:35-45; pars. Matt. 20:20-28; Luke 22:24-27). The disciples concerned did not fully comprehend Jesus' question. Obsessed with power and glory, they did not, and could not, understand what Jesus meant by the cup he had to drink and the baptism with which he had to be baptized. It did not occur to them that the cup Jesus had to drink is the cup of suffering and the baptism with which he had to be baptized is the baptism of the cross.

The way of Jesus has, then, to be the way of the cross. It is not because Jesus sought martyrdom. Nor is it because the cross is a means of self-glorification. Quite to the contrary. The reign of God Jesus preached and what it implied politically and religiously would pose such a challenge to the religious and political authorities that the latter would do whatever was in their power to counteract it with violent force. The cross is almost an inevitable outcome of the confrontation of God's reign with the kingdoms of this world. How, then, can the way of Jesus not be the way of the cross? But it is this way of the cross that proves to be the way of the resurrection.

This must be what Jesus meant when he said: "Those who find their life will lose it, and those who lose their life for my sake will find it" (Matt. 10:39, NRSV; par. Luke 14:33). Jesus could have said "for the sake of God's reign" instead of "for my sake." And probably this is what he wanted to say. We already quoted him saying: "Set your mind on God's reign and God's justice before everything else, and all the rest will come to you as well." These words disclose how God's reign is utmost in the life and ministry of Jesus. His way cannot but be the way of God's reign.

The Truth of Jesus

The truth of Jesus that has its origin in the truth of God's reign gives us glimpses into the truth of God. The truth of God! We can speak of it only in a whisper, for we know so little about it. Here our human limitations are completely exposed. Does not that story in Genesis 3—the story of human beings who attempt to know everything (good and evil) between heaven and earth, even everything about God—testify to the fact of how limited we are? Traditionally, the Christian church and its theology have derived only a negative meaning from the story. The desire to know everything is said to be the root of human sin. It is the cause of all evil. But is this all the story tells us? Is there not something else it seeks to disclose to us? The story seems also to tell us that human beings are by nature finite and limited not only in their span of life but also in their scope of knowledge. In other words, the story tells us what we are. It is a theological anthropology in a story form. One is reminded of Paul, that powerful theologian, who, at the end of his most profound and ingenious discourse on how God works in creation and what God wills for Israel and the Gentiles, had to confess and exclaim: "O the depth of the riches and wisdom and knowledge of God! How unsearchable are God's judgments and how inscrutable God's ways! For who has known the mind of the Lord, or who has been the Lord's counselor?" (Rom. 11:33-34, RSV).

This is what makes Paul a "great" theologian. A "great" theologian knows he or she knows so little of God's truth. On the contrary, a "little" theologian professes to know much about it. A "great" theologian confesses his or her ignorance when it comes to the truth of God, but a "little" theologian is confident in his or her knowledge of it. In the history of the Christian church, and particularly in the history of its missions, there have been too many "little" theologians who know too much and too few "great" theologians who confess ignorance. Sadly, in the "mission field" it has often been those "little" theologians who have defined the contents of Christian orthodoxy and exercised the power to interpret the will of God in a self-confident way.

Especially in matters related to salvation, the difference between "little" theologians and "great" theologians has become very evident. There are, on the one hand, those Christian believers who are deadly certain who is saved and who is not saved. There are, on the other, those who would agree with Paul when he wrote to the Christians in Corinth: "I do not spare my body, but bring it under strict control, for fear that after preaching to others I should find myself disqualified" (1 Cor. 9:27). What Paul says here has the danger of developing into morbid asceticism. Still, it is the reminder that in God's salvation we are confronted with the mind of God, which is beyond our reasoning, judgment, or speculation. We must quote that great theologian Paul once again. After that brilliant ode to love, unsurpassed in beauty and profundity, Paul goes on to say: "At present we see only puzzling reflections in a mirror, but one day we shall see face to face. My knowledge now is partial; then it shall be whole, like God's knowledge of me" (1 Cor. 13:12). This puzzling knowledge of God, this partial understanding of God's truth—how are we to penetrate it? We penetrate it from the truth of God's reign. Is this not why Jesus takes so much pain to tell story after story, parable after parable, of what God's reign is like? For Jesus there is no other truth than the truth of God's reign. To know what Jesus means by truth, we must know what he means by the reign of God.

The fact is that the truth of Jesus does not stand by itself. It is not a norm according to which other concepts are judged. It must be related to something else so that what it stands for may become evident. What is, then, the truth with which Jesus so closely associated himself? It is, first of all, freedom because God's reign means freedom. John's Gospel has Jesus say to the Jews: "You will know the truth, and the truth will set you free" (John 8:32). Truth here is not propositions to be accepted and theories to be followed. It is not universal norms already established to be applied to each and every situation. It is not standards and measures of all things regardless of their particular situations. It is not something fixed once for all, invariable for all times. Truth, to be truth, is time-conditioned and space-oriented. That is to say, time-space factors contribute to bringing truth into light, test it, validate it, or invalidate it. Truth, in essence, is contextual. It does not exist on its own. It *is not* all by itself. It *exists* and *is* in particular situations and contexts. And it gets uncovered and identified as these situations and contexts interact one with the other.

This must be part of what is meant by truth setting us free. Truth without freedom is untruth, because it denies human beings one of the basic conditions to be human beings. The religious truth that deprives believers of their freedom to believe in God without fear of persecution is a heresy. The political truth that denies people the freedom of conscience is a lie. What Jesus did in his proclamation of God's reign is to restore freedom to the people so that they can be true before God and in human community in what they say and do. Jesus can declare that he *is* the truth because he *has* the complete freedom that comes with the reign of God. The truth that is Jesus is the freedom from the religious and political truths that deprive people of freedom. And the truth that is Jesus is the freedom for the reign of God that belongs not to the rich and the powerful but to the poor and the dispossessed. To declare forgiveness, then, to the woman caught in adultery and condemned by the Law of Moses (John 8:2-11) is truth. To announce salvation to the tax-gatherer given up for lost by the religious authorities (Luke 19:1-10) is truth. And to intimate that anything they did for one of Jesus' brothers and sisters, however humble, they did for him although they had no knowledge of him (Matt. 25:31-46) is truth. Jesus is right. Truth, if it be truth, should set us free for the disinherited and the oppressed. At the same time, for truth to be truth it must be set free from misuse by those in power.

The truth of Jesus is further related to the justice the reign of God represents. God's justice is not justice for the powerful but for the powerless. It is not justice for the rich but for the poor. It is not the justice that takes the inequality of social status and economic situation as the starting point of competition and measures one's success and failure from that point. It is the justice that starts not with our unequal stations in life but with the equality with which God deals with us. The truth that does not conform to such justice is untruth. It is exploitation. It is the survival of the fittest. It is the oppression of the unfortunate. The truth that ignores the tragic situations of other people, that enhances the miseries of some men and women, that creates discriminations in human community is not the truth of God's reign. It is therefore not the truth of Jesus. Here justice tells us what truth must be. This is a deeper truth, the truth that touches the foundation of human existence and serves the relations between God and humanity.

It may be that this is the point Jesus tries to emphasize in his parable of the laborers in the vineyard (Matt. 20:1-16). Surely those laborers who had worked longer hours had the truth when they complained that they did not receive more wages than those who had worked less hours. They even had the justice prescribed by the conventional truth of the labor market. But there is another kind of justice, Jesus seems to be saying—justice not defined by the conventional truth but by the plight and needs of particular people, women and men against whom discrimination is committed and injustice is done. It is this justice that must redefine the truth about the rules of the labor market and determine the payment of daily wages. We have to remember that Jesus told the parable to drive home to people what the reign of God is like. It is, Jesus is saying, the justice envisioned by the reign of God that tells us what truth must be. And Jesus is this truth shaped by the justice that is to prevail in God's reign.

There is another crucial factor without which truth is not truth. That factor is love. There is such a thing as truth without love. But then it is not truth. It is an imposition of one's will on others. It is a coercion on others to think and do as one does. It is a command that cannot be disobeyed with impunity. This kind of "truth" prevails in a feudal society, in a totalitarian nation, in a hierarchical religious community. In a situation such as this, it is power, and not love, that decides what is true or untrue. What determines truth is, in a curious irony, not truth itself, but falsehood disguised as truth. Truth is robbed of its meaning. It is emptied of content to make room for the so-called truth fabricated by those in power to prostitute the human integrity of men and women under their control. Such truth is an insult to humanity, adulteration of human virtues, and corruption of the bond of love and compassion without which human relationships are in shambles.

When Jesus said that he is the truth, he had nothing to do with that kind of truth. His truth comes from the love that makes up the heart of God's reign. It is the truth that "God loved the world so much that God gave God's only Son" (John 3:16). Jesus is that love of God. He is that self-giving love of God. This truth of Jesus rooted in God's self-giving love contradicts our truth distorted and corrupted by our self-love. Paul grasped this self-giving love that makes truth what it must be when he said that among faith, hope, and love, "the greatest of the three is love" (1 Cor. 13:13). It is this truth made noble and sublime by love, the greatest among faith, hope, and love, that we witness on the cross.

Abundant Life

Jesus as the way and the truth is also the life. Here again we must stress that the life that is Jesus is the life empowered by the reign of God. Life is a preoccupation of religion. What does it mean? What is it for? Is it only transitory? Or is it eternal? Is it merely a biological process? How is life related to God? How is it related to nature? How does it function in human community? What is the power that makes life what it ought to be? Is it the power of the spirit? Life is so close to us. Life is us. And we are life. Yet life is so remote from us. It can be exploited, manipulated, tortured, even destroyed. We are not masters of our own lives.

Here one of Jesus' intriguing stories comes to our mind. It is the story of "the rich fool" (Luke 12:17-21). The man is rich and confident and knows how to make his life secure against future calamities. He builds large barns to store his grain. He is quite pleased with himself. He sits back and says to himself: "You have plenty of good things laid by, enough for many years to come; take life easy, eat, drink, enjoy yourself." Jesus' listeners must have become envious of the rich man. They must have wondered why Jesus is telling them the story. Surely this is not typical of him. But, as they are to find out very soon, Jesus is leading them to a dramatic conclusion. "You fool," God in Jesus' story says to the relaxed, contented man, "this very night you must surrender your life." Jesus' listeners cannot fail to get the point. The verb "surrender" (REB) or "is required" (RSV) "in Greek (*apaiteo*) is a word that is commonly used for the return of a loan."[5] Our life is a loan. That rich man is a fool because he does not realize this. His life is "on loan and now the owner (God) wants the loan returned."[6] He simply is not the master of his own life.

Are we, then, to give up in despair? Are we to resign ourselves to a life of uncertainty? Is life meaningless? Jesus not only speaks of life; he speaks of *abundant* life. "I came," he is reported to have said, "that they may have life, and have it abundantly" (John 10:10, NRSV). What is this life, this *abundant* life? To know what Jesus means by abundant life, one must know what he means by the reign of God. To experience that life, one must experience God's reign. To live that life, one must live God's reign in one's own life. The scope of God's reign determines the scope of Jesus' life and work. Its vision is Jesus' vision. Its goal is Jesus' goal. Is not, then, to know Jesus to know God's reign?

The abundant life that comes from God's reign is very different from the life of affluence enjoyed by those with plenty of material means. It is a life with a purpose and in Jesus' case that purpose is contained in the reign of God. A life without a purpose, though full of material things, is a very poor life. On the contrary, a life with a purpose, though lacking in material things, is an abundant life. Of course the purpose that makes life abundant is not just any purpose. It is the purpose envisioned by the reign of God—breaking fatalism, striving for justice, struggling for freedom, and believing in the fulfillment of life in God.

What has just been said will perhaps help us to understand Jesus when he is reported to have said: "Those who find their life will lose it, and those who lose their life for my sake will find it" (Matt. 10:39, NRSV; par. Luke 17:33). What a paradox! Is this not to deny our life the abundance Jesus promised to his followers in another context? Not at all. Jesus is here talking about discipleship, about bearing the cross. The key to understand what Jesus must have meant in this paradoxical saying is the phrase "for my sake." Is Jesus here demanding from his disciples personal loyalty to

---

5. Kenneth Bailey, *Through Peasant Eyes: More Lukan Parables, Their Culture and Style* (Grand Rapids: Wm. B. Eerdmans Publishing Company, 1980), 67.
6. Ibid., 67.

him? Is he asking them to pledge their faithfulness to him? Is he building a personality cult around him? I am more inclined to think that by "for my sake" Jesus means "for the sake of God's reign." Jesus himself has staked everything on it. The reign of God is everything he stands for. It is the meaning of his life. It is the focus of his ministry. To live is to live for the reign of God. To labor is to labor for it. Is there abundant life apart from the life lived for the reign of God? Is there a more fulfilling ministry than the ministry of God's reign? Here again the reign of God must shape our life, give meaning to it, and make it rich and abundant, although it may bring about loss of life. With the reign of God at the very center of what we are and what we strive for, no life will be ever lost. The reign of God dissolves the paradox in that saying of Jesus on discipleship. There is only life in the reign of God, and an abundant life at that, even if that life has to go through suffering and death on the cross.

The abundant life Jesus promised is thus the life that has overcome enslavement to the world. The world is not to be denied but to be overcome. This must be what Jesus meant when he is heard to have said to his disciples in one of his final discourses addressed to them: "In the world you face persecution. But take courage! I have conquered the world" (John 16:33). When you reach such a relationship with the world, you can really begin to enjoy the world. When you are "on top of the world," so to speak, you can begin truly to live in the world. Is this not perhaps the reason why Jesus was able to associate himself with the outcasts and the poor without having to worry about his reputation? Is this not the reason why he was able to face the religious and political authorities without fear? And is this not perhaps also the reason why he was able to go about his ministry with complete freedom even though the shadow of the cross followed him everywhere he went?

It is obvious that life is not abundant when it is lived in constant fear of death. If the reign of God means overcoming the world, it also means overcoming the fear of death. It is not death but fear of death that deprives us of freedom. It is that same fear that paralyzes us and immobilizes our creativity. Jesus was perhaps addressing himself to such paralysis of the mind when he said to his listeners: "Do not worry about your life, what you will eat or what you will drink, or about your body, what you will wear. Is not life more than food, and the body more than clothing?" (Matt. 6:25). Jesus could not be making light of food and clothing essential for our daily life. The point he was making is our obsession with them. And is such an obsession not related to the fear of death? There is no room for such obsession and fear in the reign of God. Fully committed to God's reign, Jesus is therefore able to declare that he is the life, that he came so that people may have life and have it abundantly.

Jesus Proclaims God's Reign

The central role the reign of God must play in our theology at large and in our christology in particular is more than obvious. We cannot but agree that "the challenge to discipleship, the ethical teaching, the disputes about oral tradition or ceremonial law, even the pronouncement of the forgiveness of sins and the welcoming of the outcast in the name of God—all these are to be understood in context of the reign proclamation or they are not understood at all."[7] Jesus, above all, "is the Proclaimer of the Reign of God."[8]

This is a biblical insight of utmost importance. But the Christian church and its theology have not always been guided and shaped by it. For "it remains a fact worth pondering that Jesus had preached the reign of God, while the church preached Jesus. And thus we are faced with a danger: we may so preach Jesus that we lose vision of the reign of God."[9] The danger pointed out here is a serious one. Jesus preached in isolation from his message of God's reign develops into a cult of Jesus. Jesus becomes a cultic object worshiped, venerated, and divinized. He commands the attention of popular Christian piety on the one hand and, on the other, engages the theological minds of the Christian church in speculating about his nature and essence. Either way Jesus gets detached from the reign of God he preached and gets separated from the very people who, he said, belong to it. This is the truncated Christ who bears little resemblance to Jesus, the carpenter's son, who shared the despairs and hopes of his people.

Such Jesus-cult has affected the Christian faith at least in two ways. First, faith in the reign of God becomes a faith in the "kingdom" of God to be enjoyed by Christians in the afterlife. One of the hymns still sung with deep emotion in my own church, the Presbyterian Church in Taiwan, goes like this:

> My heart longs for that beautiful land,
> That wonderful ancestral home in heaven,
> My heavenly Father has prepared it for me,
> In heaven there are many mansions.
>
> *Refrain:*
> Oh, ancestral home in heaven,
> Ancestral home in heaven!

---

7. Perrin, *Rediscovering the Teaching of Jesus*, 54.
8. Ibid.
9. Krister Stendahl, "Notes for Three Bible Studies," in *Christ's Lordship and Religious Pluralism*, ed. Gerald H. Anderson and Thomas F. Stransky (Maryknoll, N.Y.: Orbis Books, 1981), 10.

> The desire of my heart,
> Ancestral home in heaven.
> I am getting closer there.[10]

The hymn is reminiscent of what John in the Gospel that bears his name has Jesus say at one point in the farewell discourse: "There are many dwelling-places in my Father's house; if it were not so I should have told you; for I am going there to prepare a place for you" (John 14:2). But taken out of context, the saying attributed to Jesus is developed into a full-fledged faith in eternal life in heaven and becomes the center of Christian piety.

What happens is that "that wonderful land and ancestral home in heaven" is believed to be "the kingdom of God" in heaven. This leads to my second point. Faith in such a "kingdom of God" tends to foster certain Christians' lack of concern for social and political responsibilities and reinforce their negative attitude toward involvement in the world. This, sadly, is still the kind of faith held by the great majority of Christians in Asia, although they have been rudely awakened to the social and political realities of their countries in recent years. Whether in Korea or in Taiwan, for example, it is always a relatively small number of Christians who join the struggle for democracy, freedom, and human rights. They believe that the reign of God is the transforming power not only of their spiritual well-being but also the well-being of their society.

Further, the cult of Jesus has confined God's saving activity within the Christian church. Jesus is idolized at the expense of God the creator. The Christian church has often taught that to believe in Jesus is to disbelieve in what other religions teach about God and salvation. Faith in Jesus does not allow room for faith in God at work in human community outside the Christian community. The contradiction here is obvious, but most Christians in Asia seem not to be bothered by it and see no need for grappling with it.

What we have seen is Jesus divorced from his message of God's reign. That Jesus is rendered innocuous and plays no role in the struggle of women and men for justice and freedom. This Jesus is a name without the substance, a word without the reality. This Jesus could be substituted by something else—political power, cultural superiority, religious intolerance, and so on. That Jesus could also be success in life, conformity to the social and political status quo, psychological well-being, or personal salva-

---

10. The hymn is found in *Seng-Si* (the hymnal of the Presbyterian Church in Taiwan), No. 359. Philip Philips (1834–95) was its author. Since the hymn in the original English was not available, I translated it back to English from the Taiwanese version. Although my English translation must be different from its original English version, the meaning should be the same.

tion. This cult of Jesus is in fact not very different from the ways in which people outside the Christian church worship their deities as protectors of their earthly well-being and bestowers of their worldly blessings. Despite the fact that this is largely the case with Christians and churches that practice the cult of Jesus, the idea has been suggested that "Jesus preached the reign of God while the church preached Jesus conceals a disastrous error."[11] On the surface the concern seems legitimate. In the history of Christianity there has been no lack of attempts to identify a particular ideology, social and political system, religious program or structure, as the reign of God. The result is of course disastrous. What is realized is not the reign of God Jesus preached but the religious oppression and the political dictatorship Jesus would have denounced most vehemently. But an equally "disastrous error" is the error of Christian believers resigning themselves to the political and religious status quo, worshiping and adoring Jesus as the savior of individual souls and guarantor of personal peace and prosperity. This is the error of the cult of Jesus pointed out above, the cult that renders Jesus the object of personal piety unrelated to the world in which we live. Jesus becomes the private property of Christian believers shielded from the upheavals of nations and peoples. But Jesus thus protected from public affairs, Jesus shielded from social and political exposures, is not the Jesus who preached and practiced the message of God's reign.

It has, however, dawned on some Western theologians, and particularly on feminist theologians, black theologians, and Third World theologians, that this is precisely the outcome of the danger of the church so preaching Jesus that it loses the vision of the reign of God that he strove to share with his contemporaries. The awareness of this danger and the effort not to fall into it are now shaping the substance, style, and forms of much of the contemporary theology outside the confinement of traditional theology. Jesus becomes *historical* to people today through the unfolding of God's reign in the life and history of people both inside and outside the Christian church. The reign of God as historical happenings enables people today to grasp Jesus as a historical experience—Jesus, a Jew, who lived, worked, and died two thousand years ago in the Middle Eastern world of Palestine. And this historical experience of Jesus is not the experience of things past and gone. It is an experience of Jesus living, acting, dying, and rising from the dead, not just yesterday, not just the day before yesterday, not just way back in the first century, but always *today*.

---

11. Lesslie Newbigin, *Mission in Christ's Way* (New York: Friendship Press, 1987), 6. This booklet was prepared for use in the churches in anticipation of the World Conference on Evangelism to be held in San Antonio, Texas, in 1989 under the theme "Your will be done: Mission in Christ's Way" under the auspices of the Commission on World Mission and Evangelism of the World Council of Churches.

What we have in the reign of God is the hermeneutical key to the life and death of Jesus and to the mystery of God's design for humanity. It is also the theological clue for Christians to solve the puzzle of how God is at once the God of Jesus, the God of Christians, *and* the God of all human beings regardless of sex, color, or creed. Paul seems to come very close to this experience of God through Jesus when he writes those memorable words in his letter to the Galatians: "There is no longer Jew nor Greek, there is no longer slave nor free, there is no longer male nor female; for you are all one in God of Christ Jesus" (3:28, NRSV). He could have also said: you are all one in the reign of God.

The Reign of God Is Yours

So day in and day out, in season and out of season, Jesus comes back to the subject of God's reign over and over. It must have struck women and men who gathered to hear him that he was on an urgent business. In Galilee, his own native land and the scene of his ministry in the north, in Judea, a land that inspired the religious and cultural genius of Jews and rich in historical memories, and in Jerusalem, the bastion of Jewish traditions and the seat of Jewish religious-political power, Jesus dwells on God's reign as if the destiny of his hearers and the fate of their nation totally depended on it.

For most people who flocked to Jesus the reign of God was a difficult theme. It was an abstruse subject. It was a matter beyond their experience. But on the lips of Jesus that difficult, abstruse, and remote thing makes a very personal and powerful impact. Jesus speaks simply and sincerely. His manner and gestures blend quietly with the surrounding nature richly adorned with lakes, hills, flowers, and rocks. His voice is firm and earnest, penetrating into the hearts of his audience and fading into a distant echo over the fields and mountains, creating ripples of excitement and expectation in his eager listeners. They are terribly impressed and "amazed at his teaching; unlike their scribes he taught with a note of authority" (Matt. 7:29). This was the heart of his message: "The time has arrived; the reign of God is upon you" (Mark 1:15).

At first Jesus' audience must have felt no impact of his words for the simple reason that "the kingdom of God" was not new and novel in their religious vocabulary. They had, as a matter of fact, some notion of it. There was, for instance, this Kaddish prayer recited at the service of the burial of the dead:

Magnified and sanctified be God's great name in the world which he has created according to his will. May he establish his kingdom in your lifetime and in your days and in the lifetime of all the house of Israel even speedily and at a near time.[12]

We cannot fail to recall in our mind "the Lord's Prayer" in which Jesus taught his disciples to pray and say: "Your reign come, your will be done, on earth as in heaven" (Matt. 6:10; par. Luke 11:2). For Jesus' hearers the parallel between their Kaddish prayer and Jesus' prayer was not accidental.[13] So Jesus is talking about something not entirely foreign to them. The reign of God is a language with which they are not completely unfamiliar.

There is even urgency in that Kaddish prayer. To pray for God's reign to come in one's lifetime cannot be done halfheartedly. It must be an urgent plea, an ardent supplication, and an earnest expectation. This is clearly reflected in the petition of the Lord's Prayer, "Your reign come, your will be done." The day the reign of God comes will be a momentous day. That will be the day their centuries-old dream of a Davidic kingdom comes true and the promise of God for their nation is realized. Even those people listening to Jesus—women, men, and children, disqualified for God's salvation on account of their profession and status—must have also vaguely shared this religious zeal and this national hope for God's reign. Jesus seems simply to be reinforcing the urgent hope for God's reign throbbing in the veins of the nation and stirring in the hearts of the people.

After all, then, there could be nothing different in Jesus' announcement of God's reign. It seems an old dream Jesus is inviting them to dream again. But their anticipation proved premature. There is something very different in Jesus' message of God's reign. As they are to realize time and again, there is indeed something fresh and new in what Jesus said and did on many occasions that makes them sit up and listen. In his proclamation of God's reign Jesus addresses them directly and personally. "The reign of God," Jesus says to them, looking straight into their eyes, "is yours!" (Luke 6:20; par. Matt. 5:3). Now this is something really new. It is something out of the ordinary. The audience must have been startled. Murmur must have risen among them. They must have turned to each other in doubt and looked at Jesus incredulously. How can this be true? This is too big a claim for those poor peasants and social-religious outcasts to make. Their religious teachers have never taught them that way. It is beyond their wildest dream to claim the reign of God for themselves. The reign of God will belong to their nation when it is restored to its past glory. Then, and only then, God's reign will be theirs also. It will be theirs in a second-hand way. It will be theirs only because they are part of their own nation. And of course the

---

12. Perrin, *Rediscovering the Teaching of Jesus*, 57.
13. "The parallel... is so marked that it is difficult to conceive of it as accidental" (ibid., 57).

reign of God belongs to the religious community of those believers entitled to God's salvation. Sinners and Gentiles like them have no part in it. They know they are excluded from it.

To most of Jesus' hearers the reign of God is out of reach. It is a religious institution to which they are not encouraged to aspire. It is a sociopolitical establishment in which they could take pride but in which they have no part to play. This is a very strange thing, this reign of God. They love it and they hate it. It commands their awe, devotion, even pride. And yet it holds them in disdain and ridicule. The reign of God is something persons like them could "view from the distance but never touch" (*k'o wang pu k'o chi*), as one would say in Chinese. How could they, then, not murmur, be startled, and even object when Jesus tells them that that very reign of God is theirs?

But it does not take them long to realize that Jesus is not talking about a vision far removed from their everyday life of worry, pain, and frustration. He is not referring to a religious institution that judges them as sinners and beyond the hope of salvation. Nor is he talking about sociopolitical systems that consign them to the rank of outcasts. In other words, the reign of God is not the same as the kingdom of God; it is different from a political or a religious institution with the power to dictate people's daily life and to decide their eternal destiny. It is neither an extension of the present political system they have to obey blindly nor an expansion of the religious authorities they hold in awe.

Jesus must have tried very hard to drive home to them his firm belief that the reign of God is not a pious illusion, that it is not simply another religious establishment, that it had nothing to do with an oppressive political regime. The reign of God, Jesus says to them in no uncertain terms, is *yours*. It belongs to you. It is *you!* The reign of God means to be *yours*. It is closely related to you, so closely, as a matter of fact, that it means *you!* The reign of God is yours because *you* are the reign of God. This is a daring thought and a bold declaration. It certainly never occurs to any contemporary of Jesus to affirm God's reign in this way. Not even ancient prophets before him would have been able to say a thing like this. How are his listeners to understand him?

By saying that the reign of God is theirs, Jesus affirms the direct link between God's reign and people, particularly those men, women, and children, oppressed, exploited, downtrodden, marginalized, in body and in spirit, those human persons treated inhumanly, and to whom injustice is done. Jesus removes once for all the barriers set by the long traditions of their religion and by the authorities that defend and guard these traditions. Is this not evident in what he said to the religious leaders? "You shut the door of the kingdom of Heaven in people's faces," he confronted them bluntly. He then continued: "You do not enter yourselves, and when others try to enter, you stop them" (Matt. 23:13). Religion, with its elaborate rituals, doctrinal systems, and hierarchical structures, can become a barrier that separates people from God. The direct route to God is closed. When observance of rituals becomes an end in itself, God becomes dispensable. When subscription to doctrine and dogma is regarded as the test of orthodoxy, freedom of faith in God is denied. And when an ecclesiastical hierarchy sets itself between God and believers, it claims the power to dispense God's salvation. This is precisely what Jesus said to the religious authorities of his day. This strong critique of his can equally be applied to all religions, including Christianity.

The primary function of a religion is not to be a mediator between God and people. This is the conclusion we must draw from Jesus' declaration that the reign of God belongs to people and not to priests and ministers. Nor does it belong to bishops and popes. The duty of pastors and bishops is to point to people the way to God, to be of help in their search for God. Their ministry must be a ministry of encouragement, enabling those fainthearted ones not to lose heart when they lose sight of God. Theirs is to enable people to experience God's presence in them and with them. They are not to make believers forever dependent on them for their communion with God. Salvation is something that occurs between God and people. It is not mediated through the "good offices" of the religious authorities and ecclesiastical structures.

When we press further the direct relationship that Jesus asserted to exist between God and people, do we not have to have a second thought about our long theological tradition of holding Jesus as the mediator between God and people? Did Jesus consider himself as someone standing between God and people, mediating between them? John the Evangelist would have us reply in the affirmative. In his farewell discourses with his disciples Jesus, according to John, is said to have told them: "No one comes to the Father except by me" (John 14:6). Coming from John, the saying reflects more his theological insight than Jesus' own thought, more the thinking of the early Christian community than Jesus' own assertion. Besides, the idea of having a go-between especially between the superior and the inferior is derived from the feudalistic society in the past and the class society today. Did not Jesus try to break the religious traditions that block the way to God? Did he not teach and practice the faith that God is directly accessible to people? Did he not encourage people to pray to God as Abba, as parent?[14] And Jesus who stands with them, in solidarity

---

14. See my book *Jesus, the Crucified People* (New York: Crossroad/Meyer-Stone, 1989), chap. 3, "Distance between Abba and God."

with them—would he have had anywhere to stand except where people stand? The reign of God is yours! In saying this, Jesus tells them where he stands—he stands in the midst of them. In declaring this, he affirms where God is—God is also in the midst of them. And in proclaiming this, he asserts that the reign of God is the reign of God because of the people like him and his listeners—people who have no place in society and no role to play in a religious community. The reign of God, Jesus is saying, is in people, with people, and for people—the reign of God is people! This is the new and startling thing in Jesus' proclamation of God's reign. This is the good news never heard of before. And Jesus takes pains to help people realize how close they are to God's reign, that they and the reign of God exist for each other. This, in essence, is the heart of his ministry and the focus of his mission.

There is, for instance, Jesus' strong affirmation concerning the Sabbath—an affirmation that outraged his opponents and exposed him to punishment by death at the hand of the Law. "The sabbath was made for people," he declared, "and not people for the sabbath" (Mark 2:27). He was as good as his words when the test of his words came in a healing incident (Mark 3:1-6; pars. Matt. 12:9-14; Luke 6:6-10). It so happened that there was a man with a withered arm in the synagogue Jesus attended on the Sabbath. Will he practice what he preaches? Does he dare to defy the Law and heal that man? His followers must have watched him with apprehension, secretly hoping that he would not go too far. As to his opponents, they must have waited to see what he was going to do with sadistic impatience. Unperturbed, Jesus asked the man to come forward, and then turned to the congregation. It must have been a tense moment. People must have fixed their eyes on Jesus with bated breath. He did not keep them guessing for long. To the congregation and especially to his opponents he asked this question, perhaps not even raising his voice: "Is it permitted to do good or to do evil on the sabbath, to save life or to kill?"

A powerful either-or question! This is an existential question deeply related to the theological meaning of life. It is an ethical dilemma that tests one's understanding of God. It is also a moral challenge that exposes one's faith and religion to the limelight of God's saving love. Jesus received no answer to his question from his opponents. Of course not. Theologically, they were cornered. Religiously, they were exposed. And morally, they were defeated. Then Mark, the storyteller, and only Mark, gives us one of those few glimpses into the heart of Jesus in turmoil. He tells us that Jesus, "looking round at them with anger and sorrow" (Mark 3:5), restored the man's arm in full view of the congregation.

This is what Jesus means by the reign of God. In God's reign it is permitted to do good even on the Sabbath. It is not only permitted, it is expected, it is taken for granted, to do good on the Sabbath. The reign of God is meant to do good and not evil on all days and particularly on the Sabbath. In the reign of God it is permitted to save life even on the Sabbath. It is not only permitted, it is expected, it is taken for granted, to save life, no matter on what day, and most of all on the Sabbath. The reign of God means precisely this: the Sabbath is made for people, and not people for the Sabbath. By healing that man with a withered arm Jesus announces that the reign of God has come. That man, with his arm restored, his person made whole, his indignity removed, his anguish and pain taken away—that man is the reign of God. The reign of God, then, happens on the Sabbath as well as on any other day.

Jesus could not be more right. The reign of God is yours. It is yours any day, any place. It happens where people are—in the synagogue or in the marketplace. It happens any day so long as there is no day, not even the Sabbath, that can be called a day without people. It is people who make the day, and not the day that makes people. It is people who fill the day with meaning, endow it with memories, usher it in with expectation. The reign of God that is possible only on certain days stipulated by religious laws is no reign of God. It is the reign of religious authorities. And the reign of God that allows no people such as the man with a withered arm to be healed on the Sabbath is again no reign of God. It is a reign that holds them in contempt for being Gentiles, sinners, outcasts. It is a reign without God.

The Banquet of God's Reign

Jesus' hearers, long accustomed to the lofty teachings of their religious authorities about the reign of God, might not have been able to follow at once what Jesus said. It is a revolutionary teaching. How can God's reign be theirs? It is an extraordinary dream. How can it become a reality in their lives?

Jesus must have had questions such as these in mind when he tells the parable of the great banquet (Luke 14:15-24; par. Matt. 22:1-14). A *great* banquet indeed! The banquet is made great not by the privileged, but by the outcasts and by the Gentiles! As a matter of fact, those originally invited to the banquet spurned it. They are landowners, rich, confident, and snobbish. Why did they decide to decline the invitation at the last minute, after having accepted it in the first place? They each had an explanation. But it is apparent that the explanation was an excuse rather than a reason. There is no reason why the visit to the newly purchased land could not be postponed for a day or two, or the trying out of the oxen just bought could not be done the next day. And to decline the invitation on the grounds of a recent marriage, though not totally out of order, would be an indication of rudeness. Jesus must have wanted to say this when he said in the parable that "they all sent excuses."

What is, then, the real reason behind their excuses and apologies? It is not mentioned explicitly. We have to guess it on the basis of the central message of the parable and the actions taken by the host after his invitation was not honored. The banquet, they must have reasoned, may not be filled by respectable persons like themselves. Perhaps the host is an unpredictable person. One never knows what kind of people he will be inviting and the banquet may turn out to be one beneath their social status to attend. They consider themselves special people, a class by themselves. They keep a distance from people of lower classes. They perpetuate the class consciousness that divides a society and classifies people according to what they possess and not what they are as human beings. In a class society the worth of human persons is determined not by their humanity but by their materiality. It is possessions and wealth that decide what human beings are.

If this was true in Jesus' time, it is even more true in our world today. And how true it is in our capitalist society in which people are driven by material gains and greed and by the pursuit of power and recognition in society! Money talks! It can talk its way up to the highest political authorities and get them to do what it wants. And it can talk its way down to the lowest stratum of society to intimidate people without means. The irony is that the great part of our capitalist society has embraced Christianity and professes to be "Christian." It is ironical because it is precisely this kind of society that Jesus was up against. Jesus, if he were here today, would denounce this society of ours as much as, or perhaps more than, he did his own.

As it happens, the refusal of those invited to the dinner party, in the intention of the parable, is just a marginal part of the drama that unfolds very quickly. The real excitement occurs after they have decided to stay away from the banquet. The incensed host first orders his servant to "go out quickly into the streets and alleys of the town, and bring in the poor, the crippled, the blind, and the lame" (Luke 14:21). The people mentioned here are the typical components of Jesus' reign of God. They must be the guests of the banquet of God's reign and not those persons high and mighty with riches and power. They "symbolize the outcasts of Israel that were attracted to and welcomed by Jesus."[15]

Jesus wanted to make perfectly clear that the reign of God belongs to the outcasts of his own religious community. His reign of God is a powerful indictment against a religion, any religion, that makes outcasts of certain categories of people. In his time prostitutes were outcasts. Tax-

---

15. Bailey, *Through Peasant Eyes*, 100.

gatherers were outcasts. Butchers and swineherds were outcasts. For Jesus
God makes no outcasts. The word "outcast" does not exist in God's vocabulary. His God is always there ready to accept and embrace the so-called
outcasts. Jesus pointedly makes this clear in his parable of the father's love
(Luke 15:11-32). That younger son, reduced to a swineherd, "in effect com-
mits apostasy."[16] That *Jewish* father must know what he is doing when he
embraces that apostate son of his in his bosom. He is acting against the
tradition of his religion and the propriety of his society. But God is like
that father!

   Jesus in the story of the great banquet goes farther. After the outcasts of
Israel have been brought to the banquet, Jesus has the master of the house
issue a second order to his servant. "Go out on the highways and along the
hedgerows and *compel* people to come in" (Luke 14:23, RSV; italics added).
The highways and hedgerows! These are places beyond the host's village.
They are unfamiliar territories to his servant. They are strange domains
that exist outside the life and experience of the master and the servant.
And people from these foreign regions are Gentiles and therefore outcasts
in the eyes of Jesus' own religious tradition. To get those foreign outcasts
to the banquet? The master of the banquet must be out of his mind! But
this precisely is Jesus' point. The banquet of God's reign is laid out for
Gentiles as well as for the outcasts of Israel![17] This great banquet embodies
Jesus' vision of God's reign. It is a global vision. It is a vision inspired by
God, the creator of heaven and earth, God who created human beings in
God's image.

   The Christian church that is not able to envision with Jesus this vision
of God's reign cannot preach Jesus. Christian theology that is not premised
on it can only develop a theology of "salvation history" that has no room
for people from beyond its community, a theology that confines Jesus to
its familiar territory.[18] And Christians who are not able to visualize God
acting in the world outside the Christian church reduce God to a size with

---

   16. Bernard Brandon Scott, *Jesus, Symbol-maker for the Kingdom* (Philadelphia: Fortress
Press, 1981), 51.
   17. See G. R. Beasley-Murray, *Jesus and the Kingdom of God* (Grand Rapids: Wm. B.
Eerdmans Publishing Co., 1986), 173. Not all critics agree with this interpretation. There are
in fact those who "contend that such an outreach to the Gentiles was not envisioned by Jesus
and that this invitation to those outside the community is an expansion of the parable by the
early church in a situation demanding missionary activity [Jeremias, *Parables*, 64]" (Bailey,
Through Peasant Eyes, 101). One recalls in particular Jesus' charge to his disciples as he sent
them out on a mission: "Do not take the road to gentile lands, and do not enter any Samaritan
town; but go rather to the lost sheep of the house of Israel" (Matt. 10:5-6). There is also Jesus'
rather unkind response to the Canaanite woman who had come to seek his help for her sick
daughter: "It is not right to take the children's bread and throw it to the dogs" (Matt. 15:24,
26). It is significant that these words are found in the Gospel of the Jewish-oriented Matthew
only. Besides, what is one to make of Jesus' story of the good Samaritan, for instance?
   18. For a critique of the concept of "salvation history" (*Heilsgeschichte*), see "The Tower

which they can deal comfortably—a size that does not outgrow their limited Christian imagination, a size that does not make them feel ridiculously small and immature, and a size that can be manipulated by them at will. But the God reduced to that size is no longer God. That God is not the God of the reign Jesus proclaimed and practiced.

Jesus, however, must get the master of the banquet to send out his servant to the highways and the hedges, "beyond the city—that is, 'outside the theocracy,' 'to those who travel along the world's great highway, or who have fallen down weary, and rest by its hedges; into the busy, or else weary, heathen world.' Thus this reference is to the heathen world and this is made clearer because the servants go into the hedges. There were no hedges around the fields of the Jews."[19] Perhaps one may argue that the banquet is still to be held in the old familiar domain dominated by the old religious tradition and believers in that tradition. Is this what Jesus counted on? Is this what he foresaw? It is most unlikely. How could Jesus be unaware of the basic difference between this new community around the dinner table and the old community that rejected the invitation? He must have known that he was envisioning something that had no precedent in the religious history of his people.

But why "compel" these Gentiles, the "heathens" to come in? Is the servant instructed to use force, if necessary, to get them to the banquet? Is the master so desperate to fill his banquet seats that he is not even scrupulous about resorting to violence? Are these people, these Gentiles, these outcasts, to be forced to come whether they like it or not, whether they are willing or not? Here one must beware of an evangelistic twist often given to this verb "compel." This wonderful banquet God has set up could, on account of that evangelistic twist, become a violent banquet. That beautiful banquet, because of it, could turn into an ugly banquet. That delicious banquet, due to it, could develop into a bitter banquet. The invitation then becomes a declaration of war. Evangelism is carried out militantly. Militant evangelism is an all-too-familiar story in the history of Christianity. It is also present in some other religions. It is a sad story that must grieve the heart of God and confuse the souls of the "Gentiles."

No, we must not give an evangelistic twist to this key verb "compel" (*anankazo* in Greek) in this marvelous story of the banquet of God's reign. What does it mean, then, in the culture of Jesus shared in his day and the

of Babel Questions *Heilsgeschichte"* in my book, *The Compassionate God* (Maryknoll, N.Y.: Orbis Books, 1982), 23–25.
   19. J. Massyngbaerde Ford, *My Enemy Is My Guest: Jesus and Violence in Luke* (Maryknoll, N.Y.: Orbis Books, 1984), 105. The quotation cited by the author is from A. Edersheim, *The Life and Times of Jesus the Messiah* (Grand Rapids, 1947). See footnote 12 in *My Enemy is My Guest*, 146.

culture of Oriental people of today? "In the Middle East," it is pointed out, "the unexpected invitation must be refused. The refusal is all the more required if the guest is of lower social rank than the host."[20] This, however, is not all. What makes the invitation so unexpected and surprising is this:

A stranger from outside the city is suddenly invited to a great banquet. He is not a relative or even a citizen of the host's city. The offer is generous and delightful but (thinks the stranger) *he cannot possibly mean it.* After some discussion the servant will finally have to take the startled guest by the arm and gently pull him along. There is no other way to convince him that he is really invited to the great banquet, irrespective of his being a foreigner. Grace is *unbelievable!* How could it be true, asks the outsider. For me? What have I done for him? I cannot pay it back. The host is not serious! It is a most pleasant prospect, but considering who I am, he cannot mean it! The host knows that this kind of shock and unbelief will face the servant/messenger at every turn, so he instructs the same to overcome reserve and unbelief by the only method possible—with a smile grab them by the arm and pull them in.[21]

This is an accurate description of the Oriental culture of propriety. The invitation is issued, but there must be a great deal of push and pull before it can be accepted. It is a matter of social proprieties. No force is used. No violence is committed. No breach of personal integrity is made.

Grace is unbelievable! This is what that verb "compel" in the vocabulary of Oriental people means. Grace is not grace unless it is unexpected, but in our religious tradition, as in that of Jesus, we have made it something that can be expected. It is even more than that. Grace for many Christian churches can be programmed. The grace that is expected, not to say programmed, is not grace any more. It becomes something to be negotiated, bargained, earned. One has to deserve it and merit it. "You have to be converted to Christianity to be saved," preaches the Christian preacher. Conversion in the world of religions, then, often means proselytism. But is proselytism the condition of receiving God's grace of salvation? Does salvation take place only when one is converted from one religion to another religion, or more specifically from other religions to Christianity? Yes, we have to preach conversion, but not proselytism. But conversion to what? The world needs conversion to the God of life, justice, love, and freedom, that is, to the reign of God. This is the conversion preached by the prophets in ancient Israel, by John the Baptist, and by Jesus himself. Jesus

---

20. Bailey, *Through Peasant Eyes*, 108.
21. Ibid.

even removes that very condition of submission to the prevailing religious tradition of his day to be accepted by God. Human beings need to be converted to the vision of God's reign Jesus stood for, for which he lived and died. It is a vision of God in solidarity with the poor and the oppressed. It is a vision of the empowering grace of God at work in human community. And it is a vision of life in God.

Gentiles in God's Reign

To grasp that vision and to grapple with that empowering grace of God working in human community we need to explore metaphors and listen to stories from our own cultural traditions and the realities we and our neighbors share in our own society.

A Culture of Face

There is, for example, a Chinese expression that aptly sums up this Oriental culture of propriety that the word "compel" implies, that is, *mien-tze*, meaning literally "face." A discussion of the concept may give us further insights into the story of the great banquet. Chinese people from all walks of life, from the top of society to the bottom, high and low, rich and poor, speak of *mien-tze*. Chinese culture is a culture of *mien-tze*, a culture of face. It is evident in a number of colloquial expressions in everyday conversation. To preserve one's honor, for example, is "to preserve one's face" (*yow mien-tze*), and to lose honor is "to lose one's face" or simply "to lose face" (*mei-yow mien-tze* or *mei lien; lien* is the same as *mien-tze* meaning "face"). To care about honor is "to care about face" (*yau lien*, literally "to want one's face"), and not to care about honor is "not to care about face" (*pu yau lien*, literally "not wanting one's face"). To save another's face so as not to embarrass that person is "to give face" to that person (*kei mien-tze*) and to make another lose face and embarrass that person is "not to give face (to that person)" (*pu kei mien-tze*). When one speaks of someone rendering eye-service, putting up a pleasant front, or doing something for the sake of appearance, one will say that person is "creating a face" (*chuo mien-tze*). To show favor to someone with one's presence or company is "to bestow one's face" (*shang lien*) and to refuse to do so is "not to bestow one's face" (*pu shang lien*). Among the Taiwanese people there is a particular way of saying how one is extremely embarrassed by and ashamed of what one has said or done: one does not know where to carry one's face (*bin bo so-chai thang giah, bin* being the Taiwanese word for *lien* or *mien-tze*).

These are just a few very common expressions on the lips of people constantly. What a culture of *mien-tze* (face)! Face is not just face. It is everything that a person is and is not; it is what a person stands for and does not stand for. The Chinese are deeply conscious, perhaps more conscious than other peoples, of the power and function of the human face in public life. It is a most powerful and effective weapon each and every person is born with. Mastering the use of that weapon is a secret art of propriety from government officials at the emperor's court to ordinary citizens in their conduct of life and business in the family, in the street, or in the marketplace. A judge in court puts on a face that intimidates a poor defendant. A father's impassive face can be terrifying to his children. Servants in a traditional Chinese family or low officials in the government service must carry out their duties always "paying attention to their master's or superior's face" (*khan jen chuei-lien*, the word *chuei*, "mouth," added to *lien*, "face," for emphasis). This subtle power of face is not something to be made light of. There is, however, another side to it. People learn how to flatter the ego of their master or superior with a servile smile on their face. This is when face that means honor turns into face that means vanity. To have one's honor (one's face) preserved is "to have one's vanity satisfied" (*yow mientze*). Built into Chinese society, from the top down to the bottom and from the bottom up to the top, is an institution of honor and vanity shaped by infinite variations of subtle and intricate facial expressions. Face, a part of the human body, becomes a symbol and a reality of an oppressive society. This is an abuse of the power contained in the human face. The abuse corrupts human relationships and debases human integrity when things get done not because it is someone's responsibility to do them, but "for the sake of a person who recommended or requested" (*khan mien-tze*, literally, "to look at the face" of the person who recommended or requested).

To return to the story of the great banquet. Supposing it is a real story, then some of what has just been said about the Chinese culture of face can also be applied to it. After all, a Middle Eastern society in which the story has its setting shares some characteristics of that culture. The story could, then, be a typical interplay of face as honor and face as vanity. It can be retold as follows. The master of the banquet had given face (honor) to the three rich landlords by sending them an invitation to his banquet. In return he had his honor (face) preserved and vanity (face) satisfied when they accepted the invitation. In accordance with the custom the master dispatched his servant a second time to fetch them to the banquet when it was ready. Another interplay of honor and vanity. But this time around they refused to come to the banquet with excuses. What they did was "not to save the host's face" and thus to embarrass him. The host's honor (face) was slighted and his vanity (face) hurt. Then out of spite for them and to shame them (their face) he invited outcasts and strangers to fill his banquet hall, saving his face and satisfying his vanity (face). As to the outcasts and strangers with neither honor (face) nor vanity (face), they gained a little honor (face) and tasted some vanity (face) totally unexpected. That would be an experience for them to remember for a long time and to tell their friends and relatives with some pride. Retold in this way, that banquet would not be a banquet of love. It would be a banquet of saving face and giving face, a banquet of honor salvaged and vanity gained, a banquet in which the Oriental culture of face is practiced to everyone's dubious satisfaction.

It is at this point that a real life story ends and Jesus' parable of God's reign begins. The reign of God, Jesus seems to be saying, can be a matter of face, too. It is, of course, not a matter of God having God's vanity restored by getting outcasts and strangers to come into the reign. It is not a matter for these outcasts and strangers to have their vanity flattered either. Nor has it to do with God urging them to come "for the sake of someone who recommended them" (*khan mien-tze*). They in fact had no one to recommend them to God. They are rejected as outsiders unworthy of God by the religious authorities. God has taken the initiative to get them to come.

Here Jesus' parable of God's reign takes a drastic turn in our real life situation conditioned and dictated by cultural vanities. It presents a sharp contrast to our make-believe world of religions fortified with relative truths absolutized, a partial knowledge of God taken as a totality of it, a limited experience of God's salvation professed to be exhaustive. By telling the story of the great banquet, Jesus startles us by implying that God gives "face" (honor) even to outcasts and strangers. What this does to God's honor does not enter God's mind. Nor is it the concern of Jesus. His utmost concern is to show that God's love is amazing. What God does for outcasts and strangers is unbelievable, but God's grace is unbelievable. This is truly astonishing, but that is what God's salvation is.

A Korean Woman's Passion Story

We must explore this subject matter of strangers further. Strangers are Gentiles. They are people from outside the city. They are foreigners. They are *gai-jin*, outsiders, as foreigners in Japan are called no matter how long they have lived in that country, even if they were born there. *Gai-jin* are forever *gai-jin*, outsiders, even if you are a permanent resident, even if you manage to become a naturalized citizen and travel with a Japanese passport. It is the country of your ancestors that counts—be it Korea, Taiwan, or Vietnam—and not the citizenship paper or the passport you hold. This explains the countless woes of *gai-jin* in Japan, especially Koreans. Their *gai-jin*-ness affects them in matters big and small—education, intermarriage, employment. It becomes a curse. The police must take their fingerprints—done in Japan only to criminals. The history behind all this is long and painful. "During World War II," says a report titled "670,000 Koreans Call Japan Home but Say They Are Treated as Outcasts,"

> thousands of Koreans, whose country was then under Japanese rule, were forced to go to Japan to help make up for labor shortages. When the war ended, there were 2.5 million of them in Japan, most of whom soon returned home. Those who stayed became trapped in a legal quagmire. Under colonial rule they had technically been Japanese subjects. But the treaty ending the war stripped Japan of its colonies and the Koreans who remained behind lost their Japanese citizenship.... There are now 670,000 Koreans in Japan. But they are still outsiders and are frequent victims of discrimination in housing, jobs and social welfare programs.[22]

The roots of discrimination run deep. "On a street corner in Hiroshima," it is reported, "there is a stone monument that serves as a memorial to 20,000 Koreans killed in the 1945 atomic bomb attack. Nearby is the Hiroshima Peace Park, with its elaborate memorial dedicated to the Japanese who died in the blast. Korean heritage groups have tried to have their monument moved into the park, but officials say there is not enough room."[23] Thousands and tens of thousands of people both from Japan and from overseas each year dutifully and piously make a pilgrimage to the Hiroshima Peace Park on an August day, the day the atom bomb devastated Hiroshima in a flash of seconds, to pray for the peace of the dead and for the peace of the world. But how many of them pay attention to a lonely monument standing on a street corner outside the Peace Park, leaving the souls of those Koreans who died in the same blast uncared for?

This reminds me of an experience that took place one summer evening in 1986 in Tode, the industrial section of Kawasaki in greater Tokyo that extends all the way to Yokohama, the port town that played a colorful role in the history of Japan's contacts with the West in centuries past. There in a wooden house that serves as a mission station, students, pastors, and theologians, mostly from Japan, listened to a middle-aged Korean woman tell us a most gripping story of how Koreans in Japan suffer as *gai-jin:*

> My trial came when my child reached kindergarten age. Where can I send him? There was no kindergarten for Korean children in our neighborhood. But there was one for Japanese children run by the Christian church not far from where we lived. I used to pass that church every day and saw those Japanese children playing happily

---

22. *International Herald Tribune*, September 3, 1984, 5.
23. Ibid.

and well cared for. How I envied them! I told my husband about the kindergarten and timidly asked if we could put our child there. His answer was direct and curt: "Forget it!" But I could not forget it. One day I decided to go to see the pastor of the church without telling my husband. I went to the church, but did not dare to go in. I went to and fro in front of the gate, unable to bring myself to enter. I repeated the same thing for a few days. Finally I decided to be brave and went inside the church, expecting to be turned away. The pastor, after asking who I was and what I wanted, not only did not turn me away, but said, to my great astonishment, he would have my child in the kindergarten. I could not believe my ears. When I told my husband about it, he was incredulous.

The incredible thing did happen, but not without distressing incidents. The trial of the Korean woman continued. It came to a head when she decided to join the church. That was more than her husband could take. He and his fellow Koreans had borne the brunt of being Koreans in Japan. They were treated as outcasts in their land of adoption. How could his wife join the church of those people who did everything in their power to make their lives miserable? He vent on her all the anger he had accumulated for the Japanese people and often beat her black and blue. How many times she was driven to the verge of desperation! But she persevered, with the support of the pastor of the church and some church members. In the end the heart of her husband melted. He too joined the church. Before her story reached an end, he had slipped away quietly. The space he left behind him seemed filled with the pain, agony, and finally hope of a Korean person who might have destroyed himself and his family out of sheer anger and despair of living in a hostile society as *gai-jin*, as outsider and outcast. Before he committed an irreversible act of destruction, he had discovered that in God's reign there are neither outsiders (*gai-jin*) nor outcasts. That church that accepted her and her family into its fellowship is the reign of God in the land that stigmatizes certain persons as outsiders and outcasts.

God of Outcasts

Outcasts are people without hope. Gentiles are people without honor. They have no face in the religion to which they belong and in the society in which they live. A person without a face is a nonperson. He or she has no identity. She or he has no rights. But in Jesus' reign of God, God gives them "face" and bestows on them "honor" (*kei mien-tze*). But this is not all. As these outcasts and outsiders are soon to find out, they in turn give God, the host of the reign, "face" or "honor" by yielding to God's gentle urging and allowing themselves to be taken to the banquet. This is truly surprising. God, too, is without face, without identity, without personhood, until those outcasts and strangers have given it to God! God is non-God insofar as there are outcasts. God is non-God as long as outsiders remain outsiders. I know saying such things can be easily misunderstood. Do, then, outsiders make God? Do outcasts create God? Of course not. This is not what I mean. To say that God is non-God so long as there are outcasts is to say that God is not recognized as God until no one is treated as an outcast. And to say that God is non-God as long as outsiders remain outsiders is to say that God cannot be identified as God until no one is excluded from the community to which he or she belongs by birth or by adoption. And as long as certain men, women, and children are treated as outcasts and outsiders, God chooses to be the God of outcasts and outsiders.

This is quite straightforward, is it not? This is a simple logic. Is a host still a host when he or she has no guests? At most she or he would be a host only in name. This is what happened to the master of the house in Jesus' parable. When the people he had invited refused to come, he was left without guests. He was not the host he had intended to be. He could not play the host as he had planned. His "hosthood," if one can use such a term, was denied. The situation was an embarrassment to him. It made him appear ridiculous. It may be that this was just what his prospective guests had intended. This may be one of the reasons why he lost no time in taking actions to fill his banquet hall with other guests. The banquet was as important to him as to the people persuaded to come.

And as the story unfolds, the true nature of his "hosthood" is revealed: he must be the host of the masses of the outcasts and not of a few selected people, a few chosen ones predestined to enjoy special privileges in his house. By the same token, surely God does not want to be God in name only either. Can we worship a God with a mere name that has no reality? Can we entrust ourselves to a God who exists in name alone? Can we expect a God with a bare name to affect our lives and to act in our history? This God in name only is the God of the few chosen ones. It is the God of a very selective community, a God of an expensive club. This is a God not accessible to the masses of people. This God of the elected few cannot save the men, women, and children barred from that expensive club and from that exclusive community. That God can neither help those in dire physical need nor love those without privilege or prestige. But as long as there are needy people, the people with no place and status in a society and in a religious community, God has to be their God. For God to be God, God has to be with them and for them.

This seems one of the deep insights disclosed in Jesus' parable of the great banquet. That insight has to do with the whereabouts of God. Now

God, Jesus seems to be saying to us, is not anonymous. God has a name and a face: God's name is the name of strangers and God's face is the face of outcasts. If one wants to know how God is called and what God's face looks like, then one has to look at the faces of strangers, foreigners, outsiders, Gentiles. Here again Jesus gives the warning that there is in a religion, especially a well-established religion, the danger of losing God's true name and obscuring God's face, the danger of not being recognized as reflecting God's face, and the danger of representing everything except the name of God. This is perhaps what Jesus saw in his own religion. That is why he was intent on relocating where God is and reidentifying the names and faces that reflect the saving presence of God.

There is, in the last analysis, one question that is essential to religion, and one only: does it or does it not show to the world and to the people the true face of the God who forgives, comforts, and makes live, the face of God who is love, justice, and freedom? All other things are secondary—ceremonies and rituals, doctrines and teachings, structures and organizations. These are not the purpose and goal of religion. They have no autonomous value. They are important insofar as they are mirrors reflecting God's face. They are instrumental and do not and cannot take the place of God. Religion can thus be a crisis to itself, a crisis of religion contradicting itself, negating itself, and making itself harmful both to God and to the people who seek God.

A Full House

Have we exhausted the meaning of this rich parable of Jesus? No, we haven't. How can one ever exhaust the meaning of what Jesus said and did? What Jesus meant in word and in action is inexhaustible because the riches of what he was supremely engaged in—the riches of God's reign—are inexhaustible. Are we, then, not encouraged to go a little further and surmise how those outcasts and outsiders fare at the great banquet of God's reign?

One may turn at this point to Matthew's version of the parable (Matt. 22:1-14), and especially to the concluding part (22:11-13) in which a guest not in a wedding garment was quickly spotted by the king and thrown out of the banquet. It has been conjectured that this last episode "may well have been originally a separate parable, in which the lack of a wedding garment represents the failure to fulfill the will of the king who graciously invited the guest."[24] As to that concluding statement, "For though many are invited, few are chosen," it is pointed out that it "is not really an interpretation of the parable, in which only a single individual is 'not chosen' (contrary to

---

24. Filson, *A Commentary on the Gospel according to St. Matthew*, 233.

vs. 14), but a homiletic application."²⁵ There is also evidence in Matthew's account of the parable (22:1-10) that reflects the destruction of Jerusalem in 70 C.E.²⁶ What we find, then, in Matthew 22:11-13 is a "second, appended parable" employed by Matthew "to affirm that the invitation and warning in the parable are still operative after the year 70: only the person who does not suppose one has accepted the invitation once and for all now that one has been baptized, but rather lets the invitation stamp one's entire life, will continue to sit at the feast."²⁷

From the version of the parable in Matthew's Gospel we must, then, return to that in the Gospel of Luke, which presents a very different picture. There the parable ends with the host's words: "I want my house full" (14:24), and not with the incident of the person not properly dressed for the occasion singled out for judgment and rejection as in Matthew's Gospel. Here in Luke's Gospel we can almost see the master of the house greeting strangers and outcasts with a broad smile, the master in a happy and expansive mood as he sees his banquet hall filled to capacity first with the outcasts of the city and then with strangers from outside the city. This concluding episode seems more in harmony with Jesus' message of God's reign and with his ministry among the people treated as strangers and outcasts by the religious authorities.

The key word here is "full." Why does the banquet hall have to be full? It could be half full, even just one-third full, as long as the banquet is not going to be miscarried and the sumptuous food totally wasted. No, it must be a *full* banquet—a banquet brimming over with people, overflowing with women, men, and children. It must be like a banquet Jesus had with five thousand persons in a deserted place on the eastern side of Lake Galilee (Mark 6:32-44; pars. Matt. 14:13-21; Luke 9:10b-17). It must be a banquet attended by no fewer than four thousand who once ate with Jesus (Mark 8:1-10; par. Matt. 15:32-39).²⁸ The number of guests must be large. The banquet now taking place before one's eyes is not a banquet for the selected few, not for the social elite, not for the politically powerful, not for the religious insiders. These people have boycotted it. And now it has become a banquet for people—outcasts and strangers. It is a people feast. It is a completely different sort of banquet from that which was planned in the first place. The master now wants his house to be full.

The concern of the host of the banquet is clear, and coming from Jesus

25. Schweizer, *The Good News according to Matthew*, 421.

26. See A. J. Grieve, "Matthew," in *A Commentary of the Bible*, ed. Arthur S. Peake (London: Thomas Nelson & Sons, 1957), 718b.

27. Schweizer, *The Good News according to Matthew*, 422.

28. "The close similarity of this story to vi.34-44 shows that the two are variants of the same account" (Sherman E. Johnson, *A Commentary on the Gospel according to St. Luke*, Harper's New Testament Commentaries [New York: Harper & Brothers, Publishers, 1960], 140).

that concern becomes at once a challenge and an invitation. As it has been pointed out, it

> seems to be a concern to demonstrate that it is possible for the banquet to be *full* without the original guests. The occasion can be a grand success even in their absence. The noble host wants the new guests to feel total acceptance. They must not look around and say, "See how many seats are vacant. What a shame! Poor man, he is rejected by important people and has only the few of us at his banquet." No! His house must be full![29]

And seeing his house really *full*, filled to the brim, the host of the banquet is extremely glad. Those outcasts—dregs of society—make him happy. Those strangers—Gentiles outside the pale of an exclusive religious community—bring joy to him.

The full banquet and the contented host encourage us to be a little bolder in our theological imagination. What is important here is that the host makes sure that the guests "feel total acceptance." How important this is we should know at once. They are strangers and outcasts. Acceptance is a notion alien to them. They do not expect it. As to the banquet, they have not chosen to come in the first place. They have been persuaded, literally taken by the hand, to join in it. And it is such an unexpected invitation that they come just as they are in their casual wear, simple clothes, perhaps even worn-out jackets. To their complete surprise, then, they are totally accepted. They are accepted just as they are. They are not expected to be other than themselves. They are not required to wear the make-up that makes them appear different from their usual selves. Evidently, in telling the story Luke grasped the point Jesus wanted to make but Matthew missed it.

Since these people came from different places and diverse backgrounds, they must have brought different interests and concerns with them. They must have spoken different languages too. They must have also represented a variety of faiths and religions. How can the master of the house, the host of the banquet, communicate with them? How is it possible to have a meeting of minds between him and the strangers he finds in his house? What is the nature of the community he and his guests are going to make? What kind of relationships are to be forged between them?

If traditional theology is our guide, then we can almost predict the failure of the banquet even before it begins. If the missiological practice of the churches in the past is our reference, the community at the banquet is bound to be distressing from the start. Perhaps this is what Matthew's

---

29. Bailey, *Through Peasant Eyes*, 109.

version of the parable leads us to expect. There is no compromise on the part of the master of the house about the propriety these strangers must observe. They must conform to his standard, listen to what he has to say, behave in the ways prescribed by him. Those who fail to do so, even unintentionally, will forfeit the privilege of being there.

But this is not what is projected in the parable as Luke sees it. There the main emphasis is "total acceptance." The master of the house wants those strangers to feel at home. The host of the banquet wants them to feel accepted. Since no preconditions are attached to their being part of the banquet, there will be no postconditions imposed on them to be able to enjoy the banquet. And what a rich banquet it turns out to be! Rich not only in the food the master of the house has prepared, but rich in what those stranger-guests have brought to his house, rich in the community that has come into being between them and among them.

This is the way God's reign is, Jesus was saying to the people listening to him. It must be the same thing Jesus is saying to us today, to us who live in the world of different languages, cultures, and religions. What is this banquet of God's reign really like? What are we men, women, and children of diverse backgrounds to expect from it? How is it realized in our midst? To know answers to these questions, we must look around ourselves and beyond ourselves. We must learn more deeply what God must be like in our world. And above all we must learn from Jesus' message of God's reign in order to realize who God is. It is to this God of God's reign, and not to the God of our religious tradition, certainly not to the God of our own making, that Jesus wants to direct our thoughts and commitment. It is to this God that he committed himself to the end of his life. To know the reign of God is, then, not only to know God, but to know Jesus.

CHAPTER 2

NEW HEAVEN AND NEW EARTH

I saw no temple in the city; for its temple was the sovereign Lord God and the Lamb. The city did not need the sun or the moon to shine on it; for the glory of God gave it light, and its lamp was the Lamb. By its light shall the nations walk, and to it the kings of the earth shall bring their splendor. (Rev. 21:22-24)

Not a Homogeneous God

It is obvious from what has been said that to render the Greek phrase *basileia tou theou* into "the kingdom of God" does not correctly express Jesus' message of God's reign. It in fact misrepresents it. It conveys the notions of national territory, feudal system, and monarchical structure, in a word, a culture of authoritarianism. And linked with God's salvation as most Christians see it, it is given a false notion of a heavenly realm of inestimable joy and happiness reserved solely for them. It is then translated into the community on earth Christian believers establish for themselves to enjoy the foretaste of what is to come. And from time to time in the history of Christianity the church identifies itself, as in the case of the church of the Middle Ages in Europe, as the "kingdom of God" on earth to exercise the divine power and authority over secular powers and authorities.

Though the expression "the reign of God" is not totally adequate, it at least does not represent the notion of a boundary, be it political or religious. Implied in it is the faith that it is God who exercises the rule and not the ecclesiastical authorities, the confession that God exercises the rule in a very special way, uplifting the dispossessed and empowering the oppressed. This is why we have used it consistently in the place of "the kingdom of God." It has more to do with rule and power. The question is, of course, what kind of rule and what kind of power it represents. This is an important question that will engage us later in our discussion.

The reign of God in Jesus' proclamation is not a territory, a structure, or a system, in short, it is not an institution. It is, however, an institution that "the kingdom of God" has come to mean in the minds of most Christians. Once institutionalized, the reign of God takes on characteristics of the social and political institution embodied in a hierarchical structure—characteristics that contradict the very nature of God's reign, characteristics such as homogeneity, rigidity, exclusiveness, or strict control. This is why Christian churches in most countries in Asia and Africa have not yet been freed from the self-understanding inherited from their missionary past that they enjoy special favor and privilege in the "kingdom of God" on earth and in heaven. They have been half-hearted about the pluralistic nature of the world. And they continue to assume that they must strive for the homogeneity of life and faith and for the criteria of truth that can be applied universally.

Is it any wonder that a Christian church shaped by such a notion of "the kingdom of God" has something in common with a totalitarian state? A totalitarian government is built on a homogeneous political system. It seeks to mold people's lives to the minutest detail. Reporting, for instance, on Maoist China in the 1960s, an observer writes about what he saw in that land: "It is a red country, red to the very core.... In the fields, farmers till the soil with a red flag planted beside them. The walls of homes are painted red, and on them are written teachings from Chairman Mao Zedong's red Analects."[1] The whole nation is mobilized to think and behave in conformity with the teachings and policies of the Party. The mass mobilization turns the whole nation into a machine controlled and manipulated by those in power. It is the collapse of such a party machine that we witnessed at the end of the 1980s in the former Soviet Union and Eastern European nations.

But China continues an uncertain course of political development. To stem the further erosion of power the Chinese rulers had to resort to the use of violence to crush the prodemocracy movements that engulfed China in June 1989 and set back the course of democratization for at least a decade. In so doing they were practicing what their deceased leader Mao Zedong inculcated some decades earlier when he said: the function of dictatorship "is to suppress the reactionary classes and elements and those exploiters in our country who range themselves against the socialist revolution, to suppress all those who try to wreck our social construction, or in other words, to resolve the internal contradiction between ourselves and

---

1. *This Is Communist China*, by the staff of *Yomiuri Shinbun*, ed. Robert Trumbull (New York: David Mackay Company, 1968), 1.

the enemy."[2] The Chinese rulers may have succeeded, in the short run, in restoring their dictatorial rule, but in the long run they have the movement of human history toward freedom and democracy to contend with. There will be occasions later to refer again to this event, one of the most cold-blooded suppressions of people's rights and freedom in the pages of China's history.

What happens in a totalitarian society is that humanity comes to a full stop. Human relationships become terribly distorted. Human creativity is suppressed. The basic human right—the right to think—is taken away from the citizens. The right to be human is denied them. Human beings are forced to become like robots. Robots of course do not think. They are not human. They do not demand "human" rights. What we witness in history is how people refuse to be robots manipulated by those in power and rise up to assert their rights to be free and human. Political homogeneity created by a totalitarian power is an insult to human beings and a nightmare to human development. It cannot withstand the force of history to move toward the fulfillment of life in a community of freedom and justice for all.

Jesus' reign of God is not a homogeneous, monotonous, uniform, totalitarian regime. But the Christian church has often appeared more like such a regime than God's reign in Jesus' message. It has not quite understood God's reign to belong to people as Jesus envisioned it, but to bishops and priests. It has been all too ready to stifle the theological creativity of innovative theologians. It has considered it its duty to maintain the status quo and to perpetuate the language of faith that has lost its meaning for the men and women not only outside but also inside the church. It has all too often closed its eyes to God's activity in the *whole* world, and not just in the "Christian" world.

But how can we not be open to God's work outside the church as well as inside the church? How can we continue to entertain the illusion that there is no truth except the truth transmitted by the Christian church? This is particularly a soul-searching question for thinking Christians in the Third World today. This is not just an admission based on the fact that the world is pluralistic not only socially and politically but religiously and culturally. The fact that the world is pluralistic is not human invention. It is a basic fact inherent in God's creation. It is how God "in the beginning made heaven and earth" (Gen. 1:1). Theologically, then, it is impossible not to assume God's direct relationship with the world outside the church. After all, God created the world inhabited by all sorts of people, and not just by Christians.

Small wonder Jesus' vision of God's reign is anything but homoge-

---

2. Mao Zedong, *Four Essays on Philosophy* (Beijing: Foreign Language Press, 1968), 83.

neous. It consists not only of men but also of women. We already have
in Jesus a feminist theologian two thousand years ago. He did not have
the vocabulary of feminist theologians today, but by accepting women into
the community of God's reign, he practiced what we call today feminist
theology. He himself would be aghast to hear opponents of the ordination of women assert that females are not qualified to be priests because
Jesus was a male. He would be the last person to regard "sacramental-
ity" as the sole prerogative of males and would have no problem about
ordaining women to be priests. It is possible that some of his women followers could have been among his disciples, the possibility completely
obscured by the authors of the Gospels in their accounts of Jesus' call of
the "twelve" disciples. A feminist biblical scholar has reminded us: "Seeing Paul in the context of a Christian missionary movement initiated before
Paul's 'conversion'... allows us to conceptualize this movement in such a
way that women can emerge as initiators and leaders of the movements and
not just Paul's helpers, benignly tolerated and utilized by the great apostle
for his own missionary work."[3]

But the tradition of barring women from ordination is still alive and
well not only in the Orthodox churches and the Roman Catholic Church,
but also in some Protestant churches in Asia. This is why a Christian from
Hong Kong laments. She says:

> I have been in the church for almost ten years. I know some people
> who are eager to be ordained ministers, but there are a lot of diffi-
> culties and conflicts they have to face. What is worse is that women
> have more problems to face than men.
>
> Actually, there are more women in the churches than men; there
> are more female theological students in the seminaries than males.
> Yet we can see that most of the church leaders are men and there are
> a lot of male priests in the churches. Where have the women leaders
> gone? Where have the female theological students gone? Have they
> all become the "helpers" of their "heads," or have they all become
> the "wives" of our priests? Why do we not accept those women who
> are ready to commit themselves to be full-time ministers?[4]

More women than men in churches and more female theological students than male theological students in seminaries. Such "demographical"
changes of church and theological education have not only taken place in

3. Elisabeth Schüssler-Fiorenza, *In Memory of Her: A Feminist Theological Reconstruction of Christian Origins* (New York: Crossroad, 1983), 101–2.

4. Agatha Wong Mei Yuk, "The Ministries of Women in Paul's Letter," in *Asian Women Doing Theology*, Report from Singapore Conference, November 20–29, 1987 (Hong Kong: Asian Women's Resource Centre for Culture and Theology, 1989), 278.

the West but are also taking place in the East. This is bound to exert a profound impact on the church's self-understanding, from theology to polity,
from ordination to administration. If the force of the patriarchal tradition
will not yield to the ordination of women, the numerical strength of women
in church and seminaries will force open the door of ordination closed to
them.

Further, the reign of God that Jesus proclaimed is made up of outcasts and strangers. This was the subject of our discussion in the previous
chapter. Indeed, his was an ecumenical vision long before the word "ecumenism" came to be used in the modern history of Christianity. After two
thousand years Christian churches are still negotiating unity among themselves and debating their relationship with people of different religious
commitments, while Jesus was already reaching out to them and accepting
them. Contrary to the churches' endeavor toward unity, whether among
themselves or among humankind, the endeavor that puts unity before acceptance, Jesus practiced acceptance before unity. Unity is the outcome of
acceptance, and not the other way around. This is how Jesus went about
his ministry. But Christian churches in their unity efforts have not learned
this way of Jesus toward unity, be it church unity or the unity of humankind. Is there any wonder that the vision of unity becomes ever dimmer
for Christian churches?

Here a little digression into the history of ecumenism that led to the for-
mation of the World Council of Churches in 1948 is in order. This history
was inspired by

the vision of the world being my parish, the vision of evangelizing the
world in this generation, the vision of churches and confessions or-
ganically united. But the problem is that those "great" pioneers of ecumenism has their vision very much conditioned by their experience
of faith from one particular background—the white Western Christian background. Their vision was also shaped by their world-view
formed under the influence of the political and cultural domination
of the West over the rest of the world. And of course theirs was the
vision of Christianity becoming the center of the religious geography
of peoples and nations.

The ecumenical vision of the old age became, then, the ecumenical burden of our age. The sheer weight of that burden can be
staggering. The World Council of Churches' monthly, *One World*,
seems to try to bear that burden gallantly. But that magazine, *One
World*, in each and every issue, brings us *not* one world, but many
worlds. It introduces us *not* to one nation and one people but to many
nations and many peoples. And from time to time it reminds us that

Christianity does not command the spiritual world of humankind; it is in fact a divide-and-rule world in which Christians do not even have a majority vote.[5]

Needless to say, a fundamental shift is called for in Christian churches' efforts toward unity, be it of Christian churches or of human communities—a shift demanded by the reality of our world of pluralism.

The kind of unity projected by the reign of God in Jesus' parable of the great dinner we discussed in the previous chapter is something quite different. It is not the result of painstaking efforts to reach agreement on what they must believe and how they must behave. It is not the outcome of give and take in doctrinal and organizational matters. It is not the kind of unity that can be achieved through bickering with each other, nor can it come about by behaving courteously to each other, leaving differences untouched. This kind of unity is too diplomatic, too political, and too calculating. It crumbles and collapses when situations change and interests of various church bodies shift. Unity of this kind is, to use Jesus' metaphors, like "building a house on sand. The rain came down, the floods rose, the wind blew, and battered against the house; down it fell with a great crash" (Matt. 7:26-27).

The unity envisioned by Jesus grows out of human beings meeting one another at the deepest level of their lives—lives threatened with uncertainties and meaninglessness, rendered precarious by the evil forces at work in the world. It is at that level where human beings need each other's support and seek God's presence that unity emerges. That unity is built on the acknowledgment of one's own limitations on the one hand and on the other, on the richness of each other's diverse backgrounds and resources. It is a unity that develops out of the communion of people with one another and with God.

People's Creed

The reign of God, according to Jesus, is not an institution but people—people with dignity as human beings regardless of their backgrounds and entitled to freedom and justice, people affirming their full humanity and refusing to accept the conditions that belittle that humanity. This reign of God creates a new consciousness in them, emboldens them to claim to be full members of human community irrespective of their backgrounds and status, and enables them to experience God as a God who affirms them

---

5. These two paragraphs are taken from my article "The Ecumenical Calling of the Christian Church Today—Ecumenism and Paradigm-Shifts," in *Ecumenical Review* (World Council of Churches, Geneva) 41, no. 2 (April 1989): 249.

and shares their concerns and struggles. A Christian from Zimbabwe puts it this way in what he calls "The People's Creed":

> I believe in a color-blind God.
> Maker of technicolor people,
> Who created the universe
> And provided abundant resources
> For equitable distribution
> among all God's people.[6]

This is a colorful interpretation of the creation story in the first chapter of Genesis. Such an interpretation can be inspired only by a person bearing God's image on his or her person, having that divine image mutilated by the tyranny and inhumanity of racism, but now knowing how to enjoy God who is God because God affirms them with their color as much as God affirms people of other colors.

This is precisely what Jesus' message of God's reign does to people. It makes them unable to accept the image of themselves created for them and imposed on them by others. It affirms them not by comparing them with others but just as they are created by God. As long as the Christian faith is defined by others, especially by those who hold power over other people, it negates certain men and women as human beings of a certain skin color and forces them to be something other than themselves. Jesus' reign of God has nothing to do with this kind of self-negation. On the contrary, it is self-affirmation. For too long the Christian church has inculcated in people a morbid sense of self-negation. This cannot be what Jesus meant when he told his disciples: "If any want to become my followers, let them *deny themselves* and take up their cross and follow me" (Mark 8:34, NRSV; pars. Matt. 16:24; Luke 9:23; italics added). Jesus was talking about discipleship and not the worthiness of human persons. He never questioned the latter.

It is against such theological background that one begins to resonate with the assertions of black theologians in America concerning the meaning of blackness for their experience of Jesus. We find, for example, this stirring theological affirmation:

> To say that Christ is black means that black people are God's poor people whom Christ has come to liberate. . . . To say that Christ is black means that God, in God's infinite wisdom and mercy, not only takes color seriously; God takes it upon God's own self and discloses

---

6. Canaan Banana, *The Gospel according to the Ghetto* (Geneva: World Council of Churches, 1974), 8.

God's will to make us whole—new creatures born in the divine blackness and redeemed through the blood of the Black Christ.... The
"blackness of Christ," therefore, is not simply a statement about skin
color, but rather the transcendent affirmation that God has not ever,
no not ever, left the oppressed in the struggle.[7]

In such an affirmation is the joy of recovery of humanity after the long
history of suffering and humiliation. In it black people in the United States
find their Christ—the Christ who is black and not white, the Christ who is
not the oppressor like the slave masters but the oppressed like themselves,
the Christ who is not the conqueror but the liberator. This is the theological
meaning of blackness. It has to be the heart of black christology.

What we encounter in the black Christ is Jesus who enables people,
black or not, to realize their worthiness before God and in human community. This is the Jesus who associated himself with those women and
men marginalized and despised as unworthy of God's salvation and human
respect. How can this Jesus question the worthiness of those who come to
follow him? What he did was not to give it to them but to affirm it already in
them. Discipleship presupposes it and enhances it. It is not by accident that
most of Jesus' followers, including his disciples, were men and women of
lowly social status. But how they had their self-respect and self-confidence
reconfirmed in Jesus' company! It is these women and men who carried out
their ministry of witness to Jesus the risen Christ with courage and power.
Paul was right on target when he told Christians at Corinth in his letter:
"The folly of God is wiser than human wisdom, and the weakness of God
stronger than human strength. My friends, think what sort of people you
are, whom God has called. Few of you are wise by any human standard; few
powerful or of noble birth. Yet, to shame the wise, God has chosen what
the world counts folly, and to shame what is strong, God has chosen what
the world counts weakness. God has chosen things without rank or standing in the world, mere nothings, to overthrow the existing order" (1 Cor.
1:25-28). What an apt description of the Christian community Paul helped
to bring into existence, the community consisting of slaves and people of
lowly profession and position!

Jesus himself, as a matter of fact, fits this Pauline description mar-
velously. Born a son of a carpenter-father and himself also a carpenter
before embarking on his ministry, Jesus would have nothing to boast about
as Paul the Apostle was to do on occasion later. Paul, an educated man and
a Roman citizen, must have at times fretted that he himself was not quite of
the rank of men and women he was describing. But the point he was mak-

---

7. James Cone, *God of the Oppressed* (New York: Seabury Press, 1975), 136–37.

ing is that it is none other than these people—people without status and power—that "shame the strong and the wise." This is precisely what he saw as the secret of the cross, the reality and symbol of shame, pain, and death that turned into the reality and symbol of honor, joy, and life. For this reason he "resolved not to claim to know anything but Jesus Christ—Christ nailed to the cross" (1 Cor. 2:2).

No, Jesus was not talking about self-negation, negation of self-respect and self-worthiness. This is not well understood by some of those engaged in the evaluation of Christian missions. They point out that most Christian converts in India, for example, are the pariahs, outcasts or untouchables, or in China uneducated and illiterate people. They also lament that very few Brahmins or Confucian literati were attracted to the Christian faith. In this connection the Jesuit missionaries in China in the seventeenth century, especially Mateo Ricci and Michael Ruggerius the first Jesuit missionaries to set foot in that "Middle Kingdom," are held as examples to follow, for they spared no efforts to win Chinese rulers and Confucian scholars, including the emperor, even to the extent of wearing a queue and Chinese dress. Their willingness to learn from Chinese culture and their effort "to become Chinese to the Chinese," to paraphrase Paul's words in his letter to the Corinthian Christians (1 Cor. 9:19-23), are laudable. But it is also pointed out that "to identify with the elite of China meant much more than external dress. The missionaries had to avoid studiously any criticism of Confucius, the patron saint of the literati. In fact, they would come to side with a particular view of Confucius shared by a radical clique within the government. They were careful to observe all the appropriate amenities when visiting with scholars—attitudes and ceremonies considerably at variance with those in use when visiting with less highly placed persons."[8]

The price the Jesuit missionaries had to pay for their missionary strategy, in retrospect, was high. They had to take the side of the Confucian rulers in power and not the side of the men, women, and children who suffered under the social and political traditions and systems shaped by Confucianism. Both critics and defenders of missionary efforts in China or India seem thus entirely to have missed the point Paul was making in his letter to the Corinthian Christians, the point that "to shame the wise, God has chosen what the world counts folly, and to shame what is strong, God has chosen things without rank or standing in the world."

In hindsight, the missionary strategy based on the premise that conversion of the ruling elite would bring about conversion of the masses is a mistaken strategy. The awakening of the people and their struggle for

---

8. Ralph R. Covell, *Confucius, the Buddha, and Christ: A History of the Gospel in Chinese* (Maryknoll, N.Y.: Orbis Books, 1986), 41.

social and political change in some Asian countries in recent years more than prove it to be fallacious. It is not only fallacious in light of people's movements in recent years, but contradictory to the way Jesus went about his ministry of God's reign, taking the side of the poor and the oppressed. This "Jesuit error" was to be repeated again by some Protestant missions in China in the first half of the twentieth century: they associated themselves closely with the Nationalist Party's ruling elite converted to Christianity on very dubious grounds. The confusion and disappointment in some mission quarters in the aftermath of the Communist takeover of China were enormous. It is a hard lesson for the Christian church to learn, the lesson that it has been learning badly since Christianity became a state religion under the tutelage of Constantine, the Roman emperor, in the fourth century: the Christian missionary enterprise that stakes its success on alliance with the powers that be is bound to fail.

Christian missions and the Christian churches in India or China, for example, should have done all they could to interact with Brahmins or Confucian scholars. But there is a far more pressing task of enabling millions upon millions of outcast and illiterate women, men, and children to assert their humanity, to claim their rights as citizens, and to regain their respect and confidence as human beings before God and in their community. Instead, the emphasis in missionary preaching and the message at evangelical rallies and Sunday worship services is "obedience to God." But what is meant by "obedience to God"? It often means acceptance of their station in life and submission to social and political forces that make them outcast, untouchable, and illiterate. There is little of what Paul said with great passion about the foolish shaming the wise and the weak shaming the strong. Is it by accident that it is often left for secular forces to make changes in the life of the oppressed people—for example, the Communist revolution in China or the conscientization and organization of outcasts in India to stand up for their rights against their landlords?

There is nothing wrong in outcast people and illiterate persons accepting the Christian faith rather than Brahmins and Confucian literati. After all, did not Jesus associate himself precisely with such people? Did he not declare that the reign of God is theirs? If Jesus was not ashamed of them, why should the Christian church that bears his name be ashamed of them? If it was Jesus' mission to open the door of God's reign to them, why should not the Christian missions that seek to bring to them the saving love of God through Jesus do the same? This does not mean that Brahmins or Confucian literati should be excluded from God's salvation. Not at all. One recalls, for example, the story of how Jesus received Nicodemus, a rabbi, and was engaged in conversation with him about being born of the Spirit (John 3). The truth of the matter is that Jesus made it his mission to be in the company of the marginalized and the disinherited and to enable them to reclaim their humanity given by God. To deny them, then, is to deny Jesus. To be ashamed of them is to be ashamed of Jesus. It is as simple as that.

When Jesus exhorted his disciples to "deny themselves," he was talking about their commitment to the reign of God he had declared. He was demanding that they make a common cause with him in his struggle for it. And he was making clear to them that it was not going to be all rosy in the path of God's reign. Pain and suffering were going to be their lot. This is implied in Jesus asking them "to take up their cross and follow him." The translation in the New English Bible brings this out clearly and forcefully: "Anyone who wishes to be a follower of mine *must leave self behind;* they must take up their cross and come with me" (italics added). Reading these words in the light of how Jesus went about lifting up the downtrodden and empowering the powerless, I believe Jesus was stressing commitment and not self-abasement, emphasizing determination and not self-humiliation. And of course with commitment and determination come the awareness of being involved in a noble cause and the sense of self-importance previously denied them. The cross has the power to ennoble the despised and to lift up the downtrodden. It has the power to humanize the dehumanized. A strange power, this cross!

A Color-blind God

It must be pointed out too how easily human self-perception leads to God-perception! Do not the dominant religious groups, be they religious authorities, theological elite, or the religious community that has power and influence over other communities, often create God in their image and make an idol of that image? This is also evident in the history of Christian art. What theologians have done through words and concepts art has done in images and symbols. The image of God as a grand white old man with airs of power and authority is very much a part of the Christian consciousness of God, even the consciousness of some Christians whose skin color is not white. Similarly, religious paintings in the West have created the image of a white baby-boy Jesus lying in a manger watched by his parents who bore the distinctive traits of the Europeans in the Middle Ages.

Universalizing a particular image of God or Jesus does disservice to the richness of God and God's relationships to humanity and to the world. It delimits God to a certain segment of human experience. But the God exclusively shaped by that particular segment of human experience is a false God. In the realm of truth, and especially religious truth, a part does not represent the whole. We are learning from the history of Christianity that a part of the Christian church often misrepresents God and what God does in the world. The situation becomes serious when that misrepresentation is legitimized as orthodoxy and imposed on believers. That is why the truth of an "orthodox" faith and teaching often has to be defended, protected, and enforced with the power of church authorities. When the church exercises its power in this way, homogeneity is held as a religious virtue and diversity a vice.

The People's Creed we cited poses a serious question to that homogeneity of faith and theology. Theological insights contained in it challenge the homogeneous faith of many Christians and the homogeneous image they impose on God. That is why the creed confesses to "a color-blind God." This is the God of an African Christian who feels deeply and experiences in his own person what it means to be a victim of racial discrimination. Who else except black persons who have gone through bitter humiliation because of the color of their skin could be inspired to confess God to be a color-blind God? How much theology is packed into this phrase "a color-blind God"!

The theology of the People's Creed says that although we human beings, Christians not excepted, are prisoners of colors, God is not. It declares that though we are perversely conscious of them, God is not. It affirms that despite the fact that we judge human beings by the color of their skin, God does not. It makes so much sense of God as it makes non-sense of the distorted values we attach to skin color. It brings God ever so close to black humanity, the God monopolized by white humanity and *white*-washed by them. The God who is not color-blind, who has a predilection for one particular color, is a God of the *white* lie. Theological awareness such as this makes the search for God necessary all over again.

The theology derived from this People's Creed—the creed that confesses faith in a color-blind God—has more to tell us about God and about us human beings. It tells us that we are very much conditioned by colors, but God conditions them. It points out that we attach inordinate value to colors, whereas God sees no ultimate value in them. It says that for us white is white and can never be black, while for God black can be white and white can be black. For us colors are not interchangeable, but for God they are. For us colors cannot be integrated, but for God colors must be integrated. In the eyes of the human beholder shades of the skin color tell of one's social origin, even one's religious association, as in the case of the caste society of Hinduism. In the eyes of God, however, the roots of human beings, whether black, brown, red, or white, are not to be found in the shades of skin color but in the personal image of God implanted in them. To the people wounded, humiliated, and discriminated against in a society ridden with racism God is revealed as a color-blind God. And of course in the reign of the color-blind God colors of the skin play no role of discrimination. They are expressions of the richness of God's creation, the complementary nature of human community, and the interdependence of human persons.

It is, therefore, not strange at all for the People's Creed to say that this color-blind God makes "technicolor people." At first one may ask: Is this not absurd? Is this not a contradictory statement? For how can a *color-blind* God make *technicolor* people? "Color-blindness" and "technicolorness" are not compatible. They repulse each other. They reject each other. If you are color-blind, then you are not capable of technicolor. And if you are technicolored, then you are not color-blind. This is how we human beings are and how we reason. But the People's Creed reasons differently. It attaches far more importance to God's reasoning than to human reasoning, because God's reasoning is the reasoning of the heart and not of the head, the reasoning of the soul and not the brain. What rules in God's reign after all is not the reasoning based on race, color, or creed, but the reasoning derived from God's boundless love for all human beings. This is the reign of God that Jesus helped to make visible and real among the disinherited people of his day.

The deep insight into God disclosed in this simple creed amazes us. The glimpse of God it shares with us is a God who is color-blind, not because God is incapacitated when it comes to colors, but because God does not play one color against other colors. God does not favor one color at the expense of other colors either. For God each color is equally important and each shade of it is equally indispensable. God needs all colors and all shades of each color. God is like a great painter who deeply appreciates each and every color and who approaches each and every shade of a color with deep reverence. In God's magnificent painting of the creation, no color is despised and no shade of it is abused. Under God's brush each color—brown, red, black, white—comes alive. It finds fulfillment on the canvas of God, the supreme painter. God has to be, then, fully and completely technicolored. God's deep appreciation of all colors and all shades of each color cannot be contested. God does not wish to be a colorless God—God without colors. Nor is God monocolored—a one-colored God. The God of creation is God in full colors. God is a multicolored God, and not a monocolored God, who created heaven and earth and all things between them. Is not the People's Creed, then, a most ingenious commentary on the story of God's creation? Is it not a most convincing interpretation of Jesus' parable of the great dinner, more convincing than most learned and scholarly exegeses on the parable?

It is this same God who is the host of the great banquet in Jesus' parable. How could Jesus have envisioned God's reign other than that made colorful and technicolored by the outcasts and strangers "gently compelled" to come in, bringing with them their different stories and diverse tales to tell? And what a contrast this banquet makes to the banquet previously planned and then aborted! In Jesus' parable that first banquet is planned in order to be aborted. In the plot of the story the banquet to be attended by the persons of wealth and class is told to make way for the one that illuminates God as the color-blind God who made technicolor people.

What racism has done, then, is not merely an assault on colored humanity, but an attempt to abolish God. When practiced by Christians and Christian churches, it is a form of atheism more atheistic than that with which certain political ideologies and religious traditions are often accused. When enacted into social, political, or religious systems and institutions by a Christian church and its members, it becomes an idolatry far more idolatrous than the idolatry disdained and denounced in the faiths and religions of other people. The monocolored God they adore and worship is no more and no less than themselves. Racism is a form of narcissism too. What it worships is the God of narcissism. In other words, those who practice racism do not worship God; they worship themselves. Of course the reign of God has nothing to do with such a religion of narcissism. That is why it must be filled with outcasts and Gentiles—women, men, and children of all colors.

Interdependence of Peoples

The color-blind God who makes technicolor people in the People's Creed is the God of all nations. The expression "God of all nations" is not unfamiliar to us Christians. That God is "of all nations" is in fact the claim we are only too ready to make on behalf of God. Our claim, however, can be no more than a pious lip-service paid to God. It can also be used to justify our evangelistic zeal to win other people to what Christians believe and what the Christian church asserts to be true at all times and to be good in all places. That God of "all nations" can in reality be a God of "one nation," a God of "one tribe," a God of "one race." That God can be no more than an extension of a God worshiped by a particular segment of human community. The expression "the God of all nations" in this case is the God of religious imperialism, the God who goes out to conquer other nations and peoples. In traditional missiology it is this God who defines the consciousness of the Christian church and the practice of Christian evangelization.

In the world of increasing economic and political interdependence more and more of us Christians are learning that the God of all nations is not just an extension of our God. Interdependence of peoples and nations goes much deeper than political and economic interdependence. There also must be interdependence in other matters such as history, or even religion. We human beings share each other's experiences not only at the level of material welfare and political concerns, but at a much deeper level of spiritual well-being. We are follow travelers on the journey of life and history. We are bound to the common destiny of humanity. We are engaged in the search of something that is ultimate, something that can explain our life and world in transition.

Let us take history as an example. The history of one nation has its own special characteristics. It cannot be transferred to another nation. The reason is simple and evident: history does not take place in a vacuum. For history to be history it has to be rooted in the soil of a nation and in the community of a people. History is not an idea. It is a happening, or a series of happenings, that takes place at particular intersections of time and space. History is not a concept either. It is not manufactured in a historian's study or in a philosopher's brain. History is something that has to do with women, men, and children who live and die in a specific social-political space and in a certain religious-cultural environment. History is not self-subsistent. It has to be relational. To put it another way, it has to be contextual. History without a context, history abstracted from it, is no longer history. History consists of stories of human persons as individuals, as a community, or as a nation. It is the lived experiences of men, women, and children who find themselves at certain crossroads of time and space.

Strictly speaking, then, the word "history" cannot stand alone. It has to be a history of something. We speak, for example, of the history of India, the history of China, the history of Taiwan, the history of France, the history of Nicaragua, or the history of the United States. This means that the history of a nation is nontransferrable. The history of ancient Israel, for instance, cannot be transferred to the Philippines and become the history of the Philippines. The history of Japan cannot be superimposed on Thailand and replace it. Imperialism and colonialism are blatant infringements on this nontransferrable nature of the history of a nation. Whether imperialism or colonialism, they infringe upon the inviolability of a people and a nation. The colonized people had to suffer the shame and ignominy of being subjects of such anomalies as *British* India, *French* Indochina, or the *Belgian* Congo.

If the history of a people and a nation is not transferrable, is it fated to exist in isolation? Is it to be lived totally unrelated to other peoples and nations? The answer is of course no. Since the dawn of human civilization, nations and peoples have been in contact with each other through trade, religious activities, cultural exchanges, and, unfortunately, wars. Human history is a history of interactions between nations from ancient times to the present time. The fact of the matter is that peoples and nations are closely bound together in a common fate and destiny. Human beings are forced to be aware of this today as never before as ecological crisis and nuclear power threaten to bring about a destruction of global dimensions. Here we enter the realm of meanings—meanings reflected in external events and happenings that constitute history.

Interactions of peoples and nations are, thus, not limited to external things such as trade or politics. There is an inner dimension to these interactions. It is the dimension of meaning. Meaning has no boundaries. It crosses the boundaries we set arbitrarily or by force—national boundaries, cultural boundaries, ideological boundaries, even religious boundaries. It has been said, for example, that revolution cannot be exported. But the fact of the matter is that it can. Revolution is exported from one society to another society, from one country to another country, perhaps not in the way it is carried out in a particular place, but through the meaning it represented, the aspiration it fostered, and the goal it envisioned. How otherwise can one explain the Communist revolution in China, Cuba, or Nicaragua, the revolution that had its origin in the Soviet Union and transformed that country to a totalitarian Communist state? But a revolution in reverse has taken place today in most of these Communist countries. This time around it is a revolution inspired by the twin notions of freedom and democracy. All this tells us that the historical experience of a nation and a people in one part of the world is bound to exert a deep impact on those in other parts of the world. The human quest for meaning cannot be stopped either by guns, censors, or national boundaries.

Meaning also transcends time. The meaning of a particular event in the past has implications for the present and for the future. When we say we must learn from the lessons of history, we are saying that the meaning of what happened yesterday must not be lost today. Although we human beings are hopeless learners when it comes to the lessons of history, we must not and we cannot cease to learn from history. It is the meaning transcending time that makes us human beings historical beings. We cannot be conscious of being historical if we are imprisoned in a segment of time, reduced to a mathematical point of time. When time ceases to flow, when it becomes stagnant, life also comes to a standstill, is overcome by meaninglessness, and eventually dies. Time does not have to be our enemy, an enemy of our life. Its ticking away does not have to be feared as the ticking away of our life. Time carries our life from one stage to another stage in fulfillment of the meaning of our life. And in this process of time, in this movement of time, time discloses to us a time beyond time, a future beyond the present, an eternity that supersedes temporality. Here we become aware of the sacrificial and redemptive nature of time—in passing away time negates itself in order to make way for eternal time, time that can no longer be measured in terms of time but in terms of eternity.

This inner dimension of history is of special interest to those of us engaged in a theological understanding of history. The study of meaning is called semantics. Shall we, then, call our interest in history a "theological semantics of history"? Histories of nations, though particular and not transferrable, interact one with the other at the inner dimension of meaning. In our theological semantics of history we must assume that the history of ancient Israel and the history of Indonesia, for instance, have been intersecting each other at the level of inner meanings. What we have in these separate national entities are not meanings that are parallel and thus do not intersect, but webs of meanings that relate one to the other. We human beings are caught in those webs of meanings, although most of the time we are not conscious of it. These webs of meanings envelop us like the radio waves that pervade not only our living space but our living bodies as well. To fancy oneself to have nothing to do with these webs is to remove oneself from the community of meanings. To attempt to dictate the shape and contents of these webs is to distort and suppress the meanings represented by them. This is what a totalitarian regime does. A religious community too has often been guilty of fancying itself a creator of meanings, an act that leads to suppression of truths sought by other religious communities.

Theo-logical Forces in History

This is the ground of our theological affirmation that God works in the histories of *all* nations. To put it differently, there are *theo*-logical forces working in all nations and peoples, creating meanings for them and bringing these meanings to interact with each other. Such *theo*-logical forces seem to become most manifest when a history becomes involved in struggle against the diabolical powers of dehumanization and destruction.

To become aware of theo-logical forces in history and to be confronted with them is more than a mental exercise. It cannot be an outcome of reasoning and theorizing in a theological armchair. To feel these theo-logical forces, to experience them, to be grasped by them, one has to be a part of the struggle against the demonic powers at work in life and history. After all, this is how human beings come to realize the creating and redeeming activity of God working on their persons and in their community. Otherwise, it does not make sense to speak of God's saving activity. Saving from what? This is the question. In pious religious circles the answer is always salvation of individual souls from sin. And how much morbid obsession with sin on the one hand and the sin of self-righteousness on the other are bred and cultivated in the practice of religious piety! We have learned, however, that sin is not just a personal moral matter. It is more than personal, more than moralistic. It is societal, institutional, structural, and systemic. It has to do with an institution gripped by a destructive power, a society under the shadow of evil forces, a system or structure intent on the destruction of human persons.

There is an abundance of testimonies to this effect. In his novel *The Testament*, Elie Wiesel, a survivor of the Nazi holocaust, re-creates a Russian Jew, a condemned prisoner in Stalin's prison in 1952, and has him reminisce on the agony of having to bury many soldiers fallen in battle toward the end of World War II. The reminiscence takes the form of a dialogue between him, a grave digger, and God. He addresses God in a whisper:

> As a child I was a believer, because I was told that it was impossible to give You a name and equally impossible to deny You or defame You in words. Only now I know! You are a grave digger, God of my ancestors. You carry Your chosen people into the ground, just as I carried the soldiers fallen on the battle-fields. Your people no longer exist. You have buried them; others killed them, but it is You who have put them into their invisible, unknown tomb. Tell me, did You at least recite the Kaddish? Did You weep for their death?

God did not answer and the Russian Jew goes on: "My words met a stony silence. God chose not to respond. But the hoarse voice of a former companion choked within me:

> "You exaggerate, my friend; you go too far. God is resurrection, not grave digger; God keeps alive the bond that links God and you to your people; is that not enough for you? I am alive, you are alive; is that not enough for you?" "No, that is not enough for me!" I said. And I hastened to add, "In this place I have the right to demand and receive everything; and what I demand is redemption." "So do I," said my companion sadly. "So do I. And so does God."[9]

The condemned prisoner, having gone through indescribable human tragedies, was not exaggerating when he insisted that being alive was not enough. Being alive in the aftermath of the horrible death of millions of people is itself a tragedy. It is meaningless to be alive after so many human lives have been liquidated by sheer human madness. It is almost immoral to stay alive after all this. Personal salvation in this life and even in the afterlife does not make sense in the midst of all these senseless deaths.

---

9. Elie Wiesel, *The Testament* (New York: Bantam Books, 1982), 115–16.

What the prisoner demands is redemption, not the redemption of individual souls but the redemption that brings the dead back to life, rights the wrongs committed by those in power, and eradicates injustices inflicted on the powerless by demonic systems and establishments. This is what redemption means in a historical sense. It is this historical redemption that that Jewish prisoner in Stalin's prison camp demands. And it is the same redemption that millions and millions of the poor and the oppressed demand. Christianity as a historical religion should have no problem grasping redemption as happenings in human history. But traditional Christian piety has stressed redemption of individual souls at the expense of redemption that brings about love, justice, and freedom in society. And as the friend of that prisoner turned grave digger added, God too demands such redemption. The God who demands such redemption—is this also not the God Jesus proclaimed in his message of God's reign?

The key to theological interpretation of history is perhaps, then, not a theological scheme that explains what God is doing in the world. God is not bound by such a scheme. Besides, the scheme Christianity uses to frame God's saving activity discloses more the mind of the Christian church than the mind of God. That is why most Christians today still link salvation with conversion to Christianity and believe that God is related to the world only through the Christian church. Jesus, who told the parable of the great banquet, would have no sympathy for the faith that restricts God's saving activity to a single particular institution, even if that institution is the Christian church. Perhaps God's mission in the world is too colossal, too far-reaching, and too demanding to be entrusted to one religious community alone.

Jesus' reign of God identifies theo-logical forces not among the rich and the powerful but among outcasts and strangers. This is precisely what Jesus intended to say in his parable of the great banquet. If this is the case, has not the Christian church looked for those forces in the wrong places? The roots of this wrong identification of theo-logical forces go back deep in the history of Christianity. It began when Constantine the Great issued the Edict of Milan in 313 C.E. and made Christianity a legal religion of the Roman empire. From a historical perspective the development was so astonishing that it invited a comment such as follows:

One of the most amazing and significant facts of history is that within five centuries of its birth Christianity won the professed allegiance of the overwhelming majority of the population of the Roman Empire and even the support of the Roman state. Beginning as a

seemingly obscure sect of Judaism, one of scores, even hundreds
of religions and religious groups which were competing within that
realm, revering as its central figure one who had been put to death by
the machinery of Rome, and in spite of having been long proscribed
by that government and eventually having the full weight of the state
thrown against it, Christianity proved so far the victor that the Empire sought alliance with it and to be a Roman citizen became almost
identical with being a Christian.[10]

This was a truly astonishing development. But it also proved to be a fatal
development. With it began the history of the Christian church in alliance
with the powers that be.

Epiphanies of God in the *Oikumenē*

To return to the story of the great banquet. The banquet is now packed
with the histories those strangers and outcasts brought with them. It turns
out to be a banquet rich in histories. The reign of God does not store
only one history; it stores many, many histories. It is not dominated by
one single history—even if it be Judeo-Christian history—in which other
histories are excluded. It will house a great number of histories, as many
histories as there are in the *oikumenē*, in the inhabited world—the *oikumenē* not created by Christian churches but by God. The strangers at
the banquet are in fact not strangers, although they had been treated
as strangers. The outcasts at the dinner table are no longer branded as
outcasts.

To their surprise and joy they are to discover that they are members of
that household not by special human dispensation but by divine right. Their
stories are inside stories and not outside stories. Their histories are part
and parcel of the history of the banquet, inseparable parts of the history of
God's reign. In fact, God's reign consists largely of their histories. It is their
stories that make up the stories of God's reign. Once invited into the banquet of God's reign, they quickly realize that they have come to their own
home, and not to a strange house. This is an ecumenical vision projected
by the parable of the great banquet. The ecumenical movement, in this
true sense of involving "the whole inhabited world" and not just Christian
churches, did not begin in the twentieth century. It did not commence with
the inauguration of the World Council of Churches in Amsterdam in 1948.
It had already begun in first-century Palestine when Jesus told the parable
of the great banquet, stressing that the reign of God consists of strangers

---

10. Kenneth Scott Latourette, *A History of Christianity,* vol. 1, *Beginning to 1500* (New York:
Harper & Row, 1953), 65.

and outcasts, people who have no place in the history of the mainstream social and religious traditions.

This is the history of God's reign that Jesus' parable unveiled. It is human history as well as God's history. It is God's history as well as human history. It is the history of God among the nations. It is this divine-human history of God's reign that also concerned the prophets in ancient Israel. Isaiah, for instance, warned the warring nations of his time:

> Approach, you nations, and listen;
>   attend, you peoples;
>   let the earth listen and everything in it,
> the world and all that it yields;
> for the Lord's anger is turned against all the nations
>   and the Lord's wrath against all their hordes;
> the Lord gives them over to slaughter and destruction.
>
> (Isa. 34:1-2)

There are plenty of outbursts of God's anger against the nations in the Hebrew Scriptures. God is perceived to be terribly upset by what is happening in the world.

God's anger against the nations! This is the subject that has caused Christians to misunderstand what salvation means and to misrepresent how God is at work among the nations. Let us remind ourselves that in the Hebrew Bible God's anger is not reserved solely for the nations outside Israel. There is also plenty of God's wrath directed to Israel. Amos, after inveighing against the neighboring nations, turned to Israel with equal vehemence. God in Amos's perception is perhaps more vindictive against Israel than against other nations. This is what Amos said about Samaria, the capital city of Israel, in the name of God:

> Upon the palaces in Ashdod
>   and upon the palaces of Egypt,
>   make this proclamation:
> "Assemble on the hills of Samaria,
> look at the tumult seething among her people
>   at the oppression in her midst;
>   what do they care for straight dealing
> who hoard in their palaces the grains
>   of violence and plundering?"
> This is the word of the Lord.
>
> (Amos 3:9-10)

Foreign nations such as Ashdod and Egypt are called upon to be "witnesses in a lawsuit against Samaria [Israel]"![11] In saying things such as this, Amos can be accused of being unpatriotic. He can be criticized for "washing dirty linen in public," or "publicizing domestic scandals" (*chia ch'ou wai yang*), as the Chinese expression has it. In the eyes of the authorities Amos was doing something doubly unforgivable. He was not only exposing scandals in domestic public but in international public also, and "pagan" public at that. Amos was no exception. Other prophets did the same thing too from time to time. God is the God of all nations. If sins of other nations are exposed before the eyes of Israel, there is no reason why the sins of Israel should be kept from the scrutiny of other nations.

This has not been understood by the Christian churches. God's anger is perceived to be mostly directed against the "pagan" nations. In the view of some Christians God in relation to the "pagan" nations is a vindictive God who has little compassion to spare for them. God's punishment is meted out to them while God's salvation is reserved for those who call themselves Christians. But this is not the God Jesus in his parable of the great banquet is telling us about. In what he teaches and does Jesus shows no sympathy for a God who neatly parcels out punishment for the pagans and salvation for Christians.

What then, must the expression "God's anger" mean? But what does "anger" mean in the first place? True, one cannot deny that anger can be destructive. In a fit of anger violence of words and action occurs. In a moment of anger one's animal nature comes to the foreground, and one's human nature recedes into the background. Of course we cannot apply our experience of anger such as this to God. Obviously, if anger can make a human being less than human, it can also make God less than God. The God who is angry and intent on "slaughter and destruction" is not God. There must be something else in the word "anger" when applied to God. It must be referring to something other than vindictiveness and punishment.

Anger can be an expression of involvement in relationships. The involvement can be so strong that it can become destructive. But first and foremost it is involvement. There is no anger in indifference. It is simply not possible. Indifference means one does not want relationships, need a community, or seek fellowship. Indifference can in fact be more destructive than anger. It destroys the very foundation of family, community, and creation. And it destroys the very person who practices indifference. Indifference removes that person from the very thing that makes that person human, that is, relationships. It further deprives that person of the possi-

11. See the exegetical notes on Amos 3:9-11 in the Oxford Study Edition of the NEB.

bility of a relationship with God. In this sense, an atheist is much closer to God than a person indifferent to God.

There is one thing God is not capable of, that is, indifference. And there is one thing God cannot do without, that is, involvement. However one may experience and understand God, God is the God of relationships. Perhaps this is what that abstruse doctrine called the Trinity seeks to tell us about God. The doctrine of the Trinity has nothing to do with the confusing mathematics of one in three and three in one. It does not have to give rise to the academic debate on whether the God of the Trinity is a monotheistic God or a polytheistic God. It does not have to lead to the choice between one God and three Gods. However differently human beings may perceive God because of differences in cultures and religions, they have always experienced God in relationships. And the most vivid, acute, and powerful expression of those relationships is anger. Anger, used in relation to God, describes how intensely God is involved in the life and history of humankind. Anger mediates that involvement, makes it real, and enables it to endure. Is it possible that somehow the prophets of ancient Israel had some inkling of this less commonly known nature of anger? To say that God is angry with the nations is to say that God is personally present among them and deeply involved in their life and history.

If this is what anger can also mean, the word no longer conveys what it is supposed to convey. Another term must be found to express the relationship that gives meaning to human life and history and enables us to come into touch with the source and origin of that relationship. That term is "love." Anger is derived from love. It must be rooted in love in order not to be destructive. For anger not to become destructive, and thus for love not to become something other than love, anger must be other than vindictive. In this case anger is a form of love. In other words, love redeems anger from becoming destructive. It transforms anger into the power to heal, restore, and save. It is evident that the word "anger" is no longer capable of carrying this new meaning. A different world has to be found. That word is "love." Amos expressed this relation between love and anger in a most penetrating way when he said again on behalf of God:

> You [Israel] alone have I cared for
> among all the nations of the world;
> that is why I shall punish you
> for all your wrongdoings.
>
> (Amos 3:2)

It is not a matter of a balance between love and anger. Amos gives us a glimpse of the most noble form of love—God's redeeming love.

Anger and punishment in the Bible are, then, metaphorical language. They are metaphors of love. They are the other side of love. To take them literally is to misunderstand God grossly and to misrepresent what God does with the nations as well as Israel. They express the faith that things, far and near, do not happen behind God's back, that events, at home and abroad, do not take place without God's knowledge. History, with its horrors, miseries, and destructions, has to reckon with God as well as human beings. The story of bloody conflicts between nations and peoples is perceived as the story of God's anger and fury. History is an arena in which God and humanity are locked in the struggle for the dreadful stalemate to end, for the dawn to arrive, for the journey to resume again toward the future. History, in one sense, is the epiphany of God. Since anger is a strong expression of emotion and an extreme form of presence, it is entirely appropriate that anger is used to describe the epiphany of God's redeeming love in the world.

In this sense history is part of the story of creation. "In the beginning"—so begins the creation story in Genesis with these words—"God created heavens and earth. The earth was a vast waste, darkness covered the deep....God said, 'Let there be light,' and there was light" (1:1-3). What we have here is a genealogy of heaven and earth and a history of creation. And this is the story of God's epiphany in the world of chaos and confusion. God's appearance brings light into the darkness, order in the midst of chaos and hope even when despair prevails. God's epiphany is a historical happening. It changes history and redirects its course to a different direction.

These words of creation were not said just once in the beginning of time. They were not heard only once at the inception of history. They are proclaimed again and again in the course of history. They will be heard over and over as long as history lasts. Did not that same prophet Isaiah who had pronounced God's judgment on the nations hear those words echoing loudly in the dark moments of the history of his own nation? Did he not put what he had heard in most magnificent words, such as those that follow?

> The people that walked in darkness
> have seen a great light;
> on those who lived in a land as dark as death,
> a light has dawned.
>
> (Isa. 9:2)

Light in the darkness again! This is the epiphany of God in the form of light. Because of this epiphany of light, history, though a chaos, is also creation; though darkness, it is also light. The power of creation at work in the chaos and darkness of history is the power of God's presence. That is why we believe in the epiphany of God ultimately as love and not as anger. This is the God of all nations.

New Heaven and New Earth

Because of this the Bible can show us a more cheerful side of history. It can also disclose an apocalyptic vision of history with all nations and peoples reconciled to God and to one another. John, for example, that seer self-exiled on the island of Patmos when the fledgling Christian church was going through the dark hours of persecution, left behind him a vivid picture of what he had seen when he was "in the Spirit on the Lord's day" (Rev. 1:10):

> I saw no temple in the city, for its temple was the sovereign Lord God and the Lamb. The city did not need the sun or the moon to shine on it; for the glory of God gave it light, and its lamp was the Lamb. By its light shall the nations walk, and to it the kings of the earth shall bring their splendor. (Rev. 21:22-24)

What a glorious vision of history—history in its fullness and magnificence, history in which God takes full command! And is this not the vision of God's reign to which "the nations and peoples [not kings!] bring their splendor," and Jesus' vision of the great banquet at which strangers and outcasts find "total acceptance"?

What we have in this vision is the total epiphany of God in history. The seer in this vision gives us another glimpse of this total epiphany of God when he tells us in another metaphor: "I saw a new heaven and a new earth" (Rev. 21:1). With this new heaven and new earth a new history begins. In this new history, there will be no pagans, no outcasts, and no strangers. This is the ultimate vision Jesus projected in his message of God's reign. And in his life and ministry Jesus demonstrates that that vision has to begin here and now, that it can be practiced in the world today.

History, gloomy or glorious, ugly or splendid, bloody or peaceful, is the divine-human story. For this reason history must be researched, documented, chronicled, interpreted by historians. The name of Ssu-ma Ch'ien (born c. 145 B.C.E.), the great historian of the Han dynasty of China (206 B.C.E.–220 C.E.) comes to mind. By compiling *Shih chi* (or *Historical Records*), he "set a standard for historical scholarship not equaled in the West until relatively modern times."[12] To enable himself to work on that

---

12. Edwin D. Reischauer and John K. Fairbank, *East Asia: The Great Tradition* (Boston: Houghton Mifflin Company, 1958), 112. *Shih chi* "covers the history of China from the be-

history, which has since proved truly monumental not only in Chinese historiography but in the historiography of the world, Ssu-ma Ch'ien

> travelled widely in search of the historical materials then available, made a selection from them to draft his basic records, and verified his facts by comparing versions. He made use of his travels to carry out investigations all over China, and often corrected mistakes he found in the records. In this way he was able to compile a remarkably accurate history. His aim was to tell the truth, and he fought all his life against falsehood and hypocrisy.[13]

No wonder *Shih chi* became a model for later historians in China for many centuries after the death of its great compiler and author.

Great historians such as Ssu-ma Ch'ien deserve deep respect and attentive hearing. But history cannot be left only to historians. It must also be pondered, probed, and exegeted by theologians. The Bible itself gives an intensely concentrated theology of history—the divine-human story of the people of Israel and of the nations. This divine-human story is the story of God's epiphany. It is the story of God's reign that Jesus taught and practiced in his ministry. It is the story of the great banquet. It is, in short, the story of God among all nations. God among the nations! This is the God of Jesus' vision of God's reign. Strangers at the banquet and outcasts in God's reign, by telling their own stories, testify that God is the God of all nations. In that banquet hall we have a preview of the new heaven and the new earth that the seer of Patmos envisioned.

A most exciting thing has been happening in the world today. Christians in Africa, Asia, and Latin America have been emboldened to tell divine-human stories in their own countries. They of course continue to be profoundly inspired by the stories in the Christian Bible. These biblical stories that recount the history of Israel, record the life and ministry of Jesus, and share the faith of the early Christian community are the main source of their Christian faith and the powerful inspiration for their witness to the love and justice of God in their society beset with conflicts and strifes. But what have these biblical stories to do with the stories of their own nation—stories of cowardice and courage, stories of hopes shattered and visions rekindled, stories of atrocity and love, that have given them

---

ginning to Ssu-ma Ch'ien's own day and includes not only the narrative of political events but biographies of prominent men, accounts of some of the chief principalities of the Chou and some of the foreign peoples touched by the Han, chronological tables, and treatises on such phases of culture as rites, music, divination, the calendar, the economics" (Kenneth Scott Latourette, *The Chinese: Their History and Culture* [New York: Macmillan Co., 1959], 86).

13. See "Preface" by Wang Po-hsing in *Records of the Historian* by Ssu-ma Ch'ien, trans. Yang Hsien-yi and Gladys Yang (Hong Kong: Commercial Press, 1974), iii–iv.

an identity as a nation? How do they understand their own history as an epiphany of God? What does it mean to be a part of the history that is moving toward the goal of a new heaven and a new earth? While Christians in the Third World go on drawing lessons of faith from the history of Christianity in the West and its expansion to their own lands, they have to explore how they are to experience and understand their own histories in direct relation to God's epiphanies. They are forced to raise questions such as these: Do not our own stories have integrity of their own? Do ours always have to be second-hand stories, secondary stories, stories derived from elsewhere? Are our stories *not* God's stories? Are they just purely, completely, human stories—stories that cannot be hyphenated with the word "divine"?

But why, then, are there strangers in the house of the banquet in Jesus' parable? Why does Jesus want those outcasts in the city and even those strangers outside the city boundaries to come to the banquet? Why has Jesus wanted the host of the banquet to have his servant go out and gently but firmly "urge and compel" Gentiles to join him at the banquet, making them feel "total acceptance"? The reason is not far to find. It must be this: the God of Jesus is God present among *all* nations from the beginning of time. That is why in Jesus' reign of God no nation is so strange as to have no history to share, no person is so alien as to have no story to tell, no woman, man, or child is so "gentile" as to find no respect and honor. His is a vision of God's reign in which people find fulfillment in God in the company of one another. And this must be the way it is going to be when a new heaven and a new earth eventually replace the old heaven and the old earth.

A Muslim Christmas Carol

It has taken us a long time to get to this point—outcasts of the city have come in and strangers from outside the city have joined in the banquet. It has taken at least two thousand years. The fact of the matter is, however, that this sort of thing already happened at the time of Jesus. Or rather Jesus made it happen; he made a point of making it happen. It is as if he came into the world to make it happen. But what the Christian church has done all too often is to undo what Jesus did, keeping outcasts and strangers outside its walls. It has erected doctrinal barriers for them not to be able to come in. It has created institutional obstacles to keep them at arm's length. It has built rituals and rites around its faith to shroud itself in a mystery unintelligible to them. It has decreed that unless they become its members God's saving love is not available to them. In our world in which we begin to come to grips with the reality of pluralism as an integral part of creation and begin to grasp its significance for our everyday life, many Christians still hold on to the notion of a "Christian" world in which people of other faiths and cultures are somehow anomalies to be either converted or tolerated.

But inside the banquet hall of God's reign in Jesus' parable the great feast has begun—a feast of new stories and a feast of first-hand histories. At first these stories and histories seem to be more different one from the other than to have something in common. Partly this is because we have made up our minds that they should be different. But after the initial foreignness gives way to a sense of community that has developed over the banquet tables, people begin to hear something familiar in each other's stories. The suffering they go through and the hope they entertain have a strangely familiar ring to them. The souls in perplexity, once opened to one another, seem to resonate mutual concerns and fears. They begin to be aware that their stories intersect and their histories interweave at many points. They even discover that it is not their faith but their loyalty to their religious traditions and their submission to certain ideologies that separate them. In each other's company they discover that as human beings they share a lot in common not only materially but spiritually. This is the miracle of that banquet. And it is the miracle of God's reign.

There is a Christmas carol written by a learned Muslim from Egypt. Christmas carol by a Muslim? And a learned one at that? Why not? It goes like this:

> Kindness, chivalry, guidance and humility were born
> The day Jesus was born.
> His coming brightened the world,
> His light illuminated it.
> Like the light of dawn flowing through the universe,
> So did the sign of Jesus flow.
> He filled the world with light,
> Making the earth shine with its brightness.
> No threat, no tyranny, no revenge, no sword, no raids,
> No bloodshed did he use in his call to the new faith.
> A king he lived on earth,
> But wearying of his state,
> He substituted heaven for it.
> To his faith wise persons were attracted,
> Humble, submissive and weak before him.
> Their submission was followed by the submission
> of kings, common folk and sages.

His faith found roots on every land
And anchors on every shore.[14]

A Muslim who is able to write a Christmas carol like this must make us Christians think deeply.

Can a Christian write something about Muhammad, the prophet of Islam, that would equal in beauty and sincerity this Muslim Christmas carol? Perhaps not. "There is an issue that disturbs Muslims more than any other in their approach to Christians," wrote a participant in a seminar at Tripoli, Libya, in 1975. "It is the silence and reserve of Christians regarding Muhammad. He is for Muslims the last and greatest of the Prophets. Christian reticence on this subject surprises and scandalizes them. They do not understand why we refuse to grant Muhammad the respect they themselves grant to the person of Jesus."[15] Is this because of our Christian centrism? Or is it due to Christian ignorance of how others live and believe, in this case Muslims?

That Muslim Christmas carol may make us Christians dubious about the Muslim poet's theology of the incarnation; still it does recognize Jesus as "the light that brightens the world." It does not contain a lofty language of the Trinity, yet it does capture the spirit of that hymn of the early church Paul quoted in his letter to the Philippians: "Jesus Christ . . . emptied himself, taking the form of a slave, being born in human likeness. And being found in human form he humbled himself and became obedient to the point of death, even death on a cross" (Phil. 2:7-8, NRSV). Does it not give due credit to Jesus' ministry of peace and reconciliation on the one hand and hint at a veiled self-criticism of Islam on the other when it says: "No threat, no tyranny, no revenge, no sword, no raids, no bloodshed did he [Jesus] use in his call to the new faith"? We Christians have always identified in a stereotyped way as a harsh and brutal desert religion that goes out to conquer the world with the sword in one hand and the Qur'an in the other. But do we not also have to listen attentively to small voices of some Muslims trying to tell us something different?

And when the poem gets to the point where it says: "His [Jesus'] faith found roots on every land and anchors on every shore," we can hardly believe our ears. These words sound like a song of victory sung by Christians in their pews engaged in Christian mission in faraway "pagan" lands through their missionaries. But to our astonishment and to our humilia-

---

14. The carol was written by Ahmad Shwaqu, a leading Egyptian man of letters early this century. See Kenneth Cragg, *Jesus and the Muslim: An Exploration* (London: George Allen & Unwin, 1985), 41.

15. Kenneth Cragg, *Muhammad and the Christian: A Question of Response* (London: Darton, Longman & Todd, 1984), ix.

tion, these words are the words of a Muslim. "His faith" mentioned in the carol is not the faith of Muhammad, but the faith of Jesus! And "every land" and "every shore" in the carol also include a Muslim land and a Muslim shore. Do Christians in the West who now have Muslims, Sikhs, and Buddhists live in their cities and as their neighbors have the grace to say a similar thing about other religions? Do Christians in Asia and Africa who live in the midst of the people of other faiths have the generosity to say it?

"Theology" in this Muslim Christmas carol is not perfect. But is there such a thing as "perfect" theology? Not even Christian theologians are capable of it. We must leave that "perfect theology" to God. But, then, perhaps God is in no need of theology, not even a perfect theology. As to us human beings in the presence of God, all our theological efforts have to cease, not to say our imperfect theological attempts. In the presence of God it is presumptuous to continue our theological exercise. We recall Thomas, one of the disciples, who refused to believe Jesus had risen from the dead on hearsay. He vigorously argued that unless he was able to touch Jesus' risen body he would not believe. But in the presence of the risen Christ all he could say was: "My Lord and my God!" (John 20:24-29). If christology has to cease in the presence of the risen Christ, all the more theology has to cease in God's presence. It will be an act of utmost presumption to do theology before God.

Theology, not only Christian theology but all other theologies, is by nature imperfect. This has to be our basic admission when we engage ourselves in theology. Presented, therefore, with something such as a Christmas carol written by a Muslim believer, it is not for us to scrutinize the correctness of its theology but to rejoice in the effort of a Muslim to share the joy of Christians. And as Christians we must also explore the life and faith of Muslims and their community. We must learn to share the stories that Muslims tell about Muhammad, the prophet they revere and follow. Is this not how the reign of God envisioned in Jesus' parable of the great banquet grows and develops?

Living Stones

The conversation and exchange in the banquet hall must be lively and spirited. For once, those persons present, until just recently despised as outcasts and strangers, feel free and uninhibited. Social stigma has been removed from them. Religious taboos attached to them have been taken away. They are made aware that they are now full-fledged members of God's reign. They can now share their concerns and problems without having to look anxiously over their shoulders. They can look at each other straight in the eyes. They do not have to be afraid that there are people staring at them from the pedestal. What they are able to share has perhaps more to do with simple daily experience than the "theological" experience of a learned Muslim expressed in his Christmas carol. Whatever the case, it is a community of genuine sharing that has emerged in the hall.

We also find that there is an irrepressible sense of emancipation from the shackles of society and religion. Genuine humanity comes to full expression in this newfound community of God's reign. And it is entirely possible that women in the hall—women in Asia, for instance—also tell their stories to each other and even to the men present, the men the tradition taught them to fear and obey, stories of their journey from bondage to freedom in a most moving way such as these verses in a poem entitled "Stones":

This Stone

A common granite stone found everywhere in India
Women in stone quarries breaking stones, carrying stones
Hands full of blisters, while working with stones
The summer sun beating mercilessly down on them as they carry
    heavy stones
More than the stones weigh them down
Working for low wages—always less than men
The threat of being fired—being unskilled daily wage laborers
Tired while even thinking of the chores to be done in the home both
    early in the morning and late into the night
Women workers in stone quarries burdened by stones.
"The stones which the builders rejected, has become chief corner-
    stone." This is the Lord's doing; it is marvelous in our eyes.[16]

This is the story of millions upon millions of women not only in India, but throughout Asia and elsewhere. For most men in the hall it must be the first time they have heard it, although the story has been told and retold for centuries. Men just did not hear. They refused to hear. They had no ear for it.

Women are born to bear burdens. There is a kind of burden they gladly bear. It is the bearing of children. To play an active role in bringing life into the world must be at once an exciting and sobering experience. It is a sacramental experience. They are in this way in touch with the holy,

---

16. These verses are by Aruna Gnanadason of India. See *Stree* (Madras: All India Council of Christian Women/National Council of Churches in India), no. 18, August 1988, back cover.

with something sacred that they do not understand in spite of the fact that they bear it inside them. But there is another kind of burden they have to bear—the burden of being a woman enslaved to male-dominated social and religious traditions and forced to labor and toil more than men do. It is this other burden that makes the sacrament of bearing a child a curse, an extra burden. They become doubly burdened, both internally and externally burdened. They have to carry heavy stones in the quarries, toil in the kitchen, and labor in pain to bear children.

How can they not think that they are the stones rejected by the builders? Who are these builders who use them and reject them? Men of course—men who possess power at every level of the social and religious hierarchies, from the family to social conventions, to political systems, and to religious structures. But what if God is also the builder who rejects them? They are taught to believe this is precisely the case. One must have done something wrong in the previous life to be born a woman. But what a liberation to realize that this is absolutely not true! How could God who created women as well as men reject them? God made them to be chief cornerstones, to be God's co-creators of life, to be God's co-builders of human community. Women are in essence and in reality the "marvelous doings" of God; they are God's marvelous stones.

Men in the banquet hall must have a lot of repenting to do when they hear women's heartbreaking stories. The women continue their stories:

Women work in construction sites carrying stones
Heavy baskets of stones that weigh down on their heads
Walking up and down precarious ladders
Some women pregnant, some women carrying suckling babies in one
    hand
Heavy thoughts on their minds
The possibility of being paid no wage or less than usual for having
    come late for work
The fear of being raped, or being sexually harassed by the contractor
    or his henchmen
The anticipation of the hungry squabbling children and a drunken
    husband in the home
Building houses for others to live in while for them one-room
    thatched roof huts in a poor slum.
"Christ Jesus himself being the chief cornerstone in whom the whole
    structure is joined together and grows into a holy temple."[17]

---

17. Ibid.

From the quarries to the building sites. Women seem fated to carry heavy burdens. They are also exposed to physical violence by men whether at home or at the working site. This is the reality stones have to bear: oppression.

But there is another image—the image of the temple. "Christ Jesus himself being the chief cornerstone," we are told, "in whom the whole structure is joined together and grows into a holy temple." Temple is the symbol of God's presence. It is the reality of God's saving love. And it is the reality and symbol of God's own self. Does this not remind us of the temple the seer of Patmos saw in the city of God? "I saw no temple in the city," he says, "for its temple was the sovereign Lord God and the Lamb." How is this temple constructed? It is constructed with the stones rejected by the builders. Women are such stones. By inference the poor, the oppressed, the marginalized are such stones. Jesus is such a stone that becomes the cornerstone of God's reign. The temple in the city of God is to be built with such stones. With Jesus the outcasts and the disinherited will become the temple of God. And this temple is the reign of God.

This is a vision of God's reign. Each stone has a story to tell—a story of suffering and hope. No story is too insignificant to tell. No story is too trivial to share. That is why outcasts and strangers are in the banquet hall. This is a truly extraordinary vision. It is so extraordinary that the religious authorities of Jesus' day could not comprehend it. They were in fact offended by it and conspired to have Jesus put to death. But that vision did not die. It rose from the dead and has over the centuries continued to inspire men and women to be part of it. And it will go on inspiring people to live and die until the end of time.

Sound of Music in Church

All those gathered in God's banquet hall represent a community and a nation, and there is no end to the stories they can tell from the experiences of their community and from the history of their nation. China, for example, is a nation and a community with stories that fascinate us and pain us at one and the same time. And those present in the banquet hall must be spellbound, for example, by the story of a Red Guard in those dark and horrid days of the Cultural Revolution (1966–76) unleashed by Mao Zedong in his last struggle for political power and for his own revolutionary immortality. I am referring to a little-known true story told in the first person by a Red Guard.

Seen in the daytime, Trinity Church lies in ruins. Those colorful windows that used to glitter like a rainbow have been shattered [by the

Red Guards]. The red and green posters that remain on the marble
pillars and cover them like shrouds are from time to time torn off
by the wind and fall fluttering all over the place. When night comes,
the old church puts on a black veil, as it were, and gains a new lease
on life.

Such an atmosphere more or less affected even an atheist like
myself.... On the fourth night since I moved into a tiny room along
the corridor of the church, I was suddenly awakened by the sound of
music flowing into my room. Before I had the time to be surprised, I
had already lost myself in it completely.... I held my breath and quietly went out to the corridor. The music led me forward with deep
emotion like warm affectionate fingers. As if in a dream I reached
the edge of the chapel. And what did I see there among things piled
up in chaotic heaps? A huge piano! The person playing on it was hidden in its shadow.... Who knows if it is a hymn that is being played!
If there is such a thing as the kingdom of heaven, this must be it: angels hovering over the piano and covering the piano player with their
wings....

The music stopped abruptly. The chapel's decorated ceiling
seemed still whirling round to its tune.... A shadow of a small person could be seen moving over the long benches, going past a tall
cupboard and opening a small side iron door which usually remained
closed. In the moonlight that human shadow could be seen distinctly
now—head covered with grey hair, back slightly bent, wearing a
jacket even though it was summer.

Next day, I noticed an old man selling peanuts just across from the
church. His head, covered with grey hair, was buried deeply between
his knees. His jacket had spider webs on it. His fingers were tapping
his knees nervously. Once in a while someone would pass by, drop
a five-cent coin into the basket, and bend down to pick up a pack of
peanuts. But the old man would not stir himself in the slightest.

I picked up a pack of peanuts myself and asked a local person
nearby: "Where does the old man live?" "It's difficult to say where he
lives now," I was told. "He used to live in that church. He played the
piano in church for thirty years! People say he could not live without
the piano even for one day. But you see, he has been selling peanuts
here for a year and a half and has survived."

He has survived! He depends on the light gained in the stolen
hour each day to shine in the darkness of his life for the rest of the
twenty-three hours! When I dropped my coin into the basket, I felt
red all over my face with shame. But I dare not give more money,
fearing I might hurt the pride of a sensitive artist....

One day someone was there selling the peanuts in the old man's place. He told me that the old man had been taken ill quite seriously. I decided to give him a little help. I got together a few young friends of mine and rescued the piano out of the heaps of dirty things, moved it near to the side iron door, and put it against the window. . . . I also provided it with the only chair I had. . . .

A few nights passed. I heard the side door open, creaking slightly. I jumped to my feet and listened with my ears pressed to the crack in my door. What would the old man think of the improvement that has been made? Perhaps he would thank God for it.

"The piano! The piano!" A tearful voice of despair made my hands and feet freeze. I ran pell-mell to the chapel. I stood there puzzled. The moonlight was casting its dim light on the piano. As to the old man, he was on all fours in the space where the piano had been.

When I lifted the old man with some difficulty, I saw his arms were covered with dust all over. From the little side door to the dusty floor where he was lying there were traces of someone who crept past like a snail. The old man shouted tragically as if out of his mind: "They have moved away my piano! They have moved away my piano!" I shook his shoulders and stammered out: "No, Uncle, No! It's me. I moved it to. . . ."

"Quick! Take me there quickly!" The old man gripped my arm so hard that I felt sore. But he did not seem to notice I was there. "Bring me there, quick! Where is it?" I held him. But it was as if he was leading me through those broken chairs and benches. He appeared so pathetic, with his body eagerly leaning forward, but his feet shaking and not able to move. We reached the piano at last. "Where is it? Take me there quick!" The old man kept urging me.

I looked at him surprised, then lowered my head in pain. Just seeing his eyelids twitching nervously, his white eyeballs shining and his vacant face, one would know at once that he was blind. I held both his hands and led him to the piano. He was sobbing, deeply overcome with emotion. He quickly felt the piano all over with his hands as though to make sure his friend was not hurt. That icy cold piano seemed to grow warm under the touch of his fingers. It began to be filled with melodious sound. . . .

When I saw the old man could not remain standing any longer, I turned round to bring him that chair to sit on. Just at that moment the piano gave out a long sigh as if saying farewell to the old musician. His hands were trembling and his face was touching the keyboard. I bent down, trying to lift up the old man. But it was too late. For who could lift up an extinguished life? Because of that old musician I am willing that there be God.[18]

This is an ordinary story in an extraordinary time in the contemporary history of China. But it moved the heart of the hardened Red Guard enough to confess that because of that old blind musician he was willing to believe there is God. The story, after all, is not ordinary. What we hear from that Red Guard is in fact an extraordinary story of the reign of God. That old man was the reign of God. That Red Guard moved to confess God was the manifestation of the power of God's reign. In that dilapidated chapel the reign of God was the vision of God turned into reality. Perhaps this is the way God's reign works most of the time. It works in the ruins of human civilization. It works when human beings have done their best to destroy one another. And it works in the midst of despair and frustration. How otherwise are we to understand, for instance, the report made at the Fourth Chinese National Conference held in Beijing in August 1986? According to the "Working Report" presented at the conference:

- more than 4,000 churches have been opened or reopened in the last six years, in addition to the "great number" of meeting points and home worship gatherings;

- about 300 ministers have been ordained, one-sixth of them women;

- ten theological seminaries have opened with a total enrollment of 600 students;

- 2.1 million Bibles and New Testaments have been printed;

- 700,000 hymnals and 700–800,000 copies of the new Catechism have been published.[19]

These numbers are said to be on the rise. The total number of Christians, Protestant and Catholic combined, was estimated to be five million in 1986. Perhaps the accurate number will never be known, for the estimates differ widely one from the other. But "all are agreed that there are more Christians in China today than in 1949."[20]

---

18. Hsu T'in is the author of this story. See *Short Stories: A Selection*, ed. Ch'i and Lin Ye Mu (Hong Kong: Ta Tao Book Company, 1981), 1–6. Abridged and translated from the original Chinese text by C. S. Song.

19. *Bridge*, Church Life in China Today (Tao Fong Shan Ecumenical Center, Hong Kong), no. 19 (September–October 1986): 2.

20. G. Thompson Brown, *Christianity in the People's Republic of China* (Atlanta: John Knox Press, 1983), 178. Brown continues: "In the summer of 1982 the Religious Affairs Bureau estimated that there are 3,500,000 practicing Protestants. This is probably a rock-bottom figure. Other estimates run much higher. The Chinese Church Research Center in Hong Kong esti-

No matter how one may estimate the number of Christians in China today, the coming out into the open of Christians in that land is a cause of celebration. It could not have been just a windfall of China's open-door policy to the outside world. Would it have been possible without the working of God's reign, as the story "The Sound of Music in Church" seems to tell us? Was not a new heaven and a new earth being created in that ruined church, hidden away from the eyes of the public and unnoticed to Christians not only outside China but also inside it? Was it not a story of God's reign as an epiphany of God? How closely the vision of God's reign has to be related to the realities that mold our life and shape our world! To those realities, therefore, we must turn in order that we may gain further glimpses of what God's reign is and how it works.

---

mates that the number is more like 25,000,000. This is based on the number and size of house gatherings and seems highly inflated. The truth is that nobody knows, and there is no way of arriving at accurate statistics" (ibid.).

Part II

REALITY

The vision of God's reign, the vision of a new heaven and a new earth, that is, the vision of a space in which God's saving presence is manifested, is not a distant vision. It is not a vision that will be realized only in a faraway future and at the end of time. This is what I tried to demonstrate in the previous chapter. That Korean woman in Japan is part of the reign of God. That Muslim scholar able to sing a Christmas carol is part of the reign of God. And that old musician in a ruined church in China is also part of the reign of God. These stories tell us where to look for God's reign, how to identify it and what to make of it. Each story is not the whole of God's reign, but God's reign is not complete, it is not graspable, without these stories. The reign of God develops as such stories multiply. And it is God who will take all these stories, shape them, and weave them together into a final form of God's reign. In the meantime it must be our faith that each such story is indispensable to God for bringing the reign of God to fulfillment. To put it another way, the reign of God is unreal and has no meaning when it gets detached from our concrete everyday life, when it gets separated from the tortuous road of history.

This strongly suggests that there must be a close relationship between vision and reality. A vision not anchored in the reality of this world is an illusion. An illusion is created out of the inability or the refusal to face the problems of life. It is an escape into the realm of unreality from the world of reality. It takes the unreal for the real and the real for the unreal. Illusion, therefore, has no place in history. It contradicts everything that history is and that it stands for. Illusion has no memory, that essential quality of history. History is history because it remembers. But illusion thrives on oblivion. Even between one illusion and another illusion there is no connection in time and space. The fact is simply that illusion does not remember. It does not even remember itself. It has no history. It is not historical.

In Christian piety there has always been the danger of the reign of God understood as "the kingdom of God" and rendered into a concept little different from an illusion. It is a matter of historical record that even in the heyday of Christianity in Europe in the Middle Ages the society under the church's power and influence did not become "the kingdom of God." It was a world in which secular authorities and church authorities vied for supremacy, often resulting in bitter conflicts and feuds between them. In the time of the missionary expansion of Christianity in the nineteenth century the establishment of "the kingdom of God" in "pagan lands" inspired churches and Christians in the West to reach out to Asia and Africa through their missionaries. But despite the massive efforts Asia and Africa did not turn into "the kingdom of God." Christian churches were established, in most cases, as minority religious communities in the midst of the people who continued their ways of life and beliefs.

Unable to face and deal with the historical reality of the world in which it lives, the Christian church, both in the East and in the West, has come to hold "the kingdom of God" in nontemporal and nonspatial terms. "The kingdom of God" will be realized at the end of time totally unrelated to the forces of history at work in human community and in God's creation. It will come to pass suddenly, accompanied by cosmic cataclysm, replacing the old creation with a new creation. "The kingdom of God" is, in this way, an apocalyptic happening of the sort described in the Book of Revelation. And jealous evangelists are never tired of issuing a warning: those who do not believe in Jesus will perish in that horrible cataclysm. For more irenic Christians "the kingdom of God" does not conjure up the horror of fire and brimstone of those terrible last days. It is something they hope to attain when they pass from this world to the next world. It is a realm of eternal peace and bliss reserved for Christian believers. It is a place filled with gold, silver, and precious stones for those who have been obedient to God. It is a life of all comfort and blessing as a reward for being faithful members of the Christian church. It has all the glitter and splendor no human words can describe.

Whether as an apocalyptic happening or as an unworldly realm of happiness and glory, "the kingdom of God" held in Christian piety is more an illusion than a vision. It is uprooted from the reality of our daily life. It is unrelated to movements of human history. It does not interact with social and political changes. It does not deal with the world of religions and cultures of which Christianity is a part—only a part and not the whole of it. Is this what Jesus meant by the reign of God? Does it correspond to the central assertion of the Christian faith that the Word *became flesh?*

The answer is no. That is why after the vision of God's reign we must turn to the reality of the world—the reality in which and out of which the reign of God grows, develops, and moves toward its fulfillment. We must also come to grips with witnesses women and men bear to the reign of God in difficult situations. This is not to confine the reign of God to the reality we know and experience in the world. But our underlying conviction is that the reign of God as Jesus lived and practiced in his life and ministry does not "break into" history, one of the favorite expressions in traditional theology, but *breaks out* of history. The reign of God is that dynamic at work inside history through men, women, and children, that power of redemption that mends, heals, and re-creates the entire creation for the day of a new heaven and a new earth. We do not know when that day will be or what the new creation will be like. But we do know that that day is the fulfillment of all our days and that the new creation, just as the old creation, is not going to be a *creatio ex nihilo*, but a creation out of the realities that engage our life and history in this world.

CHAPTER 3

THE PLIGHT OF PEOPLE

These are the words of the Lord:

For crime after crime of Israel
  I shall grant them no reprieve,
because they sell honest folk for silver
  and the poor for a pair of sandals.
They grind the heads of the helpless into the dust
  and push the humble out of their way.

(Amos 2:6-7)

End to Theological Innocence

In 1976 the Youth Exposure for Hunger Program was held in Bangalore, India. But why Bangalore, of all cities in India? Is not Bangalore a relatively well-to-do city? With a very agreeable climate it attracts persons of means. It is a graceful city lined with willow trees, adorned with flowers, and rich in temples. It is a delight of tourists who have just escaped from the oppressive heat of Madras in the south and have been overwhelmed by the utmost indignity of human poverty in the seething city of Calcutta in the north. But the world must know that in this attractive, comfortable, and prosperous city of southern India there are thirty-two slums outside the wealthy residential areas, the busy commercial centers, and the well-trodden tourist paths.

The participants of the Hunger Program had lived for a few days in two of these slums and been "exposed" to the irony, pain, and destitution of a human community. One of them wrote after that exposure:

It was frightening to think
how people live all their lives like this.
Lives are a mockery, human beings live like animals.

> Sleeping by night in crowded room,
> or in an alley, littered with human waste.
> No job by day, the only money from the money lender.
> Women heavy with child, men crazed with drink.
> Every day the uncertainty
> where the day's one meal comes from.
> How blind have I been
> as I have walked through these slums before,
> never pausing to see the plight of people!
> How large their hearts!
> Though they eat but once a day,
> three people did not eat so they could
> share their meager fare with us.
> It was the silent suffering that pained me most.
> Who will give voice to those dumb people
> And fight their cause?[1]

The shock experienced by the participants of the Hunger Program is understandable, but the plight of the people in slums is not understandable.

With this exposure to the reality of the slums in Bangalore the theological innocence of the participants is over. Their innocence has been fostered in the church isolated from what is going on in their society. It has been cultivated by a teaching that God's salvation works almost solely within the Christian community. It is reinforced by a faith in "the kingdom of God" untouched by worries and sorrows of life and freed from fears and conflicts of this world. This innocence has been very important for many Christians. In this innocence they regard the sufferings of this world as temporary and unreal. With it they bear the hardships of life as something to endure to gain entry into the blessed world of everlasting happiness God prepares for them. It is also this innocence that helps to develop in them a passive attitude toward social and political realities. After all, these are all passing phenomena that have no place in the coming kingdom of glory and harmony.

Such theological innocence is not unique to Christians. People of other religions too are very much addicted to it. The Bhagavad Gita, for example, the great spiritual epic that has nourished Hindu spirituality for centuries, gives a vivid glimpse of what is in the deep recesses of the human quest for emancipation from the shackles of the world of transience. The epic begins with the scene of the great warrior Arjuna and his armies deployed

---

1. Harvey L. Parkins, *Root for Vision: Reflections on the Gospel and the Churches, Task in Re-opening the De-peopled* (Singapore: CCA, 1985), 103. See also chapters 1 and 5 for references to the Youth Exposure for Hunger Program.

in a battle against his kinsmen for the rule of a kingdom. Arjuna "saw in both armies fathers, grandfathers, sons, grandsons; fathers of wives, uncles, masters; brothers, companions and friends. When Arjuna thus saw his kinsmen face to face in both lines of battle, he was overcome by grief and despair and thus he spoke with a sinking heart" to Krishna, the Lord and God of love, disguised as his charioteer:

> When I see all my kinsmen, Krishna, who have come here on this field of battle,
>
> Life goes from my limbs and they sink, and my mouth is sear and dry; a trembling overcomes my body, and my hair shudders in horror;
>
> My great bow Gandiva falls from my hands, and the skin of my flesh is burning; I am no longer able to stand, because my mind is whirling and wandering.
>
> And I see forebodings of evil, Krishna. I cannot foresee any glory if I kill my own kinsmen in the sacrifice of battle.
>
> Because I have no wish for victory, Krishna, nor for a kingdom, nor for its pleasures. How can we want a kingdom, Govinda, or its pleasures or even life,
>
> When those for whom we want a kingdom, and its pleasures, and the joys of life, are here in this field of battle about to give up their wealth and their life?
>
> Facing us in the field of battle are teachers, fathers and sons; grandsons, grandfathers, wives' brothers; mothers' brothers and fathers of wives.
>
> These I do not wish to slay, even if I myself am slain. Not even for the kingdom of the three worlds: how much less for a kingdom of the earth! ... [2]

This must be a most agonizing moment in the career of this great warrior. His ambition is to conquer. His vocation is to rule. And the means to achieve his ambition and to fulfill his vocation is the destruction of his enemy. But the enemy he has to destroy to win the rule of a kingdom is not strangers but his own kinsfolk, not foreigners but his blood relations. His heart is in turmoil and anguish. His valor and courage leave him. Confronted with such heartbreaking reality, he loses the will to fight. He laments and says:

---

2. *The Bhagavad Gita*, trans. Juan Mascaro (Middlesex, England: Penguin Books, 1962), 45–46.

O day of darkness! What evil spirit moved our minds when for the sake of an earthly kingdom we came to this field of battle ready to kill our own people?

Better for me indeed if the sons of Dhrita-rashtra, with arms in hand, found me unarmed, unresisting, and killed me in the struggle of war.[3]

Arjuna is utterly confused and demoralized. What is Krishna, the Lord disguised as the charioteer, to do? Arjuna's "theological innocence" is shattered by the reality he faces. How is Krishna to deal with him? These words then come from Krishna:

Thy tears are for those beyond tears; and are thy words of wisdom? The wise grieve not for those who live; and they grieve not for those who die—for life and death shall pass away.

Because we all have been for all time: I, and thou, and those kings of men [and women]. And we all shall be for all time, we all for ever and ever.

As the Spirit of our mortal body wanders on in childhood, and youth and old age, the Spirit wanders on to a new body; of this the sage has no doubts.

From the world of the senses, Arjuna, comes heat and comes cold, and pleasure and pain. They come and they go: they are transient. Arise above them, strong soul.

The person whom these cannot move, whose soul is one, beyond pleasure and pain, is worthy of life in Eternity . . .

If any man thinks he slays, and if another thinks he is slain, neither knows the ways of truth. The Eternal in human being cannot kill: the Eternal in human being cannot die. . . . [4]

The discourse more and more takes on a spiritual tone. The battlefield becomes the arena of the human spirit in search of emancipation from the world.

This epic is an allegory, of course. It is not meant to be taken literally. But is it not an allegory such as this that prompts believers to take as unreal the reality of life and world? Here is an attempt, common to the spiritual efforts of most religions, to cross from theological innocence into the realm

---

3. Ibid., 47.
4. Ibid., 49–50.

of eternal bliss, bypassing the state of "theological" reality. The "kingdom of heaven" and the "kingdom on this earth" are two separate entities. The former is attained at the expense of the latter. But the fact is that the tears we shed are real tears. They are real because life and death are real. The life born today is real. It is real to the mother who has gone through birth pangs. As she holds that life that has been inside her and part of her she sheds tears of joy. Her tears are as real as the life she holds tenderly to her bosom. And what about the tears we shed for the death of our loved ones, relatives and friends? What about the tears that freely flowed from our eyes when we witnessed the massacre of the students and civilians in the pro-democracy movement in Tiananmen Square on June 4, 1989? The death is as real as the tears we shed. How can we, then, say that "the wise grieve not for those who live and they grieve not for those who die—for life and death shall pass away"? Yes, life and death shall pass away, but before they pass away they are really real; they are as real as the air we breathe and as real as the ground on which we stand. The destination of our spiritual journey lies beyond life and death, but it can be reached only through life and death.

This is the reality Arjuna has to face. The blood of the kinsfolk on both sides of the battleground will be very real and the death that they will be inflicting on each other will plunge those left behind in deep sorrow. Will they ever recover from it? Small wonder Arjuna, a great warrior that he is, feels that "life goes from my limbs . . . , trembling overcomes my body, and my hair shudders in horror." He exclaims in dismay: "O day of darkness! What evil spirit moved our minds when for the sake of an earthly kingdom we came to this field of battle ready to kill our own people?"

This dismay and this exclamation are in fact the beginning of the end of theological innocence. The great epic of the Bhagavad Gita could have explored how Krishna, the God of love, might impart to Arjuna, the distraught warrior, a theological wisdom to practice the way of love (*bhakti*) not only in relation to the eternal but also to the temporal. For the eternal is in the temporal and the temporal is in the eternal. Krishna, in actual fact, alludes to this in the long concluding discourse. "God dwells in the heart of all beings, Arjuna," says Krishna, "thy God dwells in thy heart. And God's power of wonder moves all things . . . whirling them onward on the stream of time."[5] Since God dwells in all beings and moves them onward on the stream of time, do we not have to seek God's will and work with God in the ongoing life and history of this world? Is not the reality of our everyday life an essential part of our spiritual journey? Is this not perhaps what Jesus

---

5. Ibid., 120.

meant when he taught his disciples to pray and say: "Thy will be done on earth as it is in heaven"?

Frightening Reality

For the participants in the Youth Exposure for Hunger Program their theological innocence is shattered by the frightening reality with which they are confronted in the slums of Bangalore. "It was frightening to think," they confessed, "how people live all their lives like this." The "frightening life" they witnessed did not exist in their Christian devotion. It did not occur to them that outside the church such a life existed. It never entered their wildest dream that "the kingdom of God" they prayed about and sang about in church had to reckon with it. But now they are rudely awakened from their innocence. What theological sense can they make of it? Perhaps for the first time in their lives they are compelled to ask this question. And the question has of course many ramifications for the practice of their faith and for the doing of their theology.

Life Is a Mockery

The first thing they have to admit is that life for these slum dwellers is a mockery. Shocked by what they see, they cannot make any sense of it. The life that makes sense to them is the life they find within the Christian community. There are the rich and the poor in the church. There are persons with more privileges and persons with fewer privileges in it. Still, the life they find in the church is a relatively decent life. And above all, it is a life supposed to give them a foretaste of what "the kingdom of God" must be like.

What they encounter in the slums, however, is entirely different. It is everything they consider "the kingdom of God" not to be. It appears to them that the slum dwellers "live like animals." This is a candid expression of their first impression. They cannot see humanity in these people. They cannot detect in these men, women, and children any human decency. What these people do and how they behave contradict everything they regard as basic to proper human life. They must have felt revulsion for these human beings "sleeping by night in crowded room" and when they step into the "alley littered with human waste." This is a far cry from what they are used to in the church.

But who defines what humanity is? The Christian church or these people themselves? Who prescribes the rules for a life to be decent? The Christian community or the community of these slum inhabitants? How is one to pass judgment on how human beings should behave in a particular place and in all places? On the basis of Christian moral values or moral values determined by a specific community? And how is one to discern redemptive meanings in human relationships? Resorting to the ready-made answer in the Christian catechisms or allowing our religious sensibility to be informed by the signals that issue from the heart of a different community?

At the initial stage of "Exposure" the participants of the program have only one answer to these questions: the Christian church. Implicitly they assume that it is the Christian faith that defines what humanity must be, that it is the Christian community that lays down rules for a decent life, and it is Christian moral values that dictate the moral values of a society and all communities. In all fairness it must be said that not only Christians have the propensity to pass judgment on life and morals as well as faiths on their terms. Those in a privileged position also do the same in relation to less privileged people. The young women and men in the Exposure Program are to learn later how wrong they have been. It turns out that it is not those slum people that are tested by their Christian precepts and standards but they themselves are subject to the testing by those men, women, and children they at the outset judged to be living like animals.

Women Heavy with Child

In the midst of what they consider to be an inhuman life, the participants of the Exposure Program notice "women heavy with child." The word "heavy" must have come to their mind with both literal and metaphorical meanings. A woman with child, a pregnant woman, is literally heavy. Her pace is slow and her steps are cautious. The burden she carries within her makes her look heavy. And she appears doubly heavy because the weight of the baby inside her adds to the weight of her already heavy burden of life. "Women heavy with child" is said more with pity than with joy. They pity her for being with child. The last thought in their minds is to go up to her and congratulate her. The sign of a new life becomes for them a depressing sign.

It is true that women in an underprivileged situation suffer doubly because they are women. This is particularly the case in an Oriental society shaped by the age-long male dominated tradition. Women have to cope with "men crazed with drink," men who vent on them their frustration and anger. They have to put up with men who have no respect for their person and who treat them as little more than a sexual outlet. Pregnancy is neither planned nor desired. Women have to accept it as a fact of life. Their life is heavy with the child inside them and with the burden of daily life they have to bear. Perhaps all these participants can see in the pregnant women in the slums is a living hell having little to do with "the kingdom of God" as they understand it.

But is it pity alone these women deserve? Do they not deserve something better? Here is a statement that makes us think deeply: "People of other lands who set foot on Philippine soil are pleased, and at the same time intrigued, to see a smiling and laughing people, especially the women. They are pleased because the smiles warm them and make them feel welcome in the country. They are intrigued since the real and full meaning behind the smiles and laughter escapes them especially when considered in relation to the poverty and dismal quality of life of the majority of the people."[6]

Why smile and laughter in a situation like this? If its meaning escapes foreigners who first set foot in the Philippines, it also escapes those participants in the Exposure Program. Those women with child may be welcoming them with a smile, but that smile to them seems a grimace. Those pregnant women with heavy gait greet them laughing, but what they hear is not laughter but a whimper. Why is this so? The reason is that visitors from outside the slums have determined that there could be no smile and laughter in the slums. As for most Christians they have decided that "the kingdom of God" filled with smiles and laughters is not possible with men and women, especially with women with children in the slums. In their theological innocence they believe that God has no business with them. But before their Exposure Program is over, they will realize that God is more present in their slums than anywhere else, that the reign of God can be more real among slum inhabitants than among regular churchgoers.

Every Day the Uncertainty

To the uninitiated minds of the participants life in the slums is an uncertain life. There is no doubt about it—that life is a very uncertain life. Unemployment is chronic. There is always the question of "where the day's one meal comes from." The only certain thing for slum dwellers is the visit of the money lender. But this is the certainty that makes sure their life is uncertain. They live from uncertainty to uncertainty. A simple little poem, "My Mother's Name Is Worry," written by a twelve-year-old child in a slum area in Korea gives a vivid picture of what an uncertain life can be:

> In summer, my mother worries about water,
> In winter, she worries about coal briquets,
> And all the year long, she worries about rice.

---

6. Lydia Lascano, "Signs of Life," in *In God's Image* (Asian Women's Resource Centre for Culture and Theology, Hong Kong), March 1989, 5.

In daytime, my mother worries about living,
At night, she worries for children,
And all day long, she worries and worries.

Then, my mother's name is worry,
My father's is drunken frenzy,
And mine is tear and sigh.[7]

How can they stand an uncertain life like this? What makes them go on living this kind of life? These must be the questions in the minds of the Christian visitors to the slums in Bangalore.

But is life uncertain only for slum inhabitants? Our friends from the Exposure Program may want to know. Is it not uncertain also for the rich and affluent? Is this not the point Jesus tries to put across to his listeners when he tells them the parable of a rich fool (Luke 12:16-20)? The rich man has accumulated a great deal of wealth and is about to sit back and enjoy it when God says to him: "You fool, this very night you must surrender your life; and the money you have made, who will get it now?" (12:20). Certainty and uncertainty are relative things. They cannot be measured by wealth, status, or privilege.

That is true. But in this parable Jesus is talking about the uncertainty of a life resulting from greed and selfishness. He must have also wanted to take the rich to the task, exposing their insensitivity to the poor and the unfortunate. The uncertainty of life in the slum is totally different. It comes from sheer lack of the basic necessities of life. It is due to the inability to have access to the means that makes life possible. It is an outcome of a life under social-political and religious-cultural forces beyond one's control. But the miracle is that many slum dwellers go on living and toiling in hope, envisioning the day when it will be different. How do they maintain their hope? Where does it come from? What does "the kingdom of God" mean to them? The visitors from the Exposure Program must have wondered out loud. Soon they will find out.

Large Hearts in a Meager Life

Romanticism ends at the slums. This is what the slums mean to most people. Even the imagination of a poet ceases to work. Slums in the minds of people outside them are associated with crime, degradation, and inhumanity. For most Christians slums mean something more: forsakenness by

7. See *My Mother's Name Is Worry: A Preliminary Report of the Study on Poor Women in Korea* (Seoul: Christian Institute for the Study of Justice and Development, 1983), 1.

God. Slums are a countersign of "the kingdom of God." They are everything "the kingdom of God" is not. Those participants in the Exposure
Program were aware there are slums in the city, but they never let their
conscience be perturbed by that awareness. As one of them puts it, "I
have walked through these slums before, never pausing to see the plight
of people!"

But they have to pause to see the plight of people. They are shocked by
the frightening sight of it. They are dismayed by the dismal life they have
to witness. And they cannot help but wonder how these human beings can
live like animals. But they soon are to find that ugliness and horror are not
the whole story. Misery and gloominess do not explain the entire life of
these slum people. A different picture begins to emerge from the depths
of the hearts of these poverty-stricken people—a picture that takes them
by surprise and astonishes them. These people

> though they eat but once a day,
> three people did not eat so they could
> share their meager fare with us.

They are moved to say: "How large their hearts!" These people who eke
out a scant living are still able to share their meager food with them. In
a harsh, crowded space of the slums they have encountered large, gentle hearts—hearts not so easy to find in the world outside the slums and
perhaps even in the church they come from.

A small space is enlarged by these large hearts. A crowded room is expanded by these gentle hearts. Is this not what Jesus meant in his message
of God's reign? They must have recalled the story of the widow's mite reported in the Gospels (Mark 12:41-44; par. Luke 21:1-4). As the story goes,
Jesus, seeing a poor widow drop "two tiny coins" in the chest at the Temple, said to his disciples: "Truly I tell you this: this poor widow has given
more than all those giving to the treasury." Two tiny coins, whose value
"was too small to be meaningfully defined in terms of modern currency"[8]
in comparison with "large sums" given by many rich people—how could
that poor widow have given more than the rich worshipers? But Jesus sees
entirely differently. He comes right to the heart of the matter when he says
that "the others who have given had more than enough, but she, with less
than enough, has given all that she had to live on." That poor widow who
gave all that she had to live on and those slum people who did not eat so
they could share their meager food with their uninvited visitors—is there

---

8. For this explanation see notes to Luke 21:1-4 in the Oxford Study Edition of the New
English Bible.

any difference between them? Jesus would have said the same thing to them as he did to the poor widow.

That poor widow had a large heart—a very large one. Those slum men and women also have large hearts—very large ones too. These two stories, separated by the span of two thousand years, these two pictures, geographically unrelated, become one story. Is this not the story of God's reign? After all, the reign of God is possible in the slums, perhaps more possible than in the affluent world outside. It is not only possible; it is real, perhaps more real than in the church. Those two coins whose value is too small to define and the meager food shared out of dearth are a reality and a sign of God's reign.

Culture of God's Reign

To find the beauty of humanity in an inhuman situation is one thing, but to set about eradicating that inhuman situation is another. To experience the reign of God among the deprived people is one thing, but to strive to remove the causes of deprivation is another. As a matter of fact, the beauty of humanity and the reign of God you encounter in the midst of deprivation and inhumanity should change you from a passive observer to an active participant. It should enable you to help release the power of God's reign and to struggle against the dehumanizing forces at work in human community. This is what the participants in the Exposure Program, touched and moved by the *large hearts* of the slum people, have come to realize when they end their reflection on their traumatic experience with a question:

> Who will give voice to those dumb people
> And fight their cause?

The question is not well put. These are not just dumb people. They shout and quarrel. But their shouts and quarrels are not organized to make impacts. Nor are they meek people not knowing how to fight. Fights break out from time to time in the slums. They fight each other, husband and wife, neighbor and neighbor, friend and friend, when their life becomes too unbearable. But their fights, directed against themselves, must be redirected against the causes that make their lives intolerable and get them on each other's nerves. They must know these causes and those who decide to join them in the fight must also know these causes.

To know these causes is to know that the plight of people is not ordained by God. It is not instituted by God the creator. It is not desired by God the savior. The plight is made by human beings. It is the by-product of the human society that has turned its back against God. It is the side-effect of the human community corrupted by the drive for power and prosperity. It is the cost certain human beings incur in pursuit of their own happiness.

The plight of people prevailing in places such as slums is the reality human beings in every age and in every place have to face. It is a nightmare that haunts humanity. It is a curse under which a greater part of human community has to live. It makes mockery of a vision of a society with justice and love. That plight of people in the slums is an insult to God—the God who created human beings in God's own image. It is a tragedy that debases human nature and defaces that image of God. That plight is a sociological problem. It is a political crime. It is an economic aberration. It is all this. But it is more than all this: it is a "theological" problem—a problem that concerns God as well as humanity. It is a theo-logical crime and hence sin because crime committed against human beings is sin committed against God. It is also a theo-logical offense—an offense against God who provides abundantly for all to share and enjoy. Did not God say to Adam and Eve in the creation story: "Throughout the earth I give you all plants that bear seed, and every tree that bears fruit with seed: they shall be yours for food" (Gen. 1:29)? These words capture the vision of a world blessed with God's abundance.

But how much we have fallen short of this vision of God's abundance for the creation and for all humanity! To know what the reign of God is like and to be part of the struggle for it we must first know how such theological offense takes form in concrete realities in human society. Here we are not concerned with theories but with lives of people. We are not dealing in abstraction but in facts. And when one speaks of facts, one naturally turns to statistics for help.[9] Statistics disclose truths about a society otherwise hidden. They untangle complicated realities of a nation in bare numbers, in simple charts, in colorful graphs. Of course there are good statistics and there are bad statistics. Good statistics are ones that reflect the plight of people and expose the culprits who have created the plight—an autocratic government, a corrupt regime, an exploitative economic system, transnational corporations. Bad statistics are just the opposite. They hide the plight of the people and extol the glory of the ruler. They falsify the state of the nation and create an illusion of prosperity. To use a Chinese expression, they "report only what is good while concealing what is unpleasant" (*pau hsi pu pau yu*). We must, then, not allow ourselves to be deceived by bad statistics, and we must learn from good statistics about the realities of the society in which we live. This is an important part of

---

9. For a theological understanding of statistics see chapter 7, "What Do Statistics Mean?" in my book *Theology from the Womb of Asia* (Maryknoll, N.Y.: Orbis Books, 1986), 78–86.

our theological task. It is indispensable if we are to share Jesus' vision of God's reign.

In a nation ruled by an oppressive government official statistics are usually bad statistics. They only tell one-sided stories—stories that depict hell as paradise, poverty as lack of wealth, hunger as imbalance of nutrition, injustice as enforcement of law and order. Needless to say, we cannot depend on official statistics to get at the reality of the life people live. We are compelled to turn to unofficial statistics—statistics made by the people eluding police surveillance and statistics compiled by outside observers and researchers whose passion is to make the facts known. It is such unofficial statistics that will concern us here.

Not every ruling power of the countries listed here will like these statistics. They will shout in anger: This is subversion! Yes, good statistics have to be subversive. Good statistics are subversive statistics. They disclose the real state of the nation suppressed by the ruling regime and expose the dire situation of the people covered up by it.

Let us look at the statistics more closely. They do not just show numbers. They have faces. They show faces of women, men, and children living in absolute poverty. But what is absolute poverty? It is a "condition of life so characterized by malnutrition, illiteracy, disease, squalid surroundings, high infant mortality and low life expectancy as to be beneath any reasonable definition of human decency."[10] Poverty becomes absolute when human beings are rendered subhuman, when they are deprived of human decency. Absolute poverty is a fearful power. It can undo what God has done: it can obliterate the very humanity God has given to human beings. It is a tyrannical power: it reduces them to petrified things begging for mercy. It is an oppressive power: it destroys human capacity to think beyond acute physical needs and to dream about the future. Absolute poverty is a despot who rules the world with relentless cruelty and unmitigated terror.

The statistics concerned reveal a staggering picture of absolute poverty in certain countries in Asia. In Bangladesh 60 million out of 80 million people live in absolute poverty. This means 75 persons out of a 100, three quarters of the population! In Burma the situation is even worse. There 25 million out of the population of 30 million have to struggle with absolute poverty, that is, more than four-fifths of the population. In the case of Indonesia slightly more than half of the population have to cope with absolute poverty, that is, 68 million out of 135 million. In Thailand

---

10. *World Development Report* (Washington, D.C.: World Bank, 1978), 11. Quoted in Julio de Santa Ana, ed., *Towards a Church of the Poor*, the work of an Ecumenical Group on the Church and the Poor (Geneva: WCC–Commission on the Church's Participation in Development, 1979), 23.

Statistics I

ABSOLUTE LEVEL OF POVERTY
IN SELECTED COUNTRIES IN ASIA IN 1979

	Population (millions)	Absolute Poor (millions)
South Asia		
Bangladesh	80.4	60.3
Burma	30.8	25.3
India	620.4	223.4
Nepal	12.9	.0
Pakistan	71.3	24.3
Sri Lanka	13.8	3.0
East & South-East Asia		
Hong Kong	4.5	0.3
Indonesia	135.2	68.4
Malaysia	12.7	1.3
Philippines	43.3	6.9
Republic of Korea	36.0	3.4
Singapore	2.3	0.1
Thailand	43.0	11.6
Pacific		
Fiji	0.6	0.1
Papua New Guinea	2.8	0.4

Source: United Nations, *Economic and Social Survey of Asia and the Pacific 1979* (Bangkok, 1980), 88. Quoted by Matthew Kurien, "Asian Issues in Perspective," in *Out of Control*, official report of the Asia Youth Assembly, Delhi, September 25–October 10, 1984 (Singapore: CCA-Youth, 1985), 67.

more than a quarter of the population are subjected to a life deprived of human decency—11.6 million out of 43 million. The examples referred to here are but part of the global reality that casts a deep shadow over the development of the so-called developing countries. "Most of the global scenarios for development," it is pointed out, "that project the future of humankind at the beginning of the twenty-first century show a large part of the human race living in conditions that could still be described as poverty. In the most recent projections made by the World Bank [1981], the low-income countries, with more than 35 percent of the world population (excluding China), will probably still have annual levels of income below U.S.$275 per capita in 1990 even on the basis of relatively optimistic projections."[11] This observation, made ten years ago, is still largely valid today.

The "untouchables" in India, for example, are the "outcasts" of society and suffer under the tyranny of absolute poverty as well as the tyranny of the caste system. There are as many as one hundred million of them, nearly 16 percent of India's population.[12] Not only the caste-structured society but nature and their gods seem unkind to them. They are the poorest of the poor who "have no food reserves. Calamities and crop destruction lead to soaring food prices, to hunger... to selling land and ornaments, and to increased indebtedness.... The poor spend much of their daily wages repaying loans, at exorbitant rates of interest, that they were forced to take in order to eat. Faced with such crises, many households become locked into a descending spiral from which they cannot escape and which pulls them below the survival level."[13] This plight of the untouchable in India is the plight the participants of the Exposure Program witnessed in the slums of Bangalore. It is at the same time the plight of the poor elsewhere in the world.

What is it like to live below the survival level? What does it do to your humanity when you are forced to live in the absolute poverty that destroys your human decency? How do you live in a human community that treats you as subhuman and even as nonhuman? Here is a voice that tells us what it is like to live as a poor untouchable:

> If you were to live the life we live
> (Then out of you would poems arise).
> We: kicked and spat at for our piece of bread
> You: fetch fulfillment and name the Lord.
> We: down-gutter degraders of our heritage
> You: its sole repository, descendants of the sage.
> We: never have a paisa to scratch our arse
> You: the golden cup of offerings in your bank.
> Your bodies flame in sandalwood
> Ours you shoved under half-turned sand.
> Wouldn't the world change, and fast

---

11. Godfrey Gunatilleke, "The Ethics of Order and Change: An Analytical Framework," in *Ethical Dilemmas of Development in Asia*, ed. Godfrey Gunatilleke, Neelan Tiruchelvam, and Radhika Coomaraswamy (Lexington, Mass.: D. C. Heath, 1983), 18.

12. See James M. Freeman, *Untouchable: An Indian Life Story* (Stanford: Stanford University Press, 1979), 5.

13. Ibid., 49–50.

> If you were forced to live at last
> This life that's all we've always had?[14]

What heart-rending words! Said by one person, these words may be just a small groan. Uttered by one hundred million persons, they become a huge murmur. Spoken by two-thirds of the world's population living in abject poverty, they turn into a colossal shout. This is a groan of pain. This is a murmur of suffering. This is a shout of protest.

The contrast portrayed in this poem is between you the rich and us the poor, you the privileged class and us the downtrodden class, you the powerful and us the powerless. Socially, politically, economically, and religiously, the community is built on this contrast. The result is that the majority of the people who are poor, powerless, and downtrodden exist for the privileged few who are rich and powerful. The latter are of course not eager to respond to the challenge the poem poses at the end: If you were forced to live at last this life that's all we've always had, wouldn't the world change, and fast? The powerful must make sure that the world does not change; that is why they impose authoritarian rule to keep the powerless always powerless. The rich must see to it that the world remains at their disposal; that is why they are not interested in the distribution of their land and wealth. The privileged must work hard to maintain their privileges; that is why they are not eager to share their privileges with the downtrodden.

Religion, especially institutionalized religion, has often proved an obstacle to change. It

> has often been a force upholding the status quo, reinforcing the stability of society and enhancing political quietism. The Hindu doctrine of *karma*, for example, promising reincarnation into a higher caste as a reward for diligently fulfilling the obligations of one's station in this life, certainly discouraged social and political protest. Protestant Pentecostal sects in the United States, Latin America, and Africa downgrade deprivation here on earth and, by concentrating on communion with the Holy Spirit and the rewards of heaven, which are vouchsafed the faithful, help reconcile their members to a lowly social and economic status. Similar doctrines encouraging either meek acceptance of suffering or withdrawal from the tribulations of human society can be found in other religions.[15]

This is the dark side of religion.

---

14. A poem by Arun Kamble, trans. Cauri Deshpaude, in *No Place in the Inn: Voices of Minority Peoples of Asia* (Hong Kong: CCA–Urban Rural Mission, 1979), 70.

15. Guenter Lewy, *Religion and Revolution* (New York: Oxford University Press, 1974), 76.

Religion itself needs to change for the world to be able to change. And a change called for in a religion must be a radical change, a change with profound theological implications for our relations with God and other people. This in essence is the heart of the prophetic movement in ancient Israel. To the chagrin and dismay of the prophets of the Hebrew Scriptures, the theocratic system of society and government did not guarantee freedom and equality for the people. It quickly develops into an oppressive political structure and an exploitative economic system, built on corruption of power and pursuit of greed. That peasant-turned-prophet Amos, for instance, became incensed. He spoke against the rich and the powerful in soul-stirring words. In the name of the Lord he declared:

> For crime after crime of Israel
>   I shall grant them no reprieve,
> because they sell honest folk for silver
>   and the poor for a pair of sandals.
> They grind the heads of the helpless into the dust
>   and push the humble out of their way.
>   (Amos 2:6-7)

I wish I could see Amos, his face, his hands, his entire person, when he shouted these words out loud in no less a place than Bethel, "the king's sanctuary and a royal shrine" (7:13). These were not his words alone. They were the words hidden in the hearts of the masses of the poor. This was not just his spirit bursting out in anguish. This was the spirit of the downtrodden unable to endure pain and humiliation any longer.

We cannot, of course, see Amos in flesh and blood, but we can see his face in the faces of millions upon millions of the poor. We can touch his hands in the hands of the dispossessed. We can meet him in countless women, men, and children, tired and emaciated. We can hear his voice too in the voice of the "untouchables" who have to endure the indignity and pain of being "kicked and spat at for a piece of bread." The language is different—that of Amos and that of the "untouchables." The imageries are not the same—those of Amos and those of the Asian poor. But the voice crying out of the suffering human beings, whether in the past or today, is the same. And these words on the lips of the poor and disinherited are not mere human words. They are words from God. They are God's words. They are human words and divine words interpenetrating each other to be heard as words of protest.

This is a culture of protest—a culture in which God and the poor meet, a culture that grows out of social oppression and economic injustice. The poem of the "untouchables" is an expression of this culture. It is the awakening of the poor to the fact that their plight is not foreordained by God but made by human injustice and exploitation. The angry out-bursts of the prophets such as Amos inspire such awakening on the part of the oppressed masses. And Jesus' proclamation of God's reign brings that culture of protest into confrontation with the prevailing culture of exploitation.

That culture of protest is, first and foremost, the culture of God's reign. Put it another way, *the reign of God is a culture of protest.* "Blessed are you who are in need," Jesus declared, "the reign of God is yours" (Luke 6:20b; par. Matt. 5:3). This is a bombshell! Beatitudes "are a series of bomb-shells."[16] They "are not quiet stars but flashes of lightning followed by a thunder of surprise and amazement."[17] Jesus' reign of God is not a moral exhortation; it is an indictment against society. It is not a wise counsel for political reform; it is a strong protest against the politics of naked power. It is not spiritual advice for change in a religion; it turns upside down the time-honored traditions of faith and practice. The reign of God, Jesus said forthrightly, belongs, not to the pious, not to the rich, not to the privileged, but to the poor, to the downtrodden, to those who do not conform to the demands of the religious establishment.

Luke has thrust to the fore Jesus' reign of God as a culture of protest much more forcefully than Matthew.[18] He has done this by posing a startling contrast between "blessings" and "woes":

6:20b: Blessed are you who are in need; the reign of God belongs to you.	*6:24:* But alas for you who are rich; you have had your time of happiness.
6:21a: Blessed are you who now go hungry; you will be satisfied.	*6:25a:* Alas for you who are well-fed now; you will go hungry.

Do we not hear in this an echo of frustration expressed in that poem of the "untouchable"? Do we not sense in this the protest of Amos, who exposed the injustices committed against the poor and the powerless by the rich

---

16. William Barclay, *The Gospel according to Luke*, rev. ed. (Philadelphia: Westminster Press, 1975), 76.

17. Deismann quoted by Barclay in ibid., 76.

18. Most critics of the Bible agree on this point. Schweizer, for example, says: "Undoubt-edly the three Beatitudes in Luke 6:20-21 are the earliest. At least the first and probably all three go back in their paradoxical forms to Jesus himself.... In Matthew the change to the third person ... and the assimilation to Isaiah 61:2 ... go back to the community. The addition of 'righteousness' corresponds to Matthew's prevailing interests (vss. 10, 20; 6:33); and the expansion of 'hunger' to 'hunger and thirst' is an assimilation to OT language (Ps. 107:9; Isa. 49:10; 65:13; Amos 8:11; cf. John 6:33). The expansion of 'poor' to 'poor in spirit' is also a later gloss" (*The Good News according to Matthew*, 83–84).

and the powerful of his day? United in this is the culture of protest that has sustained the poor in the East and in the West throughout human history. On behalf of the poor in the audience before him, on behalf of the hungry in the Palestine of his day, and, by inference, on behalf of the poor and the hungry in the world created by God, Jesus must have poured into the little word *ouai* (alas) the full force of protest against the rich in his audience in Palestine and, again by inference, in the whole world. This is strong language—could Jesus have used it? It is a judgmental word—would Jesus have recourse to it? It is an angry expression—would Jesus have no hesitation in using it? "The evidence suggests," it is pointed out, "that this form of speech was used by Jesus himself."[19] Jesus must have filled the *ouai* with all his power of protest against human selfishness and greed. And the social systems that condone and encourage selfishness and greed must have felt the full impact of Jesus' protest.

Statistics II

INCOME DISTRIBUTION WITHIN
SELECTED DEVELOPING COUNTRIES (PERCENTAGE)

Share of National Income of Population Groups

	Richest 20%	2nd 20%	3rd 20%	4th 20%	Poorest 20%
Argentina (1961)	52.0	17.6	13.1	10.3	7.0
Ecuador (1970)	73.5	14.5	5.6	3.9	2.5
Egypt (1964–65)	47.0	23.5	15.5	9.8	4.2
India (1963–64)	52.0	19.0	13.0	11.0	5.0
Kenya (1970)	68.0	13.5	8.5	6.2	3.8
Korea (1970)	45.0	22.0	15.0	11.0	6.0
Mexico (1969)	64.0	16.0	9.5	6.5	4.0
Sri Lanka (1969–70)	46.0	20.5	16.5	11.0	6.0
Tanzania (1967)	57.0	17.0	12.0	9.0	5.0

Source: See Julio de Santa Ana, ed., *Towards a Church of the Poor*, 61. The statistics come from *The United States and World Development* by Martin M. McLaughlin and the Staff of the Overseas Development Council (New York: Praeger Publishers, 1979).

Jesus did not have such statistics to work with. But he had in front of him the people from which statistics such as these could have been drawn. He did not have those percentages neatly tabulated for him, but he had

---

19. I. Howard Marshall, *The Gospel according to Luke* (Grand Rapids: Wm. B. Eerdmans, 1978), 255.

the men, women, and children, the very incarnation of those percentages, in his daily company.

This is a scandalous statistic. In Argentina the richest 20 percent of the population enjoy 52 percent of the national income whereas the poorest 20 percent subsist on a mere 7 percent of the national income. "Scandalous" is a mild word to describe this terrible inequality; this is outrageous. Sri Lanka is by no means a poverty-stricken country. But for a nation that teaches the Buddhist virtue of renunciation of the world it is a shame and an irony that such a colossal gap exists between the richest and the poorest: the former receives 46 percent of the national income while the latter survives on 6 percent. This social situation of inequality, this economic disparity between the rich and the poor, has not, despite much pious talk, changed over the years.

What does the difference between 52 percent and 7 percent say to us? What stories does the gap between 46 percent and 6 percent tell us? They tell us stories of inhumanity in our human community. They show us a world of the survival of the richest. They are stories written with human tears; they emit sighs of helpless men and women, the cries of hungry children. One sees such tears and hears such sighs and cries from the heart of the desperately poor and terribly abused woman in "Cry of Lidiya":

> They hurt me
> They bite me
> They use me
> Then throw me.
>
> Development they call it
> Threw us all out
> Field that was once ours
> Is filled with tall towers
> They promised employment
> That was six years ago
> Now they say you have no skills
> So you must go.
>
> From agency to agency
> Departments of all kinds
> Factories big and small
> My father walked day and night
> To feed seven mouths
> To keep them alive
> Skin stuck to their bones
> Waiting the great day to arrive.

I watched my father grieve
My mother's sad cry
Sisters and brothers sobbing
Exhausted, hungry, curl down and sleep
Day after day
This story went on
No more could I take it
So I ventured on my own.

Now I make enough
To send money home
To feed my family
To give shelter and home
They say they eat a good meal
At least once a day
I am kept a prisoner
For the rich man to play.

I see myself in the mirror
And say "Lidiya you are pretty"
What use is that for a husband
I'm a well-used piece of chattel
My father and mother
They love me I know
Even they feel ashamed
To call me their own.

My brothers and sisters
They say they don't know me
It would cause them shame
For in society I'm rejected
With my body I fed them
They seem to forget
But you said—"I love you"
In you I have a place.[20]

Poverty is tyranny. It tyrannizes one's spirit and body. It tyrannizes over one's entire family. And the most fearful thing is that it can destroy love, that very basis of humanity, that very heart of human relationship, that very core of the family bond.

---

20. The poem is by Sherina Niles. See *Urban Rural Action*, CCA–Urban Rural Mission News and Notes, 5, no. 2 (September 1985): 9.

Jesus must have seen how poverty could debase human nature, not only that of the poor but that of the rich also. The rich who make no scruple about exploiting the plight of the poor to satisfy their animal instincts, who give vent to their greed without compunction, abdicate their own humanity. They buy love with their wealth. But the love that can be bought is no longer love. They imprison love in the dictatorship of their riches, but the love they imprison is not love. It is subservience. It is slavery. It is a mere transaction between different interests. That kind of love reduces the persons concerned to the means and tools to achieve different purposes. Love, that sacred word that can be uttered only by persons first hand to each other and not second hand, third hand, not through intermediaries of wealth, status in life, or standing in society, has no place in a profit-centered world. Love, that holy word that can be enunciated only by women and men whose vision of life is not dimmed by ruthless ambition to succeed at the expense of others, does not fit well in a profit-oriented culture.

But that sacred word called love is precisely what God's love is. As John, the author of the Fourth Gospel, so movingly tells us, "God so loved the world that God gave God's only son" (3:16) to it. God is that sacred word, that holy word, called love. But this is not the whole story, for as John also tells us, the world did not receive that love (1:10). The world not only did not receive it; the world rejected it. The story of that love is the story of suffering and death. That story is reflected in the story of tens and thousands of women like Lidiya today. They sacrifice their bodies to feed their hungry families and send their siblings to school, but all they get in return is estrangement from them and rejection by society.

Jesus could not have been naive about the world. He could not have been ignorant about the plight of the poor. One recalls at once his parable of the rich man and the poor Lazarus (Luke 16:19-31). "There was once a rich man," as the story goes: "who used to dress in purple and the finest linen, and feasted sumptuously every day. At his gate lay a poor man named Lazarus, who was covered with sores. He would have been glad to satisfy his hunger with the scraps from the rich man's table. Dogs used to come and lick his sores." Is this not the story of the 20 percent of the population in Kenya, for example, "feasting sumptuously" on 68 percent of the national income when the poorest 20 percent have to "satisfy their hunger" with a pitiable 3.8 percent of it?

The picture Jesus portrayed in this parable is grotesque, to say the least. On the one hand an extremely rich man in his gorgeous outfit feasting to his heart's content and on the other the poor Lazarus at the gate of that rich man fighting with dogs for "the pieces of bread used by the guests to wipe their fingers, and then thrown to the street."[21] If this was the social situation of Jesus' day, it is also a social reality of the world today. The world does not seem to have made much progress in two thousand years. The situation today is even more tragic than it was in Jesus' time, if not in the nature of the tragedy, at least in the massive scale of it. "As never before in human history," it has been pointed out sadly, "humankind today confronts the stark reality of abject poverty amidst plenty, with one quarter of the world's population living in unprecedented affluence, while the rest is condemned to poverty, an impressive number of them living in absolute poverty.... On the other hand, the affluence and standard of living among the rich minority have been increasing steadily, widening the gap between the rich and the poor."[22] Is this not the very picture Jesus portrayed in the parable of the rich man and the poor Lazarus, the parable he directed at the rich minority in his audience twenty centuries ago?

If this is the reality of the past and the present, what about the future? Is the situation going to improve with the increasing ability of human "know-how" in practically every field of life? Is the gap between the rich and the poor going to disappear as the nations of the world become more and more engaged in a production-intensive economy? The prognosis gives us no cause for optimism. This is what the World Bank reported as early as in 1978:

> Given the obstacles they face, elimination of absolute poverty in the Low Income countries by the end of this century seems impossible. A more realistic target would be to reduce the proportion of their populations living in poverty to about 15 to 20 percent by the year 2000, which would still have nearly 400 million in absolute poverty. To realize even this gain will require massive efforts to raise the productivity and income of the poor.... While poverty could be reduced to low levels in the Middle Income countries by the end of this century, it will continue to plague the Low Income countries.[23]

Unfortunately, what Jesus said to his disciples on the eve of his death is still true today: "You have the poor among you always" (Mark 14:7; par. Matt. 26:11).

How could Jesus, who draws such a contrast between the rich and the poor in his parable, then say: "Blessed are you who are in need"? Those people living in absolute poverty—are they not cursed? How could Jesus,

---

21. G. H. P. Thompson, *The Gospel according to Luke* (Oxford: Oxford University Press, 1972), 215.

22. Julio de Santa Ana, ed., *Towards a Church of the Poor*, 23.

23. *World Development Report*, 11.

who must have known the indignity of the poor such as Lazarus having to fight with dogs for pieces of discarded bread, say to them: "O the happiness of you poor"? For this is what the Greek word *makarios* means.[24] Could Jesus have used a wrong word? Or perhaps Luke misrendered the Aramaic word Jesus used into the wrong Greek word? For "in Greek usage the word *makarios* was used to express the happy, untroubled state of the gods, and then more generally the happiness of the rich who are free from care."[25]

Jesus could not have intended to say that the poor men and women in front of him were like gods. This would have been a most unflattering statement. Jesus would have been preaching a religion of illusion, a religion that has no place in the world of the poor who have to cope with the bitter life of poverty. This is why the "untouchables" in India responded negatively to Gandhi's calling them *Harijans*, children of God. The word sounded to them neither complimentary nor uplifting simply because they are everything what the children of God are not intended to be. Jesus, who lived so close to the poverty-stricken people, could not have been so heartless as to tell them that they could enjoy "the happiness of the rich without care." Their life was anything but happiness. They were worn out with care. Theirs was the life typical of what Lidiya experienced in her own family when she "watched her father grieve, her mother's sad cry, sisters and brothers sobbing, exhausted, hungry." How could Jesus say to Lidiya, to her parents, to her sisters and brothers: "O the happiness of you poor"?

And there is a second part to Jesus' parable of the rich man and the poor Lazarus (Luke 16:22-31). Both men have died. But their lives after death are a complete reversal of their lives in this world. The poor Lazarus "was carried away by the angels to be with Abraham" to enjoy a truly blessed life, while the rich man found himself in Hades and began to taste a life of great torment. The tragic sense of the drama heightens when the rich man now in Hades is told that in no way could he find comfort, not even a drop of water to cool his mouth, because of the "great gulf" fixed between him and Abraham. And of course there is no way to warn his relatives who have survived him about the unbearable life in Hades.

There is some difficulty in relating this second part of the parable to its first part. The second part of the story is almost like religious folklore reflecting a widely held view of retribution: evil will be punished, if not in this world, then in the next world, and good will be rewarded, if not in this world, then in life after death. This is also a prevailing belief among Buddhists who believe that there will be an automatic repayment in afterlife of whatever one has done in the present life (*yin kuo pau yin* in Chinese).

---

24. See Thompson, *The Gospel according to Luke*, 111.
25. Marshall, *The Gospel according to Luke*, 248.

We may leave to the critics of the New Testament the question of whether the parable is a unity or consists of two separate stories.[26] The more important question for us here is whether Jesus, by telling the story, is also teaching a sort of "pie-in-the-sky" theology, diverting the poor from the miseries of their present lives to the promise of a happy life in the hereafter. In short, is he saying: "O the happiness of you poor! You will be like that poor man Lazarus, enjoying a happy life after this miserable present life!"? This could not have been what Jesus wanted to say. It sharply contradicts his message of God's reign. This would be a caricature of God's reign and do a gross injustice to it.

O happiness of you hungry! Jesus must have said this with his heart full of compassion. Alas for you well-fed now! He must have declared it with a voice quivering with anger. He offered no relief plan for the hungry. He did not set up a social program for the poor. He did not institute a service center. But in what he said and did he affirmed the humanity of the poor. By eating and drinking with the hungry he brought God close to them. Through all this he was trying to arouse conscience in his own culture. A culture that allows a poor man like Lazarus to fight with dogs for a piece of bread is a culture without conscience. A society in which a tiny minority of people consumes the greater part of the resources has lost its conscience. The poor become the conscience of a society. They carry the message of God's reign on their person—the message that the world is not what it should be, that God is on their side, that there will be no peace and freedom in human community as long as exploitation of the poor by the rich continues. For this reason Jesus declares "alas for the rich" as well as "happiness of the poor." Because of this in his parable he draws on the fable of the rich man undergoing torment in Hades and the poor Lazarus welcomed into the bosom of Abraham.

The culture of protest is then the culture of conscience. It has to be. You cannot read the words of the prophets in the Hebrew Scriptures and not be overwhelmed by the power of their conscience. You cannot hear Jesus' message of God's reign and not be gripped by his conscience in turmoil. If Jesus engages his opponents in controversy, his purpose is not to win the argument, but to arouse their conscience. This must have been what he intended when he said: "No slave can serve two masters; for either he will hate the first and love the second, or he will be devoted to the first and despise the second." Then pointedly Jesus drew the conclusion: "You cannot serve God and Money" (Luke 16:13). The religious leaders in the audience could not have missed his point. Their conscience was pricked. But instead of feeling the pangs of remorse, they "scoffed at" Jesus. This

---

26. See ibid.

prompted him to come back at them in the language they could hardly misunderstand. "You are the people," Jesus must have said with his finger pointing at them, "who impress others with your righteousness; but God sees through you; for what is considered admirable in human eyes is detestable in the sight of God" (16:15).

In Jesus the religious authorities of his day are confronted with the reign of God as the culture of conscience—a culture in which human beings become totally exposed to God. That culture says that life without conscience is a bestial life, that a religion that goes against conscience goes against God. And a culture that has lost its conscience becomes enslaved to the ruthlessness of the rich and the powerful. It serves a god called money and not God. The struggle to keep conscience alive and well in a culture is, therefore, the mission of God's reign. Jesus' message of God's reign must be at the heart of that struggle. History is unaccountable without such mission.

In contrast to the stern attitude he has taken in his dealing with the religious leaders who conduct their religious duties with their conscience closed to God's saving love, he shows infinite patience with men and women who are conscience-stricken for what they have done. This is reflected in what he is reported to have replied to Peter's question about how many times you should forgive those who have wronged you: "I do not say seven times," Jesus said to Peter, "but seventy times seven" (Matt. 18:21-22; par. Luke 17:4). This is neither indulgence nor condonation. It expresses Jesus' faith in the power of God's healing love—the love that can change a person subjected to his or her own weaknesses and empower a person who is a victim of social injustice and religious discrimination. Jesus is in this way engaged in the ministry of God's reign as a culture of conscience.

Seen in relation to the social and religious reality within which Jesus lived and worked and to the reality of the world in which we live today, Jesus must be at pains to rebuild a culture on the foundation of God's reign as he understood it. The reign of God for him is very much more a social and political vision than a religious concept. It has to be the texture of a society. It must be the foundation of a community. The reign of God is, thus, a cultural happening. It would provide the fabric of a society in which a new social and political structure could be developed. It should prepare the ground on which a more egalitarian economic order could be constructed. In a word, the reign of God, in the mind of Jesus, must be the soul of a new human community in order for justice, freedom, and equality to be realized. The reign of God, that embodiment of love and compassion, has to prevail in the heart and life of people for the construction of new human relationships.

That the reign of God represents for Jesus a culture radically different from the prevailing culture is evident in the conversation that took place between him and a lawyer (Mark 12:28-34; pars. Matt. 22:34; Luke 10:25-28). The lawyer asked him: "Which is the first of all the commandments?" To this Jesus answered quoting the *shema* (Hear, O Israel) in the Hebrew Scriptures: "Love the Lord your God with all your heart, and with all your soul, with all your mind, and with all your strength." This is the great commandment that had shaped the tradition of the Hebrew religion and dictated the religious life of people.

But Jesus' answer did not end there. He must have known that his own culture shaped by this great commandment to love God without condition had developed into a culture that fell short of love for one another, especially for the underprivileged men, women, and children. Jesus challenged this culture. He went about trying to change it. He summarized this mission and ministry of his by quickly going on to say: "The second [commandment] is this: 'You must love your neighbor as yourself.'" In Luke's Gospel Jesus tells the story of the good Samaritan, leaving no shadow of doubt as to what loving one's neighbor means (Luke 10:30-37).

For our discussion here the concluding remark Jesus made in Mark's Gospel is particularly important. When the lawyer in Mark's account—could this lawyer be different from the one in Luke's Gospel who responded to Jesus in a self-righteous manner and prompted Jesus to tell the story of the good Samaritan?—showed that he understood, Jesus commended him with these words: "You are not far from the reign of God" (Mark 12:34). Does this not make it evident that in the reign of God Jesus envisions a culture of love and compassion to replace the old culture of power, conflict, and greed? The culture of love for the neighbor as well as for God is the culture of God's reign. Jesus must have seen in this lawyer a glimmer of hope for a new culture built on the reign of God. To work toward such culture is to work toward the reign of God.

In these statistics we are confronted with the reality of our world at another level. They give us a glimpse of poverty from the local scene to the international scene, from being a national problem to an international problem, from being an isolated case to a case of global dimensions.

We find in these statistics sobering figures. Compare, for example, the GNP per capita of Mozambique and that of Switzerland in 1989. It was $80 for Mozambique and $29,880 for Switzerland! The latter is almost four hundred times as much as the former. The difference is so enormous that it is hard to imagine the gulf that separates the poor and the rich in these two countries. It is not that those who live with the GNP per capita of $80 are contented with the kind of simple lifestyle today envied by those satiated with their affluence and bored with a life that has lost its meaning. This

Statistics III

ECONOMIC & SOCIAL INDICES—
AN INTERNATIONAL COMPARISON

	GNP per capita, 1989	Energy Consumption (kg), 1989	Infant Mortality per 1,000, 1989
Mozambique	80	84	137
Ethiopia	120	20	133
Bangladesh	180	51	106
India	340	226	95
China	350	591	30
Philippines	710	217	42
Thailand	1,220	331	28
Malaysia	2,160	920	22
Korea	4,400	1,832	23
England	14,610	3,624	9
France	17,820	3,778	7
W. Germany	20,440	4,383	8
U.S.A.	20,910	7,794	10
Japan	23,810	3,484	4
Switzerland	29,880	3,913	7

Source: These statistics, based on the World Bank's 1991 report on world development, are taken from chaps. 1 and 2 of Otsuka Katsuo, *Kyosei Jidai no E-ko-no-mie* (Economy in the Era of Co-existence) (Tokyo: Shin Hyoron, 1992), 33, 36.

is not the case at all. The life of the poor is simple all right, but it is anything but the envy of the rich. It is filled with deprivation, hunger, shame, and indignity. That kind of simple life is ridden with miseries, heartbreaks, diseases, and premature deaths.

This is more than obvious when we look at the statistics closely. The statistics tell us that Ethiopia's infant mortality in 1989 was 133 per thousand, whereas that of Japan was 4. Does it have to be pointed out that the GNP of $80 or $120 per person is not a matter of a simple lifestyle, but a matter that has to do with high infant mortality? This is not all. When we look at energy consumption, we cannot but be scandalized. While a poor nation such as Bangladesh had to make do with a mere 51 kgs. of energy per person in 1989, each person in the United States consumed as much as 7,794 kgs. How are those who live in the United States to account for their energy consumption to their fellow human beings in Bangladesh, Mozambique (84 kgs. per person), or Ethiopia (20 kgs. per person)?

The situation is already bad enough, but it is made even worse when people in the poor countries are reduced to being debtors to those in the rich countries. The hard figures below show "Debt of Developing Countries" (US$ in billions)[27]:

	1990	1991
Sub-Saharan Africa	$174	$176
East Asia & Pacific	235	245
Europe & Mediterranean	184	173
Latin America	431	429
North Africa & Middle East	142	136
South Asia	115	122
Total	$1,281	$1,281

How much the developing countries owe to the developed countries! And the debt grows by the year. "For more than 80 countries," it has been pointed out, "the total debt remains staggering. In 1991, they owed about 1.3 trillion, more than doubled the debt burden they shouldered in 1980."[28] This in spite of the fact that the value of the dollar and the U.S. interest rates dropped considerably.

The irony is that the countries ridden with debts and already so poor have, in the past decade, "given more money to the North—through imports, debt repayments and dividends—than they have received. From 1985 through 1991, the world's poorest countries paid the International Monetary Fund $32.8 billion—which was $6.1 billion more than they received from the IMF's sister organizations, the World Bank and other multilateral institutions."[29] If this situation continues, no amount of hard work to develop the economy will ever enable those poor nations to be free from their debts. Just think of "sub-Saharan Africa, where more than forty impoverished countries collectively pay about $1 billion a month to service debt of about $175 billion."[30]

At this point, we have to mention those intruders from outside known as transnational corporations (TNCs) or multinational corporations (MNCs). They "are the carriers of economic imperialism. The latter is inconceivable without large-scale economic cycles in which capital, labor, raw material, semi-manufactured goods and manufactured goods are

27. These statistics are found in "Debt Swallowing Poor Countries," *San Francisco Examiner*, August 23, 1992, A-10.
28. Ibid.
29. Ibid.
30. Ibid.

moved and shuffled around. The administrator of that process including all stages of financing, exploration, research and development, extraction, processing, marketing, consumption and re-investment, at any point is a corporation. When the cycle crosses international borders, the obvious organizational solution is the transnational corporation."[31] Imperialism dies hard. It perhaps never dies. It transforms itself from one form to another. From the ashes of colonialism it has risen to be reincarnated in the neocolonialism of economic imperialism working hand in glove with the authoritarian regimes of Third World nations, exploiting the cheap labor of the poor and reaping enormous profits for itself.

TNCs and local ruling elites are the pharaohs of our time, subjecting poor and powerless women and men in Third World countries to a life of hard labor and meager wages.[32] According to an observer from Sri Lanka, "The wages they [workers for TNCs] receive are very unfair in relation to the companies' profits. Thus a shirt sold for $10 in America is paid for as if its selling price were $2 or $3 in an Asian market. Laborers are paid a dollar or two per day, whereas the same company may pay $60 per day to a worker in Europe."[33] In the case of Thailand, "as the degree of poverty is very high," it was reported in 1981, "parents especially in the rural up-country have to give up their children in exchange for money amounting to US$7–75. Some of them are sold on a contract basis, for six months or one year. Otherwise the buyer will pay the children themselves a monthly salary ($7–15)."[34] The fate of these children is tragic. If not forced into child prostitution, they are used as cheap labor for both private and government companies. There must be endless stories of hearts broken, dreams shattered, and lives ravaged while they are still innocent and fragile. The participants of the Exposure Program that set the stage for our discussion in this chapter must have heard many such stories. They must have come away from the program with a totally different vision of the reign of God.

These stories are already more than ten years old, some might counter and say, and thus ancient stories. Situations have changed, they might insist, and the life and the working condition of workers in these countries have greatly improved. Have they? Here is a story from Indonesia in the year 1992. "Over and over through the day," so the story goes,

31. John Galtung, *The True Worlds* (New York, 1980), quoted by Samuel Rayan, "Reflections from a Christian Perspective" in *Asia's Struggle to Affirm Wholeness of Life* (Hong Kong: CCA–Urban Rural Mission, 1985), 10.

32. One of the studies on TNCs in Asia is *People Toiling under Pharaoh,* eds. Kim Yong Bok and Pharis J. Harvey (Tokyo: CCA–Urban Rural Mission, 1976).

33. See Tissa Balasuriya, *Planetary Theology* (Maryknoll, N.Y.: Orbis Books, 1984), 77.

34. See *People against Domination,* a Consultation Report on People's Movements and Structures of Domination in Asia, held in Kuala Lumpur, Malaysia, February 24–28, 1981 (Tokyo: International Affairs–CCA, 1981), 42.

Tri Mugiyanti dabs paint on the soles of fresh-off-the-mold Nike sneakers. Around her on the production line, workers sit or stand elbow-to-elbow. Many are barefoot. The humid air reeks of paints and glues. The temperature hovers near 100 degrees. Breathing feels unnatural. Welcome to the Hardaya Aneka Shoes Industry factory, known as Hasi, on the outskirts of Jakarta. Each hour here, 6,700 workers crank out about 2,000 pairs of Nike shoes. Nike pays the factory $16.50 a pair for a model such as the men's Air Pegasus, which it sells to retailers for about $35, says David Taylor, Nike's vice president of footwear production. Retailers, in turn, eventually sell it for about $70.[35]

Transnational corporations and companies such as U.S.-based Nike, Inc., have "roamed through Asia for 20 years in pursuit of ever-cheaper production sources. Indonesia is the newest frontier."[36]

The exploitation of cheap labor is in itself outrageous. A pair of shoes that cost only $16.50 to make in Indonesia is sold for $70 in the market outside Indonesia. Who profits from the $53.50 difference between the original cost and the retail price? Not Tri Mugiyanti, one of the 6,700 women workers at Hardaya Aneka shoe factory. Her working conditions are as primitive and unhealthy as ever:

Stay 10 minutes in the Hasi factory where she works and your head will pound, your eyes and lips will burn. Amid the glue and paint fumes, workers without protective clothing operate hot molds, presses and cutting machines. A rubber-room fire killed one worker last year....

Tri Mugiyanti, slightly built with a heart-shaped face and silky hair that brushes her shoulders, earns 15 cents an hour for her part in the production of your Nikes. Put another way, it would take all of Tri's pay for seven weeks to buy one pair of the Nike shoes she helps to make. Contrast her wages with those of basketball star Michael Jordan, Nike's $5 million a year pitchman....

After a long day, Tri Mugiyanti, who claims she is 18 but looks barely past puberty, stands outside her home and says she is very tired. But home is hardly a place to relax. She shares one room in a slum less than a mile from the Hasi factory with three other workers. Smoldering piles of garbage line the cracked dirt paths to her

35. See Nena Baker, "Indonesians 'Just Do It,' " *San Francisco Chronicle* (Business Section, E-3), August 30, 1992.
36. Ibid.

doorway. She sleeps on a bamboo mat. For Tri Mugiyanti and the thousands of factory workers like her, there is no finish line.[37]

It makes us shudder, does it not, to know that the so-called "advanced and glorious modern civilization" of the developed nations is constructed on a story such as Tri Mugiyanti's, that it is made at the expense of a poor, working Indonesian woman such as Tri?

How, then, could Jesus have said to the men and women struggling under the burden of exploited and impoverished life: "Blessed are you who are in need"? Should he not have said instead, "Alas for you who are in need"? For they are victims of big companies, rendered hopeless by enormous national debts, by transnational corporations—companies and corporations that, in complicity with national ruling elites, take away their land, reduce them to cheap labor, and go away with the fruits of their toil, rich companies and corporations that have grown richer at their expense. "Blessed are you transnational corporations!" Jesus could have said to them if his vision of God's reign had been built on nothing but insatiable greed and ruthless exploitation.

How "blessed" transnational corporations are can be illustrated from the case of West Malaysia. This is what a 1975 study shows:

> Compared to the amount of the capital invested, the amount of profits made is excessively high. The most extreme example are National Semi-Conductor and Texas Instruments. The fixed assets and paid-up capital of National Semi-Conductor Electronics were $8.2 million and $2 million respectively in 1974, the profits made for the first and second year of its operations were $73,000 and $23 million. In the case of Texas Instruments the paid-up capital was $25,000 and the fixed assets of $8.7 million and its profits were $19 million the first 14 months of operations and $29 million the second year. The figures for the other companies are not so extreme but nevertheless high. Although much of the profits are ploughed back initially it is unlikely that the high rate of reinvestment will continue. In fact a study revealed that foreign companies have lower rates of reinvestment than local firms. Malaysian-owned manufacturing firms had a reinvestment rate of 26% compared to British, American, and Japanese firms with rates of 13%, 11%, and 10% respectively.[38]

This analysis of the operation of TNCs, seldom known to local people, discloses their normal practice.

---

37. Ibid., E-4.
38. Kim and Harvey, eds., *People Toiling under Pharaoh*, 184.

Again this is not an old story that has become history. It is still happening today. According to the story of Tri Mugiyanti from Indonesia,
"Nike will spend $180 million on advertising this year [1992]. In contrast,
it has nothing invested in manufacturing plants or equipment. Instead, the
company—which makes no shoes in the United States—contracts 35 independent shoe factories sprinkled like colonies throughout Indonesia,
China, Thailand, South Korea and Taiwan."[39] It is a myth, fabricated to
ease the conscience of consumers in the developed countries, that transnational corporations and companies contribute to the development of the
country with which they do business and to the improvement of people's
lives.

If TNCs are not interested in the development of the country in which
they carry on their business, they are not interested in using local resources
either. "The expansion of the Coca-Cola Company in India, Malaysia, and
Indonesia," for instance, "has not included the purchasing of local fruits
for soft drinks. These countries produce abundant crops of oranges, limes,
mangoes, pineapples, jak, guavas, bananas, and such fruits. But Coca-Cola
does not use them. Instead it imports powders and essences from the
United States. Asians become accustomed to drinking imported mineral
waters. Local technology is not developed. Local skills are not encouraged.
Capital flows out of the country."[40] Small wonder the gap between rich nations and poor nations continues to widen. Small wonder too that all the
victimized people in Asia can ask is: "Is there any hope for us?" The gods
of their religion keep them under the tyranny of fate and make them suffer
in submission. But now, in addition, there are gods called TNCs that make
sure their life continues to be poor, wretched, and humiliated.

"Blessed are you who are in need," Jesus said to those women and men
bearing on them the stigma of poverty. What could he have meant? There
were no transnational corporations in those days. Still, the poor had to
bear the brunt of economic injustice and were confined to a life of misery.
And Jesus went on to intimate that the reign of God belonged to them. Is
this a religion of illusion? Is this the rhetoric of a street evangelist? Is this
a tactic of religious deception? There must have been people who could
not help raising such questions.

But Jesus is not engaged either in rhetoric or in deception. What Jesus
is saying, as we have seen, is a protest. With these words Jesus inaugurated
a culture of protest. This is no illusion. This is a declaration made by the
man whose conscience is pained and angered by the exploitation of the
poor. With that declaration Jesus lets the voice of conscience be heard in

39. Baker, "Indonesians 'Just Do It,'" E-3.
40. Ibid.

his culture. And of course in saying these words, Jesus is not resorting to a tactic of deception, lulling the minds of the poor into accepting their miserable fate. He is, on the contrary, mobilizing the poor against the injustices inflicted on them by a society shaped and run by the rich and the powerful. The moral power contained in the declaration is irresistible. Jesus must have wanted to shake the poor out of their resignation. He must have tried to empower them so that they could share his vision of God's reign.

His is a moral power that enables the poor to assert their humanity in front of the rich, equips the downtrodden with the courage to stare the powerful in the face, and gives them the capacity to create, expand, and enrich the space of their life and existence. The phrase "in spirit" that Matthew attached to "the poor" in his version of the Beatitude (Matt. 5:3) must be understood in relation to this moral power to assert, to confront, to create, and to expand—the basic qualities of the human spirit, the qualities without which the human spirit is not human and without which the human spirit is not the spirit with which God endows human beings. What Jesus has done, through his declaration that kindles hope in the poor and the disinherited and takes the rich and the powerful to task, is to inaugurate *the culture of God's reign as a culture of empowerment.*

CHAPTER 4

CULTURE OF EMPOWERMENT

Jesus said, "How shall we picture the reign of God, or what parable shall we use to describe it? It is like a mustard-seed; when sown in the ground it is smaller than any other seed, but once sown, it springs up and grows taller than any other plant, and forms branches so large that birds can roost in its shade. (Mark 4:30-32)

Poor and Humiliated

In the previous chapter I pointed out that with his message of God's reign Jesus initiated a culture radically different from the prevailing culture based on inequality between the rich and the poor, privileges of the few, a hierarchy of power, and oppression of the powerless. This prevailing culture, although deeply rooted in his own religious tradition, contradicts his vision of God's reign and perpetuates the plight of people. In what he said and did concerning the reign of God, Jesus protested against it and sought to rouse the conscience of the ruling elite. Standing at the side of the poor and the powerless, he announced the presence of God's reign among them and set out to build a culture of protest and conscience. There is a tone of finality in his declaration: the reign of God belongs to you poor and oppressed people, while "it is easier for a camel to pass through the eye of a needle than for a rich man to enter it" (Mark 10:25; pars. Matt. 19:24; Luke 19:25).

A pronouncement such as this cannot but touch the hearts of people, especially the hearts of the poor and the disinherited. At last they have someone who dares to speak out for them, someone they can count on to be their advocate, and someone who is prepared to fight for their cause. They must have looked at Jesus with a flash of light in their eyes—a light long extinguished from their eyes and their hearts. Jesus must have read the meaning of the light in their eyes with mixed feelings. He must have, on the one hand, felt enormously encouraged by the light of life rekindled in them again and by their hearts grown warm with expectations. But at the same time he must have also perceived a dependent state of mind and attitude they began to develop toward him. Long accustomed to being treated with contempt and scorn by those who hold political and religious power, they had lost self-respect and confidence. "The principal suffering of the poor, then as now," it is pointed out, "was shame and disgrace. As the steward in the parable says, 'I would be too ashamed to beg' (Lk 16:3)."[1] Is there any wonder that they come to depend on others for their survival and welfare?

The culture of the poor and the oppressed is a culture of humiliation. This was the case in the society of Jesus' time and it is also the case in our time, in which "money, power and learning give a person prestige and status because they make him or her relatively independent and enable them to do things for other people. The really poor person who is dependent upon others and has no one dependent upon him or her is at the bottom of the social ladder. He or she has no prestige and no honor. They are hardly human. Their life is meaningless."[2] It is not poverty itself but the need to depend on others that poverty creates that is detrimental to the humanity of the poor. You are no longer your own master. You live on the charity of others. But what is charity on the part of the rich is nothing but a denial of humanity for the poor. It only heightens the indignity of being poor.

Nor is it lack of power itself that renders the life of the oppressed humiliating. It is when lack of power turns into submission to authority that life is deprived of integrity. You are deprived of the right to affirm the conditions that make your life and the lives of others genuinely human. You have no freedom to say no as well as yes. You are not supposed to assert your justice when injustice is done to you. And the love you deem essential to human relationship is nothing but mercy shown by the powerful to the powerless. In short, to be poor is to have no rights as human beings. And to be oppressed is to live at the mercy of the oppressor.

Dependency is deeply ingrained in the psychology of the poor and the oppressed. It makes them easy targets of derisive and unfair treatment. It renders them submissive to power and authority. It makes them passive socially and politically. When dependency on religious hierarchy as a means of salvation is taught as a religious virtue, poverty and oppression are accepted as one's fate that must be borne patiently. And what religion has not deliberately cultivated submission and dependence in believers! Jesus must have realized that to make them dependent on him for redressing their plight as poor and oppressed was to perpetuate their passive atti-

---

1. Albert Nolan, *Jesus before Christianity* (Maryknoll, N.Y.: Orbis Books, 1978), 22.
2. Ibid.

tudes toward life, to continue their submission to the authorities, and to acquiesce in the denial of their humanity. They must be made to realize that even though poor they are not to be humiliated, that even though oppressed they are not to accept oppression passively as their fate.

What they need is not dependency on others, not even on Jesus, but empowerment to be independent and human. To be independent is to be human. And to be human is to be independent. Perhaps this is one of the reasons why Jesus said to the crowds of poor men, women, and children around him that the reign of God is theirs. Humiliation of the poor and the oppressed has no place in God's reign. God's reign is not the charity God dispenses out of God's largess. It does not demand that they give up being independent and human. It is *theirs*, says Jesus, because they have an active role to play in its realization, because they have everything to do with its making. One of the things Jesus is reported to have said in his farewell discourses must be related to how he envisioned the reign of God. "No longer do I call you servants," he said to his disciples; "for a servant does not know what his or her master is about. I have called you friends, because I have disclosed to you everything that I heard from my Father" (John 15:15). Jesus shares with the poor and the disinherited the secret of God's reign. He has taken them into the confidence of God. And they are to be actively involved in bringing about the secret plans of God's reign. What wealth! What prestige! If they are in this way full-fledged independent human beings before God, how can they not also be full-fledged independent human beings in the eyes of this world?

Passive and Subservient

The social attitudes, daily concerns, and religious behaviors of the poor and the disinherited whom Jesus tried to revitalize with his message of God's reign may not be very different from those of most women and men in Asia before the wind of recent struggle for democracy swept across their countries and created in them new self-awareness. What is characteristic of the people tyrannized by oppressive rulers and exploited by those on whom they depend for their livelihood, besides a sense of humiliation, is "a sense of passive impotence before power."[3] This is a feeling of helplessness, resignation, and self-degradation. When such feeling and such sense take hold of you, the instinct for survival comes to dictate your attitudes, emotions, and thoughts. Other concerns become secondary. You learn to hold your emotions within yourselves. You at least feign apathy toward

---

3. Richard H. Solomon, *Mao's Revolution and the Chinese Political Culture* (Berkeley: University of California Press, 1971), 113.

what is happening around you. You comply with social conventions and political demands to avoid censors and risks. You take refuge in anonymity as a way of preserving a very limited space of your existence. You surrender your independence as a human being in exchange for a relatively safe and undisturbed life.

Passivity, subservience, and dependency—these are the main factors underlying what people think and do in an authoritarian society. The culture shaped and dictated by these factors can be called slave culture. It is a culture dominated by a servile spirit. Slaves survive on the whims of their master. They are not allowed independent existence. They belong to those who have power over them. They are treated as things and as property. They can be sold and bought. That is what slave trade means. Their instinct is to please their master in order to gain the latter's favor. All other concerns, including moral values and personal responsibility, are secondary. A slave culture is thus a survival culture. It is a culture that denies people's humanity and deprives them of their integrity. This is the culture of the oppressed people and the culture of the colonized nations. In this culture justice is defined by the exercise of power by masters and rulers, love is mercy occasionally shown by them, and freedom is the favor they administer grudgingly.

How deeply this kind of culture can corrupt the human nature of the oppressed people, dim their vision of freedom, and numb their will to struggle! We recall how the Hebrews in the wilderness, faced with the hardships and the responsibility of the freedom they had won, clamored for a return to the land of slavery. They vented their frustration on Moses, their leader in the exodus from Egypt, and said: "If only we had died at the Lord's hand in Egypt, where we sat by the flesh-pots and had plenty of bread! But you have brought us out into this wilderness to let this whole assembly starve to death" (Exod. 16:3). The slave culture that had developed in the course of four hundred or so years (Exod. 12:40) must have deeply affected their social attitudes, moral concerns, and psychological state as well as their religious beliefs. Perhaps at least forty years of life in the wilderness were needed to build a new culture of freedom and independence to replace the old slave culture.

The culture of the oppressed people is a passive and subservient culture. It is a culture in which they play no active and independent role. This is a sad and tragic reality not only for the enslaved Hebrews in ancient times but also for the oppressed people of all times. This is why, for instance, the presence of U.S. military bases in the Philippines for more than four decades from since 1947 to 1991 was not just a matter of geopolitics in the Pacific region and of balance of military power in Asia. For the people of the Philippines it was a profound cultural and spiritual matter. In these forty-five years these bases gave rise to a culture within the Philippine culture. "The basic facts," it was pointed out, "are that the US Military Bases occupy a vast area of the Philippine territory: the Subic Naval Base in Bataan and Zambales covers 15,000 hectares of land and 11,000 hectares of water; Clark Air Base in Pampanga consists of 49,000 hectares of land with a 22-mile perimeter. The Bases likewise constitute the biggest employer in the country outside the Philippine government. Given this formidable US presence, it only follows that the Bases give rise to a culture spawned in and around them ... which spreads to the rest of the country."[4]

This was a foreign culture imposed on the people and their country with formidable military power and "supportive of US economic interests and antagonistic to the development of a nationalistic and pro-people culture."[5] What it had done was to make the Filipino people "feel unfree and subservient to a foreign government. Freedom is not real but illusory and this ingrained perception of subservience and lack of freedom which the US cultivates in the population of the 'host country' is a true form of ideological oppression which diminishes the people's self-esteem and perpetuates an attitude of passive compliance."[6] The people were doubly unfree—they were unfree in relation to their own dictatorial government and to a foreign government through its military presence. They became also doubly subservient—they became subservient both to their own authoritarian rulers and to the foreign power. This was the culture of subservience under which the people of the Philippines suffered under the dictatorial regime of President Marcos.

Would this also have been the culture of the masses of women, men, and children with whom Jesus associated? In the Gospels these people are variously called

the poor, the blind, the lame, the crippled, the lepers, the hungry, the miserable (those who weep), sinners, prostitutes, tax collectors, demoniacs (those possessed by unclean spirits), the persecuted, the downtrodden, the captives, all who labor and are overburdened, the rabble who know nothing of the law, the crowds, the little ones, the least, the last and the babes or the lost sheep of the house of Israel. The reference here is to a well-defined and unmistakable section of the population. Jesus generally refers to them as the poor or the little ones; the Pharisees refer to the same people as sinners or the rabble who know nothing of the law. Today the same might refer to this

---

4. Alice G. Guillermo, "The Bases Culture: Subservience and Corruption," in *Kalinangan* (Institute of Religion and Culture, Manila) 8, no. 2 (June 1988): 6.

5. Ibid.

6. Ibid.

section of the population as the lower classes; others would call them the oppressed.[7]

The dreadful thing about the culture of passivity and subservience is that it tends to foster self-abasement, encourage deception, and reproduce oppression among the poor and the oppressed. It is a culture that has lost its soul and become a mere shadow of the dominant culture. With that culture human values such as compassion and integrity are suppressed. Jesus must have, from time to time, been confronted with subtle and not so subtle manifestations of such culture in his daily contacts with people.

Perhaps we can read a clue to such a culture of people in his parable of the unforgiving servant (Matt. 18:23-35). This parable is a drama, as it were, in two acts. In the first act the king confronts his servant "whose debt ran into millions." The servant must have used his position to acquire illegal money from his master's wealth and squander it. But now the day of reckoning has come. The king wants to settle accounts with him. The servant is panic-stricken and a dramatic scene develops. "The man fell at his master's feet" (18:26). The self-debasement of the servant is complete. Any sign of human dignity has disappeared from him entirely. The only thing that matters to him now is how to get himself out of this terrible predicament. "Be patient with me," he pleads with his master, "and I will pay you in full" (18:26). He knows he cannot pay back his debt at all, not to say in full. To obtain the master's mercy and gain a reprieve, he has to deceive himself and give a promise that he knows he cannot keep. It is not possible that the king is not aware of this; still he is "so moved with pity that he let the man go and cancelled the debt" (18:27).

The parable could have ended there with a happy scene—the grateful servant with his "debt in millions" remitted without condition, profusely thanking the magnanimous king full of love and compassion and pledging his renewed loyalty. Jesus has in fact set out to depict for people what the reign of God is like as he prefaces the parable saying: "The kingdom of heaven, therefore, should be thought of in this way" (Matt. 18:23). God, he is saying, is like that king who forgives. God does not just forgive; God forgives unconditionally. Your debt to God may be in the millions, but God does not count it against you. You do not need to go through all those complicated rites and rituals to be forgiven. You do not have to pay for the forgiveness of your sins by doing penance or offering sacrifices. To be forgiven is difficult enough. God does not add further difficulties by all sorts of requirements prescribed by the traditions of your religion and by your religious authorities. All you have to do is to accept God's forgive-

---

7. Nolan, *Jesus before Christianity*, 21.

ness and to be forgiving to others who may owe you a debt. This is what the reign of God is about—forgiveness without condition.

It may be that when this last thought crosses his mind Jesus decides to bring to a sharper focus a picture of anti-God's reign. Hence the second act of the drama in the parable. The principal actors in this second act are the forgiven servant and his fellow servant. The former leaves the presence of the king greatly relieved. He must have felt as if a heavy burden had been removed from his shoulders (*ju she chung fu* in Chinese). There is no more worry, no more panic. He can now breathe easily. Life is livable again. But no sooner has he stepped outside in this happy mood than he runs into his fellow servant who owes him "a few pounds" (18:28). Compared with the millions he owed to his master, "a few pounds" is a mere pittance. With his heart still grateful with the forgiveness from the king, that pittance should not have occurred to his mind. He could have exchanged greetings with his fellow servant and gone his way. Or if he did remember that wee bit of debt, he could have told the latter to forget it. He would then be practicing the reign of God.

But alas, this is not what he did. At this point the parable depicts another dramatic scene. That forgiven servant "took hold of him [the fellow servant]," so Jesus tells us, "seizing him by the throat and said, 'Pay me what you owe'" (Matt. 18:28)! Surely an act such as this is totally unexpected of him, especially when he has just been forgiven of his debt in the millions. Then the scene between him and the king repeats itself. The fellow servant is on his knees begging for mercy, saying those exact words his creditor has just said to the king. "Be patient with me," he pleads with him, "and I will pay you" (18:29). If the forgiven servant fails to practice something of the king's compassion in the first instance, this is another chance for him to do so. But, turning a deaf ear to the plea, he has his fellow servant arrested and has him "thrown into jail until he should pay the debt" (18:30).

The parable ends with a predictable conclusion. The king, when told what his servant has done, is incensed. Calling him "scoundrel," the king says to him, hardly able to contain his anger: "I cancelled the whole of your debt when you appealed to me; ought you not to have shown mercy to your fellow-servant just as I showed mercy to you?" (Matt. 18:33) With these words the king "condemned the man to be tortured until he should pay the debt in full" (18:34). The point Jesus wanted to make is clear. God forgives unconditionally, but God's unconditional forgiveness is manifested only in our unconditional forgiveness of one another. As John the Evangelist is to write later, "those who do not love a brother or sister whom they have seen, cannot love God whom they have not seen" (1 John 4:20, NRSV). This is the ethic of God's reign. An impossible ethic? It is impossible within the culture we have inherited and within which we live. But in the practice of it, God becomes visible and the reign of God becomes real.

In the second act of the parable there seems something else Jesus wants us to be aware of: oppression of the oppressed by the oppressed. This is the saddest part of the culture of subservience. A subservient culture can turn the oppressed into oppressors of one another. This is the crisis of the oppressed people particularly in their struggle for liberation from oppressive powers that rule over them. It causes suspicion one of another, creates division among them, and frustrates their efforts to reach their goal. Is this perhaps the danger to which Jesus is also trying to draw people's attention when he expands the one-act parable into a two-act parable? Is he saying that the religious elite who make life difficult for their fellow Jews, who discriminate against them on religious and political grounds, are, like that forgiven servant, unforgiving and oppressive to them? Subservience to the Roman rule has demoralized some of the Jews, corrupted their religious ethic based on the justice and love of God, and adulterated the culture that has bound them as one people with love, trust, and concern for one another. What Jesus has to face is a crisis of culture—the culture that has proved ineffective and powerless to rally people together around the double commandment of love of God and love of neighbor. What Jesus has to contend with is a culture eroding the spiritual foundation of his people under Roman colonial rule. It is into this crisis of the traditional culture that Jesus brings the message of God's reign and begins the construction of a culture with God's reign at its center.

Fear and Anxiety

Jesus, as we all know, stands on the side of the poor and the oppressed and makes a common cause with them. He makes a point of telling them that God's reign is theirs. But in doing this he is not inspired by a romantic notion of socially, economically, or religiously disinherited people. In his daily living with them he must have gained a deep experience of their life yielded to passivity and subservience, on the one hand, and on the other, to self-abasement, deception, and doing injustice to one another. It must have been his effort to enable them to aspire to a different life and culture with his vision of God's reign.

But what vitiates the life of the poor and the oppressed is not only passivity and subservience. There are also fear and anxiety. This is illustrated in a typical interpretation of the relation between superior and subordinate given by a twenty-eight-year-old factory worker from Kwangtung Province in China who works as an electrical technician in Taiwan. This is how that factory worker responded to his interviewer:

This [older] person is rather experienced in social matters; an understanding person. This other fellow is relatively young and inexperienced. They have some kind of a relationship.

What kind?

Like commercial people, but yet not like that; like landlords, but yet not. In any case, rather low level in society.

The older man is telling the younger to do something.

What kind of thing?

Not too enlightened a thing.

Why?

You can tell just from their appearances. The younger fellow is fearful; he is unwilling to do it.

What kind of thing might it be?

Just not proper. That would include many things [laughs].

What does the older man feel about the younger?

He is just telling him to do the job and not to worry about it as the responsibility is all on his shoulders.

How does the younger feel about the older?

He is afraid; he doesn't dare to do the thing.

What is the result of this situation?

He goes and does it.

Does he succeed?

From his expression he does it and fails, because he is afraid.

Afterwards what is the relationship between the two men?

The older one feels the younger is of no use.

What about the younger?

He thought it could not be avoided, doing that thing, so he did it.

How does he feel toward the old man?

Nothing in particular; he just had to do the thing.

Then what is their relationship?

The younger man is arrested.

By whom?

The police, another organization, or intelligence group. Then the older man runs away. The younger is very straightforward in telling [his captors] about the thing.[8]

The attitude of the respondent in this interview toward the relationship between the older man and the younger man, that is, between the superior and the inferior, is ambiguous and noncommittal. Even though it is apparent that the act conceived and instigated by the superior (the

8. Solomon, *Mao's Revolution and the Chinese Political Culture*, 113.

older man) and carried out by the younger (the inferior) must be illegal, the respondent does not seem willing to be openly critical of the older man.

From this interview can be drawn a variety of conclusions, but it seems to point up one particular fact of life in a society in which human relationships are shaped and dictated by a hierarchy of power and authority: social, political, and psychological inhibitions that condition the ways people think, behave, and act in given situations. What prevails in this kind of society and determines people's response is fear or "anxiety in the face of authority."[9] Considerations for moral values and personal responsibility are subject to this fear and anxiety. That is why "the young man shows no guilt at having done something improper, precisely because in the face of authority he was powerless to do otherwise. The subordinate seeks protection by investing as little of himself in the relationship as possible. There is no sense of personal responsibility."[10] And when he is arrested by the police, he "is very straightforward in telling [his captors] about the thing" he has done at the instigation of his superior. His straightforwardness, his candidness, is not motivated by his admission of his guilt and responsibility in doing something wrong. For him the situation has shifted and he is seized with fear and anxiety in the face of a different power and authority. The fear of punishment and anxiety for an uncertain future must have told him that to get the best deal out of a bad situation he has to be straightforward and candid about what he has done, implicating, of course, his former superior who has, in the meantime, run away.

Fear and anxiety take hold of people and make them numb and immobilized in an authoritarian society. Those in power know this very well, be it political power, economic power, or religious power. Fear is one of the most effective means to keep people under control and anxiety deprives them of courage and will to demand change. Once seized with fear and anxiety like that young factory worker, you become an easy target of manipulation by those who have power over you. You become socially inactive, politically compromising, or religiously submissive and reactionary. Unquestioned obedience to the political power and authority is taken for one's civil duty by citizens and even for one's religious duty by religious believers. It is little wonder that those in power use fear and anxiety as their political instruments to keep themselves in power and keep people in their place. People must cast off fear and get rid of anxiety, then, to be able to commit themselves to working for change.

---

9. Ibid., 112.
10. Ibid., 114.

124 REALITY

Unmasking Hypocrisy

Is this what Jesus realized in the company of the poor and the oppressed? Is this what he came to understand as an essential part of his mission? And is this how he went about preparing people for the reign of God? There are indications in some of what he said and did that this may have been the case. There is, for instance, his exhortation not to fear (Luke 12:2-9; par. Matt. 10:26-33). In the Gospel of Matthew it is set in the context of Jesus' "commissioning the twelve disciples" (Matt. 10:1-16) and exhorting them to confess him without fear when persecuted (10:17-25). This seems to suggest that the exhortation reflects Jesus' own confrontation with the religious authorities and/or even presupposes that the early Christian community was facing persecution. As Matthew tells it, here Jesus is preparing his disciples for courageous public testimonies when occasion arises in the future.

Luke, however, sets the exhortation in a different context: "Meanwhile," so begins his account, "when a crowd of many thousands had gathered, packed so close that they were treading on one another." This is followed by this remark: "he [Jesus] began to speak first to his disciples" (Luke 12:1). The remark must be an afterthought on the part of Luke, the author of the Gospel that bears his name. It must be the presence of the "crowd of many thousands" that is dominating Luke's mind when he sets out to compose this part of his story. Unlike Matthew, he refers neither to the commissioning of the twelve disciples nor to fearless testimonies in times of persecution. He does come to Jesus' exhortation on testifying to the truth without fear, but the reference occurs only later when Jesus himself is facing imminent arrest and trial in Jerusalem (21:12-19).

The audience Jesus is addressing with the exhortation not to fear, according to Luke, must be the "crowd of many thousands," including the disciples. It must not have been his intention to portray Jesus as having a private session with his disciples. How could such a session be possible while "a crowd of many thousands had gathered, packed so close that they were treading on one another"? Rather, Luke must have wanted us to picture Jesus in front of a big crowd and a packed audience as the background of Jesus' discourse on fear and anxiety. And this is important for us. We will see why presently.

As usual, these men and women who have gathered in great numbers to hear Jesus are mostly economically poor and politically oppressed. They are fearful of the authorities, both political and religious, and burdened with worries about their insecure lives. For Jesus these are the people who belong to the reign of God. It is they who embody God's reign in their own persons. And it is they who must bear witness to the fact that God's reign is theirs and not the monopoly of those in the traditional religious circles of respectable members of the established religion. But how can they be aware of God's reign in them and with them both as individuals and as a community as long as they are dominated by fear and anxiety? As Jesus looks at them with his message of God's reign, he can hardly suppress the question. The reign of God, Jesus must have decided, must begin with doing away with fear and anxiety in these people.

It is significant, then, that, as Luke has it, Jesus begins right away to expose the religious leaders in his discourse with the many thousands of women and men who packed to hear him. "Be on your guard against the leaven of the Pharisees," he says, "I mean their hypocrisy" (Luke 12:1). "Hypocrisy" is a familiar word in Jesus' vocabulary. He uses it again and again not just behind the back of his religious opponents but in his face-to-face controversies with them. It is a judgmental word. It is also a word bubbling with anger and frustration pent-up inside those persons down-trodden and discriminated against. It means "pretending to be what one is not," and "feigning to be pious and virtuous without really being so."

The religious authorities they hold in awe—they are hypocrites! Those who are supposed to be paragons of virtue and models of piety—they seem pious and virtuous without really being so! To hear someone saying this out loud in the open is shocking. It is not that Jesus' listeners have never suspected. In moments of desperation and dejection they too must have been tempted to shout out loud what they harbor secretly in their minds and hearts. But they have long been conditioned to resign themselves to their fate and intimidated into suppressing whatever doubts they may have about the authorities. The deep-seated fear in them for their leaders has made them voiceless and nervous. That fear is the root of their misery. It is the evil that prevents change from happening. Jesus has to tell them emphatically: "Do not fear those who kill the body and after that have nothing more they can do" (Luke 12:4). Jesus is at pains to exorcise fear from people.

As long as that fear is there, people will not be able to enjoy the free-dom of God's reign. It is an obstacle that makes it impossible for them to regain their integrity as human persons. To do away with that fear, to root it out, the hypocrisy of those in power has to be exposed. Their pretension to be virtuous and pious must be unmasked. Their assumption to be bet-ter than those men and women they disdain and oppress has to be denied. And their right to speak for God has to be challenged. It may be that this is what Jesus is doing when he goes on to say to the people: "There is noth-ing covered up that will not be uncovered, nothing hidden that will not be made known" (Luke 12:2).

This is precisely what he did in his controversies with the religious lead-

ers. "Alas for you, scribes and Pharisees, hypocrites!" he confronts them
bluntly. "You clean the outside of a cup or a dish, and leave the inside full
of greed and self-indulgence!" (Matt. 23:25; par. Luke 11:39). Jesus is not
just angry. He must be grief-stricken. Behind the mask of piety and rituals they practice greed and exploitation. "Outwardly," Jesus continues,
"you look like honest men, but inside you are full of hypocrisy and lawless-
ness" (Matt. 23:28). In this vein Jesus goes on and on. Jesus' confrontation
with the religious leaders must have taken place in public. Those men and
women, victims of the religious hypocrisy committed by their religious authorities, must have heard Jesus' stern words exposing what had been going
on behind the façade of pietism and power. They must have felt elated on
the one hand, for at last they had someone who dared to speak the truth.
On the other hand, however, they must have been alarmed, for they could
not but be aware that Jesus would have to pay dearly for what he was doing.

The unmasking of the hypocrisy of those in power and authority—Jesus
must have engaged himself in such dangerous ministry to make room and
create a context for the reign of God. In his severe criticism of the religious
leaders he must have hoped that they would repent, reform, and renew
their faith in the God of love and compassion. In his fearless confrontation with the religious authorities in public he must have wanted to open
the eyes of the poor and the oppressed. He wanted them to see what was
behind that mask of piety and power and to help them cast away their fear
of their authorities. Fear comes from the unknown. It is bred by ignorance.
To get rid of fear, then, the unknown must be made known and ignorance
be replaced with knowledge. In his open conflicts with the religious authorities Jesus must have been doing just that for the women and men kept in
fear of those who exercised control over their lives. He is engaged in what
is now widely known as "conscientization," the term referring to "learning to perceive social, political and economic contradictions, and to take
action against the oppressive elements of reality."[11]

Enabling people "to perceive social, political and economic contradictions"—this constitutes the essential part of Jesus' ministry of God's reign.
To these contradictions we must add "religious contradictions." Religion
looms large in the lives of the people Jesus has to deal with. It is the heart
of the community. In the days of Jesus contradictions that had developed
in the official religion gave rise to social, political, and economic contradictions. In story after story, in parable after parable, in controversy after
controversy, Jesus focuses on religious contradictions that vitiate the social, political, and economic realities. That is why Jesus returns to religious

---

11. See the translator's note in Paulo Freire, *Pedagogy of the Oppressed*, trans. Myra
Bergman Ramos (New York: Continuum Publishing Co., 1982), 19.

contradictions over and over, identifying them as the root of the evil that vitiates his society. To liberate the religious leaders from these contradictions, that is, from their hypocrisy, and, above all, to empower people to face them and take action against them are necessary steps toward God's reign.

Had Jesus been a revolutionary, had he been a political messiah with the aim of mobilizing the masses to turn against the oppressive religious and political powers, he could have certainly succeeded, even though the success might have been short-lived and cost many lives. The revolutionaries who struggle for power could take as a model what Jesus did to unmask the hypocrisy of the religious leaders and to dispel fear from the poor and the oppressed, and develop it into strategies and techniques to win their struggle. This could not be what Jesus wanted, but he could not have been totally unaware of the possibility. The great excitement his entry into Jerusalem caused in the crowds of people is at least an indication of what might have happened if he had seizure of political power in mind. How could both the religious authorities and the Roman authorities not have been alarmed?

The revolutionary leader who in our modern world most successfully mobilized people against the ruling power is Mao Zedong of China. The corruption of power and use of brute force that tarnished the last years of his rule apart, Mao, during his revolutionary days, was a master of enabling people to overcome their fear and institutionalizing their misery into a powerful political force. "According to Mao," it has been observed,

> the most basic of these techniques, which he asserted "won over most villages for us," was the *su-k'u* or "speak bitterness" meeting, first used during the period of the civil war and then adapted to the struggles of land reform. . . . In encouraging peasants to "speak of the bitterness" of rural life, and to "vomit the bitter water" (*t'u k'u-shui*) of injustice suffered at the hands of the rural gentry, local bullies, and warlord troops, the Party urged "the masses" to work up all the rage and resentment that by tradition was "put in the stomach." This combination of ideological study and organized class struggle makes people politically "conscious" in the sense of bringing together the *perception* of mistreatment and injustice with the repressed *emotion*. The separation of thought and feeling which Confucian culture had made the basis of "cultured" behavior was brought to an end.[12]

Jesus could have been an effective revolutionary leader. But he was no Mao Zedong, or for that matter, no political messiah that most revolution-

---

12. Solomon, *Mao's Revolution and the Chinese Political Culture*, 196.

ary leaders aspire to be. He struggled not for power but for love. He strove not for the kingdom of this world but for the reign of God. He did not agitate for class struggle but engaged himself in the healing of ruptured human relationships and promoting social values based on love, justice, and freedom. What he had was not an ambition for the power and glory of this world but a vision of God's reign in human hearts and in human community. And this makes all the difference. He envisions a human community in which power does not corrupt, wealth does not create poverty, justice for some does not become injustice for others, and love is not charity of the rich and indignity of the poor but the power that binds people in a bond of communion regardless of color, sex, or creed. No, Jesus could not have been a revolutionary who uses violence to win power. He is no messiah who struggles for political domination.

This is the reign of God as Jesus understands it and practices it. Fear should, then, have no place in it. There is no reason why people should be immobilized by it. If fear has no role to play in the reign of God, then anxiety does not have it either. This is what Jesus goes on to put across to the "crowds of many thousands" in front of him "packed so close that they were treading on one another." "Are not five sparrows sold for two-pence?" Jesus tells them. "Yet not one of them is overlooked by God. More than that, even the hairs of your head have all been counted. Do not be afraid; you are worth more than any number of sparrows" (Luke 12:6-7; par. Matt. 10:29-30).

It seems that this exhortation is a little out of context here. Jesus has just been telling people that they should not have fear in face of power and authority. But the emphasis now is not so much fear as anxiety. If God takes care of sparrows and counts the hairs of your head, if you have this God to be your God, the God who holds you infinitely "worth more than any number of sparrows," why should you have fear? This reminds us at once of some of the memorable words of Jesus brought together under what is known as the Sermon on the Mount. "Look at the birds in the sky," says Jesus, "they do not sow and reap and store in barns, yet your heavenly Father feeds them. Are you not worth more than the birds!" (Matt. 6:26; par. Luke 12:24). The exhortation to have no fear with its specific mentioning of sparrows in Luke 12:6-7 and Matthew 10:29-30 could have been a part of the Sermon on the Mount in which Jesus, after referring to more examples to illustrate his point, concludes: "So do not be anxious about tomorrow; tomorrow will look after itself. Each day has troubles enough of its own" (Matt. 6:34).

At any rate, not only fear but anxiety is what petrifies people and demoralizes them. Particularly for the poor and the disinherited over-whelmed by anxiety time has come to a standstill. All they have is the present filled to the brim with sheer needs for survival. Anxiety deprives them of that God-given ability to transcend the present and create the future. Anxiety can thus lead not only to denial of that which makes human beings human but also to doubt about the reality of God. Anxiety can reduce human beings to mere animal existence. All it makes you do is to be anxious about "food and drink to keep you alive and about clothes to cover your body" (Matt. 6:25; par. Luke 12:22).

For the poor and the disinherited deprivation of the bare necessities of life is the fact and reality to which they awake every morning. We know it and Jesus must have known it too. But as long as you let anxiety control you instead of your controlling it, so long as you allow it to dominate you instead of your dominating it, insofar as you permit it to tame you instead of you taming it, your deprivation will continue. You are too worried to be able to think what causes your deprivation. It does not occur to you that maybe it is the cultural and religious traditions rooted in a fatalistic view of life and the world that are the cause of it. You are so preoccupied with anxiety that you are not aware of what is happening around you. It does not come to your mind that perhaps it is the unjust social, political, and economic systems that contribute to your deprivation. By exhorting people not to be anxious, Jesus is not telling them to pretend there is nothing to worry about. He is not giving them an illusion of a life of blessings in a future world. It must have been his effort to empower them not to accept the life of deprivation as ordained by God and determined by their place in society and in their religious community. He must be encouraging them to raise their voice, to identify the causes that bring about their deprivation, and to struggle against these causes. This empowerment, in Jesus' view, must be part of what the reign of God means. Empowering people to fight the root causes that make them poor and hungry (Luke 6:20-21) and enabling them to laugh instead of weep, this is the reign of God. This is a powerful message. It is an empowering gospel. "These Beatitudes," observes an Orthodox Jew, "offer neither congratulations nor consolation with promises for the *next* world; they are the good news that the God of our forebears, who demands a reversal of our own thinking, will reassess all earthly values here below."[13] With that message and with that gospel Jesus seeks to build a culture of empowerment for the reign of God to become real in the life of people and in their community. And with it Jesus proceeds to equip them, in his teachings and actions, to be co-workers in the reign of God.

---

13. Pinchas Lapide, *The Sermon on the Mount: Utopia or Program for Action?* trans. Arlene Swidler (Maryknoll, N.Y.: Orbis Books, 1986), 28.

Culture of Empowerment

There is a tone of finality in Jesus' declaration: the reign of God belongs to you poor and oppressed. It carries the authority people have not felt before. It touches their hearts—the hearts of the poor and the downtrodden. But they are still poor; their stomachs are still half-empty; they are still downtrodden, not only socially but religiously. Nothing in their experience has prepared them for grasping this good news of God's reign that Jesus has declared to be theirs. What is it like? they must have asked in their hearts. What form does it take? They must have looked at each other half in excitement and half in incredulity. Does it mean peace or war? Will it bring well-being or disaster? They must have ransacked their memories for some clues of God's reign from what Jesus had been saying and doing.

Jesus must have read these questions in their hearts and from their faces. They are asking them not out of intellectual curiosity, but out of the awareness that something of enormous importance is said to be happening to them. But how is this possible? This must be what they want to hear from Jesus. Without power and status how could the reign of God become theirs? With neither institution nor structure to back them, how could they work toward the realization of God's reign? Questions such as these also reveal that they still do not know how the reign of God works and where its power is located. They need to know that the reign of God works very differently from the oppressive institutions and systems with which they are too familiar. And they have to realize that they themselves are *potentially* the reign of God, that is, God has given them the *potence*—the power—to be the reign of God. To make them conscious of that power, to help them realize that in talking about the reign of God he is talking about them and not about a religious concept, to enable them to take steps to change their life and their community—this must be what Jesus has to do. A culture of empowerment is what he sets out to build with the people—a culture without which the reign of God would remain a mere concept and a pious illusion unrelated to people's everyday life of hardships, fear, and anxiety.

God's Reign Is Like a Mustard-seed[14]

"How shall we picture the reign of God?" (Mark 4:30), Jesus asks not only his listeners but himself. He seems struggling to find words, images, and symbols of God's reign—words that empower people for God's reign, images that grip them with its presence, and symbols that sustain their faith

---

14. The exposition of Jesus' parables of the mustard-seed and the leaven that follows is a greatly expanded statement of a very brief and preliminary reflection in my book *Theology from the Womb of Asia* (Maryknoll, N.Y.: Orbis Books, 1986), 183–86.

in it. Here Jesus engages people, to use our expression today, in "doing theology" with this central subject matter of life and faith. The question is not rhetorical. It is not a question that is asked only to introduce a ready-made answer. A question that already presupposes an answer does not contain wonder and surprise. It does not stimulate people to think for themselves. It does not inspire them to take actions. It only makes them passive recipients of knowledge and information.

Jesus does not indulge in rhetoric. His questions are real questions. Together with people he explores questions and seek answers. That is why he uses different expressions, changes metaphors, lifts images out of daily life, and creates symbols that serve as a framework for understanding life and history in a new way. He seems to be illustrating this when he says, using the images that cannot fail to capture people's attention and inspire their imagination: "No one sews a patch of unshrunk cloth on to an old garment; if one does, the patch tears away from it, the new from the old, and leaves a bigger hole" (Mark 2:21; pars. Matt. 9:16; Luke 5:36). Sewing and patching old garments with new cloth! The interest of the women in the audience is aroused. How well they know they cannot mend a hole in the old garment with a piece of unshrunken cloth! The relation between old garment and new cloth—does this not point to the relationship between the reign of God and the old religious ideas and practices?

To drive the same point further Jesus makes use of other images. He goes on to say: "No one puts new wine into old wine-skins; if one does, the wine will burst the skins, and then wine and skins are both lost" (Mark 2:22; par. Matt. 9:17; Luke 5:37). Again the contrast between the new and the old expressed not in abstract concepts but in objects people handle every day! Who among Jesus' listeners is not familiar with wine and wine-skins? And who among them does not know the loss of new wine when it is put into old, worn-out wine-skins? As with new wine and old wine-skins, so it is with the reign of God and the teachings of dead traditions. Jesus must be trying to put across to people that "the truth and power of the gospel could only be lost by trying to force it into an uneasy alliance with traditional Judaism."[15] Hence his emphatic conclusion: "New wine goes into fresh skins!" (Mark 2:22).

Jesus here is not just making a fine and subtle distinction between "tradition" as "the living faith of the dead" and "traditionalism" as "the dead faith of the living."[16] With the reign of God a new age has dawned, a new

15. Francis Wright Beare, *The Gospel according to Matthew*, translation, introduction, and commentary (San Francisco: Harper & Row, Publishers, 1981), 232.

16. This otherwise very insightful distinction comes from Jaroslov Pelikan when he refers to the history of Christian doctrine as "the most effective means available of exposing the artificial theories of continuity that have often assumed normative status in the churches, and

time has arrived. It radically changes our self-understanding as human beings. It sheds new light on who God is and how we are related to God. It
requires us to reconstruct our priorities, be they religious, ethical, social, or
political. It not only has nothing to do with traditionalism, but also does not
take tradition for granted. Above all, the reign of God involves everybody,
particularly those women and men who have to mend and patch their old
garments over and over and labor and toil to provide food and wine. The
reign of God is such a down-to-earth thing. It takes place not in a cosmic
realm or in a cathedral, but in the life we live every day in our homes and
at our work places.

Doing theology in this way is very different from the way traditional
theology has gone about its task. The reign of God requires a new way
of doing theology. It will be badly served by the doctrinal approach and
propositional method, the standard approach and method of traditional
theology. That is why Jesus tells stories and speaks in parables, stories and
parables taken from the life of the people with whom he shares daily problems and difficulties. Jesus does theology of God's reign with them and
does not do it for them. He develops it out of them and does not impose
it on them. He empowers them to experience it and to claim it.

The reign of God liberates theology from the religious authorities and
official teachers. And he engages the people, that is, the poor and the oppressed, in doing a theology of freedom from fear and anxiety. Is it any
wonder that "the anxiety-free atmosphere," which is "the most important
precondition" for it, "emerges so clearly in parables. It is as though primal
confidence in life had been given a new and powerful impulse."[17] To give
the poor and the oppressed "a new and powerful impulse" for life, Jesus
speaks to them in parables.

One of the parables Jesus told to give the poor and the oppressed
"a new and powerful impulse" for life is the parable of the mustard-seed
(Mark 4:30-32; pars. Matt. 13:31-32; Luke 13:18-19). The reign of God "is
like the mustard-seed," he tells them matter-of-factly. "When sown in the
ground it is smaller than any other seed" (Mark 4:31). Is this what they—
those small people, poor and downtrodden—expected to hear? As small
as a mustard-seed? Murmurs must have arisen among Jesus' hearers. They
are small already, too small as a matter of fact. They may not be small in
physical stature, but they are small in social stature. This is a cause of their

---

at the same time ... an avenue into the authentic continuity of Christian believing, teaching,
and confessing." Then his conclusion: "Tradition is the living faith of the dead; traditionalism
is the dead faith of the living" (see his *The Christian Tradition: A History of the Development
of Doctrine*, vol. 1, *The Emergence of the Catholic Tradition, 100–600* [Chicago: University of
Chicago Press, 1971], 9).

17. Gerd Theissen, *Sociology of Early Palestinian Christianity*, trans. John Bowden (Philadelphia: Fortress Press, 1978), 105.

misery. In a status-conscious society, in a community organized around privileges, they are consigned to the bottom rank. They are persons with no privilege. And a person without privilege is a nonperson. This is their reality—their social *and* religious reality. And of course a nonperson is a powerless person. That is why they are very vulnerable. They become easy targets of exploitation, socially despised and religiously ostracized. In the eyes of the authorities they are small, powerless, insignificant people.

No, not something as small as a mustard-seed! they must have shouted in their hearts. We want something big and powerful. The reign of God, if it is to be ours, must be big and powerful. If it is to be compared to a seed, the mustard-seed is a very poor comparison. It has to be a big seed, bigger than any other seed. The reign of God to which we are to belong must be big. It must be bigger than our religious authorities to ensure that we do not come under their control again. Only a big and powerful reign of God can protect us from being dominated by them in every detail of our lives. That kind of God's reign alone could make us not afraid of them any more.

The reign of God must be more powerful than the Roman empire also. Bigness is powerfulness. The Roman empire is already big enough. That is why it is so powerful. To overpower this big power, God's reign must be more powerful than the powerful Roman empire. A small and weak reign of God is no match for it. Under such a reign of God we would be forced to continue to live under its shadow. We would be eternally colonial subjects without rights and freedom. There would be no change in our lot, impoverished and even bled to death by heavy taxes imposed on us.

If bigness is powerfulness, the reverse is also true: powerfulness expresses itself in bigness. We have a big religious tradition, Jesus' hearers must have reasoned. It is so big that it has the power to dwarf us. Our religious hierarchy is so big that it has overwhelmed us completely, always keeping small and powerless people like us at more than an arm's length. The reign of God that would bring us stature and power must, then, be bigger than our religious authorities. And the Roman empire is the embodiment of bigness. Everything it does and stands for is bigness. Big roads and big bridges throughout the empire, big armies and their weapons, big palaces and fortresses, all symbolize Rome's invincible power and might.

These reactions of Jesus' hearers may be our reactions also. Our world too has gone for bigness. Bigness is the status symbol of "high" civilization. A nation must be big—big in economy, big in industry, big in science and technology, and of course big in armaments. In particular it must be big in nuclear power. Bigness in this and in that brings power—power over other nations and other peoples. All nations are caught in the frenzy to outdo one another in bigness and powerfulness. Ours is a civilization afflicted with incurable megalomania. "Today," we are told pointedly, "we suffer from an almost universal idolatry of gigantism."[18] Bigness is power-fulness. But what idolatry of bigness, like any other idolatry, has done is to dehumanize human beings, to turn persons into nonpersons, to change people into things.

This is the really fearful nature of idolatry, and the idolatry of gigantism is no exception. This idolatry, whether practiced in politics, militarism, in-dustry, or economics, creates a priesthood of the rich and the privileged that degrades the poor and the oppressed and enhances their misery. This led an economist, the author of the widely read book *Small Is Beautiful*, to say nearly two decades ago:

> The economic calculus as applied by present-day economics forces the industrialist to eliminate the human factor because machines do not make mistakes which people do. Hence the enormous effort at automation and the drive for ever-larger units. This means that those who have nothing to sell but their labor remain in the weak-est possible bargaining position. The conventional wisdom of what is now taught as economics by-passes the poor, the very people for whom development is really needed. The economics of gigantism and automation is a left-over of nineteenth-century conditions and nineteenth-century thinking and it is totally incapable of solving any of the real problems of today.[19]

This observation is more valid today than ever, particularly in the Third World, and some of it must also have been applicable as long ago as the time of Jesus in Palestine.

To what conclusion does it lead us? According to the author we have been quoting, "an entirely new system of thought is needed, a system based on attention to people, and not primarily attention to goods—(the goods will look after themselves)."[20] How true! This must have been Jesus' con-clusion too. That is why he paid almost exclusive attention to people, especially the people impoverished, disinherited, and oppressed. That is why he declared that God's reign is theirs. And that is why he set about em-powering them to claim back their humanity and become self-reliant. The author of *Small Is Beautiful* is entirely correct when he makes a pointed statement such as this: "There is no such thing as the viability of states or of nations, there is only a problem of viability of people: people, actual per-sons like you and me, are viable when they can stand on their own feet and

---

18. E. F. Schumacher, *Small Is Beautiful: A Study of Economics as If People Mattered*, ABACUS edition (London: Sphere Books, 1974), 54.

19. Ibid., 61.

20. Ibid.

earn their keep."[21] This is exactly what Jesus must have considered to be one of his primary ministries of God's reign: to make people viable, to enable them to stand on their feet, to empower them for their rights as human beings. And he tells parables such as the parable of the mustard-seed to drive home to them that this is what he means by the reign of God.

But Jesus has not finished his parable. He has not yet come to the end of his story of God's reign. To his audience he goes on to say: the mustard-seed, "once sown, springs up and grows taller than any other plant, and forms branches so large that the birds can roost in its shade" (Mark 4:31). What a masterful way in which Jesus draws the contrast between a small beginning and a big end! It is the contrast "between an insignificant beginning and a magnificent end."[22] Whether the seed grows into a "plant" as in Mark or a "tree" as in Matthew and Luke is not important. Both plant and tree are the images of bigness in contrast to the image of smallness carried by the mustard-seed. These contrasting images can be understood at once without explanation.

His hearers should have no difficulty in visualizing the tiny mustard-seed in relation to a plant ten feet tall with great branches. This is their daily experience. They have grown so used to it that they seldom pay attention to it. But once reminded by Jesus, they suddenly realize how true that is. If this is what God's reign is like, something insignificant at the beginning but magnificent at the end, they can have confidence in it. That fragile, insignificant, small mustard-seed is not so fragile, insignificant, and small after all. To be able to grow into a tree taller than any other plant it must contain in itself power and greatness. If this is the kind of God's reign that belongs to them, then there is hope and future for them. Through a parable such as this Jesus must have evoked the faith in God from the depths of those people around him resigned to a life of deprivation and hardships. The parable makes "the oriental mind see two wholly different situations: on the one hand the dead seed, on the other, the waving corn-field, here death, there, through the divine creative power, life."[23] Is this not a very reassuring picture? Does it not empower them to work for change in their present situation?

So Jesus talks about bigness also. He affirms that the reign of God will become bigger than any kingdom and empire of the world. It will also be bigger than any religious institution. Since it is big, it should be powerful as well, more powerful than any other powerful institution, political or

---

21. Ibid., 59.
22. Eduard Schweizer, *The Good News according to Matthew*, trans. David E. Green (Atlanta: John Knox Press, 1975), 306.
23. Joachim Jeremias, *The Parables of Jesus*, trans. S. H. Hooke, rev. ed. (New York: Charles Scribner's Sons, 1963), 148.

religious. But it must be a different kind of bigness. Its powerfulness cannot be the kind of powerfulness that intimidates them. In the concluding sentence of the parable Jesus removes their fear and worry, saying that the plant "forms branches so large that the birds can roost in its shade" (Mark 4:32). With these words Jesus leaves no doubt as to what the reign of God can do: "like the tiny mustard-seed when fully grown, [it] provides protection for all who seek its shelter."[24] God's reign is, then, not an institution. It takes place when people without protection from exploitation gain protection. It happens when men and women without shelter find their shelter. It occurs when the powerless persons are empowered to struggle for their rights. *The reign of God creates a culture of empowerment.* It *is* a culture of empowerment. Jesus, who heals the sick, comforts those in sorrow, protects women and men maltreated by the rich and the powerful, *is* the reign of God. And together with these people he has created a culture of empowerment over against the culture of intimidation and exploitation.

The bigness of God's reign is the bigness of grace. Grace that is not big is not grace. Small grace is stingy grace. It is grace turned into charity. That kind of grace does more harm than good. It insults the people who happen to be the recipients of it. It humiliates them and debases them. It denies them frccdom as human beings and enslaves them in bondage. It makes them forever at the mercy of those who condescend to do them a little favor. That is right. That kind of grace, small and stingy, is nothing but a little favor the rich and the powerful show to the poor and the oppressed. And of course the grace that enslaves is no grace. It is violence. That kind of grace violates the dignity of human persons. It infringes upon their rights to be human and free. It deprives them of their independence. It makes them subservient to the riches it possesses and the power it represents.

The Christian church has not been entirely innocent when it comes to such small and stingy grace. In Europe in the Middle Ages it sold indulgences to believing men and women so that they might buy their own salvation and the salvation of their dead relatives in purgatory. It turned God's saving grace into a commodity for sale. That kind of grace made mockery of God. It set a price on the priceless grace of God. Grace on sale and salvation for sale! There had to be a Reformation that challenged the corruption of God's saving grace and the terrible misrepresentation of what God must be.

But the Christian church seems to have a short memory. When it began to expand to the world outside its base in the West in the nineteenth century, it quickly forgot the sorry episode of the indulgences of the church

---

24. Charles E. Carlston, *The Parables of the Triple Tradition* (Philadelphia: Fortress Press, 1975), 159.

of the Middle Ages. And this time around the churches and Christians, heirs to the Reformation, were not any better than the church authorities from which their reforming forebears dissented. The grace of God, at their hands, became the grace only for those converted to Christianity. The great majority of people were excluded from it. Even today not a few overzealous Christians still think, preach, and assert the same teaching. Does this mean that God's grace can only be applied to the Christians who make up a mere 5 percent of the total population of Asia, for instance? What about the rest of the 95 percent of Asian humanity? Is God's saving grace still *saving* grace when it does not work among most of the people of Asia? Is it still saving *grace* when it leaves out the majority of men, women, and children in Asia?

The big and powerful grace of God is an embracing grace. It is a grace that embraces not only men but also women. It embraces infants and children as well as adults. And it embraces both the nation and people through whom God disclosed God's self in a particular way and the nations and peoples outside the pale of Israel and Christianity among whom God has been at work in different ways. How else are we to understand Jesus when he ends his parable with these words: the plant from the tiny mustard-seed "forms branches so large that the birds can roost in its shade?" This is a reality Jesus and his audience know from their everyday life. What does it mean for Jesus? What does he want his listeners to envision on the basis of it? This is what the image of a plant grown from a mustard-seed with birds roosting in the shade of its large branches seems to imply: "out of the most insignificant beginnings, invisible to human eye, God creates God's mighty Kingdom, which embraces all the peoples of the world."[25]

God's grace is as embracing as this. Anything less embracing than this is not God's grace. What an empowering grace this embracing grace of God is! "The peoples of the world" are the Gentiles of different national backgrounds and ethnic origins. They are also men and women in Jesus' audience branded as "Gentiles" by the religious authorities and excluded from the latter's dispensation. But there are no "Gentiles" in either sense as far as God's big, powerful, and embracing grace is concerned. Is not this a really amazing grace? To be conscious of this grace, to be gripped by it, is to be empowered to be an active part of religious, social, and political transformation.

---

25. Jeremias, *The Parables of Jesus*, 149. So also C. H. Dodd (see his *Parables of the Kingdom*, rev. ed. [London: Nisbet, 1961], 154). Francis Wright Beare thinks that "this is imposing upon the parable the critic's own general interpretation of the message of Jesus." According to him the parable of the mustard-seed "does no more than stress the great difference between the size of the seed and the magnitude of the plant" (see his *The Gospel according to Matthew*, 307). But this is to restrict the parable to its "literal" meaning.

God's Reign Is Like Leaven

Have the people understood what Jesus is at pains to drive home to them? Have they grasped his vision of God's reign? Have they realized that God's reign is theirs not because it is imposed on them from above but because it grows out of them, develops from the community of the poor and the downtrodden? Do they now know that Jesus calls them blessed not because God's reign is a promise of instant riches but because it empowers them to struggle for change? By saying God's reign belongs to them, Jesus means that they are no longer to be the helpless prey of history, that they are not to be victims of fate and circumstances anymore. Jesus has not only shown them a vision of a different life and a different world. He has also stressed to them that that vision can become a reality, not in a distant future but now. Empowered by God's embracing grace, they are liberated from the history made by the powerful and free to create their own history. They are delivered from the life they live in fear of the authority over them and have become aware of the power of God's presence in them to strive for fulfillment of life. This must be what Jesus means when he says to them that the reign of God is theirs. Have they grasped this? Have they become convinced of this?

As if to make it doubly sure, Jesus tells them another parable closely related to the one he has just told them. It is the parable of the leaven. The reign of God, Jesus says, "is like yeast which a woman took and mixed with three measures of flour till it was all leavened" (Matt. 13:33; par. Luke 13:20-21). A small amount of leaven and a large quantity of flour! The parable must have struck a chord particularly with the women in the audience. As housewives they knew exactly what Jesus was talking about. As in the parable of the mustard-seed, the women and men in Jesus' audience "are invited to contemplate the great result that can follow upon a seemingly trifling cause."[26]

But how trifling is the cause and how great is the result? In other words, how big is the contrast between the beginning and the end? To leave no shadow of a doubt in his hearers' minds as to the vastness of the contrast, Jesus uses an almost exaggerated figure. "The 'three measures,'" it is pointed out, "are a vast quantity for a housewife's baking; the 'measure' ... held about twelve quarts, so that the 'three measures' of this mammoth baking would amount to thirty-six quarts (or about forty liters). This would make enough bread to feed a crowd, something close to a hundred large loaves."[27] The fact that Jesus refers to "mammoth baking" that

---

26. Beare, *The Gospel according to Matthew*, 308.
27. Ibid.

would make enough bread to feed a crowd may be an indication that Jesus is addressing not just a handful of disciples but a crowd of men, women, and children. Or is he perhaps alluding to "the feeding of four thousand" (Mark 8:1-10; par. Matt. 15:32-39) or "five thousand" (Mark 6:32-44; pars. Matt. 14:13-21; Luke 9:10b-17) that took place in an isolated place?

Jesus' listeners, who have just been initiated into the mystery of the parable of the mustard-seed, can hardly miss the point in this parable of the leaven. But just as in that parable, here too there is something besides the contrast between the humble beginning and the gigantic result. The women in Jesus' company especially know at once what it must be. They know that the leaven they place in the flour and mix with it will completely disappear into it. The leaven will lose its identity. It will be completely covered by the flour and get dissolved into the latter. The leaven will go totally out of sight. It will become entirely invisible. But it has power of fermentation. It is no small power. The power that can ferment "three measures" of flour to make enough bread for a crowd must be a tremendous power. The power that can do "mammoth baking" that produces a hundred loaves is a power to reckon with.

The logic of leaven and flour is clear. The reign of God is that "mammoth" power. Though invisible, buried out of sight, that power ferments the flour and makes the dough rise. And since that reign of God belongs to people, since it is theirs, it is they who are in possession of it. They are that power that can make a difference in their own lives and in their community. They are in command of that power that can change the social and religious status quo. This consciousness of the power of fermentation within them is the heart of the culture of God's reign. God's reign is no community of weaklings. It is no assembly of men and women demoralized with self-pity. On the contrary, the reign of God must be a community of women, men, and children who walk with their heads held high, who refuse to compromise their human dignity because they are poor and oppressed.

If such fermenting power works with as much as "three measures," even five, six, or ten measures of flour, it must also work in human society. This must be what is implied in the parable. Is this not also what the poem "The Rain and Justice" tries to say?

> It is a cold rainy night.
> I sit comfortably in my cozy house
> music pouring out of the stereo
> a glass of beer in my hands.
> I am with friends.
> I am happy.
> Our talk is of an intellectual nature—

of how we will build a better world
of what is wrong with capitalism and communism
and what kind of "ism" we will create.

Outside an old woman sits
protected from the rain by cardboard
humming a quiet song
which we hear when our stereo is quiet.
We are accustomed to her presence.
She is one of at least a million in the city.
We see something beautiful in her simple life
and her simple expectations.
Even though she is old
she still works hard every day
and seems content with the little she has.
"That is a beautiful life," we say,
as we drink our beer,
listen to our stereo
and sit comfortably in our cozy house.

Suddenly her humming turns to angry shouts.
We rush out to see.
Someone wants her to remove her cardboard
so he can park his shiny new BMW.
She won't go!
We stand with her.
There is more shouting!
There is anger!
The old lady is strong.
She won't give up her small space
and her cardboard shelter.

Finally the BMW owner tires.
If she will move her shanty
a few meters down the path
he will replace her cardboard
with plywood.
Then he can park his BMW
and her house will be stronger.

We all rejoice!
Justice has been achieved!

The old woman squats under her plywood
and hums her song again

in rhythm with the falling rain.
Once again we return to our cozy house
our beer
our stereo
and to the new "ism" we will create.

And only the rain is outraged
by this concept of justice.[28]

The scene depicted in the poem is a contemporary version of some of the scenes in the stories of Jesus' ministry two thousand years ago. It is a scene of conflict of powers that ends in the vindication of the poor and the oppressed.

The main character in the poem is the poor old woman who lives under a cardboard shelter. In spite of her poverty she lives a contented life until one day the owner of a BMW tries to force her out of her little space to park his car. This is a common scene in a society in which right and wrong, justice and injustice, are decided in proportion to the power and prestige one enjoys. The old woman seems a loser from the very beginning. She is expected to fold her cardboard shelter and move away. The man who drives a BMW, that symbol of riches and status, expects it. Most spectators, except those idealistic youth engaged in an intellectual debate on "isms" and social change in the comfort of a nearby house, also do not expect anything different. This is the unwritten code of law for the people used to the rights of the powerful at the expense of the poor and the underprivileged. This is the kind of society Jesus had to deal with in his days, and this is the background against which he proclaimed the message of God's reign and practiced it. That poor old woman could have been a typical woman or man in his audience, the people he tried to empower with the vision and reality of God's reign.

But in men and women such as that poor old woman Jesus perceives power to manifest the reign of God, the power such as the leaven that turns the three measures of flour into a hundred loaves. That power, Jesus must have known, is very different from the power with which they are familiar—the power of their religious and political rulers, the power of the rich like that BMW owner. This latter kind of power, the power that threatens and intimidates them, is anything but invisible like the leaven hidden in the flour. Invisibility is the last thing the power of this world wants. Power must become visible in all sorts of forms. Modesty is no virtue of that power. Self-effacement is not the moral quality it possesses. "He

---

28. The poem is by Max Ediger. See *Life for the People: Peace with Justice in Asia* (CCA–International Affairs, Hong Kong) 1, no. 2 (March–June 1988): 9.

[Jesus] must increase," John the Baptist is reported to have said, "but I must decrease" (John 3:30, NRSV). But this does not apply to the power that confronts people in their everyday life. It is rather the opposite. That power declares: I must increase, but you must decrease! The power that decreases is a defeated power, but the power that increases is a victorious power. The power that grows impotent is a useless power, but the power that grows potent is a power that demands recognition. The power that fades commands neither respect nor fear, but the power that aggrandizes inspires awe and reverence.

For power to be power it must increase, become potent, and expand. This is the power people feel, see, and taste. They see that power concentrated on the person of an autocratic ruler. They taste it in a repressive government. And that power takes form in police power and military power. This is the power displayed by the Roman empire in Jesus' time. This is the power exhibited by authoritarian regimes throughout human history. It is the power demonstrated by the nations of the world in ancient times and today in their geopolitical struggles. It is also the power displayed by that BMW owner. The power as the world knows it, the power that shapes the nations and changes the history of peoples, the power that exploits the poor and the weak, is often a violent power.

This power is Machiavellian in nature—a term derived from Niccolò Machiavelli (1469–1527), an Italian statesman and one of the most important political thinkers of the Renaissance, who "called for a [political] leader to use any means necessary to preserve the state, resorting to cruelty, deception, and force if nothing else worked."[29] Machiavelli could have served any despotic ruler with distinction in the past and would easily win the confidence of many autocratic rulers today. In the arena of political struggle—and is there a part of human life that does not belong to that arena?—an idealism of power preached by religious teachers unfortunately does not work. What works is naked power.

You do not have to be Machiavellian to know that the use of schemes and power is necessary to achieve your goals—from seizing political power, to defeating your political enemy, to crushing peaceful demonstrations for freedom and democracy with tanks and machine guns, to forcing a helpless old woman to give up her tiny little shelter to give you a parking space for your shiny BMW. But you have to know, Machiavellian or not, that inherent in that kind of power is a drive toward violence. That drive for power, that demonstration of power, and that use of power are demonic. That demonic power violates human lives and corrupts human community. It even challenges the sovereignty of God.

---

29. See *The World Book Encyclopedia* (Chicago: World Book, 1983).

This demonic and violent nature of power has to be taken seriously in the Christian understanding of power. Even religion itself—religion that speaks and practices love—is not free from the demonic temptation of power. The temptation takes form in coercing others to believe in a certain way, dictating how one must worship, claiming "spiritual superiority" over those who hold different religious allegiance, and consigning "unrepentant sinners and pagans" to eternal fire in Hell. Power has the capacity to profane life, even the life that has overcome profanity—the life of the holy. When the holy succumbs to the power that profanes, it becomes a curse to the unsuspecting believers. The holier the holy is, the more profane it becomes when seized and corrupted by the power of profanity. The history of religions is full of sad instances where religious authorities exercise deadly power over people. Did not Jesus' crucifixion happen at the hand of religious power turned profane? Do not the "untouchables" in India continue to suffer from the profane power of the caste religion?

The power that has turned demonic and violent is essentially exhibitionistic. It must exhibit itself. It must demonstrate itself. It must prove itself. The world, East or West, ancient or modern, has always been in the clutch of such power. That is why all nations, big and small, poor and rich, want to become militarily strong. Without dealing with the demonic nature of power, without facing the profanity and corruptibility of power—dealing with power at its roots—a conference on disarmament becomes a game of numbers, creating not balance of peace but balance of lethal power. The world has made a god of nuclear power and falls on its knees to worship that god. Nuclear power is power at its most exhibitionistic. It is a most primitive force. It is a primordial power. Its destructiveness takes a most sophisticated and thus most deadly form. It has become an idol that holds the fate of the earth and its entire inhabitants in the balance. It is an idolatry committed by the nations and peoples no matter what their political ideology may be, no matter whether they believe in God or not. The idolatry of nuclear power has become a universal religion, consuming the greater part of human resources. It is the most expensive idol worship human beings have ever invented.

An idol has to be visible. An idol hidden in the closet affects no one. It has to be put on a pedestal. It has to march at the head of a parade. It has to be placed on an altar visible to all worshipers. That is why the military parade becomes a patriotic duty on the national day. That is why the head of state—the national idol in flesh and blood—has to be surrounded with an aura of invincibility and heralded with martial music. In Japan this idol of power is institutionalized in the *Tenno* system, the system of emperor worship. The emperor as the living god radiates the power of the Japanese nation both at home and abroad. That idol must become visible, feared and worshiped, not only in Japan, but also in Southeast Asia and throughout the world. The military invasion of Southeast Asia by Japan during World War II was a religious war—the religious idol called the emperor going out to conquer Asia. As a thoughtful Japanese Christian puts it correctly, because of the *Tenno* system "the history of modernization in Japan was the very history of the invasion of Asia."[30] That invasion continues today through Japan's economic power. It is no accident that attempts are being made in Japan today to revitalize the cult of emperor worship.

Human beings are addicted to power—the power that exhibits its potency. Nations are run by politicians drunk with such power. And society is in the grip of it. This is the kind of power that people see and understand. It must have been no exception for the men and women around Jesus, themselves the victims of such power. They must have expected nothing different from the power of God's reign. They must have expected Jesus to organize that power into a revolutionary army. They must have wanted to hear Jesus proclaim it from a provisional government. And they must have hoped that that power would be institutionalized as a political machine to realize their political aspiration and national dream.

In contrast, however, to that demonic and violent power, there is another kind of power. It is the power summoned from the depths of that poor old woman to defy the demand of the BMW owner. "The old lady is strong," says the eyewitness of the episode. "She won't give up her small place and her cardboard shelter." The strength of that old woman must have surprised the spectators. It must have put the arrogant BMW owner off guard. There is something noble and inviolable in the power with which she confronts the violent power. Who could defy that power? That BMW owner could not. He had to give in and provide her with a plywood shelter in exchange for a parking space.

The power summoned out of the old woman to assert her rights is the power of the leaven in Jesus' parable. It is part of the power of God's reign. It lies hidden in the women and men oppressed by rulers and exploited by the privileged. It has to be made to work on the flour. It has to be called out to confront the oppressive powers. Jesus affirms that the power of God's reign does not share the pretension of the power of this world. The power of God's reign is not pretentious: it does not allow itself to be placed on an altar to be feared and worshiped as an idol. It does not enthrone itself to command the homage of the courtiers and wield terror over its subjects. But it is a world-transforming power, just as the leaven transforms the flour

---

30. Shoji Tsutomu, "From Power Idolatry to Full Humanity—the Pilgrimage of Japanese Christians," in *Oppressor and Victim: Japan and the Militarization of Asia, a Christian Response*, Third Asia Youth Resource Conference, Japan, August 1–13, 1982 (Singapore: CCA–Youth, 1983), 11.

into loaves of bread. The exercise of that power can be costly. It does not always bring about desired results as in the case of that old woman. That power often is the power that dies in order that others may live. Jesus himself, who possesses that power and empowers others with that power, has to die on the cross. But does not that power defy the power of death and become life-giving power and life-transforming power?

The Seed Growing Secretly

How does that power work then? How does it become theirs? How does it grow to become a tall tree that offers shelter to those in need? How does it ferment the flour and change the world? This question of how inevitably follows the question of what. Jesus is very good at raising the question of what. He tells stories and teaches in parables. He exposes the malaise of the religious authorities and points out the suffering of people. We Christians are very good at that too. More and more Christians take upon themselves the task of exposing the evils of society and injustices of the world. But unlike Jesus we are not very good at the question of how. We are slow to realize how the seed is growing and how the leaven is fermenting. From what to how there is still so much for us to learn.

It is at this point that we must turn to Jesus' parable of the seed growing secretly (Mark 4:26-29), the parable recorded in Mark's Gospel only. The reign of God, says Jesus, is like this:

A man scatters seed on the ground; he goes to bed at night and gets up in the morning, and meanwhile the seed sprouts and grows—how, he does not know. The ground produces a crop by itself, first the blade, then the ear, then full grain in the ear; but as soon as the crop is ripe, he starts reaping, because harvest-time has come.

The seed again! Jesus refers now not just to the mustard-seed, but to all seeds. Here again is the language Jesus' hearers can understand very well.

This is another version of Jesus' theology of God's reign closely linked with the life of many of his hearers who work the land. The seed they sow on the land will grow and ripen, earning them livelihood. Although this is what they have to do year in and year out, there is something in the seed that never ceases to amaze them. It is the living power in it. Seed has life! Seed is life! They are perfectly aware that they have nothing to do with that life in the seed. The seed comes with it. Life is in the seed from the beginning. And it is that life in the seed that grows and produces "first the blade, then the ear, then full grain in the ear" ready for harvest. The mystery of the life-giving and life-growing power!

In this parable Jesus brings people face to face with the question of how the power of God's reign works. As with the seed sown on the land, so is the reign of God. God's reign is not fashioned by powerful kings and does not work by show of force. It is not to be confused with observation of the Law to its minutest detail. It does not function through the hierarchical power of an established religion. Nor is God's reign brought into being by violent means. It does not have to fortify itself with more and more violence in order to carry out its goal.

But how does the reign of God work? Jesus seems to be implying that even he does not know when he says that the farmer who has sown the seed does not know how "the seed sprouts and grows." Is this not confusing? Is Jesus avoiding the question of how? Is Jesus not different from many of us who are good at describing things but are at a loss when it comes to bringing about change? Does the reign of God consist of words but not of deeds? Is it merely a matter of rhetoric and not a matter of action? Is it only religious wishful thinking that lacks social and political impact? Is Jesus implying that we can sit back and wait for God to bring us God's reign on a silver platter? Is he now saying that the reign of God does not need the culture of empowerment as a precondition of its actualization?

"How, the farmer does not know," says Jesus. But the fact that the farmer who has sown the seed does not know how the seed sprouts and grows does not mean that no one knows. It does not mean that the growth of the seed is a matter of chance, purely a case of accident. Although it is not mentioned in the parable, Jesus must have been addressing himself to the faith and trust of the people in God. Of course you people—Jesus' hearers must have understood him to be saying to them—do not know how the seed sprouts and grows, but God does. For it is God who "made the decisive beginning. . . . God leaves nothing undone, God's beginning ripens to its fulfillment. Till then it behooves human beings to wait in patience and not to try and anticipate God, but in full confidence to leave everything to God."[31]

So, God leaves nothing undone! God seems to do everything, from A to Z. The reign of God would be God's solo act. No human participation is needed. Human beings would only make things worse. God would take care of everything. All talk of empowering people would be empty talk. All effort to rouse them from a sense of impotence and resignation would be futile. All they need is tons of patience and infinite endurance. Salvation by faith and not by works! Contrary to the initial impression Jesus has given them, he appears now to be more like a preacher of salvation in

31. Jeremias, *The Parables of Jesus*, 152.

the after-life than a prophet out to change the present religious and social status quo.

God made the decisive beginning! Surely God did. This no one can question. And how decisive that beginning was! The beginning of the seed growing secretly goes all the way back to the most decisive of all decisive beginnings—the creation. It was the beginning God gave to the creation and all things in it. God created cosmos (order) out of chaos (disorder). A big, big cosmos out of a big, big chaos—what a formidable beginning! God made light shine in the darkness—a brilliant light essential to the growth of life concealed in the overpowering darkness. What an auspicious beginning! But a more decisive, more formidable, more auspicious, beginning was to arrive. It arrived when God created human beings, male and female, in God's image.

Is not the story of creation, then, related to the reign of God that Jesus proclaimed? Is it not the story of God's reign? The reign of God at the beginning of time and all times—this is the crucial element here. This thing called "the reign of God" bridges the story of creation and stories of human struggle for freedom from fear, anxiety, poverty, and oppression. It shortens the distance between the beginning of creation and the continuing work of creation here and now. It expands the horizon of our Christian vision to the horizon of God's vision. God's reign, rooted thus in God's creation, cannot be monopolized by a particular nation. Because it is based on God's creating activity that spans the whole of creation and embraces the whole of humanity, the reign of God cannot be restricted within a particular religious tradition. God's reign did not begin with Jesus. Jesus proclaimed it, made clear what it means, worked hard to bring about a new human community inspired by it. He disclosed what had already been present in the beginning of God's creation: all human beings are endowed with inviolable humanity. And that includes of course the poor, the dispossessed, the oppressed.

What follows from this is self-evident. The society that keeps the poor forever poor is opposed to the reign of God. A nation that discriminates against certain people because of the color of their skin contradicts the reign of God. The government that suppresses human rights, and arrests, tortures, imprisons, or murders political dissidents betrays the reign of God. The world that perpetuates patriarchal control over women is hostile to the reign of God. And the religious community that has no room for people of other religious communities is far from being the reign of God.

The reign of God is, in this way, a colossal undertaking. It is a gigantic task. If it needs divine labor, it also needs human labor. If it requires divine ingenuity, it can also make use of human ingenuity. If it demands divine commitment, it can also expect human commitment. Creation as the actualization of God's reign in the midst of conflicts and adversities is the joint project of God and human beings. This does not debase God as less than God. It testifies to a confident God, the God who is big enough, gracious enough, and large-hearted enough to take human beings into God's confidence and make them God's co-workers. That is why Jesus spares no effort to empower the poor and the oppressed to be the reign of God.

Nor does the fact that human beings are created to be God's co-builders of God's reign elevate them to become more than human. However hard we may try, we human beings cannot be more than human. It is our nature to be human. It is our destiny to be human. It is our calling to be human. And it is our glory to be human. Thoughts such as these must have been utmost in the mind of the psalmist who confesses and testifies:

> When I look up at your heavens, the work of your fingers,
>   at the moon and the stars you have set in place,
>   what is a frail mortal that you should be mindful of them,
>   human beings that you should take notice of them?
>   Yet you have made them little less than a god,
>   crowning them with glory and honor ...
>
> (Ps. 8:3-5)

This is a theology of creation in poetic form with profound insights into the relationship between God and human beings.

God the creator, according to the psalmist, is God, no more and no less. Human beings, crowned with glory and honor, are still human beings, no more and no less. It is as human beings, not as God, the psalmist goes on to say, that we take part in the care and development of God's creation. And after all having been said and done, our testimony and confession still is: "Lord our sovereign, how glorious is your name throughout the earth!" (Ps. 8:9) We human beings do not threaten God with our humanity. We do not usurp the glory and honor of God as creator with our labor and ingenuity. God empowers us with humanity to be God's co-workers in the renewal and reconstruction of creation.

It is as God's partners in the renewal of creation that Jesus empowers us, especially the poor and the oppressed, to be also God's partners in the construction of God's reign. If, then, we are God's partners at the sowing of seeds in the beginning and at the reaping of harvests at the end, we are also God's partners during the time between the sowing and the harvesting. God has not taken over the work entirely and left us idle between the times. If God needed us at the beginning of time and will need us at the end of time, God also needs us between the beginning-time and the end-time.

This must have been in the mind of Jesus when he told the parable of the seed growing secretly.

We are, thus, prompted to look more deeply into that parable Jesus told his audience in his usual magnificent simplicity. In the parable Jesus does say that the farmer, after having sown the seed, "goes to bed at night and gets up in the morning." It has been suggested that the emphasis here is on "the inactivity of the farmer," and that "the sower's sleeping and rising night and day are, so to speak, repeated acts of non-participation: he exerts no influence on the maturing of the seed."[32] Is this what Jesus meant—Jesus who must have known the hard life of a farmer? Is this the way he wanted his hearers to understand the parable—Jesus who must have been familiar with the daily routines of a farming family, rising early in the morning and toiling all day until darkness sets in? Jesus who draws his message from the real life of people, who identifies himself with the toil and labor of poor men and women, could not have painted a picture of a hard-working farmer doing nothing between the sowing of the seed and the harvesting of the crop. If it had been otherwise, Jesus would have been giving them a false picture of God's reign. He would have been imparting to them not a vision of God's reign but an illusion of it.

Jesus is right. The farmer does go to bed at night and get up in the morning after he has sown the seed. Rather than passivity and inactivity, this is a very picture of trust and confidence in God who alone holds the mystery of life and its growth, and not a portrayal of an idle and inactive farmer. It is surely nearer to the truth to say: "So, although he would do certain things by rule-of-thumb experience—sow after ploughing, protect the field from birds or wandering animals, etc.—for the most part after sowing he went his daily round with his prayers said, his fingers crossed and a wary eye on the field."[33] The farmer is a paragon of faith and patience indeed, "not trying to anticipate God, but in full confidence leaving everything to God."[34]

Putting these thoughts together, we may then come much closer to the heart of what Jesus wanted to put across to the people through the parable. There is indeed so much for the farmer to do after the seed is sown, Jesus must also be saying to his hearers—weeding, protecting the fields from birds and animals, keeping his eye on it, and also praying. He is as occupied as ever. The farmer is alert and vigilant. But he also knows that it is not he but God who has given the power of life to the seed he has sown. And it is God's grace that brings him the joyful time of harvest. That is why

32. Carlston, *The Parables of the Triple Tradition*, 204.
33. Norman Perrin, *Rediscovering the Teaching of Jesus* (New York: Harper & Row, Publishers, 1967), 159.
34. Jeremias, *The Parables of Jesus*, 152.

he prays. Prayer is not separable from his labor. And in prayer he gains full confidence in God. Prayer gives him the strength to wait for the time of grace—the harvest time—with patience in the midst of worry, toil, and anticipation.

This is what the reign of God is like. This is how it works. This is the way it is already at work among the poor, the hungry, and the oppressed. "The fruit is the *result* of seed"—Jesus must have gone out of his way to bring this point home to his hearers; "the end is *implicit* in the beginning. The infinitely great is already active in the infinitely small. In the present, and indeed in secret, the event is already in motion. This undisclosed nature of the Basileia [reign] is a matter of faith in a world to which nothing is yet known. Those to whom it has been given to understand the mystery of the Reign (Mark 4:11) see already in its hidden and insignificant beginning the coming Reign of God."[35]

What the reign of God does is empower people. It empowers the poor and the oppressed to strive for justice. It empowers them to claim their human rights. It empowers them to get organized to change their status quo. It empowers them to stand "with feet planted on the ground and head supporting the sky" (*tin t'ien li ti*), to use a Chinese expression. That reign of God is *already* here. That empowerment has *already* begun.

Because of the reign of God already present, there can be stories of hope grown out of a life of despair, poems of joy risen out of deep sorrow, hymns of praise sung from a heart beset by pain. These are stories, poems, and hymns of God's reign. In these hymns we perceive the plight of the poor, but we also perceive their plight turning into a cry for change. In these poems we witness the oppressed weep, but we also witness their weeping transformed into the determination to rid the world of oppression. In these stories we feel the pain of the downtrodden, but we also touch that dignity of humanity that shames the powerful. The women and men Jesus is addressing in the days past or today have, just as that farmer, not been idle between the time of sowing and the time of harvesting. With the reign of God Jesus has initiated a culture of empowerment—a culture that empowers men, women, and children to be the reign of God not only for the life to come but for life here and now. That is why the reign of God, above everything else, is a culture of empowerment.

---

35. Ibid., 152–53.

Part III

WITNESS

The reign of God is not something ready-made. It is not like a ready-made suit that needs only small alterations here and there to suit the buyer. Nor is it like a blueprint of a house drawn by an architect and given to the builder for construction. The reign of God is something that happens. When the hungry are satisfied, when those who weep laugh, when the oppressed find justice and freedom, and when those who despair of life regain hope, the reign of God becomes real. This is how we grappled with the reign of God in our discussion in the previous chapters.

If the reign of God is something that happens, it has to be sighted and identified. In other words, the reign of God needs eyewitnesses, persons who sight it and identify it, persons who are able to distinguish it from all other happenings, persons who, with theological sensitivity, can tell it from many other things that take place in the world. We are reminded of how Jesus sent back his answer to John the Baptist in prison who wanted to be assured of who Jesus was (Luke 7:18-23; par. Matt. 11:2-6): "Are you the one who is to come, or are we to expect someone else?" This was John's question. Instead of giving a direct answer, Jesus directed John's disciples who had come with the question to witness what was happening before their eyes: the blind recover their sight, the lame walk, the lepers are made clean, the deaf hear, the dead are raised to life, the poor are hearing the good news. These are manifestations of God's reign. Jesus made John's disciples eyewitnesses to these manifestations. They were to bring back to John an eyewitness report of what they saw and identified as the reign of God.

Here we are using the word "witness" in the sense of someone who witnesses something, that is, an eyewitness. It is obvious that the reign of God needs eyewitnesses, those who can see it happen before their eyes like John's disciples. But it requires more than eyewitnesses. Eyewitnesses are witnesses. But they stand aside from what is happening. There is a distance between them and the event taking place in front of them. They, in other words, are spectators. The reign of God demands more than spectators. It invites participation and involvement. Here another meaning of the word "witness"—the meaning inadequately represented by words such as "eyewitness," "spectator," or "observer"—has to be emphasized, that is, witness as someone who bears witness, who is bearer of witness. When witness is understood in this way, the distance between the event and the person who witnesses it is shortened. The bearer of witness is not just an objective observer, a disinterested reporter, or a narrator who has no stake in what has happened. To be willing to bear witness like bearing or shouldering a burden, you have to be involved in the event in one way of another. Of course you can bear witness either to it or against it. But when you bear witness to something while believing in its cause, then you as a witness become identified with that to which you bear witness.

The relation between witness and bearer of witness is subtle and important. The intensity of the relation determines the degree to which the bearer of witness is related to that which is witnessed. When the relation is so intensified that the bearer of the witness becomes completely involved in and identified with that which is witnessed, the bearer becomes the witness itself. To put it another way, the messenger becomes the message. This must be what Paul meant when he wrote to Christians at Corinth: "Wherever we go we carry death with us in our body, the death that Jesus died, that in this body also the life that Jesus lives may be revealed" (2 Cor. 4:10). Paul is referring to his own death, but he quickly identifies his own death with the death of Jesus. He is also talking about his life, but then he at once turns around and says his life is the life that Jesus lives. This is why he is able to say in another letter to the Corinthian Christians: "You are Christ's body" (1 Cor. 12:27). This is Paul's well-known "in-Christ" mysticism. Mysticism or not, there are times when the bearer of witness and the witness become one, when the messenger of a message becomes the message itself.

It is in this most intense meaning of witness that we want to explore how Jesus and many of the women and men who have come after him make the vision of God's reign visible, real, and effective in the world they live in. In Matthew's Gospel Jesus is reported to have said: "Not everyone who says to me 'Lord, Lord' will enter the kingdom of Heaven, but only those who do the will of my heavenly Father" (Matt. 7:21). The reign of God is not a matter of words but of actions. It is not disclosed as a concept but as persons—people who bear God's reign on their persons. It is not treated as an idea but as happenings that affect our everyday life. Nor is it regarded as an object of worship or a theme for contemplation either. It does not become real just by repeating a liturgical formula or performing ritual requirements over and over. It discloses itself and authenticates itself in the struggle of men, women, and children against the powers that oppress them, exploit them, and dehumanize them.

It is in this sense that Jesus is the reign of God. And again it is in this sense that many a man and woman in the past, today, and in the future together with Jesus become the reign of God. And when this reign of God moves those who oppress the powerless and exploit the poor to repent and change, that is also the reign of God. When Zacchaeus the rich tax-gatherer pledged to give half of his possession to charity and to repay four times over those he had cheated, did not Jesus declare: "Today salvation has come to this house!" (Luke 19:1-10)? Here Jesus brings salvation and the reign of God into a very close relationship. The meaning of salvation is derived from the reign of God, and not the other way around. The content of it is to be found in the content of God's reign. The quality of it is shaped by the quality of God's reign. This has been very much obscured in the faith and thought of many Christians. For them the reign of God—they prefer to call it "the kingdom of God"—is defined by what they understand to be salvation, that is, deliverance of the soul from the suffering of this world and enjoyment of eternal bliss in the bosom of God. Their reign of God is an extension of their unfulfilled desires in the present life. This, however, is not what Jesus meant by the reign of God. He directs us to be "witnesses" of God's reign not in the future but here and now.

CHAPTER 5

THE REIGN OF GOD IN ACTION (1)

> Turning to the chief priests, the temple guards, and the elders, who had come to seize him, Jesus said, "Do you take me for a robber, that you have come out with swords and cudgels? Day after day, I have been with you in the temple, and you did not raise a hand against me. But this is your hour—when darkness reigns." (Luke 22:52-53; par. Matt. 26:55)

Conflict Situations

The reign of God is, then, not a nation-state defined by territorial rights; it is a rule of love established in the hearts of people. The reign of God is not a religion competing for influence with other religions; it is the victory of justice over injustice in human community. The reign of God is not an emancipation of the soul from the shackles of this world; it is the power of God that empowers us to live in the midst of adversities and despair. The reign of God, in short, "is neither a spatial nor a static concept; it is a *dynamic concept*. It denotes the reign of God in action, in the first place as opposed to earthly monarchy, but then in contrast to all rule in heaven and on earth."[1] It is an *action* term, and not a concept term. It must be charged with energy, power, and vitality. God reigns! And God reigns on earth as well as in heaven. God reigns not only in the future but in the present. This must be how Jesus understood God's reign when he taught his disciples to pray and say: "Your reign come, your will be done, on earth as in heaven" (Matt. 6:10; par. Luke 11:2).

But how does God also reign on earth, inhabited by human beings, not only in heaven, populated by angels? How are we to perceive God's

---

1. Joachim Jeremias, *New Testament Theology,* trans. John Bowden (London: SCM Press, 1971), 98.

reign in the very midst of history full of conflicts and strife and not merely at the heavenly court where peace and concord prevail? How are we to experience God's reign in our own life—life subject to uncertainty, anxiety, fear, and death, and not just in the realm of "a new heaven and a new earth" in which "there shall be an end to death, and to mourning and crying and pain; for the old order has passed away" (Rev. 21:1-4)?

God reigns in a new order, of course. This we understand. God reigns in a new heaven and on a new earth. This we believe. God reigns in the time that has become eternity. This we affirm. And we long for a time in the future when the glory of God's reign will become fully and totally manifest. We share that new order in faith even now, although we do not know what it is going to be like. We take part in that new time even today, in spite of the fact that we have no clue as to what kind of time it is going to be and with what sorts of things and activities it is going to be filled. And here the words of Paul the apostle have a particular pertinence, words he wrote to the Christians in Rome: "Now hope that is seen is not hope. For who hopes for what is seen? But if we hope for what we do not see, we wait for it with patience" (Rom. 8:25, NRSV). Paul was a theologian of hope and his was a theology of hope.

Hope, together with faith and love, is the power to live and the power to be. If this is what Paul meant by hope, we agree with him completely. Hope means life is open-ended. To use well-known verses of a Chinese poet called Lu Yew (1125–1210), in the Southern Sung dynasty, a wanderer, "lost deep in the mountains at a river head, thinking there is no way out, sights dense willow trees and bright cultivated flowers and realizes that there must be a village nearby" (*shan ch'uen shui chin yi wu lu, liu an hua ming yu yi ch'un* in Chinese). However desperate the situation may be, there is always a new opening in life. This is what the Chinese poet wanted to say. Hope is that power that enables us to break out of the impasse of life and create an opening in the ongoing journey of life. That power helps us to overcome fatalism, does not allow us to resign to the impasse of today, and inspires us to mobilize ourselves for a new dawn. Hope is the power of life and energy for the future.

We must go on and say hope is also the power to die, for hope gives us power to believe in life through death and inspires us to envision ourselves in the presence of God and to aspire to fulfillment of life in God's love. Death is the enemy of hope. It is an ultimate enemy, and, to use Paul's words once again, it is "the last enemy to be deposed" (1 Cor. 15:26). But how can it be deposed? It is a reality of life that stares all of us in the face whether we are conscious of it or not. It haunts us and sobers us. It is something we cannot wish away even with "the power of positive thinking." Life, when death intervenes, is like when "the music is over and the people gone" (*ch'u chung jen san*), as the Chinese saying goes. But unlike music, life, overtaken by death, cannot be replayed. Hope, however, says that the music of life can be replayed, and not only replayed, but replayed with even greater richness and glory. Hope is the power that conceives us in the womb of death to give us a new life in the presence of God's eternity. Our life in God's eternity is a matter of faith and God's concern. Since this is the case, how God reigns in heaven is also a matter of faith, on the one hand, and God's concern, on the other. We do not need to worry too much about it. God can take care of it. We must unconditionally entrust God with God's reign in heaven. On our part this is a matter of "Amen"—so be it! Any speculation on this matter indicates our lack of faith. Any doubt about it is an expression of our unbelief. And if we try to have a say in it, as some Christian believers do especially with regard to the question of who will reign with God, we are doing what is not ours to do—claiming the right that belongs solely and totally to God.

We are reminded of how James and John, the brothers given a very prominent place among Jesus' disciples along with Peter, asked Jesus: "Allow us to sit with you in your glory, grant us the right to sit in state with you, one at your right and the other at your left" (Mark 10:35-40; par. Matt. 20:20-23). In the parallel story in Matthew's Gospel it was their mother who approached Jesus with the request. Whether it was the mother or her sons who approached Jesus does not make a difference to the message of the story. To be seated on the right and on the left hands means to be in the position of power and authority. This is what the two brothers, and perhaps their mother too, had in mind when they approached Jesus with their request. How Christian evangelists also are fond of preaching the reign of God in the sense of the power and authority promised to converts and Christians! The familiar refrain says that Christians will reign with God in "God's kingdom."

Jesus' answer to James and John should put to rest that kind of evangelistic refrain once for all. "You do not understand what you are asking," said Jesus. "Can you drink the cup that I drink, or be baptized with the baptism I am baptized with?" (Mark 10:38). All too easily we think of God's reign in relation to heaven and not in relation to earth, in relation to the future rather than to the present. We like to focus our concern on our place in God's reign rather than on our responsibility in it. But the truth of the matter is that

Jesus makes a connection between the coming of God's rule and *metanoia*, that is, the actual praxis of the kingdom of God. The Lord's Prayer suggests a fundamental connection between "your kingdom come" and "your will be done on earth": carrying out God's will in our mundane history has to do with the coming of God's kingdom, always in that dialectic, typical of Jesus, between "present" and "future." The latter is always greater than the present, but stimulates us in the present to religious and ethical conduct in accord with the kingdom of God.[2]

This is an important insight, although we do not want to make a quantitative distinction between the present and the future in the mind of Jesus. As I emphasized earlier, hope is the power to be, to live and to die. It has to be ahead of us, beyond us, even beyond the grave. But it has to be rooted in the present, stimulated by the present as well as stimulating it. The future has to be the growth out of the present, fulfilling it, changing it, and carrying it forward. The future is not the negation of the present but the fulfillment of it and then the transformation of it. The future is the fulfilled and transformed present. It is only in this way that we perceive the vital connection between the coming of God's reign and the doing of God's will on earth.

This leads to the importance of religious and ethical demands posed by the reign of God. The idea that religious demands are at the same time ethical demands has tended to be viewed with disapproval especially within the churches of the Reformed tradition. This must be partly the reason why a totally unethical and thoroughly demonic religious-cultural ideology and social-political structure such as apartheid is possible on the soil of the Reformed church in South Africa. "The God of the Reformed tradition," it was said, "was the God of slavery, fear, persecution, and death."[3] This God is the mutilation of the God of Jesus, and not just a misrepresentation of God. What has been preached, done, and enforced under apartheid in South Africa in the name of Christianity is, needless to say, anti-God's reign. How else are we to understand the sense of utter disbelief and outrage expressed in these words:

How is it possible that there could be any religious or, let me say, human feeling in persons who force their servants, mostly children of blacks shot dead, to sleep outside without any protection whatsoever in these cold nights, so that these unhappy wretches cover themselves with ashes, thereby inflicting upon themselves terrible burns...? How can there be any religious or even human feeling in persons—big strong men—who beat these children mercilessly with whips at the slightest provocation, or even without any reason

---

2. Edward Schillebeeckx, *Jesus: An Experiment in Christology*, trans. Hubert Hoskins (New York: Crossroad, 1985), 152–53.

3. Allan Boesak, *Black and Reformed* (Maryknoll, N.Y.: Orbis Books, 1984), 83.

at all . . . ? God knows, and I myself know, what indescribable injustices occur in these parts! What gruesome ill-treatment, oppression,
murder![4]

Yes, how is it possible? The fact is that when the Christian faith, or for
that matter any faith, chooses to disregard the ethical demands derived
from its religious demands, it becomes possible for it to betray itself and
becomes engaged in demonic practices such as what is described here by
an eyewitness.

The vital importance of religious and ethical conduct in accord with the
reign of God cannot thus be minimized. But we have to go further and say
that when religious and ethical conduct is practiced in accord with the reign
of God, we are led to recognize that the poor and the oppressed, as Jesus
declared, are the reign of God, that their struggle for freedom, justice, and
full humanity is the reign of God. The reign of God becomes manifest
almost always in conflict situations—conflicts between the poor and the
rich, between the oppressed and the oppressor, between the privileged and
the underprivileged. We must, then, question the word "coming" in "the
coming of God's reign," implying that the reign of God is to be introduced
into the present world from outside it. The fact of the matter is that the
reign of God struggles to be born in conflict situations. And when it is
born from within the midst of conflicts, the reign of God is recognized,
experienced, and embraced as freedom, justice, love, and life over against
slavery, injustice, hate, and death.

We must not, then, speak too hastily of God's reign in terms of peace
and harmony. Yes, Jesus does speak of peace. Did he not, for example,
exhort his disciples and those around him saying: "Blessed are the peace-
makers; they shall be called God's children" (Matt. 5:9)? But the fact that
peace has to be made points to a situation of conflict. Behind Jesus' "peace-
talk" is the ominous shadow of the conflict to be culminated on the cross.
Peace does not presuppose an absence of conflict. On the contrary, peace
has to be made because human beings have always been engaged in conflict. Human history, in one sense, is a history of broken peace. There
should be no hasty talk of peace, because such talk does not deal with the
root cause of conflicts and is bound to bring about even greater conflicts.

This is a lesson that the world had to learn from World War I, the
war supposed to end all wars. Instead it led to an even more catastrophic
World War II, in which more than fifty million people perished, two-thirds
of them unarmed civilians. Reflecting on the causes that led to World
War II, a political analyst admits that "a pervasive failure to stand up to

---

4. These are words of a Dutch pastor of the nineteenth century quoted by Boesak in *Black and Reformed*, 83.

Hitler" on the one hand, and "an abdication of statesmanship spanning the two decades" following World War I, on the other, "rendered the war inevitable."[5] The world was eager for peace, and eventually the world was to suffer gravely from peace ill-conceived and badly executed. According to the same political analyst, "Hitler relentlessly exploited the weakness of the international system and the guilt feelings of his opponents. A succession of Western politicians returned from meeting with him repeating his professed desire for peace."[6] Peace from the mouth of an insane political leader obsessed with aggression and war? These Western politicians, confronted with Hitler's "war-talk" disguised as "peace-talk," should have been able to recall the words of Jeremiah, that prophet of ancient Israel: "Peace, peace, when there is no peace" (Jer. 6:14, NRSV).

Jesus would have been a much more realistic politician than those Western politicians who negotiated "peace" with Hitler. Just recall what he is reported to have said: "Do you suppose I came to establish peace on the earth? No indeed, I have come to bring dissension. From now on, a family of five will be divided, three against two and two against three; father against son and son against father, mother against daughter and daughter against mother, mother-in-law against daughter-in-law and daughter-in-law against her mother-in-law" (Luke 12:51-53; par. Matt. 10:34-36). What a hard saying! It almost makes Jesus a warmonger instead of a peacemaker! But it cannot be Jesus' intention to stir up dissension, discord, and strife within a family. Even without Jesus there has always been division in families, not only in families but also in society, within a nation, among the nations and peoples. "As individuals, classes, and nations," concludes the author of *The Economy of the Kingdom*, "we tend to divide people into friends, similar to ourselves, and the others, strangers, possible threats to us. This is a way to close ourselves off from other people and also to deny the love of God toward all people. To break these divisions—mentally, socially, and economically—is the real challenge to our individual and communal lives."[7]

In saying what he has said, Jesus is not instigating further division in the world already deeply divided socially, politically, and economically, and also for reasons of race, sex, and creed. But the reign of God exposes these divisions as incompatible with what God intends for human community. What Jesus discloses in that difficult saying is the religious, or theological, dimension of human divisions. The rich, for instance, cannot exploit

---

5. Henry A. Kissinger, "Seeds Sown in Versailles Rendered War Inevitable," in the "Briefing" section of *San Francisco Chronicle*, September 6, 1989.

6. Ibid.

7. Halvor Moxness, *The Economy of the Kingdom: Social Conflict and Economic Relations in Luke's Gospel* (Philadelphia: Fortress Press, 1988), 169.

the poor without at the same time exploiting God. The oppressor cannot infringe upon the humanity of the oppressed without at the same time infringing upon God. And those who discriminate against others on account of race, sex, or creed have to know that they are also discriminating against God. In conflict situations what the reign of God is and stands for becomes ever clearer, on the one hand, and, on the other, the true nature of the forces that divide humanity is brought out in the open.

Is it any wonder that when Jesus speaks of God's reign, his eyes are fixed on earth and not on heaven? When he declares that God's reign is among us, he is pointing to the poor and the oppressed in front of him over against the rich and the powerful. And when he talks about what the reign of God means, he has to talk about the cup of suffering he has to drink and the baptism of the cross he has to go through. In other words, the reign of God for him means facing conflict situations, situations full of danger, pain, and suffering, situations created not just by individual whims or self-interest, but by the structures and systems that unleash the power of destruction against the poor and the powerless.

The reign of God emerges, then, in situations of conflict as the power that stands up to the principalities and powers of this world that threaten the lives of women, men, and children under their control. These principalities and powers are out to *over*-rule the reign of God. There are social and political forces of oppression determined to *over*-shadow it. The reigns of this world seek to *over*-whelm it. And there are demonic forces, set loose from the depths of creation, intent on plunging human community into fear and confusion, *over*-clouding the reign of God. These are the "here-and-now" realities of life and history with which people of each and every generation have to reckon. Even with the best of intentions we cannot bypass such "here-and-nows" to take refuge in a future yet to come. We cannot avoid them in the vague expectation that at the end-time God's reign will prevail. We cannot just endure them passively, telling ourselves that God's reign will become a reality, if not on earth, then in heaven.

We begin to understand why the reign of God for Jesus is not something that is to come in the future. It has to be here in the present. Jesus, like most of us Christians, must have believed that the reign of God would be active, very active, completely active, at the end of time. He must have also been convinced, again like most of us, that God's reign would be in action in its totality in heaven, *over*-ruling, *over*-shadowing, *over*-clouding, and *over*-whelming all the forces against it whether in heaven or on earth. Constantly under the shadow of the cross, Jesus must have staked his faith and hope in the fulfillment of God's reign at the end of time. Still, it is the participation in the reign of God on earth that gives us a clue as to what God's reign in heaven will be like. We can give an account of God's reign in heaven only insofar as we can give an account of God's reign in action on earth. The stories of God's reign today and not tomorrow or the day after tomorrow must be the indications of God's reign at the end-time, however imperfect, fragmentary, and incomplete these indications may be.

What are, then, these stories of God's reign in action now on earth? What kind of stories are they? How are they told? In what settings are they told? Who are storytellers of those stories? Who are the audiences of these stories? Who besides the storytellers are involved in the stories of God's reign in action here and now? And can there be disinterested audiences or spectators? Whether storytellers or spectators, whether God or humanity, whether heaven or earth, and whether the end-time or the present time, are they not all witnesses to God's reign in action? They may be active or negative witnesses, but witnesses nevertheless. They may be voluntary witnesses or involuntary witnesses; still they are all witnesses. They may be willing witnesses or unwilling witnesses, yet each of them has some part to play in God's reign in action.

There are in fact no spectators in God's reign in action. When the reign of God gets into action, chief witnesses, counterwitnesses, and accidental witnesses are all drawn into an intense drama. It is a political drama that involves certain people. It is a social happening that takes place in a particular place and at a particular time. But that drama quickly becomes a human drama affecting people far as well as near. It turns into a happening that reaches both back into the past and forward into the future, finding echoes from human community in the course of history. It can then grow into an event of cosmic magnitude making the redemptive presence of God powerfully felt in the human community, in "the whole creation... groaning in labor pains until now" (Rom. 8:22, NRSV). And the story of Jesus confronting the authorities of his own religion and the powers of the *Imperium Romanum* is the story par excellence of witnessing to the reign of God at his time and at all times.

Jesus the Witness of God's Reign

The way Jesus lived and went about his ministry is powerful witness to God's reign already present in human community. To the Pharisees looking for apocalyptic signs of God's reign Jesus said: "The reign of God is among you" (Luke 17:21). The preposition "among" is the translation of the Greek word *entos*, which can mean either *within* or *among*. But "among" is preferred, for "in the present context to translate it 'within' would mean that in answer to the Pharisees' question about when the kingdom of God would come (17:20) Jesus told them that the kingdom of God was within *them!* This would contradict everything else Jesus ever said about the kingdom of God or about the Pharisees."[8] You cannot internalize the reign of God as if it were the private property of certain individuals or a personal status symbol of being a member of a particular religious group or community. The reign of God is among you *but* not within you. This is the public and "ecumenical" nature of the reign of God.

But it does not follow that Jesus' reply—the reign of God is among you—"must be understood to mean that one day they will find that the kingdom of God is suddenly and unexpectedly in their midst."[9] The remark here implies that the reign of God is still to come, that it belongs to the future. In contrast, I want to stress that this "one day" must be today. It is not an indefinite tomorrow. That is why Jesus uses the present tense in his reply (the reign of God *is* among you) to the question asked in the future tense (When *will* the reign of God come?). To the religious leaders it happens "suddenly and unexpectedly" today because they are looking for it in the wrong time and in the wrong place. They understand it in a sense totally different from the way Jesus understands it. The poor and the disinherited among them belong to God and are the reign of God. The Jewish leaders do not know it and refuse to know it. Jesus' ministry among the sick, the outcasts, and the downtrodden is the reign of God. But those who hold religious power over people do not want to acknowledge it. They not only do not want to acknowledge it; they want to do away with it. Nothing in their religious beliefs, theology, and piety prepares them for the kind of reign of God that Jesus makes evident.

Strictly speaking, Jesus did not bring God's reign into the world, for it is already there. What he did was to engage people in the manifestation of it, to enable them to know it is there, to open their minds' eye to see it. The reign of God is among them because it "is a matter of human experience. It does not come in such a way that it can be found by looking at the march of armies or the movement of heavenly bodies; it is not to be seen in the coming of messianic pretenders. Rather, it is to be found wherever God is active decisively within the experience of an individual and people have faith to recognize this for what it is."[10] Jesus is the witness pointing to the reign of God in the very midst of the people excluded from the official religious community. And by associating with these people, eating and drinking with them, teaching them and empowering them, Jesus himself becomes the reign of God. He is the witness of God's reign in the double sense mentioned earlier. He bears witness to the reign of God and is the reign of God at one and the same time.

---

8. Albert Nolan, *Jesus before Christianity* (Maryknoll, N.Y.: Orbis Books, 1978), 46.

9. Ibid., 47.

10. Norman Perrin, *Rediscovering the Teaching of Jesus* (New York: Harper & Row, Publishers, 1967), 74.

As both the witness to the reign of God and as the reign of God Jesus is the enabler of God's reign. He is the facilitator of it. He makes real to people, friends and foes alike, that "God is active decisively" within their lives and within their society, that they are all involved in God's reign as signs of it or countersigns of it, that they all have to do with "God acting decisively" in the world as collaborators or as opponents. God's reign eliminates neutral zones within human experience, in the proceedings of human history, and in the movement of creation toward its destination. It compels witnesses of the movement of God's reign to take sides. They must be for it or against it; they cannot be neither for it nor against it. They must either work to support it or to obstruct it; they cannot be lukewarm toward it. It is not something you can take or leave at will. The reign of God commands attention and demands decision.

There is nothing strange in this. This is what the reign of God is and what it stands for. The reign of God, for example, stands for love and is love. The opposite of love is of course unlove. The reign of God cannot, then, condone unlove and defend unlove. If it does, it forfeits that very thing that makes it the reign of God, that is, love. What it can do and seeks to do is to overcome unlove with love and to transform it into love. This at once puts love in opposition to unlove. To be true to its own nature, love creates enemies. This is a most painful part of being love. In order to be love, love has to be something contradictory to its nature, making enemies. The fact of the matter is that this is the only way for love to be love. Love in league with unlove is not love. Love that is powerless before unlove is less than what love must be. And love that cannot say no to unlove cannot say yes to love.

This is the part of love that Paul has not faced in his otherwise most beautiful tribute ever written about love when he says: "Love is patient and kind. Love envies no one, is never boastful, never conceited, never rude; love is never selfish, never quick to take offence. Love keeps no score of wrongs, takes no pleasure in the sins of others, but delights in the truth. There is nothing love cannot face; there is no limit to its faith, its hope, its endurance" (1 Cor. 13:4-7). This is a sublime eulogy of love that puts most of us to shame on the one hand and, on the other, invites us to strive for it.

Love—the love that is the reign of God we are discussing here—cannot, of course, be envious, boastful, conceited, or selfish. But there are times when love has to be impatient, rudely awakening the rich and the powerful to face the consequences they bring to the poor and the oppressed. Here love expresses itself in civil disobedience, in demonstrations, in protest movements, in peaceful resistance. This is the way Jesus faced his opponents with the reign of God that is love. And this is the way an increasing number of people under socially, politically, and economically adverse

situations today are making their voices heard and expressing their determination to change the status quo. In so doing, both Jesus and these men
and women bear witness to the reign of God that is love and are, at the
same time, recognized as the reign of God.

The reign of God also stands for justice and is justice. Justice is a great
word in the Hebrew Scriptures. It is

> the fulfillment of the demands of a relationship, whether that re-
> lationship be with people or with God. Each person is set within
> a multitude of relationships: king with people, common man and
> woman with family, tribes person with community, community with
> resident alien and poor, all with God. And each of these relationships
> brings with it specific demands, the fulfillment of which constitutes
> righteousness [justice]. The demands may differ from relationship to
> relationship; righteousness in one situation may be unrighteousness
> in another. Further, there is no norm of righteousness outside the re-
> lationship itself. When God or a human person fulfills the conditions
> imposed upon them by a relationship, they are, in Old Testament
> terms, righteous.[11]

This is the standard understanding of the concept of justice that also
extends to the New Testament. In the New Testament justice is said to "pre-
sume a covenant relationship, which, for its preservation, needs the active
participation of both covenant partners. Thus, the one who upholds, and
therefore participates in, this covenant relationship is designated 'righteous'; and as in the Old Testament, those acts which preserve a covenant
relationship, either between God and human person, or between human
person and human person, are righteous, while those acts that break this
relationship are unrighteous."[12] Justice thus fortified with covenant seems
to seal relationships involving God and human beings in, as it were, a
water-tight jacket. "There is no norm of righteousness" continues the
quotation above, "outside the relationship."

If this is the case with the religious culture of both the Hebrew Scriptures and the New Testament, it is also true with many other ancient
cultures. The political culture of ancient China epitomized in the *Analects*
of Confucius comes to mind. In reply to the question about government
asked by Duke Ching of Ch'i, Confucius said: "Let the ruler *be* a ruler,
the subject *be* a subject, the father *be* a father, and the son *be* a son."[13]

---

11. *The Interpreter's Dictionary of the Bible* (Nashville: Abingdon Press, 1962), vol. R–Z,
80a.

12. Ibid., 91b.

13. See *A Source Book in Chinese Philosophy*, trans. and comp. Wing-Tsit Chan (Princeton:

Is Confucius in this statement expressing support for feudalism? Perhaps. Confucius, it has been pointed out, is asserting that people are endowed with different power and responsibility determined by their positions in family, society, and government. As to the contents of power and responsibility he is not specific.[14] This is one of the problems left unanswered by Confucius and subject to misinterpretation in support of the society built on the hierarchy of power and authority. As far as Confucius is concerned, what he regards as of primary importance is "the establishment of order." But he does not discuss in any detail "the question of the power that safeguards order, namely, the power of the ruler." The statement " 'let the ruler be a ruler, the subject be a subject,' prescribes an order in a relationship, but should 'the ruler be not a ruler,' how would the ruler's power be transferred? What form should the transfer of power take? Confucius has no answer for all such questions."[15] In the feudal political culture of China appeal has to be made to "the Mandate of Heaven" to remove the ruler who disqualifies himself as ruler by misusing his power and turning people against him.

Both in ancient Israel and in feudal China the concept of justice is understood and practiced within the hierarchical framework of power and authority. It is justice from the top down to the bottom. It is the maintenance of order in hierarchical relationships and adherence to it. But what is considered justice in this way may be injustice in another way. For justice that does not do justice to the people at the receiving end of the system of justice in hierarchical relationships is injustice. The prophets in ancient Israel were the ones who exposed this from time to time. How Nathan the prophet confronted King David with the parable of the poor man and his lamb to point out David's cowardly and shameful act is a well-known story (2 Sam. 12:1-14). But even in a case such as this, it is the injustice done by a king to one of his royal generals that is condemned. The injustice of the feudal (or in the case of Israel, theocratic) system of relationships is not challenged.

All this is not without problems. "There is no norm of righteousness [justice]," says our quotation earlier, "outside the relationship." But the relationship, whether that between God and human being or between human being and human being, defined, shaped, and practiced within a hierarchi-

---

Princeton University Press, 1963), 39. In *A Source Book*, the first two sentences are rendered as "let the ruler be a ruler and minister be a minister." But to render the Chinese word *ch'en* as "minister" in direct service of the ruler seems too narrow an understanding of the term. Confucius must have wanted to refer to "subjects" of the ruler, including all people and of course the minister and those who serve directly under the ruler.

14. See Lau Su-Kuang, *Chung Kuo Che Hsueh She* (*A History of Chinese Philosophy*), rev. ed. (Taipei: San Ming Publishing Company, 1984), 1:124.

15. Ibid., 157.

cal system of power and authority, often becomes a norm of injustice. How many crimes and cruelties, both in ancient times and today, both in East and West, have been committed within that "norm of justice" sanctioned by an order of relationships such as "letting the ruler be a ruler and the subject be a subject"? There must, then, be a norm of justice *outside* the norm of "justice" prevailing in such a political and religious culture. It is this norm outside the norm, justice outside the justice of the traditional norm, to which Jesus bears witness. It is also such a norm to which many men and women bear witness in the course of history. For Jesus this norm outside the norm, this justice outside the justice of a hierarchical society, is the reign of God. And Jesus, together with those who bear witness to it, is that very reign of God. He challenges the justice that does injustice to women, men, and children under an order of relationships that demands conformity and obedience at the expense of their rights and freedom.

So the reign of God is freedom. To bear witness to God's reign is to bear witness to freedom. To say it is to say freedom. To believe in it is to believe in freedom. To practice it is to practice freedom. Freedom of course is not an abstract concept; it is closely related to a particular meaning of the space in which we live. I stressed that the reign of God should not be confused with a territorial claim often made by Christians. Space, in relation to the reign of God, is not a fixed domain; it is movability within a community, be it political or religious. In an authoritarian society people's movability is greatly reduced. Under a totalitarian ruling power it is abolished. Your tongue is tied. Your mind is closed. Your heart becomes cold. Wherever you go, you are conscious of a shadow following you. You are rendered immobile not only physically but spiritually. To threaten your space is to threaten your being. To deprive you of your space is to deprive you of your existence.

In this way, a totalitarian ruling power can threaten your physical space and thus your existence as a human person. Similarly, an authoritarian religious authority can invade your spiritual space and thus your freedom as a human being. This is a contradiction that betrays the very nature of religion. Instead of liberating you, it enslaves you to its teachings and rules. It claims your total commitment that allows no difference of views. It demands the surrender of freedom as an expression of your loyalty. A religion can turn into a demonic force that controls the mind and soul of believers. Stories of mind-control, or rather soul-control, in the history of religions are familiar stories. Today such stories are repeated by cultic movements and fanatical religious groups.

To deprive one of the space of being, the realm of freedom whether political or religious, is against what the reign of God is and stands for. What Jesus did was to help people reclaim their space and regain their freedom. A space of freedom is created when he eats and drinks with the social and religious outcasts. When he openly defies the religious authorities that control the minds and souls of believers, he reopens the spiritual space in individual believers and in their community. And when he faces the Roman political power at his trial, he demonstrates the power of the freedom of the spirit over against the political power that finds itself in the bondage of its own power. From the prophets of ancient Israel to the Reformers of sixteenth-century Europe to the men and women who struggle for human rights in different parts of the world today, we perceive the reign of God as freedom. Jesus and "the cloud of these witnesses" are the reign of God as freedom.

Besides being love, justice, and freedom, the reign of God is also truth, power, and life. And the list can expand further. The heart of the matter is that the reign of God stands for true values over against false values, that it stands for values that put into question other values. We have already referred to the opposites of love as unlove, of justice as injustice, and of freedom as loss of space or movability. In the same way, the reign of God confronts untruth with truth and overcomes the power of death with the power of life. Here we are not talking about the triumph of God's reign over the forces that oppose it. We have learned from history that triumphalism has done more harm than good to the Christian church in its relationships with the rest of the world. What I wish to point out here is that the values that are the reign of God and what it stands for are fundamental to life. They are the foundation of history. They are recognized and affirmed as the elements without which life and history are meaningless. They also constitute the invitation, the call, the rallying point for women and men to strive for them. It is values such as these that continue to inspire people to be bearers of witness to the reign of God and to be the reign of God.

If this is what God's reign is, something happens decisively in human lives and in the world; it does not leave anyone indifferent to it. The reign of God poses a crisis to individual persons and a challenge to human community. It compels us to face the forces of evil at work in the inmost part of our psyches and in the depths of human community. And it forces us to let its values judge our values and inspires us to be part of the struggle for its cause. In his life and through his ministry Jesus was this crisis to the religious establishment and political authorities. He was the judgment of values antagonistic to the values of God's reign. And in his trial before the Jewish religious authorities as a religious offender and at the court of the Roman colonial regime as a political criminal, Jesus as the reign of God and the powers of this world as the reign of darkness are joined in battle for a decisive showdown before the eyes of the world.

The Hour When Darkness Reigns

God reigns, but darkness also reigns. This is the stage on which the trial of Jesus is set. In his account of Jesus' arrest in the Garden of Gethsemane Luke tells us that Jesus said to the chief priests and the temple guards: "...this is your hour—when darkness reigns" (Luke 22:53). Whether intended by Luke or not, these words disclose a profound insight into the cosmic significance of Jesus' trial. The trial of Jesus did not begin when he was forcefully taken to the Sanhedrin, the council of Jewish religious authorities, to be interrogated. Nor did it begin only when he was brought to the Roman colonial court for further trial and for eventual sentencing. The trial of Jesus, as all trials that have to do with witnessing to God's reign, begins in the primordial time of creation when the reign of God and the reign of darkness confront each other for domination.

The Momentous Hour of Conflict

That must be a momentous hour for God, for all creation, and for human creatures. And it also must be a tremendous hour for the power of darkness, anticipating to "hold sway and even stifle the good."[16] The trial of Jesus, and for that matter all trials that directly or indirectly reflect it in human history, is the trial of God at the beginning of creation. "In the beginning God created heavens and earth," we read in this familiar and yet awe-inspiring creation story in the Hebrew Bible, "the earth was a vast waste, darkness covered the deep, and the spirit of God hovered over the surface of the water" (Gen. 1:1). Here the whole cosmos is the court of trial, as it were. God or darkness? God reigns or darkness reigns?

This is not just poetic imagination. It is poetic, for how can a mystery of such primordial magnitude be expressed in prose? It is imagination, but not illusion or fantasy mistaken for imagination. The poetic imagination that envisions this cosmic struggle between God's reign and the reign of darkness is rooted in history. It is the horror that grips humanity, defies rational explanation, and renders ordinary everyday language useless. That is why poetry must take over. It takes up where prose leaves off. It picks up the thread broken by the power of darkness. It takes upon itself the task of witnessing to the hope of God and humanity in the midst of despair. The poet becomes the messenger of hope when he or she experiences the evil forces of destruction and survives them.

---

16. Joseph A. Fitzmyer, *The Gospel according to Luke, X–XXIV*, Anchor Bible (New York: Doubleday & Company, 1985), 1452.

It may be that the storytellers of both the creation story of the first chapter of Genesis and that of the second chapter have lived through the tragedy of life and world to become messengers of hope. These stories are, above all, stories of hope in the present and promise in the future. Perhaps it is not entirely fanciful to think that they were inspired to tell their stories after their brush with horror and death vividly depicted in the story of the flood a few chapters later (Gen. 6—8). This story of fearful destruction concludes with these words:

> When the Lord smelt the soothing odor, God said within God-self, "Never again shall I put the earth under a curse because of humankind, however evil their inclinations may be from their youth upwards, nor shall I ever again kill all living creatures, as I have just done.
> As long as the earth lasts
> seedtime and harvest, cold and heat
> summer and winter, day and night,
> they will never cease."
>   (Gen. 8:21-22)

Could this story of the flood be another version of the creation story that might have begun with "the earth being a vast waste" (Gen. 1:1) of the first creation story and with "neither shrub nor plant growing on the earth" (2:5) of the second creation story?

The destruction of lives and nature caused by the violent flood is without question the chaos and waste God must contend with. It has reduced the earth to the barren and desolate ground with which, in the mind of the storyteller of the second creation story, God must reckon. And when we realize that the heart of both creation stories is not the beginning in time of heaven and earth, but the celebration of life and the fruits of the ground to sustain that life, we begin to wonder whether these concluding words of the four lines in verse in the story of the flood express the same hope cherished by the other creation storytellers. These storytellers, in short, are bearers of good tidings. They live to tell the stories to rekindle the hope of humanity in the world of harsh realities.

Messenger of Hope

In every age in the West or in the East there are such messengers of hope from the world in shambles. In our time Elie Wiesel, a survivor of Auschwitz during the Nazi Holocaust, is such a messenger. And it is only with powerful poetic imagination that he is able to tell the horrible stories of inhumanity only human beings, not angels in heaven, not devils in hell, but only human beings on earth, are capable of. One of his stories poignantly bears the title *Night*. This is what his poetic imagination enables him to remember of his first night at the camp where systematic extermination was being carried out against the Jews:

> Never shall I forget that night, the first night in camp, which has turned my life into one long night, seven times cursed and seven times sealed. Never shall I forget that smoke. Never shall I forget the little faces of the children, whose bodies I saw turned into wreaths of smoke beneath a silent blue sky.
>
> Never shall I forget those flames which consumed my faith forever. Never shall I forget that nocturnal silence which deprived me, for all eternity, of the desire to live. Never shall I forget those moments which murdered my God and my soul and turned my dreams to dust. Never shall I forget these things, even if I am condemned to live as long as God. Never.[17]

Never shall I forget! This is a promise. This is a vow. This is a cry from the abyss of hell created by human hands.

But who wants to remember such things? It is a miracle that Elie Wiesel survived those horrors. Is that not enough? Who likes to be haunted by them for the rest of one's life? But the problem is that there will be no miracle of survival again if such horrors are obliterated from human memories, when it is believed that they never took place, that they only occurred to someone in hallucination. This would be a more horrible thing to happen than those indescribably horrible things that happened at the heart of "civilized" Europe during the bloody and obscene World War II. If these things were forgotten, if they were believed to be just nightmares with no reality in the waking hours of humanity, then there would take place in the future even more horrible things—things beyond words, things that would render even poetic imagination totally numb and stupefy it into eternal silence. That would be the victory of the power of darkness. That would be the triumph of insanity over sanity. That would be a total surrender of humanity to inhumanity. That is why Elie Wiesel has to become "messenger to all humanity."[18] He has to describe those indescribable things. He must exploit his poetic imagination to the last ounce of its power to tell those unbelievable things. Never shall Elie Wiesel ever forget! And of course never shall God ever forget! Never! Hope for the future of humanity can

---

17. Elie Wiesel, *Night*, trans. François Mauriac (New York: Bantam Books, 1982), 32. The first edition was published in 1960.

18. This is the subtitle used by Robert McAfee Brown in his excellent study, *Elie Wiesel* (Notre Dame: Notre Dame University Press, 1983).

only come from the memories of that terrible past. Salvation of the world and of the whole of creation is possible only when these incredible things are not to be repeated. In Elie Wiesel's own words:

> Let us tell tales so as to remember how vulnerable human being is when faced with overwhelming evil. Let us tell tales so as not to allow the executioner to have the last word. The last word belongs to the victim. It is up to the witness to capture it, shape it, transmit it and still keep it as a secret, then communicate that secret to others.[19]

In telling the tales of the Nazi Holocaust, Elie Wiesel summons all humanity to be witnesses of the struggle between the reign of God and the reign of darkness.

Jesus himself, in that dark night in the garden of Gethsemane, must have realized that the struggle between God's reign and the reign of darkness had begun in earnest. Surrounded by "a crowd armed with swords and cudgels" (Mark 14:43; par. Matt. 26:47), "the chief priests, the temple guards and the elders" (Luke 22:52) and "a detachment of soldiers" (John 18:3), Jesus must have known that he had become a prisoner of the reign of darkness. He must have remembered, to quote Elie Wiesel, "how vulnerable human being is when faced with overwhelming evil." The evil to which the crowds, religious agents, and Roman soldiers who came for Jesus succumbed must be the evil to which humanity surrenders body and soul ever so often in the course of history. Surely it must be the same evil that turned certain human beings into savage beasts at those camps of death instituted by the Nazi rulers. But the miracle is that the reign of God has not been overwhelmed by the reign of darkness. Somehow light shines out of the darkness that seeks to extinguish it, just as at the creation light broke out of the siege of darkness, enabling the creation to resume its course toward the time of fulfillment. John the Evangelist sums all this up when he says: "The light shines in the darkness, and the darkness has never mastered it" (John 1:5).

We Cannot Forget—A Memorial Message

There are individuals such as Elie Wiesel who have survived the horrendous power of evil to bear the message of hope for humanity and there are thousands and hundreds of thousands of people, most of whose names will never be known, caught up in the mighty tide of history to become bearers

---

19. Elie Wiesel, "Art and Culture after the Holocaust," in *Auschwitz: Beginning of a New Era? Reflections on the Holocaust*, ed. Eva Fleischer (New York: KTAV Publishing House, 1977), 403–16. The quotation, found on 403, is from Brown's *Elie Wiesel*, 37–38.

of both the tragedy and the hope of their own nation and of the human community at large. And almost as if by chance the reign of God discloses itself from the depths of conflict between tragedy and hope. I am referring particularly to the peaceful student demonstrations for freedom and democracy that ended in a bloodbath at Tiananmen Square, the Gate of Heavenly Peace, in Beijing in the months of May and June 1989.

As the student demonstrations went on, a fierce power struggle was taking place inside the Forbidden City, the old imperial palace adjacent to the square, between the moderate faction represented by Zhao Ziyang, the general secretary of the Communist party, who urged conciliation, and the hard-liners headed by Deng Xiaoping, the eighty-four-year-old paramount leader of China. Deng was adamantly opposed to conciliation.

> "I have 3 million troops behind me," a source quoted Deng as saying. "I have all the people of China," answered Zhao. Deng dismissed him: "You have nothing."[20]

Calling over one billion people of China nothing? Deng must have gone out of his mind—Deng, one of the revolutionary leaders who led the *people's* revolution to victory in 1949, Deng who has been for many years head of China's *People's* Liberation Army. His retort against Zhao was ominous, and the events that unfolded proved it was truly ominous. It reminds us of Ch'in Shi Huang Ti, the first emperor of the Chi'n dynasty in ancient China, who, according to an old Chinese folktale, "regarded his subjects as so much grass and weeds" and who built the Chinese Wall at the cost of tens of thousands of human lives.[21]

What caused the students to take to Tiananmen Square and as many as three thousand of them to stage hunger strikes was corruption in the government and suppression of freedom and democracy. They "were joined by railway workers, coal miners, textile spinners and truckloads of grizzled peasants. Contingents of protesters arrived from government offices, such as the Foreign Ministry, the Bank of China and even the cadre school of the Chinese Communist Party.... More than one million demonstrators, by official count, jammed the streets of Beijing."[22] Viewed from outside, the Communist rulers seemed not quite to know how to respond to the hunger strikers and demonstrators. This was interpreted as a sign of hope.

Then came June 4. The hard-line "revolutionaries" from the days of the Long March in the 1930s struck, after the dust of the power-struggle

---

20. See *Newsweek*, May 29, 1989, 16.
21. See my *Tears of Lady Meng: A Parable of People's Political Theology* (Geneva: World Council of Churches, 1981; Maryknoll, N.Y.: Orbis Books, 1982).
22. *Newsweek*, May 29, 1989, 20.

within the Party had settled. They had Tiananmen Square sprayed with machine guns, leaving behind thousands of unarmed students and civilians dead. The massacre was as traumatic as it was entirely unexpected. China plunged back to the rule of terror and the clouds of darkness descended on it and its people once again. "The government has won the battle here to-day," said a weeping student, "but they have lost the people's hearts."[23] In these words, said in anger, desperation, and despair, one cannot help hearing echoes of what Confucius said about government twenty-five hundred years ago. This is what one reads in the *Analects:*

> Tzu-kung [one of Confucius's disciples] asked about government. Confucius said, "Sufficient food, sufficient armament, and sufficient confidence of the people." Tzu-kung said, "Forced to give up one of these, which would you abandon first?" Confucius said, "I would abandon the armament." Tzu-kung said, "Forced to give up one of the remaining two, which would you abandon first?" Confucius said, "I would abandon food. There have been deaths from time immemorial, but no state can exist without the confidence of the people."[24]

Brushing aside the political wisdom of the ancient sage, the Communist rulers in Beijing chose to retain the armament and abandon the confidence of the people. Little wonder some Chinese intellectuals, thoroughly disillu-sioned by the Party that again resorted to the barrel of the gun to maintain one-party rule and to crush brutally the peaceful pro-democracy demon-strations of the people, predicted that the Communist regime is bound to collapse in the not so distant a future.

During those weeks in which people demonstrated their hope, courage, and solidarity there was no lack of moving images in Tiananmen Square and in the streets of Beijing—the erection of the goddess of liberty in the square right under the huge portrait of Mao Zedong; students, civilians, and doctors helping hunger strikers; demonstrators talking to the soldiers and offering them food and drink. But there was one image that stands out most vividly and will remain in the memories of people for a long time to come—the image of a young man in white shirt standing in front of a column of tanks, trying to stop them from carrying out their savage order. It is an image that moves heaven as well as earth, gods as well as human beings. It is heroism so unpretentious and yet so audacious that it stunned the soldiers and brought the tanks to a temporary standstill. These words of an observer speak it all:

---

23. *Newsweek*, June 12, 1989, 26.
24. *The Analects*, 12:7. See Wing-Tsit Chan, *A Source Book in Chinese Philosophy*, 39.

One man against an army. The power of the people versus the power of the gun. There he stood, implausibly resolute in his thin white shirt, an unknown Chinese man facing down a lumbering column of tanks. For a moment that will be long remembered, the lone man defined the struggle of China's citizens. "Why are you here?" he shouted at the silent steel hulk. "You have done nothing but create misery. My city is in chaos because of you." The brief encounter between the man and the tank captured an epochal event in the lives of 1.1 billion Chinese: the state clanking with menace, swiveling right and left with uncertainty, is halted in its tracks because the people got in its way, and because it got in theirs.[25]

The power of the lone man versus the power of the gun! Is not that man a witness to the redemptive power of life and history? Is he not even for a brief moment part of that redemptive power itself?

That moment of confrontation is a moment of eternity. It is not just a fleeting moment. It is not a moment that will be swallowed up in the flux of time. We do not know what eternity is as a concept, an idea, or even as a belief. Is it an endless time? Is it an infinite continuity of time? But how is it different from time? How and when is time transformed into eternity? When does time cease and eternity begin? But is eternity still eternity when it has a beginning? If it has no end, it should have no beginning either. Otherwise, we would be speaking of eternity in terms of the past, the present, and the future. But these—past, present, and future—are the components of time and not of eternity. In short, we do not know what eternity is if we try to comprehend it in relation to time.

Eternity is grasped by us—no, it grasps us—when it makes its epiphany in the midst of life and history. It is like night-blooming cereus that appears and then quickly disappears (*than-hwa yi hsian* in Chinese). But what an epiphany! In that brief moment of epiphany eternity commands the total attention of those who witness it, just as those who witnessed the confrontation of the lone man before the column of tanks. That brief moment is eternity. It redeems time from the tyranny of human insanity. It transforms human tragedy into divine comedy. It restores hope to the human community devastated by despair. It rekindles life in the human heart given way to disillusionment. The epiphany of eternity in a brief moment of time is the epiphany of redemption. It is a proclamation that the world is redeemable, that human community is redeemable, that human beings are redeemable. That brief moment of epiphany is not a moment in time. That moment is

---

25. *Time*, June 19, 1989, 10.

eternity. It is the reign of God. For a brief moment eternity reigns. And that reign of eternity will be remembered forever and ever. "The reign of God," said Jesus, "is in the midst of you." Jesus was the witness to epiphanies of God's reign. He himself was that epiphany. And he enables us to be his co-witnesses to the epiphanies of God's reign. He inspires us to be part of those epiphanies. There has been more than one epiphany of eternity in human history. These epiphanies of eternity lived, witnessed, and remembered are the subjects of our theology of history and the themes of our confession.

In the aftermath of the Tiananmen massacre two Chinese poets wrote a memorial dedicated to those men and women who perished at the square on June 4. We cannot forget! This is their message not only to the dead but to the living:

> You are already dead. It seems not so long ago in that Square under the blue sky, when mothers were pushing carts and frantically calling you. But you had already risen so high, watching the kites dancing in the spring sky.
>
> You are already dead. Yet it is not so long ago that we said, let's go to the square and speak what's on our minds. In the company of many people we then walked to the trees beside the subway station.
>
> Not so long ago we shared a bowl of soup together, cooked instant noodles, slowly letting it go down our throats. In the rain we moved from one tent to another with umbrella in our hands.
>
> And then, you died.
>
> Sudden lights nailed you to the brick floor. Your legs broken, you crawled, shouted, and were crushed under the iron tracks of armor vehicles.
>
> We cannot forget that moment when the gun was fired. You looked on stunned, the hands that had clapped clutching the chest covered with a sudden burst of blood. You were all sitting neatly on the ground, and they shot at you neatly in the face....
>
> You are dead. We cannot forget you. You were only slightly younger than us, walking with your head held high and laughing like children. We cannot forget you. They drove you into a *cul-de-sac* and killed you for no reason at all....
>
> They say they have won. They think once they have reduced you to ashes and washed away the blood, you become nothing forever, eternally silent, unable to tell the frightful injustice done to you....
>
> We are alive standing before you. They can also kill us. But they do not know we also died the moment the gun was fired in the Square, in the family of ours called China. We surrender our hearts to you, to

the dead, so that you may live again in us. We will, like you, raise our hands high and complete the task you were not able to complete.[26]

"We cannot forget you!" This is a promise. This is a prayer. And this is a commitment to carry on the struggle crushed by cold-blooded murder conducted by aging leaders desperately clinging to power won with the barrel of the gun.

This is a promise, and not revenge. Eternity makes its epiphany not to avenge humanity but to reconstruct the promise devastated by human atrocities. It can be said that human history is a history of revenge in the name of "the Mandate of Heaven" in China, in the name of "God's will" in the history of Christianity, in the name of "religious faith" continuing bloodshed between Sikhs and Hindus in India, between Muslims and Christians, between Jews and Palestinians in the Middle East, and between Protestants and Roman Catholics in Northern Ireland. In this respect, human history, political or religious, is a history of "eye for eye and tooth for tooth." Revenge, often under the pretext of justice and truth, unleashes the power of destruction in us to strike at our enemies and render a blow to our opponents. It is an ugly power lurking in the depth of individual persons, biding its time in the arena of political struggle and hiding behind the façade of holiness in a religious establishment.

For Jesus, however, the reign of God is promise and not revenge. Did he not say, "You have heard that they were told, 'An eye for an eye, a tooth for a tooth.' But what I tell you is this: Do not resist those who wrong you" (Matt. 5:38)? Jesus cannot be either teaching an ethic of the weak or proposing an art of compromise without regard to what is true and false and what is right and wrong. He must have been deeply aware of the destructive power of revenge, the power that destroys not only others but also oneself. In the person consumed by revenge, even for a just cause, something is already dead—love. Love cannot coexist with revenge. In fact love is destroyed by revenge. If love without justice only gives rise to greater injustice, justice without love turns the human heart into a hard stone and deprives human beings of feelings. Can there be, then, love with justice and justice with love? Yes, Jesus would say. That is the way of God's reign—the way not of instant success and triumph, but of long suffering and pain. It is the way of the cross. And is not the cross of Jesus the supreme epiphany of God's reign—the epiphany of God's eternity in the temporality of this world?

We cannot forget. These words from the hearts of the Chinese poets in deep sorrow are also a prayer. What is prayer if not our remembering

---

26. The memorial was written by Ku Ch'en and Yang Lien. See *The Nineties* (Hong Kong), special issue, June 16, 1989, 8. Translation from the Chinese text by C. S. Song.

of things before God and God's remembering of us in times of despair and hopelessness? Memory is a great gift God has given. Just as we misuse other gifts, we do also misuse the gift of memory. We allow our memory to be filled with hatred for others, regrets for the past, or disappointments of life. We become prisoners of the past, unable to live with hope in the present and to create a future yet to come. We then deprive memory of its power—the power of transcendence. Memory becomes a prison house. Our life comes to be imprisoned at a certain intersection of time and space, losing dimensions and perspectives. We become psychopaths confusing reality and illusion.

But this is not all that memory is. Memory, when charged with the power of transcendence, liberates us from enslavement to the past and empowers us to strive for the future. It fills the present, not with hate and regrets, but with the sense of call to struggle for change in our lives and in our society. This is memory at its most constructive, creative, and forward-looking. And it is such memory that should play a central role in prayer. In prayer we remember the past not for the sake of the past but for the sake of the present and future. God also remembers us in our prayer not merely to remind us of our sins and failures but to urge us to live the present and build the future. Here is this prayer in the Psalms:

> Remember, LORD, your tender care and your unfailing,
>   for they are from ages past.
> Do not remember the sins and offences of my youth,
>   but remember me in your unfailing love,
>   in accordance with your goodness, LORD.
>   (Ps. 25:6-7)

In this ardent prayer the psalmist seems to have grasped the twofold meaning of memory—memory as enslavement to the past and thus unredemptive and memory as the creative power of life and thus redemptive. God is God because God is capable of not remembering our sins and offenses of the past on the one hand and, on the other, remembering us in God's unfailing love. Dwelling on our sins in an almost morbid manner in our prayers and in the teachings of our churches demonstrates our lack of faith and trust in God's ability to know what to remember and what not to remember. We have, in our life of faith and in our theology, projected too much of ourselves on God, making God a reflection of us who often forget what should be remembered and remember what should be forgotten.

The memory that redeems the past and creates the future is also what concerns the prophet known as Second Isaiah, who lived during the time when Jews were taken to Babylon in exile. That prophet tells us something very strange:

> Stop dwelling on past events
> brooding over days gone by.
> (Isa. 43:18)

The message must have infuriated some of the Jews who lived in shame and indulged in remorse in the land of exile. Do we not have this heart-rending song that moves its hearers' hearts, inducing their tears and enveloping them in anguish?

> By the rivers of Babylon we sat down and wept
>   When we remembered Zion.
> On the willow trees there we hung up our lyres,
>   for there those who had carried us captive
>   asked us to sing them a song,
>   our captors called on us to be joyful:
>   "Sing us one of the songs of Zion."
> How could we sing the Lord's song
>   in a foreign land?
>
> If I forget you, Jerusalem,
>   may my right hand wither away;
> let my tongue cling to the roof of my mouth
>   if I do not remember you,
> if I do not set Jerusalem
>   above my chief joy.
> (Ps. 137:1-6)

We cannot help recalling the Jews in Hitler's concentration camps were demanded by their captors and executioners to make music for them. The scene is as tragic as it is heartbreaking. What we see is the profanation of the sacred. What we hear is the blasphemy of the divine. And mingled with the music that wells out of the depths of human suffering and pain, we hear the Nazi officers clapping their hands. What can be more obscene and demonic than this! No, we cannot sing the Lord's song in a foreign land. We cannot forget Jerusalem. We must set it above our chief joy.

And yet, loyalty to our nation and faithfulness to our religion can also dim our vision and close our minds to new possibilities. Was this not perhaps the danger to which that prophet in the land of exile was referring when he told his fellow exiles to "stop dwelling on days gone by"? The prophet could not have been more to the point. In this case the days gone by are the days of defeat by a foreign power, the days of promise aborted, the days of future derailed from its course. A people conscious of having been in God's special favor cannot be reconciled to the shame and pain of captivity. That is why they cannot sing the song of Zion in their captors' land. All they do is "brood over" the past glory and pride no longer theirs.

If we cannot forget what has happened, if we remember it in our prayer, it is not to brood over it but to prepare ourselves for something new. That is why the prophet continues to say in the name of God and on behalf of God:

> I am about to do something new;
> this moment it will unfold.
> (Isa. 43:19)

If we do not expect God will do a new thing, then we do not have to pray. God already knows our past. We do not need to remind God of that over and over. Could this be what Jesus was trying to say to his disciples when he said to them: "In your prayers do not go babbling on like the heathen, who imagine that the more they say the more likely they are to be heard" (Matt. 6:7)? How much of "the heathen" in our Christian prayers! And in our prayers if we do not anticipate that a new thing "will break from the bud" (NEB), then it is useless to pray. For God is always ahead of us, beckoning us to be part of a new creation. How otherwise could John on the island of Patmos have heard "the one sitting on the throne" saying to him: "I am making all things new!" (Rev. 21:5)?

The two Chinese poets, their memorial words turned almost into a prayer, are not yet over their trauma. They are still very much haunted by the memories of their friends brutally murdered at Tiananmen Square. But they are not "brooding over" their memories. They do not promise not to forget that tragic event on June 4 to lock themselves in perpetual mourning of the lives lost and of the high hopes dashed to the ground. They do not turn their memorial into a prayer in order to indulge in the dream shattered to pieces. They promise not to forget their comrades who died in the prodemocracy demonstrations because they have a commitment to make and honor. It is the commitment that they will continue the struggle to accomplish what is yet to be accomplished—freedom and democracy for China.

Promise without commitment is not promise. At best it is a mere empty word that carries neither determination nor conviction. At worst it is a word from a treacherous mind to create false expectation and illusion. When the Chinese poets mourn their fallen friends, they are making a promise with commitment—a commitment to carry on the struggle for a new future. A promise with a commitment such as this denies the oppressive powers the last word. It is a promise that can become a reality in the life of a people and in the history of a nation. Because there are men and women like these two Chinese poets who can make a promise with commitment, human history has hope and a future. Pessimism, then, is not the answer to setbacks in the cause of human freedom and social change.

But there are prayers without commitment. How much of Christian prayer is this kind of prayer! Most of our prayers are half-hearted prayers because we do not believe in the cause for which we are praying. Some of us Christians pray for the coming of God's "kingdom" but refuse involvement in the cause for social change. There are Christians who believe that the "kingdom" of God is an entirely religious matter having nothing to do with the realities of life. Such Christians are no better than that lawyer who came to Jesus with a question on eternal life (Luke 10:25-37). He knew everything that was taught in the Law about eternal life, but he saw no relation between his faith in eternal life and the commitment of that faith in the present life, between loving God and loving one's neighbor. "Go," Jesus told him at the conclusion of the story of the good Samaritan, "and do as he did." What Jesus was trying to drive home to the lawyer was not so much imitation of the good Samaritan as commitment to involvement in the transformation of life and society.

What we hear in the words of the Chinese poets is a prayer with commitment to the cause for which many young people gave their lives. They want to unite their hearts with the hearts of the dead in order that the dead can resurrect in them to pursue with them the struggle they began. To give one's heart to others—there is no commitment stronger than this. It is a commitment with one's soul, mind, heart, and body. It is a total commitment. In a total commitment such as this, a commitment to the transformation of human community, we perceive a religious commitment. A prayer with commitment breaks down the barrier between what is religious and what is secular, what is spiritual and what is worldly. This is the prayer that Jesus taught us: "Your reign come, your will be done, on earth as in heaven."

"In Memory of Me"

The promise, prayer, and commitment the Chinese poets expressed in their memorial dedicated to the men and women who perished at Tiananmen Square take us back to the instituting of Jesus' memory in the celebration of the Lord's Supper. We have the words of the institution first left us by Paul in his letter to the Christians at Corinth: "For the tradition which I handed on to you came to me from the Lord himself," Paul writes, after chiding them for their misuse of the Lord's Supper:

that on the night of his arrest, the Lord Jesus took bread and, after giving thanks to God, broke it and said: "This is my body, which is for you; do this in memory of me." In the same way, he took the cup after supper, and said: "This cup is the new covenant sealed by my blood. Whenever you drink it, do this in memory of me. For every time you eat this bread and drink the cup, you proclaim the death of the Lord, until he comes." (1 Cor. 11:23-26)

Our attention is drawn to the phrase "in memory of me."[27] What kind of "memory" could this be? To put it differently, how is Jesus to be remembered? How does he want us to remember him?

In the history of Christian doctrine the church has remembered Jesus as prophet, priest, and king. It is certain that he would object strongly to being remembered as king. There is nothing in what he said and did that could lead us to call him king. It is the Christian church, from its earliest inception, that crowned him as king. Would he, then, have minded being called priest? Perhaps he would prefer the title "rabbi"—teacher. He appeared on the scene as a rabbi who astonished people with his teaching, "for, unlike the scribes, he taught with a note of authority" (Mark 1:22; pars. Matt. 7:29; Luke 4:32). In other words, he was rabbi of rabbis, a teacher who turned the tradition of his religion upside down. A revolutionary rabbi he was. Then he was regarded as prophet. This is what his disciples told him when he asked them how people took him to be on their way to the villages of Caesarea Philippi (Mark 8:27-30; and pars.) Of all three titles "prophet" is that with which Jesus would probably have had least difficulty. Jesus has, of course, been remembered as Lord, Messiah, Son of God, and so on. But would any of these titles, including that of prophet, have been the way Jesus wanted to be remembered by when he invited those present at the Last Supper to share with him the bread and wine "in memory of me"? At that critical hour of his life when he was aware of his impending arrest and possible death, would he have been concerned about his title? Would titles such as king, messiah, even prophet, have crossed his mind? Probably not. What occupied his mind must have been entirely something else.

It is the cause for which he lived and labored that must have been utmost in his mind during those last hours with his followers. That cause is now threatened with defeat with his final confrontation with the religious and political authorities. What unfolded after the Last Supper is that "Jesus' message, his way of living his life and in the end his very person were in fact rejected. In a straight historical sense Jesus failed in his life's project."[28] If there were moments in which Jesus could not help being pen-

---

27. In some Lukan texts the same phrase, "in memory of me," also occurs.
28. Schillebeeckx, *Jesus*, 640.

sive during the supper, it must have been because he was aware of a very possible failure of his "life's project." I believe these are the most critical moments in the whole life and ministry of Jesus. It is possible that this could have been the subject of his conversation with his followers at the supper, although none of what he might have said about it is to be found in the passion narratives of the Gospels. It is also possible that Jesus went over with them some of what he did and said concerning the reign of God during the past three years.

How is, then, this cause of God's reign to survive his death, not only to survive, but to grow and develop? As he himself remembers how that cause inspired the people around him and made a difference to the lives of some of them, his followers sharing the supper with him must remember it after he is gone. As long as it lives in the memories of people, it will not fade into oblivion and disappear from history. Hope is nurtured in the memory of a cause. Vision is sustained by it. Efforts to change the present are inspired by it. And future is created out of it. The experiment of the cause of God's reign may fail from time to time, but as long as it is retained in the memories of people to inspire their faith in it, it will erupt every now and again from the depths of human memories to assert itself, to demand attention, to claim following, and to work toward transformation of life and society. Human memory has this power to command life and history. When Jesus shared bread and wine with his followers as his body and blood at the Last Supper, he was instituting a sacrament of memory. He was making sure that the cause of God's reign becomes the sacrament of life and history in the memories of his followers. Once the reign of God becomes sacramentalized in the memories of people, it will not be forgotten. It will be remembered from one community to another community, from one generation to another generation. It will remain a vital force in the movement of history. It will be the conscience of society, exposing injustices and opposing oppressions. It will be the source that evokes the best and noblest in humanity to strive for love, justice, and truth in a world of conflict, exploitation, and greed. And it will be a foretaste of eternal life, life of lives, a life to fulfill our lives that in each and every instance are unfinished and unfulfilled lives.

The historical fact that the Last Supper took place under the shadow of the cross and in anticipation of it tells us further what the Lord's Supper we observe in memory of Jesus must be. The cross, in a very real sense, is a sacrament of death. It does not only signify death, it administers death. It not only symbolizes death, it *is* death. In that sense the cross spells finality. There is no life beyond the cross. There is no history after it. It is the end of all meanings. It is the triumph of the power of death over the power of life. Those who contrived to have Jesus sent to the cross and those who ordered him to be crucified on the cross must have known this finality of the cross. They were certain that Jesus and what he represented would perish from history and from human memories. How could they have been more mistaken!

To anticipate that sacrament of death, to forestall it, to desacramentalize it, at the Last Supper Jesus instituted the sacrament of life. Before death becomes final, life must assert its finality. Before death claims its victim, the victim to be must claim death as his victim. What took place at the Last Supper is thus an enactment of life. It institutes life in the presence of death and ensures it against death. It claims that life is final, but death is not. It declares that life is eternal while death is not. It proclaims that no power on earth, not even the power of death, can stop the march of life from frustration to fulfillment, from defeat to victory, and from here to eternity. The cross, then, is no longer the sacrament of death. It becomes an extension of the Last Supper. It becomes part of the sacrament of life. On the cross death is overtaken by life.

If the cross is the sacrament of life, it is also the sacrament of hope. This is again the way we must understand the Last Supper. Just as life that emerges as a sacrament over against death, hope too realizes itself as a sacrament in relation to hopelessness and despair. Jesus at the Last Supper must have known that if hope did not become a sacrament in the memories of his followers, the reign of God to which he bore witness would fade soon after his death. For hope to become a sacrament is for it to become a permanent part of life, an enduring element of faith. Hope as a sacrament is the power of life and energy for the future. Without it life is not life and future is not future.

This must have been what Paul wanted to say to the Christians in Rome when he wrote in his letter: "For I am convinced that there is nothing in death or life, in the realm of spirits or superhuman powers, in the world as it is or the world as it shall be, in the forces of the universe, in heights or depths—nothing in all creation that can separate us from the love of God in Christ Jesus our Lord" (Rom. 8:38-39). This is a big claim to make. But if hope is a sacrament, if it is part and parcel of life and faith, then one can make an even greater claim than the one Paul was making. The reign of God is the claim Jesus has made. It is the claim greater than the claim Paul, or for that matter, any of us, can dream of making. To sustain this claim of God's reign, to make it grow, and to carry it out in the world, hope has to be a part of that claim. How true this is when Jesus stares at the cross from the table of the Last Supper!

"For Nelia"

This is also true for many a woman and man for whom the reign of God means the sacrament of life and hope. This was certainly the case for Nelia Sancho, a political detainee at Camp Bicutan in the Philippines under martial law during the dictatorial rule of Ferdinand Marcos. For her the poem "For Nelia" was written:

> Why are you so hard? they ask.
> Why do you not bend a little?
>
> They call it grace
> Swaying like the bamboo
> with the wind.
>
> Listen to it weave
> the music of compromise
> While it kisses the ground
> at your feet.
>
> Even the bamboos however
> could only bend so much.
>
> When the storm comes
> listen to their cracking.
> They break one by one.
>
> You could only bend so much.
> I would prefer to be a rock
> smothered by the years
> but unswaying.
>
> Why are you so hard? they ask.
> Why do you not bend a little?[29]

One hears a deep cry of human suffering in this poem. One is also moved by the human will not to bend to the injustice and terror that cause that suffering.

The reign of God can be likened to many things. In fact Jesus himself likened it, as we have seen, to the mustard-seed and to the leaven. He also compared it to "the treasure lying buried in a field" (Matt. 13:44-46), to "a net let down into the sea catching fish of every kind" (Matt. 13:47-50). These are all images from daily life. God's reign for Jesus is such a

---

29. *Pintig: Poems and Letters from Philippine Prisoners* (Hong Kong: Research Centre for Philippine Concerns, 1979), 130.

"mundane" matter. Jesus made the awareness of God's reign a matter of everyday life, faith in God a matter of the heart, and religion more a matter of living than a matter of rituals to be observed and doctrines to be recited.

Had Jesus been born today as an Asian, how would he have likened the reign of God to his fellow Asians? He would have likened it, among other things, to the bamboo swaying in the wind. Bamboo is an eternal part of the Asian landscape. The fields spread far beyond the horizon are dotted with bamboo groves. And bamboo is planted in the small courtyard of a house in a crowded metropolis to bring nature and thus sanity back to the city dwellers who have forgotten the smell and taste of rustic air and beauty. "How shall we picture the reign of God?" Jesus would have asked. And without waiting for an answer, this is what he would have said: "The reign of God is like the bamboo swaying with the wind." The beauty and grace of God's reign is the beauty and grace of bamboo.

But then the storm arrives and the hurricane rages. The bamboo no longer sways gracefully with the wind. In the raging wind and in the torrential rain the bamboo bends until it "kisses the ground at your feet." This is a surrender to the fearful power of nature. And this is a compromise with demonic forces in human community. But neither surrender nor compromise saves the bamboo. The bamboo cracks. It breaks. As to God's reign, it does not surrender; it does not compromise. Would it crack and break like the bamboo under terrible pressure? A different image is called for. Another metaphor is needed. "I would prefer to be a rock," concludes the poem for Nelia Sancho, "smothered by the years but unswaying." The reign of God is like a rock, hard and solid before the forces that threaten to crack it and break it, unbending in a typhoon and unswaying in a tempest.

Those who have the power to crack and break their victims such as Nelia Sancho do not comprehend this. With sardonic smiles on their faces they ask: "Why are you so hard?" They want you to bend to the ground and kiss their feet. With the power to inflict pain and death on their victims they shout in your ears an obscene question: "Why do you not bend a little?" But you know your limit. To know that limit is theological wisdom. Not to go beyond that limit is political will. For if you bend a little more, you crack and break. Reaching that limit, the swaying bamboo must turn into an immovable rock. That moment to transform from the swaying bamboo to a solid rock is an eschatological moment. It is a decisive moment on which other moments depend, a moment to be remembered for all eternity.

Nelia Sancho grasped that moment. That is why she is remembered. In the company of many millions and millions of men and women throughout history she remains in the memories of God's reign as one whose life becomes a sacrament of hope not only for herself but for her fellow Filipinos. Paul must have understood this deeply when he concluded the words of the institution of the Lord's Supper saying: "For every time you eat this bread and drink the cup, you proclaim the death of the Lord, until he comes" (1 Cor. 11:26). "Until he comes"! This is not future but eternity. This is not something yet to happen. It happens now and will continue to happen. When the reign of God manifests itself as the sacrament of life and hope in and through the lives of people, Jesus is present. *He has come.* And he comes again and again, testifying that within human history is the history of the reign of God. Jesus comes in the memories of men and women who are transformed by it and who bear witness to it. The story of God's reign in action continues, therefore, not only into the next chapter but until Jesus comes.

CHAPTER 6

THE REIGN OF GOD IN ACTION (2)

> Now the chief priests and the whole council were looking for testimony against Jesus to put him to death; but they found none. For many gave false testimony against him, and their testimony did not agree. (Mark 14:55-56, NRSV)

Many Gave False Testimony against Him

The reign of God is not overcome by the reign of darkness. At the Last Supper Jesus instituted it into the memories of his followers. It becomes a sacrament to be remembered and manifested in human community. John the Evangelist sums this up in this pithy statement: "The light shines in the darkness, and the darkness has never mastered it" (John 1:5). This is the history of the reign of God within the history of the world. It is a history made with the sweat and blood of those who are both witnesses and bearers of God's reign. The reign of God is the meaning of history. It makes the light of God's saving love shine out of the darkness of human attempts to extinguish that light.

That is how we in retrospect must understand the trial of Jesus, the trial contrived to make an end to Jesus' claim of God's reign. It begins at the Sanhedrin, the Jewish supreme religious council of high priests, lawyers, and elders. By putting Jesus on trial, the council is putting God's reign on trial. Intent on doing away with Jesus, who addressed himself to the malaise of the prevailing religious tradition and practice, the whole council is blind to the fact that Jesus is the presence of God's reign. This is the tragedy that happens when religious authorities identify themselves with the truth and reject any other claims to the truth. But as we have seen, the reign of God manifests itself in the midst of attempts to discredit it, deny it, and reject it. As a matter of fact, the suppression of God's reign only contributes to its epiphany, to use the language from our discussion in the previous chapter. This is a supreme irony in the conflict between the reign of God and the powers of this world, on the one hand, and, on the other, the ground of our faith in the ultimate triumph of God's reign in history.

The trial of Jesus should not have taken place at the Sanhedrin in the first place. The Sanhedrin is no ordinary place. It is the highest religious court. It is where the best minds of the Jewish religion must have been concentrated. It is the heart of the religious tradition founded on the Exodus in the ancient past still remembered as God's deliverance of a people from slavery in Egypt. It is the center of Jewish spirituality where the sorrowful should be able to find comfort, the weak have their strength renewed, and the errant helped to find their way back to the God of mercy. If one wants to know the truth of God, one must go to the Sanhedrin. When one seeks to have justice done, one should be able to find it there. And when one needs the assurance of God's saving love, where else could one go except to the Sanhedrin?

The Sanhedrin is the last place where a person is taken by force and tried as a criminal. It should not be the place where falsehood is fabricated, injustice committed, and intrigue against the innocent hatched and carried out. How could it become an arena dominated by the darkest thoughts hidden in the depths of human hearts? And how could it stoop so low as to make a pact with the devil in an effort to silence the prophetic voice that speaks in the name of God's reign and on behalf of the poor and the dispossessed? The Sanhedrin must be, of all places, where the reign of God in love and justice prevails in the reign of darkness dominated by poisonous hate, unscrupulous power struggle, and shameless distortion of truth. It must be the final arbiter of truth in disputes over the issues of life and questions of faith.

But Jesus was taken to the Sanhedrin for trial like a criminal. And it is there in that court of justice and the council of truth that those accountable to God and to people had some persons give false testimony against him. "We heard him say," they said, " 'I will pull down this temple, made with hands, and in three days I will build another, not made with human hands' " (Mark 14:58; par. Matt. 26:61). This accusation, and a fatal accusation at that, does echo something of what Jesus is reported to have said in the account of his "cleansing of the Temple" in John's Gospel (2:14-22). The religious authorities must have remembered that incident with much chagrin. Their indignation must have been aroused again when they finally had Jesus brought before them. At last they were able to lay their hands on the man who dared to invade the very seat of their authority and challenge their religious practices. That incident must have sealed their determination to destroy him. All they needed was a pretext, a false reason, concealing their true intentions and justifying their premeditated act of murder.

According to John the Evangelist, Jesus did say in that heated confrontation with religious leaders something that provided the basis for the false testimony now brought against him. In John's account this is what Jesus said: "Destroy this temple, and in three days I will raise it up again" (John 2:19). This was enough. It was in fact more than enough. These few words became a powerful weapon in the hands of his accusers. Jesus might have said them. If he did not, they could have invented them and put them in his mouth. It is not what Jesus actually said that matters. Also it mattered little what Jesus might have meant by what he is testified to have said. Their power and authority must be maintained at any cost, even at the cost of truth. It must be protected by every possible means, even by means of distortion and lies.

But the fact that power cannot be maintained without distortion of truth exposes the terrible insecurity of power. The fact that authority must be protected with lies discloses the perverse nature of authority. This is what happens in the world of politics. This is how an authoritarian regime keeps itself in power. This is the open secret of a dictatorship. That it could also happen to religion, to any religion, is a matter of deep sadness. From primal religions to world religions, from primitive belief systems to highly sophisticated systems of religious teachings and rituals, truth is always at the risk of being betrayed, justice prostituted, and love perverted.

As a matter of fact, a rigid formulation of truth often impoverishes truth itself. A carefully orchestrated liturgical practice has the effect of numbing believers' religious sensibility. And a tightly controlled and regulated religious hierarchy is vulnerable to unscrupulous political scheming. What one witnesses here is a secular political power disguised as divine power to force believers into submission and conformity. This is what the Sanhedrin did to Jesus. There he was confronted with the religious leaders determined to maintain and carry out the official verdict on him for allegedly blaspheming God and desecrating the Temple.

But false testimonies leveled at him did not tally one with the other. Lies are lies precisely because they do not follow the logic of truth and reality. They are fabricated to distort the truth and to misrepresent the reality. By nature they cannot be authenticated. It is the power sanctioning lies that authenticates them. But is authentication in such a case different from falsification? And they of course carry no authority in themselves. It is the authority backing them that makes them appear authoritative. But authority such as this has no credibility. To know, then, what truth is, one must know who is naming the truth. To be sure that one is in touch with reality, one must look behind that reality for a clue as to who is identifying it. It is one of the sad facts of our world that truth is not free from untruth and reality is not free from unreality. Again it is in conflict with untruth that truth gets manifested. Also it is in exposing unreality that reality becomes recognizable.

Popular History versus Official History

The religious drama unfolded at the Sanhedrin where Jesus was tried raises, therefore, the question of who is telling the story—Jesus or his opponents? The question has far-reaching implications when applied to history. What is history if not the telling of stories? Stories are the matrix of history—stories of individual persons, a community, or a nation. History is human beings telling stories about themselves and about others. The accuracy of history depends, then, on who is telling the story, who is interpreting it, and who is making a version of it. Is the story told, for example, by the king or by the prophet? Is it narrated by the autocratic ruler or by the oppressed people? Does it speak for those who practice injustice and violence or does it echo the voice of the victims of injustice and violence? Is it a story of the rich or a story of the poor? In short, does the version of the story come from those who hold power or from those who have no power? This is the test of the verity of history.

The question of who is telling the story leads to the distinction between "popular" history and "official" history. Generally speaking, stories told by the king, the ruler, the rich and the powerful, become parts of "official" history taught in school, recited on official occasions, and preserved in the national archives and annals. To question it, to deviate from it, or to challenge it, is to play with fire. It is to commit unpatriotism, betrayal of national interest, and treason against the powers that be. In contrast, stories remembered and circulated by the ruled, the powerless, and the poor do not, of course, enjoy an official status. They are circulated among the people by word of mouth, passed on in handwritten copies, and preserved not in national archives and records, but in the memories of people. The history strung together from these stories is "popular" history—popular not in the sense of enjoying fame or gaining acclaim, but in the sense of having to do with *populus*, people, that is, women, men, and children who have to live and struggle under the shadow of ruthless power, exploitative economy, unjust social-political structures, or religious-cultural traditions. The distinction between popular history and official history must play a critical role in the theological semantic of history. That semantic must be based on our "theological bias" for popular history. Here is a poem written by a Filipino father about his daughters. It is an example of the stories that make up popular history:

My daughters shall not
Grow up beautiful
But they will inherit
The Wealth of my story
Neither will they be happy
For the hours of their day
Shall be counted
By ten times the troubles I now bear
But they will not weep
Nay, theirs shall be a countenance
Of firm defiance.[1]

What a history is contained in the story this little poem tries to tell! That history confronts us with a defiant soul of a Filipino father in prison.

It tells us about the struggle of men and women for freedom and democracy in those dark days of dictatorship. It shows us a society dominated by the demonic powers of oppression. This is the popular history of the people of the Philippines. It had to be written on a tissue, on a leaf, on a match box, and smuggled out of prison. It did not find its way into the official history manufactured by those in power. But it found its way into the hearts of hundreds of thousands of people both inside and outside that country. That little history was a big indictment against the regime that ruled the people with iron fists. That short history told a long story of people's suffering and their determination to be free.

Popular history, like this poem, consists of testimonies of people. Since official history is a history of self-justification, without popular history truth will never be known, justice vindicated, and right distinguished from wrong. Because of it, we can talk about theology of history. Thanks to it, we can come to grips with God's saving activity in the world. It forces our theological language to be the language of the victims of political oppression, economic exploitation, and racial, sexual, or religious discrimination. It compels us to listen to tales of longings told by those in despair. In popular history we are in touch with the restless human spirits seeking emancipation from the bondage of life.

If this is the case with the history of nations and peoples, it is also true with regard to the history of Christianity. It is time church his-

---

1. The poem is by Augustin Pagusara. See *Pintig: Poems and Letters from Philippine Prisons* (Hong Kong: Research Centre for Philippine Concerns, 1979), 18.

tory was retold as stories of countless Christian believers whose names
would never be known but without whom the history of the Christian church would be a history of power struggles within ecclesiastical
hierarchies and in the arena of theological controversies. This is particularly urgent for Christian churches outside the Western world. Each
Christian community in Asia, for example, should lose no more time
in recovering its own stories that cannot be found in the memoirs and
reports of Western missionaries, in the archives of the mission boards
of the "mother" churches, or in missiological writings of theologians
in the West. A very different history of the church will emerge out of
such first-hand experiences and accounts of struggles, social-political or
religious-cultural, that many Christians have to go through in a world alien
to Christianity.

You Are the Man!

The Christian Bible contains testimony after testimony against the powerful and the rich. What we read in it over and over is popular history over
against official history. The tension between these two histories is often
so great that they come to head-on collisions. The history of the prophets
in ancient Israel is born out of such tension and collisions. The prophetic
movements we encounter in the Hebrew Scriptures are basically people's
movements. These movements constitute the core of popular history over
against official history, that is, the history of kings and rulers. God is experienced as a God acting on behalf of the poor and the disinherited, seeking
justice for those to whom injustice is done, empowering the lowly and the
humiliated with the power of love to fight the violence committed against
them.

One of the most dramatic stories comes from the confrontation of
Nathan the prophet with King David (2 Sam. 11). King David had abused
his power and authority as head of the nation. He had committed adultery with the wife of Uriah, one of his military officers absent from home
on the battlefield. After he had failed in a cover-up attempt, he instructed
Joab the commander of the army to "put Uriah opposite the enemy where
the fighting is fiercest and then fall back, and leave him to meet his death"
(11:15). His order was carried out and Uriah was killed in the battle. With
Uriah dead and the period of mourning over, "David sent for her [Uriah's
wife] and brought her into the palace; she became his wife and bore him
a son" (11:27).

In the official history told by court historians this most despicable and
cowardly act committed by the king would either not have survived or have
been told in such a way as to justify what the king had done. The official

history of the incident reconstructed from a few clues one finds in the Book of Second Samuel would be something like this:

King David recalled Uriah, one of his military officers, from the front for a first-hand report on the campaign against Ammon and Rabbah. David asked him for news of Joab, the commander, and the troops and how the campaign was going (11:6-7). The king, commander-in-chief, could hardly wait to be briefed on the progress of the military operation and to express his personal concern for his fighting men. A model king indeed!

And of course his concern was extended to Uriah, an able and trusted military officer, who hurried back from the battlefield at the king's order, visibly tired but in high spirits. After the briefing was over, he said to the officer: "Go down to your house and wash your feet after your journey" (11:8). Uriah, being a responsible soldier in total solidarity with the fighting men he left behind on the front, declined the favor and "did not return to his house; he lay down by the palace gate with the king's servants" (11:9). The king, ever benevolent and magnanimous, sent words urging him: "You have had a long journey; why did you not go home?" (11:10). Still, Uriah the officer was not persuaded. This was his reply: "Israel and Judah are under canvas, and so is the Ark, and my lord Joab and your majesty's officers are camping in the open; how can I go home to eat and drink and to sleep with my wife? By your life, I cannot do this!" (11:11). A model soldier indeed!

The king, intent on doing his fighting man a favor, would not take no for an answer. He was not so heartless as to send him back to the front at once. He not only permitted Uriah to stay another day (11:12), but "invited him to eat and drink with him" (11:13). No greater honor could a soldier receive from the king, his commander-in-chief! Ever grateful and high-spirited, Uriah then returned to the front to resume his fighting duty.

The official history would have ended here, extolling the virtue of the king and praising the loyalty of his military officer. There would not be a word alluding to the king's illicit relationship with Uriah's wife. His letter sent to Joab, the commander, with an instruction to have Uriah killed in the battle would have of course been shredded. And perhaps there might have been a footnote saying how the king personally saw to it that the widow of his faithful soldier was well provided for.

But an official history such as this could not have remained unchallenged. The challenge came from a popular history, the story told by people by word of mouth first and then gaining publicity through the action taken by Nathan the prophet. The confrontation between the prophet and the king is the confrontation between popular history and official history. True to the spirit and style of a popular storyteller, Nathan began with a story taken from the daily lives of people, a story seemingly unrelated to what the king had done. "In a certain town there lived two men," Nathan began,

> one rich, the other poor. The rich man had large flocks and herds; the poor man had nothing of his own except one little ewe lamb he had bought. He reared it, and it grew up in his home together with his children. It shared from his food, drank from his cup and nestled in his arms; it was like a daughter to him. One day a traveller came to the rich man's house, and he, too mean to take something from his own flock or herd to serve to his guest, took the poor man's lamb and served that up. (2 Sam. 12:1-4)

A simple but poignant story pointing up the injustice done by the rich and powerful to the poor and powerless, a story that could not fail to provoke anger even from King David. "As the Lord lives," he exclaimed, "the man who did this deserves to die!" (12:5). But little he knew he was condemning himself with his own words. Without wasting any more words Nathan came straight to the point and said to the king: "You are the man!" (12:7). All pretension gone, King David collapsed before the towering figure of Nathan the prophet. Even his kingly power and authority could not protect the official history from the challenge of the moral power and authority of a popular history.

Nathan must have been a remarkable storyteller. And it is storytellers like him who had the capacity to dethrone an official history from the seat of pretension, arrogance, and oppression with a popular history. Without the stories of people told by the prophets, what would have been there in our Bible to make it exciting and moving? Without them, how are we to know ways in which God's saving activity was perceived and experienced by people in those ancient times? Popular history is the history of people's testimonies against the official history of kings, dictators, the powerful, and the rich. It is the stories of men, women, and children in struggle against the powers that oppress them and dehumanize them.

"I Saw All Israel Scattered on the Mountains"

Another example of popular history in the struggle against official history is found in the account of the battle Ahab, king of Israel, is about to wage against the Aramaeans (1 Kings 22; par. 2 Chron. 18). The story begins with

King Ahab declaring the reason why an attack must be launched against Aram. "You know that Ramoth-gilead belongs to us," he intoned to those assembled at his court, "and yet we do nothing to recover it from the king of Aram" (22:3). This sounds very familiar even today—recovery of the lost territory! This is an official creed. This is a matter of national honor. When the king declares it, who can disagree with it and not be tried for treason? When the president announces it, who can dissent from it and not be branded as unpatriotic? But in human history how many wars have been waged and how many lives have perished all because of this official creed, this national honor!

The four hundred "prophets" summoned to advise the king knew they were expected to give religious blessings on the war about to be waged. Here a curious thing happens—politics feigns piety! Politics suddenly shows interest in religion. It makes a show of humility, summoning prophets to the royal court, inviting religious leaders to the palace, sending for theologians to the presidential office. A great honor for religion? In appearance, maybe, but in reality it signals danger. In many cases when politics condescends to religion for advice, religious leaders would be elated with a sense of self-importance and would spare little thought on a trap that may have been set for them. This is particularly the case in a feudal society or in an authoritarian country. They would even begin to talk politics with some flair. What matters now is power politics and not religion without political power. Religion and politics thus enter into a pact—a pact that compromises both religious faith and political wisdom. This is precisely the danger. When a political decree gains religious sanction, it becomes even more official. And the more official it becomes, the more brutal and terrifying the consequences are going to be. History, from ancient times to the present day, is not short of complicities between politics and religion that change the course of history and plunge the world into confusion, madness, and destruction.

An official history is now manufactured at the court of Ahab, king of Israel, with the full support of the four hundred prophets summoned by the king. With one voice they said to the king: "Attack Ramoth-gilead and win the day; the Lord will deliver it into your hands" (1 Kings 22:12; also 22:6). One of them, Zedekiah son of Kenaanah, even wanted to excel others in his support of the war. He made himself horns of iron and declared in the name of God: "With horns like these you will gore the Aramaeans and make an end of them" (22:11). Religion, when blinded by power politics, is capable of most murderous language. It must have been a soul-stirring scene at the king's court with four hundred prophets predicting defeat for the Aramaeans and victory for their king in the name of God.

But there is another history—a popular history—to be heard from a lone prophet called Micaiah. This solitary figure must have appeared even more solitary in the midst of the four hundred prophets loudly clamoring their support for the king's decision for war. But as the event unfolded, it became clear that Micaiah was not alone. What he had to say must have been what people outside the king's palace wanted to say. His fear must have been the fear of the men who would be conscripted to fight the war. His anxiety must have been the anxiety of the wives and mothers who would lose their husbands and sons to the war. And with him must have been also the God misrepresented again and again in human quests for greed, power, and glory.

It was this prophet Micaiah who spoke up against the war. Instead of victory he predicted defeat. "I saw all Israel," he must have said in a solemn voice quivering with pain, "scattered on the mountains, like sheep without a shepherd" (1 Kings 22:17). This must have been how the people thought the war would be. This was the "popular" version of the outcome of the attack on Ramoth-gilead. The king, his generals, and the four hundred prophets were of course enraged. Micaiah was arrested and put in prison. "Official history" always seems powerful. It has the power to intimidate popular history, to silence it, to imprison it. But that power always proves self-destructive. It cannot destroy others without destroying itself. In contrast, popular history—written with the blood and lives of people—seems powerless. But strangely enough, in its powerlessness it has the power to purge a nation and redeem a people on the brink of destruction and death. The popular history for which Micaiah stood was vindicated in the shambles of the official history fabricated by the king, his courtiers, and the four hundred prophets. Israel was roundly put to rout. King Ahab died from the wound inflicted by a stray arrow and "the dogs licked up his blood, and the prostitutes washed themselves in it" (1 Kings 22:38, NRSV).

Episodes such as this between prophet Micaiah and King Ahab or the one between Nathan the prophet and King David discussed earlier tell us that history not checked and balanced by popular history is a distortion of what must have happened. It can be a false history distorting facts and misrepresenting realities. Is it not true that most "official history" is such history? Much of the "official history" is in fact unofficial history. It lacks legitimacy and commands no immediate credibility. A theology of history cannot be constructed on the basis of it. For it to be credible, it has to go to popular history and learn from the latter. It has to discern how popular history, branded as "unofficial history" and censored by "official history," turns out to be the "official" history—a history genuinely reflecting what people have to go through and how they fare in the world of conflict and confrontation of powers.

A Friend of Sinners

Jesus on trial at the Sanhedrin, then, is popular history on trial. This is how we must understand the confrontation between Jesus and the religious leaders. Tried with him is a host of the women and men with whom Jesus has been associated—prostitutes, tax-collectors, sinners, people who are poor, men, women, and children who are socially and religiously discriminated against. His opponents accused him saying: "Look at him! A glutton and a drinker, a friend of tax-collectors and sinners!" (Matt. 11:19; Luke 7:34). Jesus had no apologies for being a friend of "sinners." He himself made it known that this was precisely what he wanted to be. He declared, when challenged by the leaders and officers of the established religion: "I did not come to call the virtuous, but sinners" (Mark 2:17; pars. Matt. 9:13; Luke 5:32). And as if to make sure everyone, including his opponents, heard him and understood him, he told a parable to illustrate the point he was making. "Two men went up to the temple to pray," Jesus began in his usual manner as a storyteller,

> one a Pharisee and the other a tax-collector. The Pharisee stood up and prayed this prayer: "I thank you, God, that I am not like the rest of humankind—greedy, dishonest, adulterous—or, for that matter, like this tax-collector. I fast twice a week; I pay tithes on all that I get." But the other kept his distance and would not even raise his eyes to heaven, but beat upon his breast, saying, "God, have mercy on me, sinner that I am." It was this man, I tell you, and not the other, who went home acquitted of his sins. (Luke 18:10-14)

The contrast between the two men is never greater. But this is not just a contrast between these two persons. It is a contrast between two prayers, two traditions, two histories.

On the one hand is the Pharisee who "radiates self-confidence from the beginning."[2] His prayer does not radiate his own self-confidence only, however. It radiates the self-confidence of his proud tradition, the religious hierarchy, and the whole complexity of rituals and teachings. In other words, the prayer is the epitome of the entire official history. As such it is not so much a prayer to God as an articulation of the self-understanding of the religious authorities that have assumed the right to speak on God's behalf and the power to regulate the lives of believers. It is an affirmation of what the authorities regard as right and proper. This is an assertion of self-righteousness disguised as prayer.

---

2. Josef Ernst, *Das Evangelium nach Lukas* (Regensburg: Verlag Friedrich Pustet, 1977), 496.

The tone of judgment is unmistakable. "I am not like the rest of human-kind," says the Pharisee, "greedy, dishonest, adulterous." This is typical of an official history. The term "official history" itself is a judgmental term. It judges other stories as flattering and thus unofficial and excludes them from its fold. "The rest of humankind" in this case includes all men, women, and children outside the religious community with exclusive membership. In actual fact "the rest of humankind" is the great majority of humanity. When it comes to Asia, "the rest of humankind" outside the Christian church is 95 percent of Asia's population. It is a lot to exclude from the official history of Christianity. The percentage varies from country to country, of course. In Thailand "the rest of humankind" are the Buddhist believers who make up 99 percent of the population. In Indonesia it will have to refer to the 85 percent of the population who are Muslims.

And this is a very sweeping judgment to make. The judgment is not based on sociological studies. It is not the result of a public opinion survey. Nor is it a conclusion after a careful analysis and reflection. An official history is "official" because it needs none of these things. It does not have to be tested. It does not allow itself to be questioned. Appeal to reason and common sense is forbidden. An official history refuses to consider there may be some persons among "the rest of humankind" who are not greedy, dishonest, adulterous. And it will not allow the suggestion that within the rank and file of those enjoying privilege, power, and authority there are some who are greedy, adulterous, dishonest. What matters is not "orthopraxis" but "orthodoxy," to use two contrasting expressions in the vocabulary of Latin American theology.

The tax-collector in Jesus' parable, however, stands for another kind of history—unofficial history. Even the tax-collector himself seems to be resigned to the unofficial nature of who he is and what he does. He accepts the fact that he has no place in a respectable society, not to say in the community of those who are saved. He has braced himself for prayer at the Temple, but "keeps his distance and would not even raise his eyes to heaven, but beats upon his breast"—the very gesture and expression of repentance.[3] This is all he says in his prayer: "God, have mercy on me, sinner that I am." There is no derogatory mentioning of others. Nor is there self-assertion at the expense of "the rest of humankind."

The story of this tax-collector is the story of the "sinners" Jesus be-friended. His history is the history of women, men, and children estranged from society and alienated from exclusive religious circles. Jesus identified himself with that history we call "popular history." It is this popular his-

---

3. Ibid., 497.

tory of the tax-collector and not the official history of the Pharisee that Jesus affirmed and commended. "I tell you," he said, "it was this man and not the other who went home acquitted of his sins." The tax-collector *is acquitted*. His story is legitimized. His history is accepted as official in the reign of God. And with him other "sinners," Gentiles, prostitutes, the dispossessed, are also acquitted, their stories legitimized and their histories accepted as official.

Is not this history the history of the reign of God? Just recall Jesus' declaration that the reign of God belongs to the poor, the hungry, the persecuted. And also remember how Jesus announced God's salvation to Zacchaeus the tax-collector (Luke 19:1-10). The history of "sinners" is accepted as the history of God's reign. And what could be more "official" than the history of God's reign? How could a self-styled "official" history such as that of the Pharisee not turn out to be a history with no legitimacy and credibility?

Illumined by a background such as this, the trial of Jesus before the Sanhedrin is in reality not the trial of Jesus as an individual person who offended the religious authorities with his radical interpretation of the religious traditions and teachings and with his unconventional ways of life and ministry. It is the trial of men, women, and children who live on the fringes of society and religion but who are at the center of God's reign. It is the trial of the popular history of these people. It is the trial of God's reign, which they constitute and represent. But the tragedy is that those religious leaders who engineered that trial cannot see beyond Jesus as a challenge to their power and authority. In the face of Jesus they do not see the faces of the people outside the Sanhedrin. In the claims of Jesus they do not hear the claims of the poor and the dispossessed. In the agony and anger of Jesus they do not perceive the agony and anger of the oppressed. In short, they refuse to admit that perhaps Jesus stands for what is truly true and genuinely good in their faith and tradition. They are not willing to concede that Jesus is the bearer of witness to God's reign, that he is that very reign of God.

A religious claim must be proved wrong and outrageous by a counter religious claim. This is how the Sanhedrin went about its trial of Jesus. Their counterclaim, as we have seen, is focused almost solely on what Jesus allegedly said about the Temple. "Destroy this temple," he is reported to have said, "and in three days I will raise it up again" (John 2:19). These words, even if actually said by Jesus, now gained a different nuance in the witness of those brought in to testify against him. They pointed their finger at him and testified that this is what he had said: "*I will destroy* this temple that is made with hands, and in three days I will build another, not made with hands" (Mark 14:58, NRSV; emphasis added).

Is this what Jesus in fact said? Did Jesus mean that he himself, and not with anyone else, he alone, singlehandedly, would destroy this formidable Temple that had taken forty-six years to build and was not yet completed, and would build it up again within a mere three days?[4] Despite his anger provoked by what he saw done at the Temple, Jesus could not have been prompted to declare: "*I will destroy* it!" His purpose was not to destroy the Temple but to cleanse it. His aim was not to pull it down but to transform it, making it once again the house of God instead of a marketplace (John 2:16). His mission was to restore the Temple that had turned into a den of robbers to what it should be: a house of prayer (Mark 12:17; pars. Matt. 21:13; Luke 19:45). His opponents could not have misheard Jesus. In that immediate encounter when Jesus was face to face with them and they were face to face with Jesus, they must have understood him not to be bragging as if he had the power to do whatever he wished to the Temple, that heart of Jewish piety, that awesome center of Jewish history, and that massive symbol of the hope of the Jews, including Jesus himself. They must have realized in the thick of the controversy that these words were directed to them as a challenge—a challenge that sought their conversion from their religious ways.

"Destroy this temple." Those words "are in effect a conditional sentence."[5] "According to John in the present passage," it has been pointed out, "Jesus only said that *if the Jews destroyed* the Temple, in three days he would raise it up."[6] The onus of a catastrophe such as the destruction of the Temple is on the religious authorities. This must be what Jesus was trying to say. It is not he who is to be responsible for such a catastrophe. Even so, he could not have meant that those who hold religious power over people would literally and physically destroy the Temple. It was not they but the Romans who were going to do that eventually, in 70 C.E. By destruction Jesus must have meant desecration. The desecration of the Temple takes place before his eyes—the Temple has turned into a marketplace, and instead of being a house of prayer it has become a den of robbers. The complicity of the Jewish authorities in the desecration is more than obvious. And it must have been an open secret that a lot of corruption

---

4. "The main Temple building, which contained the Holy Place and Most Holy Place, had been rebuilt by Herod the Great in eighteen months, beginning in 20–19 B.C., but work on the other parts of the total Temple area had been going on during the rest of the forty-six years and was not ended; the entire group of buildings was not completed until about A.D. 64, shortly before Romans destroyed the Temple in A.D. 70." See Floyd V. Filson, *Saint John: Layman's Bible Commentaries* (London: SCM Press, 1963), 43.

5. C. K. Barrett, "John," in *Peake's Commentary of the Bible*, ed. Matthew Black and H. H. Rowley (London: Thomas Nelson, 1962), 848b.

6. J. H. Bernard, *A Critical and Exegetical Commentary on the Gospel according to St. John*, International Critical Commentary (Edinburgh: T. & T. Clarke, 1928), 1:93.

took place in the business transactions ostensibly conducted for the sake of worshiping in the Temple. Jesus touched the most sensitive nerves of the religious hierarchy and they were not going to let him get away with it. The official history is severely challenged. To maintain the "officiality" of their history, and with that officiality their power and authority, the popular history, the history of the people and the history of God's reign, must be opposed and silenced, by any possible means, even the distortion of facts and false accusation.

Justice and Law

The nerve center of power cannot be touched with impunity. This is true with political power. Political power, despite its ideological fanaticism, formidable machinery of control, and exaggerated show of force on every possible occasion, has very sensitive and vulnerable nerve systems. To calm their nervous systems, authoritarian rulers resort to oppression. To reinforce those vulnerable systems, they act and react with intimidation, torture, imprisonment, or execution. It is not very much different with religious power. This latter is also capable of the same atrocities and an irrational course of action.

It is to that nerve center of the Jewish religious authorities to which Jesus exposes himself. "Alas for you, scribes and Pharisees, hypocrites!" Jesus is remembered to have lashed out at the religious leaders (Matt. 23:1-36; par. Luke 11:37-52). "You snakes, you vipers' brood!" (Matt. 23:33, NRSV), he castigated them. "What have we done to deserve such vituperation?" the religious leaders must have protested in indignation. Jesus is direct and specific, however. He does not prevaricate. He does not soften his tone with metaphorical language. Nor does he change his prophetic posture to a diplomatic posture. Jesus expresses himself in such a forthright manner that his followers must have "broken out in a cold sweat" (*nieh yi pa han*, in Chinese, literally, to squeeze out a handful of sweat). "You shut the door of the kingdom of Heaven in people's faces" (Matt. 23:13), Jesus accuses them. They treat God's reign as if it were a kingdom, a territory under their control, or a piece of real estate at their disposal. They take it for granted that they are in control of the entrance way to it.

Jesus goes on and confronts his opponents with the fundamental question of what the law is really about. "You pay tithes of mint and rue and every garden herb" (Luke 11:42; par. Matt. 23:23), Jesus conceded. They must have been meticulous about it. We remember that Pharisee in Jesus' parable who prayed and said: "I fast twice a week; I pay tithes on all that I get" (Luke 18:12). How zealously he keeps the law! He is in fact overzealous. "The Law prescribes fasting only once a year,"[7] but here he is, fasting twice a week! All in all, the religious leaders are model observants of the law. They should be commended. But, instead of commending them, Jesus saw in their practice of tithing nothing more than legalism that fosters self-righteousness and spiritual pride. Again in that parable of two men going up to the Temple to pray, this is what Jesus sharply denounced when he had the Pharisee pray to God and say: "I am not like the rest of humankind, for that matter, like this tax-collector."

"You," Jesus addressed them with the directness that no one had dared. "You neglect justice and the love of God" (Luke 11:42; par. Matt 23:23). This surely is the heart of the matter. Is there law that neglects justice? Is law still law when it ceases to do justice to "justice"? But what does Jesus mean by justice? For Jesus, "the *krisis* (justice) is the act of judging righteously, a *krinein* (judge) that ever defends those who are wronged and thus is synonymous with *dikaioun* (declaring as righteous) and parallel with *sozein* (to save)."[8] Justice, in Jesus' view, is not the state of being righteous, a state that easily leads to self-righteousness, but the act of judging righteously, a judgment based on facts and respect for truth. Law is justice when it defends the wronged party, particularly when the latter is poor and defenseless. It is injustice when it harbors the guilty party because the latter is rich and powerful.

Jesus is not against the law as such. "Do not suppose that I have come to abolish the law and prophets," he declares. "I did not come to abolish, but to complete" (Matt. 5:17). What he was against is the law without regard for justice—the law practiced by those who hold power and enforced on those who are powerless. He had no quarrel with the law; it is with those who turn the law against the defenseless that he was quarrelling with. It is not so much the law as the religious rulers who use the law to their advantage that he was at odds with. In what he said against the religious authorities of his day we hear a strong echo of what the prophets pronounced to their leaders in ancient Israel. In him we seem to hear these stirring words of the prophet Amos:

> You that turn justice to poison
> and thrust righteousness to the ground,
> you that hate those who bring the wrongdoer to court
> and abominate them who speak nothing less than truth....
>
> (Amos 5:7-10)

---

7. Ernst, *Das Evangelium nach Lukas*, 496.

8. R. C. H. Lenski, *The Interpretation of St. Matthew's Gospel* (Minneapolis: Augsburg Publishing House, 1964), 908.

The law is confused by those who administer it. It is perverted by them. It is used by them as an instrument of oppression. By perverse use of the law they foster suspicion among people and encourage intrigue in society.

Society is full of cases of how law is used to intimidate the poor and the powerless and to protect the rich and the powerful, of how it is manipulated to defend the wrongdoers and punish the wronged, of how it serves the interests of the ruling class and humiliates the ruled. A case in point is what is called Legalist School in ancient China. The Legalist School "accepted no authority except that of the ruler and looked for no precedent. Its aim was political control of the state and the population, a control to be achieved through an intensive set of laws, backed up by generous rewards and severe punishments."[9] The Legalists who belonged to the school "were primarily interested in the accumulation of power, the subjugation of the individual to the state, uniformity of thought, and the use of force. It is not surprising that they were instrumental in setting up the dictatorship of Ch'in (221-206 B.C.E.), in unifying China in 221 B.C.E., and in instituting the tightest regimentation of life and thought in Chinese history."[10] An example such as this is of course not unique to China. It is an all too familiar story that one hears both in the East and in the West over and over from ancient times to the present day. Dictatorship is born out of making law serve power and authority.

Unfortunately, political history such as this is not entirely foreign to religions. A religion that is expected to put people right with God and with one another—this is what justice (*krisis* in the New Testament and *mishpat* in the Hebrew Bible) means primarily—puts them wrong with God and one with another. It rules its adherents with unreasonable demands and controls their life and faith with fear. It regulates their duties to the most minute details. The Jewish regulations, for example, "demand that the tithes be paid on even the small flavoring herbs of which a family might grow a few, such as mint, dill, and cumin."[11] The rabbinic tractates, though compiled at the beginning of the third century C.E., "illustrate the kind of mentality to which Jesus refers here."[12] These tractates, we are told, "have laid down a general rule about tithes: Whatever used for food, kept watch over, and grown from the soil is subject to tithes."[13]

All such religious minutiae must have proven burdensome, especially to the people who had to eke out their living with difficulty. It must be for

---

9. Wing-Tsit Chan, *A Source Book in Chinese Philosophy* (Princeton: Princeton University Press, 1963), 251.

10. Ibid.

11. Lenski, *The Interpretation of St. Matthew's Gospel*, 908.

12. Joseph A. Fitzmyer, *The Gospel according to Luke, X–XXIV*, Anchor Bible (New York: Doubleday & Company, 1985), 948.

13. Ibid.

this reason that Jesus was prompted to say: "Alas for you lawyers also. You load people with intolerable burdens, and will not lift a finger to lighten the load" (Luke 11:46). What an irony! Religion, instead of lightening the burdens people bear both physically and spiritually, loads them with even heavier burdens. What Jesus pointed out with such candidness regarding his own religion is also true of Christianity and of other religions. These words of Jesus should be an essential part of a critique of religions. They tell us what a religion must not be. They show us where a religious tradition can go wrong. They remind us that religious authorities can betray God in the name of God and can do disservice to people by giving them a distorted experience of God—an angry God, a vengeful God, an autocratic God, a God who makes endless demands.

Two histories are thus brought into sharp contrast at the Sanhedrin. On the one hand is Jesus, who represents the poor, the disinherited, and the oppressed. The false testimony brought against him is at the same time a false testimony against such people. It testifies that people are not impoverished, that they are not exploited, that they are not oppressed. And if they find themselves outside the community of the saved, they themselves are to blame. Since they engage in activities and professions forbidden by the religious traditions, they exclude themselves from the protection of their religion. It is because they are Gentiles or make themselves Gentiles that they are disqualified from being members of the religious community. The question is not raised as to why they are engaged in those activities and professions and as to why they are Gentiles and make themselves Gentiles. Besides, those activities and professions forbidden by the religious authorities, are they to be condemned outright? Is to be a Gentile itself a cause of religious condemnation?

It is popular history that Jesus represented at the Sanhedrin. This popular history is none other than the history of God's reign. When the religious authorities testified against Jesus, they were testifying against popular history. And as they testified against popular history, they were at the same time testifying against the reign of God. They were in fact saying that the reign of God does not belong to the poor, that it shows no preference for the oppressed, that it does not deal with those laden with burdens of life and conscience. The reign of God, and they would prefer to call it the "kingdom of God," is the power to judge those at odds with the religious establishment. "The kingdom of God" is the manifestation of ecclesiastical authority against those who question the truths it represents. It is the domination of people according to the rules and laws established by the traditions. For them Jesus is everything their "kingdom of God" is not. And the men, women, and children, particularly the "sinners," in his company deserve no place in it. The ecclesiastical authorities sit in judgment of Jesus and the people who represent the popular history of the nation. They are the defenders of the official version of "the kingdom of God."

What we see at the supreme council of priests and teachers is the confrontation of the popular history of Jesus and the official history of the religious authorities. Much was at stake, especially on the part of the official history. It had to maintain its officiality. It had to defend its legitimacy. It had to assert its power and authority. In contrast the popular history that Jesus carried with him to the trial had no officiality to maintain; its "popularity," its being of people, in itself made it more "official" than any other claim to officiality. That popular history did not have to defend its legitimacy. The fact that it was the history of the people in suffering, pain, and helplessness proved its legitimacy. And it had no need to assert its power and authority. In actual fact, it did not have the kind of power and authority that official history claimed and exercised. Its power was of an entirely different kind: it was a moral power, a power derived from the saving love of God. Its authority was also of a completely different kind: it was an authority grown out of the humanity touched by the compassionate hand of God.

This may be the reason why Jesus did not feel compelled to speak out in his own defense. He kept his silence most of the time. It was the religious authorities jealous of their own power and anxious to assert their authority that had to speak. And when they spoke, it was not true testimony but false testimony that they made. It was not the reign of God that concerned them but the kingdom of their power and prestige. "Are you the Messiah?" They finally came out with the only question that had haunted them. This was the one essential question that mattered to them.

The question must have long disquieted them. In comparison, the accusation that Jesus boasted to destroy the Temple in three days merely set the stage that enabled them to raise this question. They must have been impatient to get to the heart of their concern. They could hardly wait to get to this question. The Temple faded into the background. The high priest and other religious leaders knew the Temple was standing there intact, Jesus or not. It was the question of messiahship, the question of someone ordained by God to save the Jewish nation from their political adversities and to restore the kingdom of Israel to the colonized nation. But the Jews, they reasoned, do not need someone like Jesus to destabilize their already precarious relations with the Roman colonizers. Besides, who could play the messiah, if ever one were needed, except the religious leaders themselves? This man called Jesus, brought before them for interrogation, must be a messianic pretender. They had dealt with many messianic pretenders before and had acquired enough experience to deal with this one. Jesus, this man from Nazareth, must be silenced.

The Grand Inquisitor

This scene of Jesus' trial before the Sanhedrin reminds us of the famous story of the Grand Inquisitor in Dostoyevsky's *The Brothers Karamazov.* "The action of my poem," Ivan Karamazov, a professed atheist, said to his younger brother, Aloysha, a deeply religious person incapable of harboring evil thoughts against anyone, "takes place in Spain, in Seville, during the most terrible time of the Inquisition." In his infinite mercy, Jesus

> once more walked among men and women in the semblance of human being as he had walked among people for thirty-three years fifteen centuries ago. He came down into the hot "streets and lanes" of the southern city just at the moment when, a day before, nearly a hundred heretics had been burnt all at once by the cardinal, the Grand Inquisitor, *ad majorem gloriam Dei* in "a magnificent auto da fé... " He appeared quietly, inconspicuously, but everyone—and that is why it is so strange—recognized him.... The people are drawn to him by an irresistible force, they surround him, they throng about him, they follow him.

Then what happened in Palestine fifteen hundred years ago happens once again in Seville, in southern Spain, in the fifteenth century. Jesus blesses the women, men, and children who are following him. He heals the sick, comforts the sorrowful, and raises the dead. The Inquisitor, an old man of nearly ninety, sees all this. He has him arrested and locked in "the dark, narrow, vaulted prison in the old building of the Sacred Court."

A most bizarre scene is to unfold between Jesus and the old Grand Inquisitor that very night of Jesus' arrest and imprisonment.

> Amid the profound darkness, the iron door of the prison is suddenly opened and the old Grand Inquisitor himself slowly enters the prison with a light in his hand. He is alone and the door at once closes behind him. He stops in the doorway and gazes for a long time, for more than a minute, into his face. At last he approaches him slowly, puts the lamp on the table, and says to him:
>
> "Is it you, You?"
>
> But receiving no answer, he adds quickly: "Do not answer, be silent. And indeed, what can you say? I know too well what you would say. Besides, you have no right to add anything to what you have said already in the days of old. Why, then, did you come to meddle with us? For you have come to meddle with us, and you know it. But do you know what is going to happen tomorrow? I know not who you are and I don't want to know, but tomorrow I shall condemn you and

burn you at the stake as the vilest of heretics, and the same people who today kissed your feet, will at the first sign from me rush to rake up the coals at your stake tomorrow. Do you know that? Yes, perhaps you do know it," he added after a moment of deep reflection without taking his eyes off his prisoner for an instant.[14]

This is a most profound commentary on Jesus' trial, a commentary inspired by the notorious Spanish Inquisition in the fifteenth century. It came from a novelist and not from a biblical scholar. This is powerful "contextual theology." It makes the trial of Jesus contemporaneous—a happening that takes place again and again within the history of Christianity and also outside it.

"Are you the Messiah?" The religious authorities that tried Jesus asked him. The question must have obsessed them. "Is it you, You?" the Spanish Inquisitor fifteen hundred years later asked Jesus. The question must have disturbed him deeply. These two questions, though formulated differently, are in fact one and the same question. What concerned both the Jewish authorities and the Spanish Inquisitor is the identity of Jesus. But what they are really interested in is not objective truths about Jesus but their own power and authority. Jesus healed the sick, assured God's forgiveness for the repentant, sided with the poor and the oppressed. Instead of seeing in all this manifestations of God's reign, the religious authorities in Jesus' time and in later times such as the time of the Inquisition confronted Jesus as someone who undermined their authority and challenged their power. In the story of "the Grand Inquisitor" we witness once again the conflict between popular history and official history, between the reign of God and the power of the ecclesiastical authorities, between the men, women, and children in physical and spiritual need and the ruling hierarchy intent on maintaining its privilege and power.

Jesus did upset the social, political, and religious status quo. Jesus *means* new interpretation of the time-honored traditions. "The sabbath was made for human being and not human being for the sabbath" (Mark 2:27), he declared. Jesus *means* recovery of the true spirit of the law. "You have heard," he taught people, "that they were told, 'Love your neighbor and hate your enemy.' But what I tell you is this: Love your enemies and pray for your persecutors" (Matt. 5:43-44). Jesus *means* a fundamental change of values. He is reported to have concluded his parable of the rich fool who vainly sought security in his wealth with these words: "So it is with those who store up treasure for themselves but are not rich toward

---

14. Fyodor Dostoyevsky, *The Brothers Karamazov*, trans. David Magarshack (Harmondsworth, England: Penguin Books, 1982), 291–93.

God" (Luke 12:21, NRSV). Jesus also *means* life lived in its fullness and authenticity. "Those who find their life," he is remembered to have told his disciples, "will lose it, and those who lose their life for my sake will gain it" (Matt. 10:39, NRSV; par. Luke 17:33). In all this Jesus *means* what God's reign must be: God's reign is love and not vengeance, it is forgiveness and not condemnation, it is justice and not exploitation, it is humility and not arrogance, and, above all, it is life dedicated to the cause of God's reign.

Because of this, and perhaps precisely because of this, the religious authorities then and now have to direct that question at Jesus, "Are you the Messiah?" "Is it you, You?" But it may be that they do not expect an answer from Jesus. That is why the Spanish Inquisitor "adds quickly: 'Do not answer, be silent.'" In other words, they know the answer already. That question about Jesus' messiahship is their own question to begin with; it is not Jesus' own question. Implied in their question is this: Are you the Messiah in the line of King David? In that case you are a self-styled messiah. Are you the Messiah who wishes to command the religious and political allegiance of our nation? Then you are nothing more than a messianic imposter. Or are you the Messiah who seeks to restore political independence to Israel? Then you are just a messianic pretender. We, and not you, are the messianic hope of our people. Our religion, and not yours, is the messianic religion. Our tradition, and not your innovation, is the messianic tradition. Our law, and not your absurd interpretation of it, contains the messianic truth—the truth about God's salvation.

The trial of Jesus at the hands of the religious authorities both in the first century and in the fifteenth century, or for that matter, in any century, is not the trial of Jesus. It turns into the trial of the religious authorities themselves, the trial of those who try him. It is the trial of their power and authority—the legitimacy of their power and the credibility of their authority are on trial. It is the trial of the traditions which they represent and with which they protect themselves. It is the trial of the religious systems that can condemn a person with a false testimony, that can pass a verdict on an innocent person on the basis of what they determine that person to be.

A subtle reversal of role has taken place. Jesus the accused becomes the accuser, and the accusing religious authorities becomes the accused. Jesus the judged is the judge, and the judging religious authorities become the judged. And in this role reversal at the Sanhedrin Jesus, who did not respond to the false testimony, who said nothing in defense against vicious accusations, proves an eloquent witness to God's reign—the reign of love, justice, and freedom in the midst of the people oppressed, impoverished, and fallen victims to the powers and principalities of this world. That role reversal and that eloquent testimony to God's reign were to happen again when Jesus was taken to Pontius Pilate, the Roman governor, for a political trial. And it is this same role reversal and the same witness to God's reign that take place again and again today at military tribunals where men and women, whether Christian or not, are put on trial for their struggle for justice, freedom, and democracy.

For the time being, however, the religious authorities that tried Jesus seem to be having their way. Dostoyevsky brilliantly captured the scene of the mock trial and exposed its outrageousness when he made the old Spanish Inquisitor say to Jesus his prisoner: "Why, then, did you come to meddle with us? For you have come to meddle with us, and you know it." The members of the Sanhedrin who tried Jesus could have said the same thing to him. These words are said to intimidate Jesus. They harbor a stubborn insistence that there is no room for someone like Jesus in their way of life and religion. He has no right to be involved in their social and religious affairs. He has no role to play in the destiny of their nation. "Are you the Messiah?" Of course you are *not* the Messiah. "Is it you, You?" Of course it is *not* you, You. Then came the threat of death from the old Inquisitor: "Tomorrow I shall condemn you and burn you at the stake as the vilest of heretics." Does this not echo the verdict the Sanhedrin handed down to Jesus—the verdict that said: "He is guilty; he should die" (Matt. 26:66; par. Mark 14:64)?

The Question of Kingship

The scene of Jesus' trial changes quickly. Having found him guilty of blasphemy, the religious leaders "bound him and led him away to hand him over to Pilate" (Mark 15:1; pars. Matt. 27:2; Luke 23:1). But just as the trial of Jesus before the Sanhedrin turned out to be the trial of the religious authorities—the trial that exposed their all-out effort to obstruct the reign of God, the trial of Jesus before Pilate becomes "the trial of Pilate, for he stands self-revealed as he attempts in vain, first to avoid the issue, and then to escape responsibility for the decision."[15] Here again the role reversal has taken place. The judge becomes the judged and the judged becomes the judge. The sovereign proves to be a prisoner of political power and the prisoner in full freedom the bearer of witness to the truth of God's reign. Just as the trial court at the Sanhedrin becomes a court of witness to God's reign, the trial court at the palace of Pilate the Roman governor turns into another court of witness to God's reign. It is the witness of popular history, the history of the poor and the oppressed, against official history, the history of the rich and the mighty.

---

15. Alan Cole, *The Gospel according to St. Mark: An Introduction and Commentary*, Tyndale New Testament Commentary (London: Tyndale Press, 1981), 232.

If what concerned the Jewish religious authorities most was the question of Jesus' messiahship, what troubled the Roman political authorities most was the question of Jesus' "kingship." Was not Jesus at his entry into Jerusalem hailed as king by the welcoming crowds? And now are not Jewish leaders themselves accusing Jesus of claiming to be a king before the Roman colonial ruler? "We found this man," they are bringing charges against him, "subverting our nation, opposing the payment of taxes to Caesar, and claiming to be Messiah, a king" (Luke 23:2). These are all political crimes. They must have pronounced the word "king" with particular emphasis, for kingship was a sensitive subject that could bring grave consequences to the person who dared to make a bid for it in defiance of the Roman power. Eventually Jesus was to "suffer under Pontius Pilate," says the Apostles' Creed, and to be crucified on the cross bearing the inscription of the charge "The king of the Jews" (Mark 15:26; pars. Matt. 27:37; Luke 23:38).

"The king of the Jews"! This inscription on Jesus' cross was of course not a compliment to the Jewish people. Coming from the Roman colonial governor, it must have been used to humiliate them. It even could have been meant to be sarcastic. "Look," the Roman colonial rulers were saying to the Jews through that inscription on the cross, "what happened to your king!" The Jewish leaders must have realized that they were trapped. They were politically outmaneuvered by shrewd Roman politicians. They, according to the account in John's Gospel, protested: "You should not write 'King of the Jews,' but rather, 'He claimed to be king of the Jews.'" But it was too late. Pilate rebuffed them and declared, perhaps with an imperial air, "What I have written, I have written" (19:21-22). Pilate beat the Jewish leaders at their own game. An alleged king of the Jews was executed on the cross, the form of execution carried out on a criminal. This was a national shame. Pilate dealt a terrible blow to the honor and dignity of the Jewish people. The day Jesus was crucified as a political criminal was the day the Jewish leaders brought shame and humiliation to their people and handed a political victory to their colonial ruler. In their zeal to protect their power and privileges they refused to acknowledge the presence of God's reign in the midst of their people and did everything in their power to do away with Jesus. In this way they became, tragically, unwilling collaborators of Roman colonial rule.

The execution of Jesus as "the king of the Jews" must also have served as another warning to Jewish political adventurers. It must have been carried out as a case of "killing one as a warning for a hundred" (*sha yi chin pai*), to use a Chinese phrase. It was a stern warning of a similar fate to would-be political rebels. To be a king of the Jews was to be "a political authority, a rival of Rome itself."[16] And Rome, of course, could not tolerate it. Keeping in mind the imperial power of Rome over its colonial nation sheds a different light on Pilate's attitudes and behaviors during the trial of Jesus at his palace. This is a picture of Pilate different from that portrayed by the writers of the Synoptic Gospels—depicted out of "a general tendency to place the blame for Jesus' death squarely on the shoulders of the Jewish leaders."[17] As for Pilate, the Roman procurator, he was merely pressured into complying with the demand of the Jewish leaders to have Jesus put to death.

The Jewish authorities were no doubt determined to get rid of Jesus as a messianic pretender. But was Pilate a mere passive accomplice in the tragic death of Jesus on the Roman cross? He could not have been just the passive or unwilling accomplice that the Passion stories in the Gospels make him out to be. The fact of the matter might have been just the opposite. Pilate must have seized the opportunity to take the matter into his own hands and to have Jesus crucified as a potentially dangerous political subversive. For Pilate, a Roman governor who was no stranger to Roman power politics, this could have been a case of "making the wall crumble with the help of the favorable wind" (*sun hong sak to chhiu*), as people in Taiwan would say.

Pilate, in all probability, played an active political role in the execution of Jesus in a seemingly passive fashion. And he played that role to the end, perhaps with some relish. The writers of the Gospels inadvertently give us a very intriguing picture of a power politician serving under the authoritarian government of imperial Rome. It is a picture strikingly similar to that of the judges and prosecutors in court today trying political dissidents under constraint of the power and authority above them.

Pilate must have been in control of the situation. The Jewish leaders manipulated and incited the crowds to turn against Jesus. And now Pilate manipulated the Jewish leaders to be solely accountable for the death not only of a "messianic pretender" but of a potential "political rival," thus ensuring the *Pax Romana* within his jurisdiction. The event that unfolded showed how adept Pilate was at political intrigue. He presented Barabbas, possibly a Zealot arrested and imprisoned for violent acts against Roman colonialists, and Jesus, then demanded the Jews choose between the two. "Would you like me," he asked, "to release for you the king of the Jews?" (Mark 15:9; pars. Matt. 27:17; Luke 23:18). Did not Pilate know what was

---

16. Fitzmyer, *Luke X–XXIV*, 1475.

17. This is the conclusion reached by Lietzmann in his essay "Der Prozess Jesu," in *Sitzungsberichte der Prussischen Akademie der Wissenschaft* (Berlin, 1934), 313–32. See G. R. Beasley-Murray, *Jesus and the Kingdom of God* (Grand Rapids: Wm. B. Eerdmans Publishing Co., 1986), 296.

going to be "the outcome of such a choice from the start"?[18] Was he totally unaware that "there was much in Barabbas, the nationalist and man of violence, to win him the vote over Jesus"?[19] Pilate could not have been as naive as he sounded. He did not ask the crowds, already incited by the religious leaders against Jesus, "Do you wish me to release Jesus for you?" Instead, he used in his question an expression that touched the raw nerves of the Jewish authorities. It was "the king of the Jews" he offered to release for them.

Pilate could not have been serious when he referred to Jesus as "the king of the Jews" on such a volatile public occasion, unless he himself was foolish enough to court the wrath of Caesar. He must have asked the question half taunting his colonial subjects and half threatening them. Pilate, the Roman procurator of Judaea, was in Jerusalem during the festival of Passover to maintain law and order. He must have been vigilant. He must have been informed about the religious and political unrest in the Jewish community caused by the action taken by the Jewish authorities against Jesus. After the crowds asked for the release of Barabbas instead of Jesus, Pilate put to them another question: "Then what shall I do with the man you call king of the Jews?" (Mark 15:12; par. Matt 27:22).

"King of the Jews" on the lips of Pilate once again! But this second time he qualified it by saying, "the man you call king of the Jews." I, Pilate, did not call him "king of the Jews." It is you, the Jews, who almost crowned him as your king—a heinous political crime in the eyes of the Roman empire. Did you not almost "seize him to proclaim him king" (John 6:15) after he had miraculously fed the five thousand in the wilderness of Galilee (6:1-13)? And when Jesus entered Jerusalem on a donkey, did you not give him a royal welcome and shout: "Hosanna! Blessed is he who comes in the name of the Lord! Blessed is the king of Israel!" (12:13)? What shall I, then, do with your king, the king of the Jews? Pilate was the master of the situation. He got the Jews into a dilemma: to press their religious and political charges against Jesus and have "the king of the Jews" humiliated and brutally executed, or to withdraw their charges and preserve a semblance of national honor.

The trial of Jesus at Pilate's tribunal ended with the crowds shouting, "Crucify him! Crucify him!" Then came the final act of the trial that could only be performed by a consummate politician. According to Matthew's version of the Passion story, Pilate "took water and washed his hands in full view of the crowd, saying, 'My hands are clean of this man's blood; see to that yourselves'" (Matt. 27:24). This is like adding insult to injury.

---

18. Cole, *The Gospel according to St. Mark*, 234.
19. R. Mc.L. Wilson, "Mark," in *Peake's Commentary of the Bible*, 817b.

The symbolic act of washing the hands in water to show one's innocence of bloodshed was not unfamiliar to the Jews. They must have known from the Book of the Law that when a murder was committed, "all the elders of the town nearest to the dead body shall wash their hands over the heifer... [and] solemnly declare: 'Our hands did not shed this blood, nor did we witness the bloodshed...'" (Deut. 21:7). Pilate too must have been "acquainted with this Jewish symbolic act, and this their own custom he uses with great impressiveness... right in the presence of... the multitude so that all might see and understand."[20]

What makes the trial and sentencing of Jesus infinitely tragic is that neither the Jewish leaders nor the crowds they had incited saw and understood the political meaning of that ritual act of theirs effectively played by the foreign ruler before them. They were completely carried away by their frenzy and with one voice cried: "His blood be on us and on our children" (Matt. 27:25). Pilate must have been a little surprised by the way Jesus' trial proceeded at his court without his bearing direct responsibility for the final verdict. He must have congratulated himself for being able to come out of it so clean. But the fact is that Jesus was crucified as a political criminal and that history remembers him to have "suffered under Pontius Pilate." The trial of Jesus was as much a political trial as a religious trial. His murder by crucifixion was as much a political murder as a religious murder.

From Trial Court to Witness Court

Most of the time during his trial before the Sanhedrin and at Pilate's tribunal Jesus was silent. At one point the High Priest urged Jesus to speak out in his own defense. "Have you no answer," he was prompted to ask Jesus, "to the accusations that these witnesses bring against you?" (Mark 14:60; par. Matt. 26:62). But Jesus "remained silent and made no reply" (Mark 14:61; par. Matt. 26:63). At stake is his life. In jeopardy is the cause of God's reign. And in limbo is the fate of those who followed him and looked up to him for regaining their rights. Jesus should have mustered the strength of his spirit and the power of his speech, if not to defend himself, then to defend the poor and the oppressed who, he said, personified the reign of God.

But Jesus remained silent. He made no reply. Is this not strange? Is this not extraordinary? This reminds us of the strange and extraordinary advice he once gave to his disciples:

But before all this happens, they will seize you and persecute you. You will be handed over to synagogues and put in prison; you will be

---

20. Lenski, *The Interpretation of St. Matthew's Gospel*, 1095.

haled before kings and governors for your allegiance to me. *This will be your opportunity to testify. So resolve not to prepare your defence beforehand, because I myself will give you a mouth* (power of utterance) and wisdom as no opponent can resist or refute. (Luke 21:12-15)[21]

This is very uncommon advice. It is not the kind of advice that one would give to a person on trial in court.

Seated behind the judgment seats are the judges who represent the power and authority of the state. As individual persons they are not different from other people, not even from the defendants before them. Like others, they have their private desires and secret ambitions. They have worries and anxieties about many things of both personal and official nature just as you and I. But when they put on the state authority, they become transformed. They have the power to condemn you or acquit you. They have the authority to imprison you or to set you free. This, in fact, is what Pontius Pilate said to Jesus: "Surely you know that I have authority to release you, and I have authority to crucify you?" (John 19:10).

"I will give you a mouth," says Jesus to his disciples if ever they find themselves put on trial by their enemies, that is, Jesus promises to give them the power of utterance. But the judges too have a mouth. What they have at martial law court is not the mouth that ordinary citizens use to speak, eat, laugh, or sigh. It is a mouth given by the state with a tremendous power of utterance. It speaks for kings and presidents. It announces the decrees of a military regime. It declares the mind of an autocratic ruler. And all this with an air of legality and constitutionality! That mouth invokes the authority of the law and stresses the inviolability of it. It recites the litany of virtues derived from obedience and allegiance to the powers that be. It gives praises to the law and order that ensures freedom, or rather ensures lack of it, for the citizens. And of course it renders strong support to the false testimony fabricated against the defendants. The outcome of all this is too obvious. At the end of the mock trial would come from that powerful state mouth the predetermined verdict: Guilty! That mouth will pronounce the verdict with a tone of finality. You are the enemy of the state. You have subverted the cause of the nation. You have violated the security of the people.

It was to such a court that Jesus was brought for trial, as we have seen. The Sanhedrin turned into such a court for his trial. Pilate's tribunal was

---

21. Emphasis added. The passage quoted here combines the renderings of the REB and the RSV. The exposition that follows is based mostly on my essay "The Politics of Resurrection: Truth-Power and Love-Power in the Court of Testimony," in *Proclaiming the Acceptable Year*, ed. Justo L. Gonzales (Valley Forge, Pa.: Judson Press, 1982), 27–40.

not any better. And it is in such a court that many men and women are tried for their struggle for freedom and democracy. A court can be a formidable instrument that serves the whims and interests of certain power holders. Before it, defendants have lost all their freedoms except the freedom of their mouth. Their mouth is not yet incarcerated. They still have some power of utterance. They must make full use of this last freedom they still have. They must now open their mouth in their own defense. They must defend their innocence. They can declare how much they love their nation and its people, although the way they express their love is very different from their rulers and judges. They can stress that their zeal for the welfare of their country is no less strong than that of their compatriots. Their sincerity, their eloquence, and their argument may still move the judges and soften their hearts. Who knows?

To speak in one's own defense at a trial is the most natural thing in the world. It is a must. Too much is at stake to keep one's mouth shut. Bleak lonely years of prison life may be ahead. Much worse than that also can happen. This is why defendants must speak out. They must hire defense lawyers to defend their case. This is the time they must put their mouth to full use. They must muster their power of utterance before the court sitting in judgment of them. But Jesus advised his disciples to the contrary. "Make no preparation for your defense!" The advice contradicts common practice. It offends common sense. Brought to trial before the court that serves the dictates of autocratic power and not the conscience of the judges, with no preparation for your own defense?

What are we to make of advice such as this? Does Jesus want us to practice the ethics of the Sermon on the Mount (Matt. 5) or on the Plain (Luke 6) at a law court? Does he counsel us to apply this ethics when we are put on trial for not committing a crime but for advocating peace, love, and justice? Is Jesus saying to us: "Turn the other cheek! Give your shirt as well as your coat! Walk the second mile!"? That Jesus might have meant this is not impossible. But there must be a deeper meaning in his advice not to prepare for your defense at the court that tries you as a messianic pretender when all you have done is to put the reign of God before the religious authorities. Why are you advised not to defend yourself at the tribunal that condemns you for sedition when all you have done is to strive for the basic human rights of freedom and justice?

The fact of the matter is that the court, be it the Sanhedrin, which conducted Jesus' trial, Pilate's tribunal, which sentenced Jesus to death, or the martial law court that tries human rights advocates and political dissidents, is no longer a court that hears your defense but a court that has to hear your witness—witness to the truth. Jesus was right. You do not need to prepare your own defense. You do not need to hire a defense lawyer to fight your case. What you are doing in the full view of the court, in the full knowledge of the public outside the court, is witnessing to the truth. The truth itself will empower you to be a witness to it. It will inspire you with the power of utterance to testify to it. It is for the sake of the truth that you must break the silence and speak in the full hearing of the audience both inside and outside of the court.

Jesus himself was such a witness before the Sanhedrin. He was also such a witness before Pilate's tribunal. When the chief priests and doctors of the law demanded to know whether he was the Messiah, Jesus no longer kept his mouth shut. He broke his silence and said: "It is you who say I am" (Luke 22:70).[22] The "Messiah" on the lips of the Jewish authorities meant Davidic kingship. Of course Jesus did not profess himself to be the Messiah in that sense. That is why he had to speak out and throw the question back at them. "It is you, and not I, who say I am the Messiah." Jesus refused to be a political messiah. Again and again he had to fight back the temptation to be one. From time to time he had to discourage people from taking him for one. Because of this, he must have disappointed his followers, including his own disciples. Jesus was anything but a political messiah.

And Pontius Pilate must have decided to take full advantage of the political blunder committed by the Jewish leaders out of their blindness to the truth of God's reign. It is now his turn to ask Jesus: "So you are the king of the Jews?" (John 18:33). This is a serious question. It contains the charges of sedition against Rome. It is also a threatening question. Rome has no leniency for anyone plotting a revolt against itself and making a claim to kingship. Of course Jesus did not make a political claim to be a king. The charge is the distortion of his message of God's reign and defamation of his ministry among the people. As before the Sanhedrin Jesus at this point broke his silence too and retorted: "Is that your own question, or have others suggested it to you?" (18:34). This counterquestion of Jesus must have caught Pilate by surprise. He exclaimed: "Am I a Jew?" Then he went

---

22. Here I follow Joachim Jeremias's view that the Lukan version is more original. In his words, "If we compare the two independent versions of the confession before the supreme council in Mark 14:62 and Luke 22:69, the Lukan can be seen to be simpler; unlike Mark 14:62 it has still not been influenced by the early Christian Christological pattern of exaltation and parousia. That Luke 22:69 represents an earlier formulation is, moreover, confirmed by Acts 7:56.... The exclamation of the dying Stephen corresponds with Luke 22:69... in content, but rests on the independent tradition" (Joachim Jeremias, *New Testament Theology,* trans. John Bowden [London: SCM Press, 1971], 273). There are other New Testament scholars who hold the view that the Markan version is earlier. Beasley-Murray, for example, argues: "It is plausible to view Mark's version of the parousia saying in the trial as the most original version available. Matthew's version is essentially the same as Mark's, and Luke's version is most likely an adaptation of the tradition reproduced by Mark that is attributable either to Luke himself or to his source" (*Jesus and the Kingdom of God,* 303).

on to put the blame on the Jews for the charges. "Your own nation," he said, "and their chief priests have brought you before me. What have you done?" (18:35).

This is a lame pretext. Of course the Jewish leaders delivered Jesus to Pilate, accusing him of political subversion. But Pilate could not have been entirely in the dark and uninformed about the activities of Jesus in Galilee and in Judaea. One did not have to be a Jew to become concerned about the possible outcome of Jesus' activities. At this point the trial took a dramatic turn. If Pilate really wished to know what Jesus had done, Jesus must tell him. "My task," Jesus declared, "is to bear witness to the truth" (18:37). The trauma of trial becomes a drama of witness! The charges of sedition fade into the background and the question of the truth comes into the fore. And Pilate, the Roman governor, found himself confronted, not with a political criminal charged with sedition, but the truth Jesus stood for.

"What is truth?" (18:38), Pilate asked Jesus. Did he ask the question because he did not know what truth meant? Maybe. But more likely he already knew what truth was. For persons like him—persons who hold power, be it religious or political—there is no truth but their truth. They have the monopoly of truth because they have the monopoly of power. And truth must serve power, not power the truth. This must be the truth Pilate knows. But the truth of Jesus is totally different, not just in some aspects or merely in some ways, but in kind. It is a truth Pilate, and for that matter the rulers who rule not by justice but by force, not with humanness but with brutality, does not know. Jesus must now tell him what truth is. He must give a strong witness to it.

Jesus' truth is that his "reign does not belong to this world" (John 18:36). Is his reign, then, a reign that belongs to heaven? Is it a heavenly reign, a reign that has nothing to do with this earth of ours? Is it a utopian reign, a reign of "not place" ("utopia" is from the Greek *ou*, "not" + *topos*, "place"), a reign that has no spatio-temporal meaning in the world here and now? Confronted with the formidable Roman authority, has Jesus suddenly become a utopian preacher, a preacher of utopia, a preacher who denounces the world of time and space as a world of illusion? Flinching from that gruesome instrument of Roman justice, or rather Roman injustice—death by crucifixion—is Jesus trying to explain that his reign is a utopian reign, a reign of "not place," a reign emptied of all social and political implications for the life of people?

If this is what Jesus meant, would he not be denying what he had done? Would he not be rejecting what he had said and taught? Would he not be betraying those women and men who followed him because of his message of God's reign? Is he now saying that they—the poor, the hungry, the persecuted, the oppressed—are blessed not because God's reign is theirs in the midst of their tears, frustrations, sorrows, and hardships, but because they will find consolation after this life in heaven? How many Christians in the past understood Jesus to be saying just such things. And how many Christians today still understand Jesus to be saying that this is what God's reign is about!

But some significant change has been taking place even among the so-called evangelical Christians, especially those in the Third World. Twenty-five "evangelical" mission theologians from the Third World, meeting at a conference held in Bangkok said this:

> We expressed our human solidarity with the poor, the powerless, and the oppressed of the world, with those who are followers of other religions and with all people everywhere. We recognized that we are all made in God's image, yet fall short of God's glory. Christ came, lived, died, and rose again for us all. We are all under the sovereignty of the Lord Jesus Christ, whom we are committed to proclaim to all, especially our brothers and sisters in the Two Thirds World.[23]

This is one of the thought-provoking reflections that have begun to be heard from "evangelical" theologians. A space seems to be opening up for constructive interactions between Christians of different theological persuasions. And it is "the poor, the powerless, the oppressed, and the followers of other religions" who are instrumental for such opening within the divided Christian confessional bodies and theological camps. Is this not the case of "the poor, the powerless, the oppressed, and the people of other religions," most of them are outside the pale of Christianity, showing us Christians where Jesus is and what he is doing? Solidarity with them seems to disclose to Christians, even to "evangelical" Christians, fresh meanings of Jesus' message of God's reign. Is it not in this sense that the poor, the oppressed, the powerless, and even people of other religions have good news for Christians?

At any rate, Jesus could not have been detracting from what he had said and done during his public ministry by his statement to Pilate the Roman governor: "My reign does not belong to this world." He must have meant that his reign, that is, the reign of God, is totally different from the Roman empire. It does not rule by brutal power but by the power

---

23. *Sharing Jesus in the Two Thirds World: Evangelical Christology from the Contexts of Poverty, Powerlessness and Religious Pluralism*, papers from the First Conference of Evangelical Mission Theologians from the Two Thirds World, Bangkok, Thailand, March 22–25, 1982, ed. Vinay Samuel and Chris Sugden (Grand Rapids: Wm. B. Eerdmans Publishing Company, 1983), 279.

of love. It does not play cold-blooded power politics; it plays the politics of justice. It is not an instrument of oppression and fear, but an instrument of freedom and peace. Its mission is not to conquer life with death but to overcome death with life. And it brings to people, not despair, not resignation, but strength for the present and power for the future. Its task, in short, is to empower women, men, and children with the meaning of life in this life as well as in the life to come. The reign of God, Jesus is saying, is a crusade against meaninglessness and lostness, and it is a crusade for meaning-full-ness and purpose-full-ness of life. It is a campaign against totalitarian social, political, and religious power, and it is a campaign for the empowerment of the powerless. God's reign is a revolutionary movement that makes God's presence in love and justice really real in the world through the pain, agony, and suffering of the cross. This is the truth of God's reign. This must be what Jesus wanted to tell Pontius Pilate when he said: "My reign does not belong to this world."

Jesus' advice to his followers begins to make sense. "This will be your opportunity to testify," he said. "So resolve not to prepare your defense beforehand." He himself did not defend himself before the Sanhedrin or at Pilate's tribunal. What he did was to "testify" to the truth of God's reign on earth as well as in heaven—the power of God's presence in love and justice in this space and time of ours as well as in the eternity of God. What happened during that Passion week of Jesus was the transformation of the court that tried Jesus—both Jewish and Roman—into the court of Jesus' testimony.

This is truly astonishing. What is equally astonishing is that such a transformation continues to take place today after two thousand years. From Korea to Taiwan, from China to the Philippines, men and women, among them Christians, brought to trial on the charges of subversion and sedition, have changed military courts into courts of testimony. From trial courts to testimony courts! What unfolds before one's eyes are different courts altogether. The court is no longer the space and time in which martial law reigns supreme. There in the massive concentration of state power martial law is suspended. The testimony court called into being through those women and men put on trial for their struggle for human rights of freedom, justice, and democracy has created a new space and a new time in which a new law takes command—the law of love!

This is a really amazing spectacle. The judges sitting in judgment of the defendants before them, like Pilate in the ancient time, appear awesome and intimidating, but look affected and unreal. When the testimonies of the defendants fill the courtroom—testimonies of how people suffer under oppressive power, how they have become victims of social, political, and economic injustices—the judges and representatives of state power must feel indicted and judged. To the audience both inside and outside the courtroom, it is as clear as day that the defendants are innocent and that the ruling power is guilty. It is this miracle in the court of martial law, the miracle of the trial court being transformed into a testimony court, the most astonishing miracle Jesus performed before the Sanhedrin and at Pilate's tribunal—a miracle more astonishing than his healing of the sick and his raising of the dead—it is a miracle such as this that empowers powerless men, women, and children to become a formidable nonviolent revolutionary moral force to overcome the military power of an autocratic regime, to discredit illegitimate rule by an authoritarian political party. It is a miracle such as this that has ushered in the era of people in Asia and in many countries in the Third World today. The moral power of that miracle is the spirit and energy of the people's revolution that breaks the rule of military dictators and brings about the rule by the people. In the testimonies of people today one hears the echo of Jesus' testimony to God's reign before the religious and political authorities of his day.

And the testimony of Jesus echoed in the testimonies of people, the testimonies of people echoing the testimony of Jesus, will continue from today to tomorrow, even to the time when God's reign will be fully present on earth as well as in heaven. Thus,

> It is not over...
>
> Not Pilate's sentence, not the jostling of the soldiers who divided his garments, not even the cry from the cross was the last word.
>
> The accusers of old are dead. The witnesses have gone home. The judge has left the court. The trial of Jesus goes on. His is a trial that is never finished, and one in which the role of judge and accused are strangely reversed.
>
> Tribunals assemble, tribunals disband. The bailiffs, the informers, the accusers, the witnesses, the procurators, the executioners are still with us.
>
> Many have come in his name, and have joined the accusers; and there arose new false witnesses among them—yet even so, their testimony agrees not.... The words "His blood be upon us and upon our children!" have come true—a thousand times. But no valid answer has yet been given to the question "What will you that I do with the king of the Jews?"; only the cry "Crucify him! Crucify him!" echoes throughout the centuries.
>
> Rabbi Eliezer ben Hurqnos, Eliezer the Great, said of Jesus: He owns his share in the Age That Is Coming...

It was not finished. Sentence was passed, and he was led away. Crucified, dead, and buried, yet risen in the hearts of his disciples who had loved him and felt he was near.

Tried by the world, condemned by authority, buried by the Churches that now profess his name, he is rising again, today and tomorrow, in the hearts of men and women who love him and feel: he is near.[24]

---

24. Paul Winter, *On the Trial of Jesus* (Berlin: Walter de Gruyter & Co., 1961), 208.

Part IV

TRANSFIGURATION

Change is a fact of human life. It implies growth and development. A human person grows from infancy to youth and develops into adulthood. But change also contains an element that threatens human life—decay. Decay is present throughout the process of growth and development. It begins as soon as life comes into being. It grows with life and develops with it until it overtakes growth and development. And it continues its work until life succumbs to death. This process of human life from birth through growth and development and then to decay is shared by nature. Nature and all lives in it go through the same process of birth, growth, development, and decay. In this respect human life is part of nature. We human beings share our destiny with nature.

But there is something in nature that human life does not have—the power of rejuvenation. When autumn comes followed by winter, nature shows every sign of decay: fields become barren, leaves fall from trees, and the sun loses its luster. Even birds flee in search of food and warmth. But come spring, life returns to nature. Flowers begin to bloom and trees start to bud. Even birds return to sing and play. You may call this a cyclical life—nature in ebb and flow in perpetual rhythms. But this is not just a meaningless repetition that does not signify anything new. The life that returns after the bleak winter is a new life, ready to enliven nature and to enrich it, bringing into being a new cycle of life.

Human life may not have the power of rejuvenation, but it has something that nature does not have—the power of transformation. Literally, the word "transformation" means change of form. One at once thinks of someone putting on make-up or donning specially designed clothes such as a clown does for a show. Here the change occurs externally. The appearance has changed. Or in the case of the mask dance, putting on the mask changes the appearance of the person into that of the character the mask is supposed to represent. The change in the external form is immediate and direct. It is evident for all to see. This is what happens in the theater, from the amateur theatricals played on the street on festival occasions to the plays, dramas, and operas performed by professional artists in ornate theaters and opera houses.

Transformation, however, is not merely change of the external form. It affects the inner nature of the person or thing concerned. Here the natural process of birth, growth, and decay no longer fully explains human life. We have to speak of maturity in addition to, or rather in spite of, growth and decay. This must be what Paul meant when he wrote in his letter to the Corinthian Christians: "When I was a child, I spoke like a child, thought like a child, reasoned like a child; but when I grew up, I had finished with childish things" (1 Cor. 13:11). Our biological life and our spiritual life, though inseparable, take the opposite direction: while the former gradually heads for decay, the latter grows into maturity. Our outer life exhibits signs of aging, but our inner life can grow more mature as we gain in years.

In a completely different setting and from an entirely distinctive background Confucius of ancient China seems to imply a similar understanding of life in its inner transformation when he says: "At fifteen my mind was set on learning. At thirty my character had been formed. At forty I had no more perplexities. At fifty I knew the Mandate of Heaven. At sixty I was at ease with whatever I heard. At seventy I could follow my heart's desire without transgressing moral principles."[1]

The progression of human maturity does not take place in such a schematic fashion and each stage on the way is not followed by the next stage in such a chronological order. It is truer to say that the stages identified by Confucius interact with each other at each stage as we grow in maturity. And apart from unusually endowed sages such as Confucius, even at seventy we are still perplexed by the mysteries of life and universe and do not always follow our heart's desire without transgressing moral principles. That there is transformation of our inner self and basic nature taking place, however, must be what Confucius tried to show through these stages of life he described.

From external change to inner transformation—this is what makes human life more than biological. But inner transformation, when it does take place, does not remain hidden in the inmost recesses of the heart. It is bound to affect the external appearance, first the persons who have experienced it and then the relationships and institutions, be they social, political, or religious, to which they are related. Inner transformation brings about outward change. The Reformation in sixteenth-century Europe is a case in point. Whatever transformation Martin Luther had to go through was

---

1. *Analects* 2:4.

to result in a revolutionary change within the Christian church and in the history of Christianity. In the social and political realm we also witness radical changes in society and politics when individuals are transformed by their aspirations for freedom and democracy. There is always an element of unexpectedness in the transformation of people and society.

There is also an experience of the miraculous in it. To give expression to the sense of unexpectedness and the experience of miraculous, the words such as "change" and "transformation" are no longer adequate. To signify what amounts to a deeply religious sense and experience, we must look for another word. That word is "transfiguration." The dictionary meaning of this word is basically the same as the word "transformation." But there is something in it that makes it different from the word "transformation." There is an irrepressible feeling of surprise attached to it. A sense of awe and transcendence is a very real part of it. Although what is transfigured is continuous with life and history, it nevertheless reveals something new in life and history. It discloses a totally different dimension that endows life and history with a new meaning and gives them a sense of purpose. It calls for a fresh evaluation of our past and a renewed commitment to our journey toward the future.

The story of Jesus' transfiguration at once comes to mind (Mark 9:2-10; pars. Matt. 17:1-9; Luke 9:28-36). As Jesus "was transfigured, his clothes became dazzling white, with a whiteness no bleacher on earth could equal" (Mark 9:2-3). To this account of the brilliant light radiating from the transfigured Jesus Matthew adds how "Jesus' face shone like the sun" (17:2). Luke tells us in his version of the story that "the appearance of Jesus' face changed" (9:29). What we have here is a literary device to describe an extraordinary change that has come over Jesus, making tremendous impact on the people and the world affected by it. Peter, James, and John, three disciples Jesus had taken with him to the high mountain where the transfiguration took place, were completely overwhelmed. Peter could only find himself suggesting to Jesus that three shelters be built, one for Jesus, one for Moses, and one for Elijah. Mark then tells us in parenthesis: "For he did not know what to say; they were so terrified" (Mark 9:6). The transfiguration was something totally unexpected, something no everyday experience could explain.

The story of Jesus' transfiguration, in its original setting, was perhaps closely related to the story of his resurrection, as some New Testament scholars would have us believe. It could have been a post-Easter account of how his followers experienced Jesus, who died on the cross in pain and agony, as the risen Christ in glory. It might have also been an account of how they themselves were "transfigured" by the risen and transfigured Christ and became the bearers of witness to his life, message, and ministry.

And it could have been at the same time a recognition of the ways in which the world around them with its structures of powers and authorities, its complex relationships, its systems of values and beliefs, are to be affected and changed.

What we read in the story of Jesus' transfiguration may, then, be a dramatic example of changes that can take place in real life and in the course of history, although most of these changes are usually not easily recognized and identified. Certainly they are not as dramatic as Jesus' transfiguration experienced by his disciples. But they do share the power and glory of that transfiguration. In other words, the reign of God, which Jesus identified in the poor, the oppressed, and the disinherited, for which he himself lived and died, does make a difference to the people and to the world touched by it. The power of God's reign is that power of transfiguration. Its glory is the glory of transfiguration.

In what follows we want to explore ways in which the power and glory of transfiguration in human communities is manifested. These are mostly painful and agonizing ways, but somehow the power of transfiguration is felt and its glory is revealed in the midst of pain and agony. What is faith if not the ability and imagination to perceive and experience the crucified Jesus as the transfigured Christ?

CHAPTER 7

THE REIGN OF THE MAGNIFICAT

Tell out, my soul, the greatness of the Lord,
rejoice, rejoice, my spirit, in God my saviour;
so tenderly has God looked upon God's servant,
    humble as she is.
For, from this day forth,
all generations will count me blessed,
so wonderfully has God dealt with me,
    the Lord, the Mighty One.

    God's name is Holy;
God's mercy sure from generation to generation
    toward those who fear God;
the deeds God's own right arm has done
    disclose God's might;
the arrogant of heart and mind God has put to rout,
God has brought down monarchs from their thrones,
    but the humble have been lifted high.
The hungry God has satisfied with good things,
    the rich sent empty away ... (Luke 1:46-53, NEB)

Not the Mary in the Holy Pictures

During an informal Sunday worship service in a Central American country, the following "liturgical exchange" took place between the priest and the people:

PRIEST: Today is September 12. Does that date mean anything to you?

RESPONSE: Three years ago yesterday Allende was killed in Chile
                 and the Chileans lost their leader. Now they are suffering
                 repression.

RESPONSE: Allende's death makes me think of Mao.

RESPONSE: Their deaths make me think of the death of Martin
                 Luther King.

PRIEST: Why do you think of the deaths of those three together?

RESPONSE: Because all three of them were concerned about the
                 oppressed peoples.

PRIEST: Doesn't the day mean anything but *death* to you?

RESPONSE: Well, today is also the Feast of the Holy Name of Mary.
                 So this day also makes me think of her.

PRIEST: Is there any connection between Allende and Mao and
                 Martin Luther King and Mary?

RESPONSE: I guess that would depend on whether Mary was con-
                 cerned about oppressed peoples too.

PRIEST: Let me read part of Mary's song, the Magnificat, in
                 the beginning of Luke's Gospel: "God has scattered the
                 proud in the imagination of their hearts, God has put
                 down the mighty from their thrones, and exalted those of
                 low degree; God has filled the hungry with good things,
                 and the rich God has sent empty away."

RESPONSE: Bravo! But, Father, that doesn't sound at all like the Mary
                 we hear about in the cathedral. And the Mary in the "holy
                 pictures" certainly doesn't look like a person who would
                 talk that way.

PRIEST: Tell us about the Mary in the holy pictures.

RESPONSE: (*displaying a picture*): Here she is. She is standing on a
                 crescent moon. She is wearing a crown. She has rings on
                 her fingers. She has a blue robe embroidered with gold.

PRIEST: That *does* sound like a different Mary from the Mary of
                 the song! Do you think the picture has betrayed the Mary
                 of the Song?

RESPONSE: The Mary who said that God "has exalted those of low
                 degree" would not have left all of her friends so she could
                 stand on the moon.

CORPORATE RESPONSE:
> Take her off the moon!

RESPONSE: The Mary who said that God "has put down the mighty from their thrones" would not be wearing a crown.

CORPORATE RESPONSE:
> Take off her crown!

RESPONSE: The Mary who said that God "has sent the rich empty away" would not be wearing rings on her fingers.

CORPORATE RESPONSE:
> Take off her rings!

RESPONSE: The Mary who said that God "has filled the hungry with good things" would not have left people who were still hungry to wear a silk robe embroidered with gold.

CORPORATE RESPONSE:
> Take off her robe!

ANGUISHED RESPONSE:
> But, Father, this is not right! (*embarrassedly*) We're, we're doing a striptease of the Virgin.

PRIEST: Very well, if you don't like the way Mary looks in *this* picture, what do you think the Mary of the song would look like?

RESPONSE: The Mary of the song would not be standing on the moon. She would be standing in the dirt and dust where we stand.

RESPONSE: The Mary of the song would not be wearing a crown. She would have an old hat like the rest of us, to keep the sun from causing her to faint.

RESPONSE: The Mary of the song would not be wearing a silk robe embroidered with gold. She would be wearing old clothes like the rest of us.

EMBARRASSED RESPONSE:
> Father, it may be awful to say this, but it sounds as though Mary would look just like me! My feet are dirty, my hat is old, my hands are rough and my clothes are torn.

PRIEST: No, I don't think it is awful to say that. I think the Mary you have all described is more like the Mary of the Bible

than the Mary we hear about in the cathedral and see in
all the holy pictures.

RESPONSE: I think she would be more at home here in the slum with
us than in the cathedral or the General's mansion.

RESPONSE: I think her message is more hopeful for us than for them.
They are mighty and rich, but she tells them that God
puts down the mighty from their thrones and sends the
rich empty away.

RESPONSE: And we are at the bottom of the heap and very hungry,
but she tells us that God exalts those of low degree and
fills the hungry with good things.

PRIEST: Now let's see, how could we begin to help God bring those
things to pass?[1]

The death of Mao is of course entirely different from that of Allende and
Martin Luther King. Allende and Martin Luther King died martyrs to the
cause of liberation of people from political oppression and racism. But
Mao died a dictator, having thrown China into the turmoil and chaos of
the Cultural Revolution, the China he and his fellow Communist leaders
had won from the Nationalist regime after a long and bloody civil war. Mao
is an example of how a revolutionary leader who wins liberation for people
could turn into a dictator who takes away the freedom he has won for them.
It is an irony of history that a revolution that overthrows a dictatorship
often itself turns into dictatorship, to the dismay and despair of the people.
   But this should not detain us more than a fleeting moment here. The
members of the congregation involved in this liturgical exchange were
not engaged in a comparative study of societies deeply affected one way
or another by these three charismatic leaders. Nor were they conduct-
ing a postmortem analysis of the lives of these three personalities who
profoundly changed the people and their countries. They were not doing
what Chinese call *kai koan lun tin*, meaning when one's coffin is covered, one's deserts can be properly judged. As the exchange between
the priest and the members of the congregation in the liturgy went on,
it became evident that Mary and the song traditionally ascribed to her
and known as the Magnificat were the heart of their concern. And the
theology the liturgy implied and struggled to articulate turned out to be

1. This "liturgical exchange" was used by Robert McAfee Brown to illustrate what he
called "a hermeneutic of engagement" in his book *Theology in a New Key: Responding to Liberation Theology* (Philadelphia: Westminster Press, 1978), 98–100. The congregation concerned
was not identified for reasons of safety in a country under dictatorial rule.

most refreshing and thought-provoking. It is a theology rich in meaning and authentic in practice, rendering theologies full of jargon poor and hollow.

The image of Mary captured in this unusual Sunday worship service is revolutionary in every sense of the word. What happens here is a revolt against the cult of the Virgin deeply rooted in the religious culture of Roman Catholicism from the Middle Ages to the present day, from France or Italy to Brazil, to the Philippines. The cult is epitomized in the "holy pictures" displayed at the worship service—the pictures of the Virgin Mary "standing on a crescent moon, wearing a crown and a blue silk robe embroidered with gold, and having rings on her fingers." Mary in this popular cult, assiduously fostered by the religious authorities through the centuries, has commanded Christian believers' allegiance, filled their spiritual lacunae, induced them to resign themselves to their lot, and prompted them to shun struggles for justice and freedom in a socially, politically, and economically oppressive society. If the cult has served the official church well, it has also rendered the state invaluable service. In the name of the God who demands absolute obedience and promises joy and blessings in the life to come, church and state have conspired to perpetuate oppression and exploitation.

To question this Mary of the cult, then, is to question the faith of the church. To doubt this Mary is to doubt the traditions of the faith. To depart from this Mary is to depart from the centuries-old teaching of the church. As one of the responses puts it, referring to the Mary of the "holy pictures": "That *does* sound like a different Mary from the Mary of the song! Do you think the picture has betrayed the Mary of the song?" The word "betray" used in the response is a shocking word. It points to duplicity on the part of the church. It even contains a sense of resentment. As a matter of fact, the sense of betrayal is strongly reflected in what many women Christians and theologians say about Mariology today. "The cult of the Virgin/Mother," said a participant of the conference on "Asian Women Doing Theology" held in Singapore in 1987, "resulted in the theft and redefinition of the meaning of both words. It brought the consequent fear and denigration of birthing and of female sexuality, and the suppression of female independence."[2]

A sense of frustration, even chagrin, is apparent in a remark such as this. The fact is that this is not an outburst of isolated individual women Christians. As women in the church, whether Protestant, Roman Catholic, or Orthodox, look critically into the way the teachings of their church have

---

2. Barbara Menzies, "Mariology: A Pakeha Perspective," in *Asian Women Doing Theology*, Report from Singapore Conference, November 20–29, 1987 (Hong Kong: Asian Women's Resource Centre, 1989).

distorted the male-female relationship and even debased their humanity by idolizing Mary, the mother of Jesus, as an eternal Virgin and as an object of worship, how can they not be appalled? How can they not resent it when they discover that in such a crucial matter as religious faith they have been misinformed, misled, and even deceived? This is the case with an increasing number of women Christians in Latin America, Asia, and Africa. In the words of a Latin American lay Catholic woman theologian, the cult of the Virgin "has produced an aberration of devotion to the Virgin Mary. Mary is the synthesis of both aspects, virginity and motherhood. Thus she symbolizes the traditional ideal of woman (in a male-supremacist reading of her life)."[3]

Aberration of religious devotion! Each and every religion has aberrations of religious devotion. Christianity is no exception. The cult of the Virgin is one of the aberrations that have developed in the course of its history. In a true sense religious reformation is an effort to redeem religious devotion from aberrations. What has been happening in new theological developments in the West and in the Third World is theological reformation. It tells us that a radical reorientation in our understanding of the gospel is no longer an optional matter. It is a matter of Christian responsibility and theological integrity. The witness of Christians in the Third World and the theological fruits they bear today testify to that responsibility and integrity.

The Mary of the "holy pictures" standing on a crescent moon not only betrays Christian believers, particularly women Christian believers. That Mary has done something far worse: that Mary has betrayed the Mary of Nazareth, the historical Mary, Mary the spouse of the carpenter called Joseph, Mary who gave birth to a son named Jesus, even the Mary of the Magnificat. That Mary of "the holy pictures" is a religious fiction that has no basis in historical reality. The Mary who wears rings on her fingers and is dressed in a blue silk robe is a caricature of Mary, the wife and the mother who had to bear many of life's burdens and endure the lot determined for women by social and religious traditions. That Mary is a spiritual substitution for the challenge to the fate ordained for women not by God but by humans. That Mary suppresses and mutes the protest against the world that is not what it should be—the world in which only the rich and the powerful can survive.

And the Mary of the "holy pictures" wears a crown! Does this not remind us of "the gold-crowned Jesus" to which we referred at the outset of

---

3. Ana Maria Bidegain, "Women and the Theology of Liberation," in *Through Her Eyes: Women's Theology from Latin America*, ed. Elsa Tamez (Maryknoll, N.Y.: Orbis Books, 1989), 21.

our quest for "the real Jesus"?[4] If that gold-crowned Jesus is not the real Jesus, then the Mary wearing a crown cannot be the real Mary either. The gold crown on the Jesus encased in the cement statue has to be removed, if we remember, before Jesus can gain the freedom to speak to Leper and Beggar, to the suffering men and women. That crown has to go in order for Jesus to regain his humanity, so that he can be with women, men, and children, disinherited and marginalized. The Jesus fossilized in church traditions cannot help. The Jesus crystallized in the creeds and dogmas of the past cannot save. For that is not the *historical* Jesus, not the *contemporary* Jesus. And the Jesus who is not historical and contemporary is not the *real* Jesus, but an unreal Jesus, not the *living* Jesus, but a dead Jesus.

A similar thing developed in relation to the Mary of the traditional Christian cult at the Sunday worship service of a congregation in Latin America. The men and women at the worship service rediscovered the *historical, contemporary*, and, thus, *real* Mary—the Mary who is not standing on a crescent moon but in the dirt and dust where they are standing, the Mary who does not wear a crown but an old hat like them to keep the sun from causing her to faint, the Mary who wears no silk robe but worn-out clothes just like them. The cult of the Virgin is broken. "It may be awful to say this," a response arose in the midst of the worship service, "but it sounds as though Mary would look just like me!" This is an important statement. An awakening of faith enabled them to make it. It signals a beginning of a new journey of faith in a society in which religion contributed to the spiritual poverty and economic exploitation as much as politics.

And the faith sealed in the past is freed to make sense for the present. For the first time in their lives these men and women in the congregation learned that Mary is a mortal human being like them, having to toil under the heat of the sun and to bear the curse of poverty. "It may be awful to say this," they responded in their liturgical exchange, "but it sounds as though Mary would look just like me!" The process of freeing themselves from the cult of Mary was not yet complete. They were still a little hesitant. That is why they were apologetic about what they were going to say. That is also why what they were about to say had to be preceded by "as though," a tentative phrase. But tentative or not, hesitant or not, they already made a big stride in their faith. They began to see a close relationship between Mary and themselves, between what they are and what Mary was, between where they are standing and where Mary was standing. "Mary," they are now saying, "would look just like me!" A historical tie has been forged between them and Mary. They and Mary become contemporaries to each

---

4. See "Prologue" in *Jesus, the Crucified People* (New York: Crossroad/Meyer-Stone, 1989).

other, not in the insulated setting of traditional piety but in the rough and tumble of the world in which they live.

The priest himself played a pastoral role that was at once liberating and reassuring. He responded to their hesitation with the assurance that the Mary they discovered to be very much like them is the real Mary, the Mary of the Bible. "The Mary we hear about in the cathedral and see in all the holy pictures" is not the real Mary. For the priest, ordained in the cathedral and inheritor of the tradition of devotion to the Mary of the holy pictures, this must be a frightening thing to say. It is nothing short of a spiritual turnabout, a theological *metanoia* (repentance), and a religious revolt. He must have been glad that at last he was able to say it, that he did not have to go on betraying himself, members of his flock, and above all Mary herself. Liberated from the cult of the Virgin Mary, he regained his integrity as the shepherd of his flock and as the messenger of the reign of God.

The bold step taken by the priest and members of his congregation enables them to take a fresh look at the Magnificat. As Mary has become for them a historical person, the Magnificat too takes on now a historical significance. It contains a message of hope for the people like them who are exploited and oppressed. They are now able to hear Mary tell them that "God has brought down monarchs from their thrones and sent the rich empty away." First they realize that the real Mary is the Mary who identifies with them in their life of hardship and in the history of their suffering. And now they are able to identify themselves with the message of Mary expressed in the Magnificat. Mary's Magnificat is their Magnificat. Her message is their message. Her experience is their experience. Her liberation is their liberation. And her determination not to submit to oppressive powers is their determination also.

This "mariological" conversion has to result, at the same time, in a "christological" conversion. The negation of the cult of Mary has to lead to the negation of the cult of Jesus. The encounter with the historical Mary brings about the encounter with the historical Jesus. And the meeting with Mary as their contemporary enables them to recognize Jesus in the midst of them as their contemporary. The bond of humanity—fragile, uncertain, corruptible, and finite humanity—is forged between Mary, Jesus, and themselves. And a united front to strive for the common cause of God's reign is also established among them. They can now count on each other in the effort to bring about the change envisioned in the Magnificat.

This liturgical exchange is a vivid testimony that Christian faith is not an escape into the illusion of a cult of Mary or Jesus; it is a vision of God and human beings working toward the transfiguration of the world. Faith is not a substitute for disappointments in life; it is the courage to live as fully as possible in the midst of adversities. Faith does not end where hope collapses and despair sets in; it rekindles hope in us to greet humanity with the promise of life, reconstructs the vision of a future world, and generates the strength to strive for the fulfillment of meaning in God. This is the faith of the Magnificat. The reign of God is the reign of the Magnificat.

Song of God's Reign

The Magnificat is the song of God's reign. It is the anthem of God's presence. It is the hymn of God's salvation.

> Tell out, my soul, the greatness of the Lord,
> rejoice, rejoice, my spirit, in God my savior.

With these opening words a mighty chorus rises from the heart of humanity to fill the entire creation—the space-time of God's saving activity. It is a chorus of praise. It is a chorale of jubilation. And it is an oratorio extolling God's salvation.

It is a fact of great significance that the Magnificat is put in the mouth of Mary, a woman, and not in the mouth of Joseph, a man. In a patriarchal society it is the man, the husband, the father, who takes all the credit for the birth of a child. And when the marriage fails to produce a child, especially a male child, it is not the man, the husband, who does not go through birth-pangs, that takes the blame, but the woman, the wife, who experiences the extreme pain of birthing. The religious tradition within which Jesus was born was a patriarchal tradition. It was a male-dominated society. How, then, did these words of the Magnificat come to be associated with Mary? The Magnificat could not have come from men. It must have its origin in a circle of women including Mary—women who longed for freedom from the tradition and society oppressive to them. The "woman power" contained in it was so overwhelming that Luke must not have found it possible to change it from a song of Mary to a song of Joseph, from a women's hymn to a men's hymn. The Magnificat is the triumph of women's spirit over men's domination. It is a reaffirmation of their inalienable right as children of God on a par with men.

For some women this "triumph of the spirit," this "reaffirmation of their inalienable right," has to be won through the painful experience of separating from their men, their husbands. The cost of asserting "I am a woman" is high, as these words testify:

> I emerged as a "woman" *only when* I chose to be free of bondage in marriage ... disrespected, discriminated against, redundant. Then I

became a woman—fighting to live, to retain my humanity. I chose to become myself again. My struggle to become a "woman" is a struggle to personhood—to become human.[5]

That a woman has to face hostility in the struggle for her humanity, that she has to sever the bond of marriage in order to recover her personhood, is, in one sense, a deep tragedy. It is men who are accountable for the tragedy.

But she can be a woman now. The cost is very high, but it is worth it. Woman can be woman in her own right. Her personhood does not have to be derived from man. She is human because she is woman, not because she is part of a man. She is a person because she is a woman, not because she is a helpmeet of a man. This freedom to be woman is the basis of a new relationship with men, the foundation of a new society, and the ground of a new order and structure of a religious community. "I am a woman" is therefore a twentieth-century version of Mary's Magnificat.

It is a fact of an even greater significance that the Magnificat is sung not by a woman rich and high, a woman of means and privilege. Even in a patriarchal society and in a male-dominated religious community there are women of influence because of the wealth they possess and the privileges they hold. In league with their rich and powerful men and husbands they can be oppressors not only of their sisters but also their brothers. But the Mary of the Magnificat did not belong to this group of oppressive women. She was God's servant, "humble as she was." Humility here is not merely religious humility, the kind of humility exploited by men to keep women in submission to men under the pretext of submission to God. This has at last dawned on some women Christians and theologians in Asia. In the statement issued by the participants at the Asian Women's Theology Conference in 1985 we find these words:

> Mary has been depicted as passive and submissive. This is a masculine perception of idealized femininity which has been inflicted on us and which many of us have tried to internalize. When imitated, Mary becomes an extremely useful means of domesticating women and other oppressed people.... What makes it worse is when this kind of model is held up for the poor and for women particularly, reinforcing their subordinate position in the family, society and in the church.[6]

Mary freed from the cult of Mary, Mary divested of silk robe and gold rings—this authentic Mary, this liberated Mary, must be the Mary who

---

5. Susan Joseph, "I Am a Woman," in *In God's Image* (c/o World Student Christian Federation, Hong Kong), September 1988, 88; emphasis added.

6. See *In God's Image*, December 1988, 9.

compels us to redefine human relations in the family, the organizational principles and structures of society, and the meaning and ordering of the Christian church. We can no longer avoid the radical implications this Mary poses for us, for the church, and for the world. "The Magnificat in the 20th century," says most pointedly the statement just quoted, "is the song of liberation for all humankind."[7]

And it is a fact of far-reaching significance that the Magnificat reaches beyond humble and oppressed women to humble and oppressed human beings, women or men, men as well as women. The Magnificat is a hymn of the disinherited and the oppressed. Mary was one of such people. The author of the affirmation "I am a woman" is also one of them. Those women Christians and theologians at the Asian Women's Theology Conference of course belong to them. But in a class society, whether in the East or in the West, in the South or in the North, there are men beside women who are disinherited and oppressed. In a socially and politically authoritarian country men as well women are subject to oppression and humiliation. And children too, or rather children in particular, easily fall victims to the adult world of racial conflicts, struggles for political power, insanity, and war. "Child of War," a poem by a Sri Lankan woman, is a chilling testimony to what has just been said:

> Grey faces
> Frozen with premature knowing
> They stand on piles of
> Bombed-out rock
> Bewilderment and shock
> Soft minds
> Scarred by blasts of
> Barrel bombs and shells
> Listlessly to heap and mend
> Doomed frontiers
>
> Stretch so bleak and bare
> Scorched palms and
> Yellow grass everywhere
> They crawl on fours
> Like rats that search for grime
> With eyes upswept
> To dart to rubble mines.

---

7. Ibid., 12.

> Child of War
> Child without light
> Struggle on
> High above
> Your wishing star
> Shines beyond.[8]

The Magnificat must be a song of children of war too. It sings for the "wishing star shining beyond" in the midst of rubble and destruction created by war. Sung by them, the poem becomes a magnificat of freedom from fear, a song of deliverance from hunger, and above all a hymn of liberation from the violence of war. The Magnificat is a freedom song for all humanity. And it is significant that it is sung by a woman in the first instance, or at least even Luke, a male writer in a patriarchal society, was moved to ascribe it to a particular woman, Mary. How the Spirit of God works in mysterious ways!

Hymn of Joy and Freedom

Affirmed in these opening verses of the Magnificat are, however, not only the personhood of women, the longing of the disinherited, the vision of the oppressed, but also trust and joy in the great God. God is great not because God is almighty, but because God saves. God is great not because God intimidates, but because God comforts. God is great not because God bursts out in terrible anger from time to time to punish those deemed disobedient to God, but because God upholds the weak and lifts up those who are fallen. And God is great not because God is decked with glory and power, but because God "tenderly looks upon God's servant, humble as Mary is." This kind of greatness is of course totally different from the kind of greatness with which we are all too familiar—the greatness of an autocratic ruler that shatters the confidence of people and makes them afraid, the greatness of the religious authorities that threatens believers with punishment and eternal death in hell. The greatness of God sung in the Magnificat has nothing to do with that kind of greatness. It restores confidence to people. It empowers the downtrodden. It enables the humble men and women to be able to burst out in joyous singing once again from the bottom of their hearts. This is the greatness of God's reign.

The Magnificat has to be, then, a hymn of joy. "Rejoice, rejoice, my spirit!" This is the call of the spirit in ecstasy. It is a summons to all human

---

8. The poem is by Ranjani Mendis and to be found in *Life for the People*, Ecumenical Peace Program in Asia (CCA–International Affairs, Hong Kong) 1, no. 3 (September–December 1988): 26.

spirits to join in the ecstasy of the soul. The word "ecstasy" has become a word of reproach within the mainline Protestant churches. We have banned it from our public worship. We shun it in the privacy of our spiritual life. We are afraid of it as if it will seduce us into self-intoxication or speaking in tongues. As a result we have become incapable of getting excited in our life of faith. Being averse to irrational behaviors at worship services of some Christian sectarian groups, we become so restrained in public demonstration of emotion that our conduct of worship does not display joy inside us—the joy that comes from fellowship with one another and from communion with God.

But there is no reason why ecstasy should not be reintroduced into our life and faith. According to the dictionary ecstasy, among other things, is "a feeling of overpowering joy." When joy overpowers us, we clap our hands. When it overwhelms us, we burst into song. When it takes hold of us, we are transfigured. We are transported into deep communion with God, the source of our life and being. Joy such as this gives us the power to live in the world with courage and hope. Paul must have experienced this kind of overpowering joy to be able to say to the Christians at Philippi: "I wish you joy in the Lord always. Again I say: all joy be yours" (Phil. 4:4).

As a hymn of joy the Magnificat is a song of freedom. To be able to rejoice in the midst of hardships is a sign of freedom. To find joy despite adversities of life comes from the power of freedom. To feel overpowering joy even when life faces humiliation and hostility must be a liberating kind of freedom. This is an inner freedom made possible not merely by discipline and the will-power of human beings but by God, the very source and origin of freedom. God and human beings are closely related in freedom. Human beings can be free and must be free because God is free. The reverse is also true. God is not free until we human beings are free. God is free, free at last, when we human beings become free, free at last. The Magnificat is the song of God's freedom as well as ours. It is our chorus of praise and jubilation, and it is also God's.

It is this hymn of joy and freedom, this song of God's reign, that becomes the Magnificat of Mary, a woman destined to give birth to the life that was to be the most powerful happening in the whole of human history. Mary, an already engaged but not yet married woman, was to bear a child. To be an unwed mother? She was confused and frightened. And she was helpless. She could already feel the accusing fingers pointing at her. She would have to brace herself against merciless social customs and severe religious laws—customs and laws that had for centuries humiliated women, made them submissive to men, and treated them as inferior objects.

Joseph, a Man of Principle

It is, for example, stipulated that a bride found not to be a virgin when brought to her husband's home is to be stoned to death (Deut. 22:20-21). There is of course no such stipulation for a bridegroom. It is a law made by men to keep women in their place that Mary had to face. A law such as this is an insult not only to the integrity of women but to their humanity. It makes women live completely at the mercy of men and their whims. In the case of Mary, would death have been her fate if Joseph, her fiancé, had not been merciful as well as upright? According to what Matthew tells us in his Gospel, "Being a man of principle, and at the same time wanting to save her from exposure, Joseph made up his mind to have the marriage contract quietly set aside" (1:19). This little remark has not caught much of our attention. In the Nativity story, from the annunciation of the angel to the birth of Jesus, Mary is the central figure. It is she who commands our attention, inspires our devotion, and evokes our imagination. Joseph plays only an insignificant role and quickly fades into the background. We casually pass over this little remark about Joseph without further thought—a remark Matthew inserted in his story.

But the remark cannot be passed over casually. This is the only place that tells us something about Joseph. He is said to be "a man of principle" (REB) or "a righteous man" (NRSV). Only a few words. But these few words seem to have a magic power to bring Joseph back to life. In this brief and only description of him we encounter a real person with strong character. He must have been known to be a man of principle, that is, a man of right conduct, a man of integrity. This must have made him a man of moral character as well as a devout believer. Religious devotion and moral uprightness must have combined to make him a well-respected member and a highly regarded artisan in his community. Within a religious community, moreover, one's moral character is closely associated with strict codes of sexual conduct. "A man of principle," then, is a person who, among other things, adheres strictly to the codes of sexual conduct prescribed by the law and enforced by the religious authorities.

How would Joseph, a man of principle, not have taken Mary's pregnancy as the result of her unfaithfulness and wanted to set aside the marriage contract (Matt. 1:19)?[9] They had been engaged, but not yet mar-

---

9. See Raymond E. Brown, *The Birth of the Messiah: A Commentary on the Infancy Narratives in Matthew and Luke* (Garden City, N.Y.: Doubleday, 1977), 127. In Brown's view, "... while Joseph's sense of obedience to the law forced him in conscience to divorce Mary, his unwillingness to expose her to public disgrace led him to proceed without accusation of serious crime. He was upright *but* also merciful. This theory demands no special understanding on Joseph's part about the origins of Mary's pregnancy; he assumes that she was unfaithful. It also makes perfect sense of the angel's instructing Joseph not to be afraid to take Mary his

ried. It was the intervention of the angel, so Matthew tells us, that saved her from punishment by the law. Without that intervention, Mary's fate would have depended entirely on Joseph's discretion and mercy. It would have been decided on the basis of how Joseph would live up to his principles. Contrary to the common perception, Joseph's role in the story cannot, thus, be minimized. The development of the story must have owed much to him. The outcome of it would have depended entirely on his decision. So important was the part he could have played in the whole matter that, to use a Chinese expression, "each step he would have decided to take would have affected in a significant way" (*chu choo ch'in chung* in Chinese) the unfolding of the drama surrounding the mystery of Jesus' birth, life, and future ministry. Had Joseph taken steps to nullify the marriage contract, the whole subsequent history would have been an entirely different story.

History and theology have not done justice to Joseph as a key player in the Nativity story. The potential threat he might have posed to the official view regarding Jesus' birth must have cost him his place in the development of the Christian faith. But already in the Gospel narratives Joseph quickly faded out of the scene and eventually was forgotten entirely. He was not only forgotten by the writers of the Gospels, he was also set aside by Christians and theologians in the history of Christianity. His place in the drama of God's saving activity must be restored. He must have come to realize the extraordinary significance of the unusual circumstances in which the conception and birth of the child took place. And he must have decided, early in the development of the unusual event, to be fully behind Mary and supportive of her against the criticism and even opposition his religious community would be directing at him. Although this is not said by Matthew in his account of the story, this must have been partly what he meant when he attributed Joseph's acceptance of Mary's pregnancy to the intervention of the Holy Spirit (Matt. 1:20). And if Mary agonized over the turn of events that were to take place later in the life and ministry of their son, Joseph too must have agonized over them. Joseph might not have lived to see their son crucified on the cross. If he had, his heart would have been torn in extreme grief as Mary's was at the foot of the cross. Joseph must have been, then, more a man of faith than a man of principle. Or he was a man who knew how to put faith above principle and not principle above faith. In this way he became instrumental in the birth of Jesus in cooperation with the Spirit and in solidarity with Mary.

It is against a background such as this, however, that we can realize how extraordinary the Magnificat is as a song of joy and a hymn of free-

---

wife into the home—the law was not being broken because Mary was not an adulteress; she had conceived through the agency of the Holy Spirit with her virginity intact" (ibid.).

dom. The odds against Mary are enormous. The age-long tradition of her religion is against her. The all-important law threatens her life. And above all, she has to face Joseph, no longer someone she could love and trust without question, but someone who, as "a man of principle and a righteous man," could have personified the vindictive power of the law in the male-dominated society. At least this was the Joseph with whom she had to reckon before he was addressed by the Spirit as to the nature of Mary's conception. Mary is a powerless woman before her religion, before her society, and before the man she is engaged to marry. She must have felt utter dejection. And the feeling of humiliation as a woman must have overwhelmed her.

The Spirit Encased in the Female Form

This story of the powerless and helpless Mary is the story of countless women in the West and in the East, in ancient times and in the present day. In the poem "Powerless?" we hear an echo of women through the centuries, including Mary, lamenting their powerlessness and helplessness:

> My spirit was encased
> At birth
> Within the Female Form.
> My role models
> From childhood
> Others encased in the Female Form.
>
> A Female Form
> Is powerless.
> Economically,
> Politically,
> Physically,
> Religiously,
> Domination of the Female Form
> Has always been the norm ... [10]

Frustration reflected in these words is deep. The agony of the spirit "encased in the Female Form" is profound.

The history of women, be it in the East or in the West, is the history of the spirit encased in the female form struggling for emancipation from the society, family, and religion that treat them as less than human and thus as men's property. Violence has been committed against the person

---

10. Ranjini Rebera, "Powerless?" in *In God's Image*, October 19–25, 1985, 120.

and body of women through "witch hunting in Europe, foot binding in China, sati [widow burning] in India, female genital mutilation in Africa."[11] Horror stories of the crimes committed against women in these inhuman practices reveal the very dark side of human cultures and tell how human community can be in the grip of terrible evil powers. With regard to the practice of witch hunting in Europe,

> here is a typical case of Agnes, who was tortured in Tetanwang, Germany. On August 11, 1600, she was hoisted repeatedly in the strappado (a torture consisting of hoisting the subject by a rope, sometimes with the wrists fastened behind the back, and letting the victim fall to the length of the rope).... She bore this heroically, confessing nothing and pardoning those who had falsely accused her, even though she had been hoisted eleven times, ten of them with a fifty-pound weight. Ten weeks later she was hoisted again and was told that her own mother had accused her; then her courage gave away. Four days later she made an unsuccessful attempt at suicide.... Both she and her mother were burnt.[12]

How gruesome the practice must have been! Very often the practice was carried out by the religious establishment, "by priests, lawyers and physicians, both Catholic and Protestant. At times they vied with each other to be more fanatical than the rest."[13] This is one of the dark chapters in the history of Christianity in Europe. Could it be that it is this irrational, inhuman, and anti-God part of the Christian church dominated by male priests and theologians that still lingers on in the objection to the ordination of women in certain churches in the name of tradition and on the grounds that Jesus was a man and not a woman? It is entirely right that the "study of witches [witch hunting] is part of the entombed history of women—it needs to be fully unearthed so that European society and the church can openly acknowledge this guilt, make compensations to the women and not to repeat it in other forms."[14] The same must be said about foot binding in China, sati in India, and female genital mutilation in Africa, in which both secular and religious forces join to subjugate women to the basist desires and whims of men.

But, strangely, throughout human history men have also idealized and idolized the female form, all for their own purposes, be they social, political, economic, biological, religious, or spiritual, completely oblivious

---

11. See Jessie Tellis Nayak, "Institutional Violence against Women in Different Cultures," in *In God's Image*, September 1989, 4.

12. Ibid., 7.

13. Ibid.

14. Ibid.

to the frustration and agony of women bearing the female form. The story of women has indeed been the story of the cult of the Virgin. It is a story of conferring a "divine" status on them while suppressing their real humanity, piling one lofty attribute after another on them on the one hand, and, on the other, reducing them to be passive objects in the male-dominated world. The cult of the Virgin may, in a sense, be an expression of the divided state of the male psyche, making women the objects both of their highest ideals and their lowest instincts. The "human" world is the world of men and not of women. Women do not belong to this "human" world. They are either "divine" or "sub-human." In either case women are not free to be human, to develop their human potentials, to fulfill their human aspirations, and to be full partners with men in society.

Some statistics reveal that even today women are still not free in a world that operates on "male principles." For example:

Two out of three of the world's illiterates are now women, and while the general illiteracy rate is falling, the female illiteracy rate is rising. One third of all families in the world are headed by women. In the developing countries, almost half of all single women over age fifteen are mothers. Only one third of the world's women have any access to contraceptive information or devices, and more than one half have no access to trained help during pregnancy and childbirth. Women in the developing world are responsible for more than 50 per cent of all food production (on the African continent women do 60 to 80 per cent of all agricultural work, 50 per cent of all animal husbandry, and 100 per cent of all food processing). In industrialized countries, women are still paid only one half to three quarters of what men earn at the same jobs, still are ghettoized into lower-paying "female-intensive" job categories, and still are the last hired and the first fired; in Europe and North America, women constitute over 40 per cent of the paid labor force, *in addition* to contributing more than 40 per cent of the Gross Domestic Product in *un*paid labor in the home. As of 1982, 30 million people were unemployed in the industrialized countries and 800 million people in the Third World were living in absolute poverty; most of those affected are migrant workers and their families, youth, the disabled, and the aged—and the majority of those categories are women. Approximately 500 million people suffer from hunger and malnutrition; the most seriously affected are children under age five and women. Twenty million persons die annually of hunger-related causes and one billion endure chronic undernourishment and other poverty de-

privations; the majority are women and children. And this is only part
of the picture.[15]

This observation supported by statistics brings home to us the lamentable
situation of women even today. But this is "only part of the picture." What
would, then, the whole of the picture be? If a partial picture such as this already staggers our minds, would not the whole picture, if it could be known,
defy our imagination?

The picture portrayed here simply does not tally with that of "the Mary
in the holy pictures" displayed during the worship service at a church in
Latin America. That sublime Mary is totally unrelated to the women depicted in this observation. She is an "a-typical" woman, a woman who has
existed only in Christians' religious imagination but never in human history. That Mary has been part of Christian piety for centuries, but never
been part of the reality of the world. That Mary has to be liberated from
the bondage of the church on the one hand and, on the other, set free from
captivity in the male psychic prison. Struggle for that liberation did not begin today; it must have been the concern of the Mary of the Magnificat
two thousand years ago. And that struggle is part of Jesus' struggle for the
reign of God.

The Arrogant Put to Rout

There is another reality with social and religious consequences against
which women must struggle—barrenness. The wife who cannot bear a
child is socially despised and religiously put on probation, so to speak. In
contrast, the woman who gives birth to a child, and especially to a son, even
if she is of low status in family or in society, gains respect and power. This
was true in the ancient Hebrew community and is true in Asian society today. The familiar story of Sarah, Abraham's wife, and Hagar, the Egyptian
slave girl, at once comes to mind (Gen. 16). Sarah, according to the story,
"had borne Abraham no children." This is not only a serious family problem but a grave religious matter. Abraham must have understood it so. The
community in which they lived must have also taken it that way. And Sarah
herself believed it to be having to do with God when she said to her husband: "The Lord has not let me have a child" (Gen. 16:2). Childlessness is
believed to be God's doing in response to specific situations to show God's
displeasure and disapproval. Thus God "closed all the wombs of the house
of Abimelech" (Gen. 20:18, NRSV), king of Gerar, who had taken Sarah to

---

15. Robin Morgan, "Planetary Feminism: The Politics of the 21st Century," in *Sisterhood
Is Global*, comp. and ed. with introduction by Robin Morgan (Garden City, N.Y.: Anchor
Press/Doubleday, 1984), 1–2.

be his wife, showing God's disapproval of what he had done. And in the conflict between the two sister-wives of Jacob for the latter's favor, God took the side of Leah and "opened her womb, but Rachel was barren" (Gen. 20:31, NRSV). Socially and religiously, then, how important it is for women to be able to bear children! Barrenness for women was and still is in some societies today a social disgrace and a religious stigma.

In compliance with the custom of her day this is what Sarah, who was barren, had to propose to Abraham, her husband: "Take my slave-girl [Hagar]; perhaps through her I shall have a son" (Gen. 16:2). The story that ensued has all the ingredients of a tragicomedy. Sarah must have felt vindicated when Hagar, the slave-girl, became pregnant. But her elation was short-lived. Finding herself with child, Hagar, the slave-girl, gained a new status in the family and won respect in the community. This, however, is the beginning of a comedy turned into a tragedy. As the storyteller tells us, "when Hagar knew that she was pregnant, she looked down on her mistress" (16:4). The rest is an all too familiar story. In jealousy and anger Sarah "ill-treated Hagar and she ran away" (16:6).[16] The rest is a human story with a heightened drama, but it is beyond our concern here.

There is good reason, then, to think that the Magnificat of Mary could have been the Magnificat of Elizabeth, her cousin, who "was barren . . . and well on in years" (Luke 1:7), although Luke, author of the Gospel that bears his name, placed the Magnificat in the context of Jesus' conception and birth. In fact, the striking resemblance of the Magnificat to the song of Hannah (1 Sam. 2:1-10) and the almost identical situations of Hannah and Elizabeth, Mary's cousin, becoming pregnant at an advanced stage of their lives led some Bible critics to suggest that the Magnificat was sung, not by Mary, but by Elizabeth.[17] Humiliated, stigmatized, and in anguish because she was not able to bear children—thus, had she been a Chinese woman, "committing the gravest of three cardinal offenses against filial piety for producing no male heir"[18]—Hannah was in the temple at Shilo pouring her heart out before God in tears. Miraculously, her wish was granted and she gave birth to a son. Her prayer of thanksgiving turned into a hymn, a song of joy. She sang:

---

16. Although "ancient law codes provide for punishment if a pregnant female slave claimed equality with her mistress, Sarah has exceeded the limit of justice" (cf. commentary on Gen. 16:4-16 in NEB).

17. For the discussion of this problem see, for example, Josef Ernst, *Das Evangelium nach Lukas*, 4th ed. (Regensburg: Verlag Friedrich Pustet, 1976), 84, and R. E. Brown, *The Birth of the Messiah*, 334–36.

18. The three cardinal offenses against filial piety in traditional Chinese society are failure to support parents when they are alive, failure to give them a decent burial upon their death, and failure to produce a male heir.

> My heart rejoices in the Lord,
> in the Lord I now hold my head high;
> my mouth is full of derision of my foes,
> exultant because thou hast saved me ...
> (1 Sam. 2:1, NEB)

Joy is the theme of this hymn. It brims over from this song. This is Hannah's Magnificat. Her social disgrace has been eliminated. Her religious stigma has been removed. This could have been the Magnificat of Elizabeth, mother of John the Baptist, too. They could have said in joy, using the words of the Magnificat attributed to Mary: "The arrogant of heart and mind God has put to rout!" They were vindicated. They were no longer objects of derision. They could now walk with their heads held high.

How could Hannah and, for that matter, Elizabeth refrain from bursting into the praise of God when their barrenness was removed? One could of course argue that both Hannah and Elizabeth, just as other men and women, were not free from the tradition that binds the destiny of women to the fertile womb. Theirs was a culture, like other Oriental cultures, that could not think of a woman apart from motherhood. "Motherhood," says the Talmud, "is the main goal of a woman; it is the most fulfilling experience she may ever have, her greatest creative achievement."[19] To be barren is not to be able to attain the main goal of a woman. To be deprived of motherhood is not to reach the greatest creative achievement as a woman. Liberation for a woman in such culture is to have the "curse" of childlessness removed.

Of course, liberation for women as we understand it today is not to be defined solely in relation to motherhood. Inability to bear children is a biological-medical problem and not a social-religious issue. Besides, to put the whole blame on the wife is neither just nor right. Often it is the husband's biological-medical defect that is the problem. What is needed is medical help and not recourse to religious explanation. Still, for Hannah and Elizabeth and for millions and millions of women in cultures that stigmatize women for childlessness, to be pregnant was to be liberated from the curse under which they had to live.

Besides, motherhood, just as barrenness, can be enslavement of a woman as well as liberation for her in a society in which the entire burden of childrearing and housekeeping is borne by mothers. Such has been the case in most Oriental societies not only in the past but even today. In response to the question "What are your experiences in the home as wife and mother?" Lita, a Filipino woman, replied:

---

19. See Menachem M. Brayer, *The Jewish Woman in Rabbinic Literature* (Hoboken, N.J.: KTAV Publishing House, 1986), 102.

Like many other women, I know how it is to be a working wife and mother. After working eight hours in the factory, I rush to the market to buy something for the supper. I get home and cook supper. Supper is the only time I get to talk with my husband and children. After supper I wash the children and put them to bed, after which I can then fetch water to do the laundry. When morning comes, I prepare breakfast and pack our lunches for work, do a hurried cleaning of the house and then run to work in order not to be late.[20]

This is the way most women in Asia still live today. One cannot help wondering what joy motherhood brings to women as wives and mothers.

But still, how can one deny to women such as Hannah, Elizabeth, or other countless women in traditional societies the sense of joy and the experience of liberation when they are at last able to be rid of the stigma of barrenness? To be free from the curse of barrenness far outweighed the burden of childrearing. To be liberated from the stigma of childlessness made hardships of life easier to bear. How can we find fault with them for finding liberation in motherhood? "Tell out, my soul, the greatness of the Lord, rejoice, rejoice, my spirit, in God my savior...," so goes the song of Mary. This could have very well been the song of Elizabeth too, a song of liberation.[21]

Whether it is Hannah, Elizabeth, or even Mary, they are victims of the social-cultural conventions and the religious traditions that penalized women for being women, humiliated their humanity, and made them submit to the dictates of men. It must be within such social and religious experiences that they came to know what God's salvation meant. That salvation is not a guarantee that they will be freed from the fetters of religion and culture that make them unfree. That liberation does not necessarily promise that they will win equality with men. It can be followed by other fetters that motherhood would bring them. But liberation, short-lived or more enduring, is liberation. Human history is made possible by countless small liberations. The transformation of a society, a revolution of political systems and structures, or a change in religious and cultural mores is

---

20. *In God's Image*, March 1989, 10.

21. It is possible that the Magnificat also could have expressed Elizabeth's own experience. Eduard Schweizer, for example, observes: "Without this verse [1:48b: For, from this day forth, all generations will count me blessed], the hymn could originally have been Elizabeth's. This theory is supported by v. 48a and the parallelism with the song of Hannah (1 Sam. 2:1-10), as well as by v. 41 (Elizabeth's being filled with the Holy Spirit) and v. 56 ('her' referring to Elizabeth, while Mary is named explicitly). Was the conclusion of v. 41 together with vs. 46-55 circulated as a hymn of Elizabeth, like v. 67 with the hymn of Zachariah? Was it Luke who placed the Song in the mouth of Mary, adding v. 48b, to make Elizabeth more clearly subordinate to her (cf. Gen. 30:11)?" (*The Good News according to Luke*, trans. David E. Green [Atlanta: John Knox Press, 1984], 33–34).

brought about by the accumulation of each and every liberation achieved and experienced by individual persons and by a community. Can we not, then, say that the struggle of women today for their rights and integrity as human beings is already foreshadowed by women such as Hannah, Elizabeth, or Mary? Can we also not say that such struggle of women is part of the struggle of God's reign in the message and ministry of Jesus?

Change of Power Relations

The Magnificat has not ceased in human history. If it was sung by Mary, mother of Jesus, it was also sung by Elizabeth, mother of John the Baptist, and by Hannah, mother of Samuel the prophet. And if it was on the lips of Mary, it has also been on the lips of many a woman in the East and in the West, at present as well as in the past. Human history is a history of the Magnificat. It is the story of the song of Mary. Earlier we quoted a poem by a woman from Australia. It was a song of anguish. It was a hymn of helplessness. But as the poem goes on, it is transformed into a song, a hymn, of the Magnificat. For she continues:

> But power exists
> When power is given.
> Power controls
> By submission,
> By acceptance.
> I grant power
> To People
> To Systems
> To Society
> To Structures.
>
> Now my spirit
> Re-awakens and revives
> As a plant
> Crushed within powerful stone
> That refuses to be crushed
> But pushes its way,
> At first hesitantly,
> Then with confidence
> To reach out
> To the Source of its life—
> The sun.
> I too refuse to abdicate
> To grant power

To be crushed.
I reach out exultantly
To the Source of all life![22]

In comparison with the song of Hannah and Mary's Magnificat this poem is rather modest in its claim and sober in its tone. But one cannot miss the excitement, however subdued, of recovering one's authentic self—the self not shaped by what the male-dominated world desires and demands, but by God, the source of all Life.

The problem is always power. And the author of this contemporary version of the Magnificat faces it from the outset. "Power exists," she says. We can in fact go a step further and say: power *is*. In the beginning, to paraphrase the opening words of John's Gospel, was power. Not only in the beginning, but perhaps even before the beginning, power was. Power does not come into existence. Power is being and as such it brings all things into existence. That power, in the biblical faith, is God. *God is power*. This is how human beings already in the earliest times experienced what they came to call and worship as God. God as creator and savior is God's self-manifestation as power. It is an awesome power. And it is also a loving power. Here the most basic nature of power becomes evident. For power to be power it has to manifest itself, to become other than itself. Power realizes itself in things different from itself. The power that remains within itself and cannot break out of itself is an emasculated power. It contradicts its own very nature and becomes self-destructive. This is when power turns demonic. It not only destroys itself but those drawn into the sphere of its activity. Authoritarian systems and structures, be they social, political, or religious, are the manifestations of power in its demonic form.

But the manifestation of power does not have to be demonic. It can be creative and redemptive. This is why God as power is perceived to be the creator and redeemer. God as creator and redeemer is God breaking out of Godself, God manifesting Godself. God realizing Godself in that which is not God. This must be the theological meaning underlying the story of creation, from the story of "genesis" in the Hebrew Bible to the stories of creation of one kind or another in almost all ancient human communities. The genesis story in Hebrew Scripture seems to have grasped this important theological insight when it says as the work of God's creation nears completion: "Let us make human beings in our image, after our likeness" (Gen. 1:26). Human being is thus not God. We are other than God. We are *human* beings and not divine beings. But we are part, and an extremely im-

---

22. Ranjini Rebera, "Powerless?" in *In God's Image*, October 19–25, 1985, 120.

portant part at that, of God's self-manifestation in that which is not God. This is the theological basis of anthropology.

To use the expression of the poem we are considering here, God "grants power." The power that God grants is the power to live and the power to be. It is the power of life. The order of the created universe is the ordering of this power of life from inorganic lives to organic lives, from inanimate things to animate things, from impersonal objects to personal subjects, from unconscious beings to conscious beings. There is of course something beyond this "natural" ordering of power. There are degrees of intensity in which this God-given power gets expressed and embodied in the world. I am referring to the power to reflect, think, plan, develop, even create. It is this power that enables us human beings to dream dreams, to develop community, to organize society, and to build civilization. To use the words of the poem again, this power is granted "to people, to systems, to society, to structures."

Power thus acquires social-political values and religious-cultural demands. This is the power we have come to know—the power that realizes itself in systems and structures, be they social, political, religious, or cultural. But there is something here that changes the nature of the God-given power when that power becomes institutionalized in systems and structures. It becomes less and less God-given. It creates its own values and makes its own demands independently of its source and origin. Paul was right when he said in the thirteenth chapter of his letter to the Romans that "all authority comes from God." This is a theo-logical understanding of power as something granted by God. But he was no longer right when he continued to say that "the existing authorities are instituted by God." Here Paul did not take into account the change in the nature of power when it gets instituted into social, political, and religious systems and structures. As a matter of fact "the existing authorities" are *not* instituted by God. We cannot then follow his admonition that "every person must submit to the authorities in power" without further ado.

The values and demands that systems and structures establish have the strong tendency to become the ideological basis of maintaining the status quo and of strengthening the existing order of power and authority. The often quoted speech of Ulysses in Shakespeare's *Troilus and Cressida* is an eloquent expression in support of the existing order over against the chaos that might erupt in the event that order collapses:

> The heavens themselves, the planets, and this center,
> Observe degree, priority, and place,
> Insisture, course, proportion, season, form,
> Office, and custom, in all line of order: ...

How could communities,
Degrees in schools, and brotherhood in cities,
Peaceful commerce from dividable shores,
The primogenetive and due of birth,
Prerogative of age, crowns, scepters, laurels,
But by degree, stand in authentic place?
Take but degree away, untune that string,
And hark! what discord follows....
Strength should be lord of imbecility,
And the rude son should strike his father dead;
Force should be right; or rather, right and wrong—
Between whose endless jar justice resides—
Should lose their names, and so should justice too.
Then everything includes itself in power,
Power into will, will into appetite;
And appetite, a universal wolf,
Must make perforce a universal prey,
And last eat up himself.[23]

What could be a more effective argument against the right to challenge the powers that be and the attempts to change them?

But the heart of the matter is precisely the nature and manifestation of the power defended by those in power. This is the order, justice, and peace seen by the rulers and not by the ruled. What is regarded as justice at the top of the hierarchy of power may be injustice when it reaches the bottom of the hierarchy. The order created by those who hold power may be oppression when applied to those without power. And what is upheld as peace by those who enjoy privileges may in fact be the cause of division and hostility in a society in which the majority of people are deprived of the basic necessities of a decent life. Human history is in fact a history of disruption, collapse, and eventually replacement of the power that maintains the order, justice, and peace in support of the ruling elite, from kings to ministers, from emperors to magistrates, from presidents to local officials.

How strong and prevailing this "ideology of order," the ideology that "power, broken loose from order, must prey upon itself"[24] throughout human history! Here is a statement from a context entirely different from the context of the speech just quoted. It is from *The Great Learning* (*Ta Hsueh*), a Confucian classic used as a required text in Chinese education,

---

23. Quoted by Godfrey Gunatilleke, "The Ethics of Order and Change: An Analytical Framework," in *Ethical Dilemmas of Development in Asia*, ed. Godfrey Gunatilleke, Neelan Tiruchelvam and Radhika Coomaraswamy (Lexington, Mass.: D. C. Heath, 1983), 3.
24. Ibid., 4.

which has exerted a profound influence from the early fourteenth century to the twentieth:

> From the Son of Heaven down to the common people, all must regard cultivation of the personal life as the root or foundation. There is never a case when the root is in disorder and yet the branches are in order. There has never been a case when what is treated with great importance becomes a matter of slightest importance or what is treated with slight importance becomes a matter of great importance.[25]

At first sight the statement sounds plausible. It follows "the Way of Great Learning" based on the tradition built on almost preordained social, political, and religious order, with people at the bottom and the state at the top presided over by the ruler as "the Son of Heaven." But when this order is put into question, the values and demands derived from it are also put into question. The relationship between order and disorder maintained in the traditional society—the order upheld by the ruler and the disorder created by challenge to that order—cannot remain intact. The disorder created by the challenge to the existing order may have to be accepted as a necessary process to bring about a new order that does justice to the values and demands for which people at the bottom aspire and struggle.

What is inculcated in this Confucian classic is cultivation of private virtues as the foundation of a society to the neglect of the injustice and corruption that inhere in systems and structures. "An ethos of this nature," it is observed very pointedly,

> placed the emphasis on personal perfection and the spiritual liberation of the individual within a given system. To that extent, it deflected attention from the imperfection of the system and the social structures themselves. Such an approach could easily lead to a moral complacency that acquiesced in social evils readily accepted as imperfections of the system. It could become an ideology for the legitimation and rationalization of inequality and social oppression. At each stage of human history, the order-oriented ethos accepted and legitimized the imperfections and deformities of that time—slavery, serfdom, or any other exploitative socioeconomic system and structure of power.[26]

---

25. Wing-Tsit Chan, *A Source Book in Chinese Philosophy*, trans. and comp. Wing-Tsit Chan (Princeton: Princeton University Press, 1963), 87.
26. Gunatilleke, "The Ethics of Order and Change: An Analytical Framework," 4.

How true this is! Is it not to break such ideology of order that power is also granted to the people who suffer from the institutions and structures built on that ideology? It is this power granted to people that is the heart of the Magnificat sung by Mary, by Elizabeth, by Hannah, and by those women and men who become conscious of the power granted to them and who decide not to accept the ideology of order as their civil duty. It is obvious, then, that the spirit of the Magnificat is the spirit awakened in all people who struggle to be free from oppressive systems, structures, and traditions. The Magnificat is a vision that belongs to all humanity.

I Will Not Compromise!

What is called for, then, is a change of power relations as the result of the human spirit "reawakened and revived" from submission and resignation, the spirit that "refuses to be crushed and reaches out to the source of its life." The struggle of the human spirit for a change of power relations is a long and hard struggle. How can it not be long and hard when "monarchs have to be brought down from their thrones and the humble to be lifted up," to quote the Magnificat. Human history consists of countless stories of the struggle to replace oppressive powers with the power that brings about freedom and justice through the people involved in the struggle.

This is how the story of Mariakutty Thoman, a sixty-eight-year-old Syrian Christian woman, a primary school teacher from India, was lived and told. After her parents' death, she dedicated her life to the well-being of her brothers, only to find that she was denied a share in the family property she had helped to build and was reduced to a nobody and nothing in the eyes of the law and of the community. This is why her long struggle against the law, her brothers, and her community started. It took her to the People's Council for Free Legal Aid where the following exchange took place between her and a judge:

> JUDGE: How old are you?
> MARIAKUTTY: Sixty-eight years.
> JUDGE: Is this the time to fight with your brothers? How much longer will you live?
> MARIAKUTTY: I will answer that question if you give me in writing how long *you* will live. If the Lord so desires you may go before I do. . . .
> JUDGE: You must be prepared for great sacrifice: (a) You must forget the cost of trees [on the land] which are valued at seven lakh rupees [one lakh is a hundred thousand rupees] and have now been cut down and sold, (b) the cost of the ancestral houses which have

been demolished, (c) and of immovables which are the share of the girls but which no longer exist.

MARIAKUTTY: This I am not prepared to do, as without them there is only barren land left. They [her brothers] divided the spoils as soon as they read in the newspapers that I had filed a Writ in the Supreme Court. Why do you not ask my brothers to make any sacrifice? . . .

JUDGE: You have become a heroine among the women of Travancore and Cochin. Now you must show that you are capable of great sacrifice.

MARIAKUTTY: Thank you for the compliment. I am prepared for reasonable sacrifice. But don't forget that I have fought for equal rights. Now I cannot be forced to accept a pittance. Women all over this state will be watching my case. I must show them that I fought for Equality—and that equality is not negotiable.

The case was not resolved. The judge who presided over it "suggested one and half lakhs as my share. My brothers were not agreeable. Women were not worth that much. I too was not agreeable." Her struggle continues. "A woman," she writes, "is worth an amount equal to that which is given to her brother. A brother's share is between five and six lakhs. I WILL NOT COMPROMISE."[27] Those with power, in this case the woman's brothers and the judge, have not yet been brought down from the seat of power. But in her determination to carry on the struggle, she, a humble old woman, is already lifted high. She will no longer accept submission to the demands of the others as the price for her case. Her sense of justice and her defiance to the injustice done to her have changed the power relations between her and her brothers, between her and the judge, and even between her and the law of the land—the law that takes the side of the powerful against the powerless, the law manipulated to benefit men at the expense of women.

"I will not compromise!" In this declaration of the old woman we have a manifesto of the reign of the Magnificat. And of course the reign of the Magnificat is the reign of God. The reign of God includes "noncompromise" when the weak are exploited, when the poor are downtrodden, when the oppressed cannot "raise their heads above the sky" (*chhut-thau-thi* in Taiwanese, meaning the overcoming of overwhelming hardships, despair, or resignation in adverse situations), and, in the case of this Indian woman, when the law is bent and distorted to satisfy greedy men and to humiliate women. When she declared, "I WILL NOT COMPROMISE!" not in a whisper but in a loud voice, not in small letters but in

---

27. The story is to be found in *Stree* no. 14 (March 1984): 9–11.

capital letters, she was singing her Magnificat and witnessing to the reign of God. She was part of the great number of people who struggle to change the power relations that have shaped their tradition and defined the social values and ethical standards of their society.

The stakes are high, not only for herself, but for all women in India. She had to tell the judge that "the women all over this state will be watching my case." Surely not only women in her state but all women in India would be watching her case in suspense and hope. Even as the struggle for women's rights continues, "not only is women's status lower than men's," it has been pointed out, "but the gap between the two is now widening."[28] Each and every compromise makes this already widening gap even wider. The sixty-eight-year-old Mariakutty Thoman was speaking for all long-suffering women of India when she declared before the judge that "equality [between women and men] is not negotiable."

Many things in life can and must be negotiable. For public safety and for the welfare of the community one's personal desires must be negotiable. Individual needs must be negotiable for the sake of the needs of a greater number of people. But there are a few things that are not negotiable. One of them is equality between women and men. That equality is ordained by God and is the law of the universe. It is the very basis of creative relationships between women and men. Treating women as less than men hampers those relationships, and regarding men as more than women destroys them. In either case both women *and* men are less than human. In order, then, for women to be truly women, they must be equal to men and not less than men. At the same time, for men to be truly men, they must be equal to women and not more than women. It is only when women and men are equal partners in life that they can enjoy one another as truly human beings for better or for worse, for richer or for poorer.

Elephants and Women-power

The Magnificat, it has been pointed out, "was a general hymn applicable to the downtrodden of Israel."[29] This has become evident from what has already been said. This links Mary immediately to Elizabeth her cousin, to Hannah of the former days. It also relates her to the prophetic movement in the history of ancient Israel on the one hand, and, on the other, to the history of God's reign that has already begun with the conception and birth of her son Jesus. What we witness here is the vision of the Magnificat enlarged to join with the vision of the reign of God.

---

28. Katherine K. Young, "Hinduism," in *Women in World Religions*, ed. Arvind Sharma (Albany: State University of New York Press, 1987), 97.

29. R. E. Brown, *The Birth of the Messiah*, 335.

This is already a big leap of faith contained in the theology of the Magnificat. It becomes the theological focus for us Christians when we try to identify the saving activity of God in human community, to surmise the meaning of human history. For this very reason, the Magnificat has to break out of the history of Israel and the history of Christianity to be linked up with the experiences of life and history outside its immediate frame of reference. The vision of the Magnificat is expanded further to merge with the vision of God's reign in the *Oikumenē*, in the whole inhabited world. What the Magnificat contends and celebrates "describes the human situation in general."[30] Because this is what the Magnificat does—describing the human situation in general—it also describes the human situation in particular living contexts. The Magnificat is not a theological principle construed in the realm of abstraction. It grows out of the human soul touched, moved, and embraced by God—the soul struggling with the harsh realities of the world, the soul threatened by the evil forces at work in human community, and the soul that finally finds assurance and confidence in God. Mary's was such a soul. Elizabeth's was also such a soul. Hannah's too was such a soul. And all women, men, and children in distress who have found reasons to celebrate life experience movements of such soul within them.

The fact of the matter is that the Magnificat is the hymn of praise sung at the epiphany of God's reign. As such, it must be Jesus' Magnificat as well. If he had known it—would it be totally out of place to suggest that Jesus must have come to know it?—he would certainly have said "Amen" to it. Did he not himself proclaim that God's reign belongs to "those who are in need, those who weep now and those who are persecuted" (Luke 6:20-23 and Matt. 5:3-10)? What could have been a better description of his ministry with the poor and the disinherited than the Magnificat? What could have been a more profound "mission statement" of his work of empowering the powerless and the oppressed? And what could have been a more challenging manifesto of what he had taken upon himself to do? Did he have the Magnificat in mind when he, at the beginning of his mission in his hometown of Nazareth, announced good news to the poor, the sick, the prisoners, and the broken victims, quoting the stirring words from the prophet Isaiah (Luke 4:18-19)? He must have.

One of the crucial expressions in the Magnificat is "low estate" (RSV) or "humble" (REB), to which we referred earlier. It is the rendering of the

---

30. Schweizer, *The Good News according to Luke*, 35. Equally instructive is the observation made by René Laurentin: "The conjunction of God and humanity extends thus from the two women [Mary and Elizabeth] who prophesy, to the whole people, without opening up to the universalism which will be expressed later in the canticles of Zachariah (like 1:7a) and Simeon (2:32)." See his *Truth of Christmas*, trans. Michael J. Wrenn (Petersham, Mass.: St. Bede's Publications, 1986), 157.

Greek word *tapeinosis*, meaning humility, humiliation, barrenness, poverty. Who are those humble ones, or humiliated ones rather, those people who belong to low estate? They are the "poor ones" (the *Anawim*), that is, "those who could not trust in their own strength but had to in utter confidence upon God: the lowly, the poor, the sick, the downtrodden, the widows and orphans."[31] It is these "poor ones" who dominate the main concern of the Magnificat. And of course they are the women, men, and children with whom Jesus associated himself. If the Magnificat is a song of these "poor ones," it must have also been Jesus' own song. If it is a hymn of jubilation for the disinherited and the oppressed, it must have been Jesus' own hymn too.

God "lifted high the humble," so goes the Magnificat, and "satisfied the hungry with good things" (Luke 1:52-53). "Blessed are you who now go hungry," says Jesus in the Beatitudes, "you will be satisfied" (Luke 6:21; par. Matt. 5:6). The Magnificat and the Beatitudes—do they not only speak the same language but express the same longing, the same vision, for the reign of God? Those "poor ones" are still poor. Some of them still suffer from hunger. Their rice bowls may still be empty. Their thatched huts have not turned into palaces, and never will. The Magnificat is not a song of magic. The Beatitudes do not encourage people to indulge in illusion. But a big difference has occurred to them. They can no longer be humiliated because they are poor. They cannot allow themselves to be despised anymore because they are not members of a high society. They have regained their humanity. This is what the Magnificat celebrates, and this is what the Beatitudes proclaim.

This is the basis that makes a change of power relations possible and even necessary. After the Magnificat and the Beatitudes a change of power relations between the rich and the poor, between the ruler and the ruled, between the powerful and the powerless, is no longer an option but an imperative. It is not something that may take place sometime in the future but must take place now. Does this mean that the change will occur all of a sudden with God's miraculous intervention? Is it going to be a change without tears? Does it lead to the expectation that a revolution will take place without sweat, toil, and cost? Does this mean that "the poor ones" have become the "rich and mighty ones" to be driven in turn from the seat of power and riches in the next revolution?

The change of power relations extolled in the Magnificat and anticipated in the Beatitudes does not mean any such things. Yes, the "poor and

31. R. E. Brown, *The Birth of the Messiah*, 351. "The word Anawim," explains Brown, "represents a plural from the Hebrew *'anaw*, which along with its cognate *'ani*, is a word for 'poor, humble, afflicted.' Also of importance is the abstract noun *'oni*—lowliness, poverty" (ibid., 35, 350).

humble" ones have gained power, but it is not the political and economic power of the "rich and mighty" ones that they have won. What they have won is the power to be human, the power to claim their humanity, the power to assert their dignity as human beings. It is the power that enables them to declare before the court that serves the powerful with a loud clear voice: I WILL NOT COMPROMISE! This is the moral power with which the powerful must reckon. This is the spiritual power that challenges the arrogance of the rich. This moral power and this spiritual power are nothing but the power of God's reign at work in the life and history of humanity.

A story from Kumarikatta of Assam, again from India, illustrates this dramatic change of power relations in that community. For a long time land in Kumarikatta was occupied by some tribes and cultivated by them. But the people who depended entirely on that land for their living were often threatened with eviction by the local authorities. They had fought the threat until one day when they received an ultimatum saying that the authorities "would bring in a herd of elephants to trample the huts. The elephants came. The village people gathered outside the huts. There was a tense silence...."

This was the day of reckoning for the poor and harassed villagers. Confronted with the powerful elephants to carry out the destruction of their community ordered by the authorities, they felt utterly helpless and almost gave in to resignation. But something totally unexpected happened. "Suddenly," so the story goes,

> with no discussion and without the advice of any so-called organizers, village women rushed out of the crowd and started to embrace the elephant's trunks and legs, chanting prayers that they usually sang on a particular *pooja* (sacred) day. This *pooja* was devoted to the elephant god and it was customary for these women to stroke the elephants and rub sandal paste, *kumkum*, and flowers on them with devotion and love. These women started to imitate the same ritual, with full devotion. The elephants responded in turn by accepting this with their conventional grace. They refused to move further. No one—the authorities, the social workers, or even the men squatters—could do anything. The elephants turned back—and the women, men, and children returned to their huts.[32]

This is a drama of the Magnificat. There is even participation of nature in this human drama with the appearance of the elephants.

---

32. This is a true story, told by Devaki Jain, "India: A Condition across Caste and Class," in *Sisterhood Is Global*, 309.

The elephants, those giants of animals, were brought in to intimidate the village people into submission to the demands of the authorities. But the next thing we see is that these same elephants, affected by the religious devotion shown them by the women, refused to carry out the work of destruction. They became friends of the hard-pressed village people. And the situation that emerged reminds us of the idyllic scene of peace and harmony depicted by Isaiah the prophet in Hebrew Scripture:

> Then the wolf will live with the lamb,
>   and the leopard lie down with the kid;
> the calf and the young lion will feed together,
> with a little child to tend them.
>   The cow and the bear will be friends,
>   and their young will lie down together;
> and the lion will eat straw like cattle.
> The infant will play over the cobra's hole,
>   and the young child dance over the viper's nest.
> There will be neither hurt nor harm in all my holy mountain;
> for the land will be filled with the knowledge of the LORD,
>   as the waters cover the sea.
>
> (Isa. 11:6-9)

This is another version of the Magnificat—the Magnificat with its cosmic implications. This is a grandiose vision that involves human beings, nature, and all of God's creation. And it is that vision that became partially real in the story of the elephants taking part in the struggle of the people in an Indian village for their right to live on their land.

As the drama unfolded, it was women who took command of the situation, contrary to the custom and tradition of a society in which men command everything, including the life and destiny of women. This alone was a change of the power relation between men and women sanctioned by the religion of the country. The male villagers in that confrontation with the naked power of the authorities proved entirely helpless. They remained silent, not knowing what to do. The power to act left them. The courage to protest deserted them. And they gave up the responsibility to defend their families and their community from the intruders.

But the women were different. They acted. Was it their mother-nature that gave them courage to break silence and act in the interest of men and children as well as themselves? Both in the case of Mary and Hannah "motherhood" had very much to do with their song of the Magnificat. It must have been through the experience of motherhood that they came to realize how God was present in their lives in a saving way. It could have been the same with those tribal women in that village in India. Their capacity to conceive life, their ability to give birth to it, and their power to nurture it and make it grow must have enabled them to act spontaneously and fearlessly at the time of crisis. Perhaps because of this, the song of the Magnificat had to be sung by Mary, and not by Joseph her husband, by Hannah, and not by her husband Elkanah, or by the women and not by the men of that Indian village.

This change of power relations in the story of the conflict between the people of the village and the authorities transformed the nature of the confrontation: a political confrontation became a religious ceremony, a sacred (*pooja*) ritual! This is truly remarkable. A political struggle became a "sacramental" action. The women, as they used to do in religious ceremonies on a *pooja* (sacred) day, began to chant prayers and embrace the trunks and legs of the elephants that were expected to wreck their huts and make havoc of their lives. Then something extraordinary happened. These elephants came representing the physical power of the authorities, but now came under the power of the women's devotion and love. They came to serve the political power of the authorities that had sent them, but now were affected by the religious power displayed by the women. The elephants "refused to move further and turned back." No one dared to intervene in this dramatic turn of events, not even those men from the authorities. As a result, the village gained time to recover from the crisis and to prepare itself for the worst yet to come.

In all these stories, from the story of Mary to the story of Hannah and the story of the women in an Indian village, we encounter the power of the Magnificat as a sacramental power. By "sacramental" power we mean the power that turns our struggle to live as human beings into a religious vocation, the power that heals the wounds inflicted on powerless men, women, and children by the society and the tradition that take the side of the rich and the powerful, the power that restores justice to those to whom injustice is done, and the power that injects hope into our lives threatened with the power of death. It is this power that enables women such as Mary, Elizabeth, and Hannah to sing the Magnificat. It must have been that same power that seized the women of the village, enabling them to approach the elephants with religious devotion and love.

This sacramental power that changes power relations is the power of God's reign. It is the power that was manifested in the life and ministry of Jesus. It is the power of transfiguration.

CHAPTER 8

TRANSFIGURATION OF LIFE

Six days later Jesus took Peter, James, and John with him and led them up a high mountain by themselves. And in their presence he was transfigured; his clothes became dazzling white, with a whiteness no bleacher on earth could equal. They saw Elijah appear, and Moses with him, talking with Jesus. Then Peter spoke: "Rabbi," he said, "it is good that we are here! Shall we make three shelters, one for you, one for Moses, and one for Elijah?" For he did not know what to say; they were so terrified. Then a cloud appeared, casting its shadow over them, and out of the cloud came a voice: "This is my Beloved Son; listen to him." And suddenly, when they looked around, there was no longer anyone else to be seen. (Mark 9:2-8; pars. Matt. 17:1-8; Luke 9:28-36)

Metamorphosis of Human Conditions

The reign of God does not consist of concepts; it consists of power for the powerless and the disinherited. The reign of God is not manifest through theological ideas that justify and maintain the traditions of the past; it becomes manifest through movements of people to be free from the shackles of the past, to change the stalemate of the present, and to have a role to play in the arrival of the future. The reign of God is, in essence, movement toward metamorphosis of individual persons and human community. Our preceding discussion shows this is what the reign of God must be.

The story of Jesus' transfiguration gives us a rare glimpse of the metamorphosis that lies at the heart of his message and ministry of God's reign. The story has been understood in a variety of ways as "a legendary development of a Resurrection-story which has been read back into the earthly life

262

of Jesus,"[1] or as "an epiphany story whose purpose is to express the doctrine of Jesus' divinity, i.e., a creed in narrative form."[2] It is also thought to be related to "the eschatological vision of Jesus' exaltation at God's right hand."[3] These are some of the ways in which the early Christian community and the churches through the centuries have tried to understand the story, although it is "in fact no longer possible to reconstruct exactly what happened."[4]

The story is not a history in the strict sense of the word. It reflects more the faith of the community or the church in the risen Christ than something that happened at a certain place and time. This does not mean, however, that the story has no frame of reference in the life and ministry of Jesus. As a matter of fact Mark, the author, has provided the historical framework or context for the story of Jesus' transfiguration with another story—the story of Jesus and his disciples on their way to the villages of Caesarea Philippi (Mark 8:27-33).[5] He "has prefaced this [the eschatological vision of Jesus' exaltation at God's right hand] with the disciples' enthusiastic and ill-informed identification of Jesus as Messiah (Mark 8:29), which is immediately balanced by Jesus' assertion that his role in relation to the coming of God's kingdom can be fulfilled only through suffering and death (8:31)."[6]

To get at the meaning behind the story of the transfiguration, it is more important perhaps to have it related to the story on the way to Caesarea Philippi than to the story of the resurrection. What surrounds the transfigured Jesus on the mountain would be, it seems, not so much the empty tomb as the cross. "The purpose of the heavenly manifestation," it has been pointed out, "is the announcement of the passion or even heaven's confirmation of Jesus' announcement of passion."[7] The transfigured Jesus in the presence of his three disciples is going to be the crucified Jesus before the eyes of the world! The transfiguration anticipates the crucifixion! It does not have to be a projection of the experience of the resurrection. Nor does it have to be a story based on the faith in the risen Christ. The close association of the story of the transfiguration with the passion of Jesus discloses

1. C. E. B. Cranfield, *The Gospel according to Saint Mark* (Cambridge: Cambridge University Press, 1959), 292.

2. Sherman E. Johnson, *A Commentary on the Gospel according to St. Mark* (London: Adam & Charles Black, 1960), 155.

3. Howard Clark Kee, *Community of the New Age: Studies in Mark's Gospel* (Philadelphia: Westminster Press, 1977), 75.

4. Hugh Anderson, *The Gospel of Mark* (London: Marshall, Morgan & Scott, 1976), 223.

5. For our discussion of this story see chap. 7: "Who Do You Say That I Am?" in my *Jesus, the Crucified People* (New York: Crossroad/Meyer-Stone, 1989), 144-63.

6. Kee, *Community of the New Age*, 75-76.

7. Joseph A. Fitzmyer, *The Gospel according to Luke, I-IX*, Anchor Bible (New York: Doubleday & Company, 1981), 792.

to us an important message: suffering can be overcome, evil powers of this world can be defeated, and death cannot be the last word. In short, human conditions can be changed.

One may, then, speak of "transfiguration experiences." Transfiguration is not something that occurs once and once only. It has to be a recurring experience because there will always be suffering to overcome, evil powers to defeat, and death to reckon with. The history of humanity and the world has to be a history of the transfiguration. This must be the reason why "in all the Transfiguration narratives, the transfiguration is temporary."[8]

The transfiguration experience is a temporary experience, an experience at a particular place and at a particular time. It is not an out-of-space and out-of-time experience. It is, in essence, not an out-of-the-body experience. Not to realize this is to misunderstand the meaning of the transfiguration. Peter and the other two disciples did not understand this temporal nature of the transfiguration. They were unable to relate it to the suffering of Jesus. No wonder they failed to share the "divine ecstasy" Jesus must have experienced each and every time he was able to overcome the fear of suffering and death. All Peter could do was to suggest to "make three shelters, one for Jesus, one for Moses, and one for Elijah" (Mark 9:5 and pars.). He completely failed to understand the temporariness of the transfiguration experience. That experience cannot be institutionalized into a permanent structure or made into a fixed part of piety. Each time it has to be a new happening experienced in a different situation under a different circumstance.

In this way the story of the transfiguration must be an integral part of the story of Jesus' passion (suffering). It cannot be separated from the ways in which Jesus and the people, poor, disinherited, and oppressed in his time and at all times, confront the powers that inflict suffering, pain, and death on them. In the story of the transfiguration we are not suddenly gazing at a Jesus unknown to us before, a real Jesus in contrast to the Jesus with whom we are familiar, a Jesus disclosing his true nature hidden from us previously. No, we are looking at the same Jesus—Jesus who in conflict with the powers of this world himself becomes the epiphany of God's reign and who is able to identify its epiphanies in the life and history of human community.

Does it not follow that the story of the transfiguration is in reality another version of the story of the reign of God? The reign of God can be understood as consisting of stories of the transfiguration, that is, stories of how human conditions are changed under the impact of God's saving power working in human community in different ways. What we encounter

8. C. S. Mann, *Mark*, Anchor Bible (New York: Doubleday & Company, 1986), 360.

in the Gospels is how that power of God is at work in the life of individuals and of a community in and through Jesus. His vision of God's reign evokes restlessness in people's consciousness with regard to the present situation. His presence provokes a desire to overcome the stalemate in their lives. His action inspires courage to transform society. If the reign of God is the heart of Jesus' transfiguration, it must also be the heart of the metamorphosis of human conditions.

Forgiveness of Sins

Human conditions are not what they should be. This is anything but novel wisdom. Ever since the dawn of human consciousness, this has been one of the thoughts that has puzzled and tormented human beings. The contradiction between the awareness of human potency vis-à-vis the world in which we live and the threats of impotence, decay, and death has always engaged the human mind. If we cannot resolve the contradiction, at least we have to be able to explain it. And human beings have explained, from the remote past to the present day. In most cases it is to religion that people turn for explanation.

One of the classic attempts at explanation is of course the story of Adam and Eve in the third chapter of the Book of Genesis in the Hebrew Scriptures, known as the "Story of the Fall." This, in fact, is not so much a story of human fall from God's grace as a story of how ancient Hebrew storytellers understood the reason that human conditions are not what they should be. Why, they must have asked, does a man have to gain his bread by the sweat of his brow (Gen. 3:19)? Why must a woman bear children in labor and pain (3:16)? And above all the question of death! "Dust you are, to dust you will return" (3:19). There are, on the one hand, endless possibilities of what we human beings can do. On the other hand, however, there is an inevitable end to human life that brings everything to an eternal halt. The story of "the Fall" tries to explain this not by holding Adam and Eve accountable; both in fact denied responsibility. Instead the blame is laid squarely on the snake that seduced Eve to eat the fruit from the forbidden tree.

The snake is the culprit. And what does the snake represent if not the potent power, among other things, that does evil as well as good? "To the Chinese," it has been pointed out, "snakes are at the bottom of all magic power, while the Hebrew and Arabic words for magic come from words that mean 'snakes.' "[9]

---

9. Mircea Eliade, *Patterns in Comparative Religion* (New York: New American Library, 1958), 168.

It is this snake, this animal with magic power, that is the ultimate cause of human suffering, pain, and death. Is this perhaps what is implied in the divine pronouncement of curse on the snake in our story? "I shall put enmity between you and the woman," says God to the snake in the Genesis story, "between your brood and hers. They will strike at your head and you will strike at their heel" (Gen. 3:15).

Sickness—a condition in which human beings should not be—is, then, as much of a religious matter as a physical matter. It is symptomatic of the hostility the evil power has created within and among human beings, between human beings and the world of nature, and of course between human beings and God. Some folk medicine still practiced in Asia and Africa seems to understand this religious nature of sickness better than modern medical science. "For the West," says a doctor trained in the Western science of psychotherapy, "the connection of health with orders other than that of the body and the mind no longer exists. It is generally forgotten, for instance, that not too long ago, the ministrations of the priest on the deathbed and the doctor on the sickbed were both termed clinical. However, with the irresistible march of scientific naturalism over the last one hundred years, the domain of the clinical has been finally and firmly usurped by the doctor, and the priest forced into exile."[10]

Priests are returning from their forced exile, armed, however, more with technical knowledge than with theological depth. Little wonder "there are many in the West today who regret the disappearance of the sacred from the healing sciences and its removal generally from the world of everyday life."[11] In Asia, however, the sacred has not disappeared totally from the healing sciences despite the fact that it has also come under the irreversible impact of modernization in recent decades. This must be the reason why folk medicine still flourishes and shamans continue to perform the function of both priests and healers.

It is not our interest here to explore folk medicine or the art of healing performed by shamans. Our concern has to do with the religious nature of sickness. Sickness, if it is more than a matter of the body and the mind, if it also has to do with the evil power that disrupts the relationships surrounding human life, is then an obstruction of the reign of God. Sickness clouds the human vision of the reign of God. It calls for a halt to the march of God's reign. It deprives the reign of God of meaning and reality. In short, it can be a formidable challenge to God's reign. The removal of this obstruction, then, is necessary for the reign of God to become manifest. Sickness

---

10. Sudhir Kakar, *Shamans, Mystics and Doctors: A Psychological Inquiry into India and Its Healing Traditions* (New York: Alfred A. Knopf, 1982), 5.
11. Ibid.

is an enemy of God's reign. The conquering of it has to be an essential part of the ministry of God's reign.

Is this not the reason why Jesus is so much preoccupied with the ministry of healing? Is this not why he is often engaged in exorcism? Jesus is not a physician. Nor is he a shaman. His chief business is to give witness to the reign of God and to practice it. But since sickness poses a challenge to the reign of God, healing has to be part and parcel of his ministry. He has to engage himself in a metamorphosis of the human condition. His healing is theological healing, the healing of the relationships ruptured by the evil powers. It is a ministry of transfiguration—transfiguration of the conditions that corrupt human beings and their community, that threaten the well-being of God's creation.

How does Jesus go about this ministry of transfiguration? The story of the healing of the paralytic (Mark 2:1-12; pars. Matt. 9:1-8; Luke 5:17-26) in the city of Capernaum offers us deep insights into how Jesus relates a change of human conditions to the reign of God. As Mark the Evangelist weaves different strands into one complex whole, the story is developed into two distinct but closely related foci: healing of the paralytic and forgiveness of sins. "Jesus said to the [paralyzed] man," Mark tells us, "'My son, your sins are forgiven'" (Mark 2:5). Perhaps anticipated by Jesus, the pronouncement touched off a controversy between him and his opponents. Mark the storyteller continues:

Now there were some scribes sitting there thinking to themselves, "Why can the fellow talk like that? It is blasphemy! Who but God can forgive sins?" Jesus knew at once what they were thinking, and said to them: "Why do you harbor such thoughts? Is it easier to say to this paralyzed man, 'Your sins are forgiven', or to say, 'Stand up, take your bed, and walk'? But to convince you that the Son of Man has the authority on earth to forgive sins"—he turned to the paralyzed man—"I say to you, stand up, take your bed, and go home." And he got up, and at once took his bed and went out in full view of them all, so that they were astounded and praised God. "Never before," they said, "have we seen anything like this." (Mark 2:6-12)

No one has indeed seen anything like this, not the spectators, not the paralyzed man himself now healed, and of course not Jesus' opponents!

What is so extraordinary about the whole episode? Why are they so astounded by what has taken place? It is not the healing itself. Healing of bodily ailments and curing of physical illness are not that astounding. This is what physicians do. But relating the healing of sickness to forgiveness of sins is what is at stake here. This of course has its danger. It is the danger of leading people to think that sickness is brought about by the sins committed, if not by the sick person, then by those closely related to him or her, such as the parents. The causal relation between sickness and sin is a prevailing notion deeply rooted in people's religious consciousness. It is precisely this notion that Jesus emphatically denies in the story of the man born blind told by John the Evangelist (John 9:1-38). To his own disciples who, like others, firmly believed that the man's blindness was caused either by his own sins or by his parents' sins, Jesus declared firmly: "It is not that he or his parents sinned; he was born blind so that God's power might be displayed in curing him" (9:3).

If blindness is not a mere physical phenomenon, neither is it a punishment for the sins one is supposed to have committed or inherited. What comes first is not the religious discussion of the cause of blindness but the curing of it. It is in the curing of it that the religious dimension of the human ailment becomes manifest. This must be what Jesus meant when he said that "the man was born blind so that God's power might be displayed in curing him." Jesus was not saying that there is a purpose in the man's being born blind—the displaying of God's power. This would be a very cruel theology, a theology not less cruel than that of regarding sickness as punishment for sins. This could not have been Jesus' theology. Jesus must be stressing that the healing of the physical ailment, when it does take place, is a restoration, a metamorphosis, of the human condition.

Another story that shows us insights into Jesus' theology of healing is the story of Jesus curing ten people afflicted with leprosy (Luke 17:11-19). It has been pointed out that

> the lepers did not ask Jesus to heal them. They only wanted Jesus to show them compassion, acceptance. "Jesus, Master, take pity on us." Show us the human face of mercy. Show us the human side of pity, compassion, tenderness, sympathy. To be a leper, in the world of the Bible, is to be an unclean person. They were isolated from family, the community, and consigned to live in villages or on reservations outside the city. Once diagnosed as unclean they were shown little compassion by the professional healers of the day. Lepers were to keep their distance. The greatest fear deriving from the situation of affliction was that they may never be able to return to the community. Or if they did return, they would always carry the stigma of their affliction. Small wonder, then, that the request to Jesus was "Make us clean; show us compassion."

The expected result is a return to full membership in the community."[12]

The story goes on to tell us that these people did not just receive pity and sympathy from Jesus. They were healed and restored to be full members of the community.

Healing in the faith and theology of Jesus is the power of God's love and compassion working in human community. And wherever God's power is perceived to be at work, there the reign of God is. That the blind man is made to see and the lepers are made clean and have the stigma of uncleanness removed from them witness to the presence of God's reign. No, it is more. They are not just witnesses to something that happens to them. They themselves, healed, made whole, and restored to full relationships in family and community, are the reign of God. By pronouncing healing on the sick people, Jesus is pronouncing them to be God's reign, just as he pronounced the poor, the disinherited, the oppressed, to be the reign of God.

The stories of Jesus healing the sick contain different metaphors highlighting healing as the manifestation of God's reign. In the story of the man born blind just cited, the power of God at work is the metaphor for the reign of God. In the story of healing the paralyzed man, forgiveness of sins is the metaphor with the emphasis more on forgiveness than on sins. It expresses "the total acceptance of the person by God."[13] And what we see in the healing of the ten lepers is the power of God's love and compassion restoring their health and the health of the community that discriminated against them. In all this, restoration and acceptance are what the reign of God is about—restoration of the broken community and acceptance of men, women, and children regardless of their conditions. The reign of God is what it is because it does not recognize the distinction between the acceptable and the unacceptable. There are no so-called unacceptable people in the reign of God. In proclaiming the paralyzed man forgiven, for example, Jesus is proclaiming that he is accepted, totally accepted, despite himself, in spite of his sins. And his healing is one of "the signs of the kingdom of God [that] are present in, with, and around Jesus...."[14]

If the healing of individuals is in this way deeply rooted in the reign of God as Jesus understood it and practiced it, the healing of the human community is no less closely related to it. How sick a human community

---

12. I owe this observation to my colleague Dr. Archie Smith, professor of pastoral counseling and psychology at the Pacific School of Religion, in his unpublished paper entitled "The Church and Family's Challenging Journey into the Confusing Wilderness of Mental Illness."
13. Klaus Seybold and Ulrich B. Mueller, *Sickness and Healing*, trans. Douglas W. Stott (Nashville: Abingdon, 1981), 166.
14. Hugh Anderson, *The Gospel of Mark*, 101.

can become! A society is sick when injustice is done to the poor and the disinherited. A community is sick when oppression, be it political or economic, deprives the powerless of freedom and well-being. And a human community is no longer human when women, men, and children are discriminated against on account of race, sex, or creed. When the world turns into the arena of the survival of the fittest, the fittest being those who hold political and economic power, it is neither fit nor healthy for human beings. And in Jesus' time the fittest included those who held religious powers.

It must be for this reason that Jesus turns from healing the sick people to healing the sick society. If the sick need metamorphosis of their conditions, the sick society needs it all the more. Seen in this way, the Beatitudes (Luke 6:20-23; par. Matt. 5:3-12) cease to be an ethic only for an ideal future. A society must become the reign of God in which the poor as well the rich are blessed. A community should strive to be the reign of God in which no one goes hungry. And the world can be the reign of God when people are not persecuted and oppressed for what they believe and what they affirm. Jesus must have envisioned a transfiguration of the human community, no longer dictated by ruthless power but shaped by love and compassion.

Some of the parables Jesus told make it even clearer and more concrete what he envisions to be the reign of God as a transfigured human community in his Beatitudes. A society is on the way to change for the better when every effort is made to recover the lost souls. This must be what Jesus was urging when he told the parable of the lost sheep (Luke 15:1-7; par. Matt. 18:12-14). A community experiences a metamorphosis when a father, in his boundless love, overcomes social conventions and religious inhibitions and receives back to his house his wayward son. This is the image of God's reign no one can miss in his parable of the father's love (Luke 15:1-9). There is also the parable of the laborers in the vineyard (Matt. 20:1-16). It portrays a world transfigured not by labor disputes and wage negotiations but by the willingness to make love and concern for those in need the basis of a new human community.

But the metamorphosis of human conditions and the transfiguration of human community is not just a parable that has no basis in the real world. This is precisely the point the story of the last judgment (Matt. 25:31-46) seems to emphasize. True, in the real world the general practice may be for people to pretend not to be aware that there are those who suffer hunger and cold and those who are persecuted and imprisoned for freedom and justice. But there are also men and women, though far fewer in number, who go out of their way to render help to the victims of exploitation and oppression. The conviction that prompts them to act is this:

> Not to love is violence
> Not to find the way for a lost child is violence
> Not to find water for a thirsty child is violence
> Not to find solutions for hungry people is violence
> To let violence have its way is violence.[15]

How much violence, then, is committed each and every day! But there are also those who take actions against such violence. It is to such people that the king on the throne says: "Anything you did for any of my brothers and sisters here, however insignificant, you did for me" (25:40). The king here is of course not a feudal lord who rules with ruthless power. The word "king" should be substituted by the name of Jesus. And the name of Jesus should be further related to the reign of God. The story means then to say that as long as there are people, even though few in number, who go about offering help to the helpless, the reign of God becomes manifest and transfiguration of the world becomes a real possibility. Is not transfiguration of the world in fact the result accumulated from such deeds?

As a matter of fact, the life and ministry of Jesus consisted of a series of actions, big and small, that gave witness to the real presence of God's reign. The healing of the servant was an occasion for the Roman centurion to confess his faith in God's saving power working in and through Jesus (Luke 7:1-10). When he accepted Zacchaeus, the tax-collector (Luke 19:1-10), he shattered the barriers that made God's salvation inaccessible to outsiders. Such acts that give rise to a change of the human condition must have proved to be more threatening to the religious and political authorities of his day than armed revolts and rebellions. They arrested him and crucified him, believing that they put an end to the attempt to change their society. But contrary to their expectation, this cross, an instrument intended to stop a metamorphosis of the human condition, became the very source and power of that metamorphosis. The cross continues to inspire a transfiguration of men and women to what the reign of God stands for and a metamorphosis of the oppressive and corrupt status quo.

A transfiguration of the human condition is not something spectacular accompanied with power and glory. There is, in fact, more pain than joy, more suffering than glory. If this is the way of God's reign, how can we expect something different as we become involved in efforts to change the human condition in which we find ourselves? Some Christian women in Bangladesh, a country in which women are held to be inferior to men in the social and religious traditions, seem to understand this as they grapple with the gradual change of their conditions:

---

15. Cho Hai from Korea. See *Life for the People: Peace with Justice in Asia* 1, no. 3 (September–December 1988): 3.

> Sisters,
> Our world is not one we have personally chosen.
> It is not one we have much control over.
> All seeds have potential for growth: So do you and I.
> So all village women.
> If we want society to view us differently,
> We must first view us differently...
> Isn't that so?
> If we believe we have the potential for growth,
> Then we must grow. Isn't that so?
> Women are organizing into groups.
> We are solving our own problems.
> We are managing our own affairs.
> By doing these things our self-confidence grows.
> By doing these things our view of ourselves is changing.
> By doing things slowly,
> Our world expands... [16]

Our world expands! The poem concludes that our world changes and our world is transfigured.

The poem does not idealize or fantasize about the world these Bangladesh women want to see expand, change, and be transfigured. It is a world they did not choose to live in nor is it in their power to control. And centuries of traditions, social, political, and religious, have made not only women but also men victims of dehumanization. Even this kind of world is still possible to change only if people realize that "all seeds have potential for growth" and are determined to "develop their potential for growth." They must begin to take things into their own hands, get organized, and manage their own affairs. They should stop being like robots submitting to the whims of their gods and to the oppression of their rulers. The process is slow and can be painful. But this is the only way for their world to change, be transfigured and expand. This is the way of the cross. This is the way of transfiguration.

Exorcism of Evil Powers

Jesus was not only engaged in the transfiguration of the world; he was also very deeply involved in the transfiguration of the human body and mind. He had to come to grips with the sickness that invades humanity. Sickness makes havoc of the human body. There is also sickness that demonizes it.

---

16. See ibid., 59.

This is the sickness that invades the human mind, known as demon possession in the old days and as mental illness today. If Jesus had to deal with the sickness of the body, how could he avoid grappling with the sickness of the mind? And in grappling with it, he had to engage himself in the exorcism of evil powers. That is why there are as many stories of Jesus healing sick minds as there are stories of him healing sick bodies in the Gospels. It is in confrontation with demon possession that the transfiguration of human condition encounters violent powers. Here the reign of God has to reckon with violence just as Jesus had to come into a head-on collision with it.

Demon possession has of course no cultural boundaries; it is a universal phenomenon that affects the health of individual persons and of society everywhere. "In most parts of the world," it has been pointed out, "the belief in possession by spirits and demons has been historically the dominant theory of illness and especially of conditions that we call mental illness. The Arabs and the Chinese, the Hebrews and the Greeks, have all believed in some form of spirit possession."[17] If the belief in possession by the spirits and demons is widespread, East and West, ancient and modern, "the indications of spirit possession have traditionally covered a wide range—from an alteration in the possessed person's state of mental and physical well-being to such florid manifestations as trances and other dramatic states of altered consciousness."[18]

My Name Is Legion

The world in which Jesus lived is no exception to this understanding of sickness and particularly of mental illness as spirit or demon possession. As a matter of fact, "cases of 'possession' were a common phenomenon during Jesus' time. The sick people were thought to be ruled by demons that resided within them and coerced them into self-destructive behavior."[19] One of the most dramatic examples is the story of "the Gerasene demoniac" (Mark 5:1-20; pars. Matt. 8:28-34; Luke 8:26-39), an extraordinary story vividly portraying human conflicts with the spirit-world and culminating in Jesus' overcoming that world.

The story is made up of different elements unrelated to each other before they were woven into a composite whole. What is of primary interest to us here is the encounter that took place between Jesus and the demoniac. When Jesus

---

17. Sudhir Kakar, *Shamans, Mystics and Doctors,* 24.
18. Ibid.
19. Seybold and Mueller, *Sickness and Healing,* 116–17.

> came ... to the country of the Gerasenes ... a man possessed by an
> unclean spirit came up to him from among the tombs where he had
> made his home. Nobody could control him any longer; even chains
> were useless. ... No one was strong enough to master him. Unceas-
> ingly, night and day, he would cry aloud among the tombs and on the
> hillsides and gash himself with stones. (Mark 5:1-5)

What a horrid scene is portrayed here! The man under the control of the
evil spirit is no longer a human being. "The utter lostness of the man," the
man who is no longer a human being, is beyond remedy because he lives
among the tombs, that is, beyond the boundaries of human habitat.

This is what the evil spirit can do to human beings. It has the power to
change human conditions totally and to make human beings less human,
even subhuman. The strange thing, however, is that when rendered less
than human or subhuman, human beings can demonstrate "superhuman"
power and do what they cannot do under normal circumstances. In the case
of the Gerasene demoniac in the story, he "snaps his chains and breaks
the fetters" (Mark 5:4) used to restrain him. He of course poses danger to
himself, for he "gash himself with stones" (5:5). He must have also caused
fear and panic in the community by "unceasingly, night and day, crying
aloud among the tombs and on the hillsides" (5:5). In the grip of the power
of the evil spirits the whole community suffers. Its health is impaired. Its
peace is disturbed and its harmony is broken.

Here is a vivid account of a similar situation from an ancient Chinese
medical source compiled between 100 B.C.E. and 100 C.E. describing "erup-
tions of a form of insane behavior which threatened both society and the
individual." When outbursts of insanity or demon possession occur, the
person concerned

> will discard his clothes and run around, mount heights and sing, or
> get to the point of not eating for several days. He will leap walls and
> ascend rooftops. In short, all the places he mounts are beyond his or-
> dinary abilities. ... He will talk and curse wildly, not sparing relatives
> or strangers. Not wishing to eat, he will run about wildly.[20]

The life of a person possessed by an evil spirit behaves and acts in a strange
and often destructive manner. That person is no longer himself or herself.
The disruption has occurred within that person and between that person
and the surrounding world.

---

20. Martha Li Chiu, "Insanity in Imperial China: A Legal Case Study," in *Normal and
Abnormal Behavior in Chinese Culture*, ed. Arthur Kleinman and Tsung-Yi Lin (Dordrecht,
Holland: D. Reidel Publishing Company, 1981), 75–94, 75.

The evil power that possesses a human person is an antihuman power—a power that puts itself against what it means to be human. By possessing human persons, it takes them captive, uses them, and in the end destroys them. This destructive power of the evil spirit is vividly described by the father of the son who, in the presence of Jesus, was thrown "into convulsions, fell on the ground and rolled about foaming at the mouth"; often the evil spirit had "tried to destroy him by throwing him into the fire or into water" (Mark 9:20-22). Mental illness, believed to be caused by spirit or demon possession, is not just a matter of physical disorder or a malfunction of nerve systems. It is violence committed against a human person. It is a disruption of the harmony essential to human physical and mental well-being.

Jesus must have seen in spirit possession everything that contradicts what the reign of God is and stands for. It is hostile to the reign of God. It confronts the reign of God with a claim to human persons and their community. In the case of the Gerasene demoniac, this contradiction is strongly reflected in the fact that he lives among the tombs "believed to be the abode of demons."[21] Jesus confronted with the demoniac who lives among the tombs is the reign of God confronted with the abode of demons. It is no mere sickness with which Jesus has to cope. What he is faced with is the challenge to the reign of God by the reign of demons personified in the demoniac. It is the challenge to the realm of light by the realm of darkness.

This is not just a struggle between the Gerasene demoniac as an individual and Jesus also as an individual. Behind the demoniac is the whole realm of antihuman forces at work to demolish human community and God's world. Represented by Jesus is the realm now become manifest as the reign of God. Is this the reason why the demoniac, challenged by Jesus, discloses his name as "Legion"? The word "legion" reminds one that "a Roman legion numbered from 4000 to 6000 men."[22] If the name "Legion" does not refer directly to the Roman legion, at least it is symbolic of the formidable power it represented. It is not just a "very large number"[23] that is meant here. It is a power that dehumanizes individual persons, perverts human relationships, throws a society into confusion, and challenges God's power and authority.

It is this power of the "Legion" that makes havoc of human community in the course of history. That power becomes concentrated in autocratic rulers and authoritarian social and political systems. That power can also come to embody itself in a religious hierarchy and establishment. What

---

21. Anderson, *The Gospel of Mark*, 148.
22. C. E. B. Cranfield, *The Gospel according to Saint Mark*, Cambridge New Testament Commentary (Cambridge: Cambridge University Press, 1959), 179.
23. Anderson, *The Gospel of Mark*, 149.

we witness in ruthless dictators is no other than that Gerasene demoniac "no one is strong enough to master" (Mark 5:4) until confronted by the power of God's reign. In the particular incident of the Gerasene demoniac Jesus faces it with the power of God's reign. He is not a solitary hero out to conquer the world all by himself and through his own power. Surrounding him are the women, men, and children he identified as the reign of God. And with him and in him is that very source of the power of God's reign—God.

If this is true with Jesus in his confrontation with the demonic powers of his day, the demonic powers that came to be personified in political domination by Roman colonial power or in the control of people's faith and life by the religious authorities, it must be also true in similar confrontations throughout human history. With each defender of freedom is the community of men and women longing for freedom. Behind every advocate for human rights is the community deprived of rights to be human. And in the company of each and every martyr, political or religious, are those people fallen victim to the rulers and their ruling machines possessed by the demonic powers.

This leads us to the question of different ways in which power is exercised and manifested. After all, to reign power is needed, whether to reign by God's saving power or to reign by the destructive power of the evil spirits. In the political realm the power to rule has to be won and consolidated. This is the case in a democratic political system. In this system power is relativized. That is what democracy means essentially. It is a political system in which the power to rule cannot be monopolized by one single party. It is also a system of government that is accountable to the political views and choices of the people. Under the democratic system of government the power to rule can be replaced by the process of law or by a general election in which people freely express their political choices.

There is a built-in mechanism within a truly democratic system that prevents the power to rule from turning demonic. The power represented by the reign of God within this kind of political system is the moral power of the people that checks and balances the power to rule. It reinforces the power of conscience at work in society to make sure that the power that rules does not turn demonic. It joins forces with the voices that speak out for justice. It will not tire of stressing that the power of rulers is the power ordained to serve people.

By the Finger of God

But there is another kind of power that comes into conflict with the power of God's reign. It is the power exercised by an autocratic ruler. For that power to turn demonic is inevitable. In this case the power to rule absolutizes itself, although by nature it is only relative. There is simply no such thing as an absolute power to be held by any human being. Absolute power is thus a pretension. And what demonic power is not a pretension? Something becomes demonic precisely when it pretends to be anything other than itself. This is the theological meaning of spirit possession. Evil power by nature is parasitic. By itself it is nothing. It has no power. It is not self-productive. It is not the power that creates. It comes alive only when it succeeds in possessing something other than itself, particularly human persons. And how much the world has to suffer when the whole society comes under the domination of those possessed by the evil spirit.

Confrontation of God's reign with demonic political systems and religious practices, then, cannot be avoided. The power of God's reign has no alternative but to expose the demonic nature of the power to rule. It reveals the latter's secret—its pretension and thus its illegitimacy and immorality. The power that pretends to be what it is not is an illegitimate power. It is also an immoral power. It not only corrupts itself. It also corrupts others and the whole human community. That is why an authoritarian society is a society of lies. Speaking out for the truth becomes treason. Standing for justice is treated as rebellion. And taking sides with the poor and the oppressed is said to be inciting social unrest.

Jesus' opponents, therefore, miss the point entirely when they accuse him and say: "He is possessed by Beelzebub and he drives out the demons by the prince of demons" (Mark 3:22; pars. Matt. 12:24; Luke 11:15). This is a very malicious charge. According to the charge Jesus is in league with the demons. He is a pretender. His power has no legitimacy. His authority is of demonic nature. The charge has no basis in reality, of course. What Jesus does is to heal body and soul. What he strives for is the transformation of human community to reflect the love and goodness of God. And what he envisions is the reign of God in which justice prevails. Did he not himself describe his own ministry to John the Baptist through the latter's disciples when he said to them: "The blind recover their sight, the lame walk, the lepers are made clean, the deaf hear, the dead are raised to life, the poor brought the good news" (Matt. 11:5; par. Luke 7:22)? This is the work of transformation. It is the ministry of transfiguration. Jesus must have wanted to ask those who accused him of being a party to the demonic powers how this could be the work of the demons.

But this "Beelzebub controversy" gives Jesus the occasion to affirm the relationship between his ministry of exorcism and the reign of God. In Luke's Gospel Jesus is reported to have declared: "But if it is by the finger of God that I drive out demons, then the reign of God has already come upon you" (Luke 11:20). With these words the controversy reaches a theological climax.[24] The nature of Jesus' exorcism becomes evident. It is by the finger of God that he casts out demons. It is God who makes change in the human condition happen. It is God who enables transformation of society to become a reality. And it is God who works to renew the creation for the purpose for which it is created—reconciliation of all things in creation to one another and to God. The destructive power of the demons can be overcome. It has no final say. It is a real power, but it cannot be more real than the power of God. It is a fearful power, but it cannot be so fearful that it can dominate even the power of God. It is a power intent on undoing the work God has done, but God sees to it that it cannot prevail in the end.

Jesus is the witness to this power of God. He himself embodies that power of God. And he goes about empowering the poor, the disinherited, and the oppressed with that power of God. For Jesus exorcism is not magic. It is not a secret way of outdoing the evil spirit. His exorcism takes place in the open. What he does is to mobilize the healing and saving power of God at work in human community in confrontation with the demonic power that possesses certain individual persons, drives them insane, keeps them completely under its control, and wrecks human community. This is no other than the work of the reign of God.

Transfiguration as Liberation

"Jesus exorcises the demons from the possessed person," it has been pointed out, "and in this way liberates him."[25] Jesus did a lot of this, as the Gospels tell us. But Jesus did much more than that. We have, therefore, to expand this statement and say that Jesus exorcises the demons from the possessed world and liberates it—the world possessed by demons, under the control of the tyrannical power of dictators, at the mercy of powerful political and economic forces, and dominated by social, cultural, and religious traditions that continue to discriminate against people on the grounds of race, sex, and beliefs. This must be the theological conviction that led the Presbyterian Church in Taiwan to adopt a new confession in 1986, which says in part:

> We believe that God has given human beings dignity, talents and a homeland, so that they may share in God's creation and have responsibility with God for taking care of the world. Therefore, they have social, political and economic systems, arts and sciences, and a spirit that seeks after the true God. But human beings have sinned and they

24. Josef Ernst, *Das Evangelium nach Lukas* (Regensburg: Verlag Friedrich Pustet, 1977), 375.

25. Seybold and Mueller, *Sickness and Healing*, 117.

misuse these gifts, destroying the relationship between themselves, all creatures and God. Therefore, they must depend on the saving grace of Jesus Christ. God will deliver humankind from sin, will set the oppressed free and make them equal, that all may become new creatures in Christ and the world, God's kingdom, full of justice and joy.[26]

The expression "God's kingdom," or "the reign of God," occurs only once in the whole confession, but it brings to a focus not only the letter but also the spirit of the confession.

The language of the confession may be a little too irenic to resound with Jesus' powerful declaration: "If it is by the finger of God that I drive out the demons, then be sure the reign of God has already come upon you." But the irenic tone of the confession is only deceptive. For the Presbyterian Church in Taiwan to be able to confess its faith in the reign of God full of justice and joy, it has had to be engaged in exorcising the demons of social and political powers that has kept Taiwan and its people in the captivity of fear and oppression. It has had to reckon with the political taboo

26. Here is the English translation of the whole Confession:

We believe in God, the only true God, the Creator and Ruler of human beings and all things. God is the Lord of history and of the world. God judges and saves. God's Son, Jesus Christ, the savior of humankind was conceived by the Holy Spirit, born of the Virgin Mary and became our brother. Through His suffering, crucifixion, death and resurrection, He manifested God's love and justice, and through Him we are reconciled to God. His Spirit, which is the Holy Spirit, dwells among all peoples until the Lord comes again.

We believe that the Bible is revealed by God, the record of God's redemption and the norm of our faith and life.

We believe that the Church is the fellowship of God's people, called to proclaim the salvation of Jesus Christ and to be an ambassador of reconciliation. It is both universal and rooted in this land, identifying with all its inhabitants, and through love and suffering becoming the sign of hope.

We believe that through the grace of God human beings are brought to repentance, their sin forgiven, that they may glorify God through lives of devotion, love and dedication. We believe that God has given human beings dignity, talents and a homeland, so that they may share in God's creation and have responsibility with God for taking care of the world. Therefore, they have social, political and economic systems, arts and sciences, and a spirit which seeks after the true God. But human beings have sinned and they misuse these gifts, destroying the relationship between themselves, all creatures and God. Therefore, they must depend on the saving grace of Jesus Christ. God will deliver humankind from sin, will set the oppressed free and make them equal, that all may become new creatures in Christ and the world, God's Kingdom, full of justice and joy.

"This translation, based on the original Romanized Taiwanese text authorized by the 32nd General Assembly, was officially adopted by the General Assembly, Faith and Order Committee, on January 10, 1986." This note and this text of the Confession are to be found in *The Church and Political Reform*, Report of a CCA–International Affairs Consultation in Bangkok, October 26–29, 1988 (Hong Kong: CCA–International Affairs, 1989), 42–43. In reproducing the Confession, I took the liberty to replace "He" with "God."

of speaking against the authoritarian rule of the Nationalist regime and to contend with the religious taboo of "interfering" in social and political matters. Where did this compulsion for the Presbyterian Church in Taiwan to break the silence come from? How did it get the encouragement to be the voice of the voiceless people in those dark days in which fear and intimidation and not justice and joy prevailed on the island? The source of that compulsion was the finger of God. The origin of that encouragement was the power of God.

This is how many Christian communities in the world today, especially in the Third World, have learned to confess their faith in the presence of God's reign in the midst of them in difficult social and political situations—situations quite similar to the situations in which Jesus and his contemporaries found themselves, but very different from the contexts in which the Christian church from the fourth century onward had to wrestle with its creeds and confessions. I believe one of the fundamental differences is this. The creeds and confessions of faith enunciated by the ecumenical councils in the early centuries are in large part the outcome of internal doctrinal controversies and the struggle of orthodoxy against what came to be branded as heresy. Those great confessions of faith to which the Reformation of the sixteenth century gave rise are also largely of an intra-ecclesial nature. In contrast, what many Christian churches in the Third World, the Presbyterian Church in Taiwan among them, are confronted with is not so much "Christian" heresies as "secular" heresies fostered by an absolutism of political power. The heart of the contention is, then, not doctrinal orthodoxy or theological purity but the question of power—the political power of a secular state and the saving power of the reign of God.

What some Christians and churches in the Third World have found themselves doing in recent years is very much like what Jesus found himself doing in his time: exorcism of the demonic powers that have become institutionalized in the social, political, and economic structures that deprive the majority of men and women of their freedom and human rights. Movements for democracy are movements against the demons called social and political domination of the few over the majority of citizens. A consultation on "the Church and political reform in Asia" convened by the International Affairs Committee of the Christian Conference of Asia in Bangkok in 1988 puts it well when it sums up the discussions:

> Over the past decade, the Christian Church (both Catholic and Protestant) in many Asian countries has become more vocal about issues judged to adversely affect the life of the nation and its citizens. This concern is manifested in some cases by statements, fact-finding stud-

ies and documents issued by the Church in response to national crises or socio-economic issues. In other cases, religious bodies or individual Christians participate in government initiated political changes, particularly those changes which promote more freedom and democracy for all citizens. And increasingly the Church is adding its voice by joining with other groups (local, national and international) to actively oppose and alter policies deemed obstacles to the Christian vision of fullness of life for all people as attested in the scriptures.[27]

This is an important theological insight from those Christians and churches that have come to see the close link between their faith and the social and political responsibilities they have to face with their fellow citizens in their society and in their nation.

They are, however, aware that they are dealing with a divisive issue here. "What in the Christian faith," they ask themselves, "compels followers to undertake such activity in the name of Christ?" Or what is "the relationship between church and state when, in some cases, the separation of church and state is seen as desirable or even essential for the protection of religious liberty and rights, especially in pluralistic societies where one religious group may be dominant"?[28] The second question—a question that has been a bone of contention for the Christian church for centuries—has to be subordinated to the first question. In most countries in Asia the question that really matters is not the relationship between church and state, the question that has had to be asked again and again in the West when Christianity has grown to be a political power beside, above, or in alliance with the power of the princes, kings, or presidents. The critical question for the Christian churches that do not share that complex history of church and state in the West has to be related to the source of power that compels Christians to practice their faith not only within the church but outside it.

What truly matters is the nature of the Christian faith that demands public actions raised in the first question. The consultation under discussion answers the question by reaffirming the conviction that "obedience to the gospel demands participation in support of those who are oppressed or marginalized." It also reiterates the assertion that "participation in political life is an aspect of religious liberty." But the insight of particular importance seems to be this:

---

27. See *The Church and Political Reform*, 89.
28. Ibid.

Commitment in faith to the coming of God's kingdom on earth ne-
cessitates taking moral positions on political structures and processes
as well as actions emerging from those positions.[29]

It is the reign of God and what it stands for that compels Christians to
join in movements for a change of the human condition prevailing in a
particular society.

The reign of God is not the church, but it can be the church when the
latter becomes an epiphany of God's reign. As an epiphany of God's reign
the church joins with other epiphanies of God's reign in a society and in a
nation. And together these epiphanies of God's reign mobilize the power
in the human community to bring about the fall of autocratic powers, inaugurate a new era of freedom and democracy, and rekindle the hope of a
world built not on exploitation and domination but on mutual support and
enrichment. As Christians and churches we learn to say with Jesus, "If by
the finger of God we drive out the demons, then be sure the reign of God
has already come upon us." The reign of God is the power that exorcises
the demons of social oppression, political authoritarianism, and economic
exploitation.

What is, then, this power of God's reign that exorcises the pretensions
of the powers of this world? How is it possible for that power to bring about
changes in the human condition in face of the demonic forces that often
drive a society and its people to the verge of insanity? There is an allusion
to the nature of that power in the Confession of the Presbyterian Church
in Taiwan when it says: "We believe that through the grace of God human
beings are brought to repentance, their sin forgiven." The power of God's
reign is the power to forgive. It is this forgiving power that, as we have seen,
makes Jesus' exorcism different from that practiced by shamans or healers.

What a contrast this forgiving power of God's reign also poses to the
powers of this world! Forgiveness is of course not contained in the vocabulary of an autocratic power. That power punishes. It imprisons. It destroys.
But the power of God's reign forgives. Forgiveness is not weakness. It takes
a tremendous power to forgive. It must have taken a superhuman power
for Jesus to forgive those who engineered to have him nailed to the cross.
It is not human to forgive in that kind of situation. That forgiving power
manifested by Jesus on the cross is divine power. It was God enabling Jesus
and empowering him to forgive those who had him crucified.

The power to forgive, then, has to be a strong spiritual power. It is
the power of the spirit and not the power of the body. Forgiveness is not
a physical force. Those who use physical force cannot forgive. They can

---

29. Ibid., 90.

only coerce, defeat, and conquer. Only those who possess the power of the spirit can forgive. That spiritual power cannot turn into the power to hate. Nor can it prostitute itself into violence. But this is not always the case in the world of conflicts. The power that creates violence often gives rise to the violence to counteract that power of violence. What ensues is the conflict between violence and counterviolence. This is a profound tragedy of human history. Of course there is no power of the spirit in those who commit violence against others. They are possessed by demonic powers. But the tragedy is that the power of the spirit in those forced into counterviolence can also turn into physical force. To be an epiphany of God's reign the church must resist to the end allowing its power of the spirit to become the power of the body. In this way it can be a sign of hope in a conflict-ridden world. In this way too it can be the power of God's reign that works the miracle of healing a society undermined by hate. In and through that power of the spirit to forgive God discloses the nobleness of the human heart in touch with the source of God's healing power. That power to forgive makes the metamorphosis of the human condition possible. And of course that power has to reckon with suffering just as Jesus had to reckon with it in his life and ministry and, above all, in facing the cross.

The power of God's reign that empowers Jesus and the men and women who follow him is a reconciling power. This is another point we need to explore here. The Confession of the Presbyterian Church in Taiwan professes that "the Church is called ... to the ministry of reconciliation." The ministry of reconciliation is the heart of Jesus' mission. As Paul puts it in his second letter to the Christians at Corinth, "God was in Christ reconciling the world to Godself." This ministry of Jesus must be our ministry also, since, as Paul goes on to say, "God has entrusted us with the message of reconciliation" (2 Cor. 5:19). Reconciliation, according to Paul, is the beginning and end of God's mission in the world. It is the sum-total of God's involvement with humanity. Human beings have shattered, to use the language of the Confession, "the relationships between themselves, all creatures and God." Without reconciliation transformation of the shattered relationships remains either mere talk or an illusion.

Reconciliation is a big subject. It is the heart of the Christian gospel. It is the center of the Christian faith. And it is the pivot of Christian discipleship. If this is what reconciliation must be, it compels Christians and churches to take seriously the ethical demands of their faith, to explore situational implications of it, and to strive for contextual practice of it. Here a word of warning to the church is in order. The church that exercises its prophetic responsibility toward the world with ethical demands must also direct, from time to time, the same responsibility toward itself. We remember this is what Jesus said to the religious leaders of his day:

"How can you say to your neighbor, 'Let me take the speck out of your eye,' while the log is in your own eye?" (Matt. 7:4, NRSV; par. Luke 6:41). How much the church, committed to prophetic witness in the world, is in need of such "prophetic self-criticism"! This is true of all churches, including the Presbyterian Church in Taiwan whose new confession of faith is discussed here.

We recognize that reconciliation understood in this threefold relationship that involves us human beings, creation, and God poses an enormous challenge. Reconciliation between God and human beings has traditionally preoccupied Christian piety and engaged Christian theology. It develops into doctrines of redemption and theories of atonement primarily concerned with the Christian community of redeemed believers separated from other human communities. But is reconciliation that does not go beyond the Christian community still reconciliation? Is it the reconciliation Jesus practiced in his life and ministry? Is it the message of reconciliation with which Paul says God has entrusted us? Reconciliation of Christians with God that brings about ir-reconcilability between them and others is no reconciliation. More and more Christians have come to realize this when they have to learn to coexist with people from other cultural backgrounds and religious traditions.

And the reconciliation of Christians with God that becomes so internalized that it turns a deaf ear to social and political contradictions cannot be the reconciliation intended by God. It is not the reconciliation Jesus risked his life to bring about in his community. It has nothing to do with what he believed to be his mission when he declared at the beginning of his ministry, quoting that soul-stirring passage from the Book of Isaiah, the prophet:

> The spirit of God is upon me because God has anointed me;
> God has sent me to announce good news to the poor,
> to proclaim release for prisoners and recovery of sight for the blind;
> to let the broken victims go free,
> to proclaim the year of God's favor.
>
> (Luke 4:18-19)

This is a far cry from reconciliation without tears and pain, the reconciliation that leaves oppressors unrepentant and injustice done to the victims of oppression unrequited. This kind of reconciliation only helps to perpetuate the status quo and becomes an obstacle in the transformation of life and world. Jesus would have nothing to do with it. It in fact represents everything against what he strove to bring about in his community.

In the world of conflicts and strife and not in the world of illusion enter-
tained by some Christians, reconciliation means liberation. This must be
what Jesus meant in his proclamation. To be reconciled to God means to
be whole again both in body and in spirit. It seeks freedom from economic
exploitation. It demands freedom for those women and men imprisoned
for the sake of conscience. It is conditional upon the setting free of victims of oppression. When things such as these happen, then reconciliation
becomes a reality, then the year of God's favor has arrived—the year of
liberation. Ultimately, reconciliation is liberation from the power of death
into the power of life. Reconciliation means, then, transfiguration of life.
It means rising from the dead. It means resurrection.

Life in All Fullness

Here we have come full circle. We began with Jesus' vision of God's reign.
How this vision has to be tested within the hard reality of life and the world
and, in the case of Jesus, under the shadow of the cross was the subject
that occupied us next. And since the reign of God takes place in human
community, our discussion led us to the witness to the epiphanies of God's
reign, beginning with Jesus and continuing with women and men through
the centuries. What has become evident to us is that the reign of God is
manifest when change occurs for the better in relationships that involve
human beings, the world, and God. We called this change transfiguration.
The story of Jesus' transfiguration is no other than the story of the reign of
God. And as the story of God's reign, it is also the story of the resurrection.
It is the story of how life can be lived in all fullness in spite of hardship,
suffering, and even death.

What is this life in all fullness like? How is the reign of God related
to this life in all fullness? An expression of faith made by the Christian
Workers Fellowship of Sri Lanka at the Eucharist gives us a glimpse of
that life in these words:

> We have made memorial of your death, O Christ
> Your resurrection's symbol we have seen
> Now filled with your undying life.
> In this Sacrament we have been
> United to you and one another.
> As we in fellowship have shared this food—
> Your gifts and symbols too of humankind's work
> So may all people for the common good
> Share in all the products of our earth!
> With this manna for our march we go

> Hopefully, joyfully to serve you more
> In the struggle to free all
> And in that struggle power to wrest
> For the working people then
> In the interests of all.
>
> In this way by your grace we can
> Help build a new society, a new humankind,
> A new heaven and a new earth.
> In your strength we now go forth.[30]

The prayer comes from men and women engaged in the experiment of life in all fullness, a life that shares in the life Jesus lived, the life of transfiguration in the midst of conflict and suffering.

The resurrection is not a denial of the past. It is sacrament of tears shed, pain sustained, and death remembered. This sacrament affirms that the tears shed are not in vain, that the pain sustained is the birthpang of hope, and that death is remembered not to be feared but to be transformed into life. Jesus is reported to have said to Martha grieving the death of Lazarus her brother: "I am the resurrection and I am life" (John 11:25). To celebrate the sacrament of life in the face of death is an act of faith. To believe in life resurrected from the ruins of human conflict comes from God who is the power of transformation. And to work toward change in the human condition is a calling in response to the vision of God's reign.

The entire life of Jesus is an act of that faith. His ministry is shaped by that power that transforms human conditions, be they individual, social, or religious. And his calling comes from that vision of God's reign that envisions the transfiguration of life and creation. The resurrection is, then, not a resuscitation of dead bodies. It is the rejuvenation, the renewal, or, even better, the re-creation of life—life of the entire creation. It is a second act of creation in contrast to the first act of creation. The expressions "first act of creation" and "second act of creation" can be misleading. They suggest that creation of life and re-creation of it take place at the beginning of time and at the end of time. The fact of the matter is that creation and re-creation are not to be regarded as something like quotation marks, marking the beginning of a quotation and the end of it, while having nothing substantial to do with the quotation itself between them. This is not what the resurrection as a sacrament of life means. The resurrection is a sacrament because life has to be created and re-created in this space and

---

30. Quoted by Jeffrey Abayasekera in "Ecclesiological Issues Emerging from the Experience of Para-Church and Action Groups: The Experience of the Christian Workers Fellowship," *Tradition and Innovation: A Search for a Relevant Ecclesiology in Asia* (Commission on Theological Concerns–CCA, 1983), 66–67.

time of ours. And it is a sacrament of God's reign, the sacrament Jesus enjoyed with the poor and the oppressed during his ministry, the sacrament he celebrated with his mother, his disciples, and his followers before he went out to the final showdown with the religious and political authorities,[31] and the sacrament he himself became on the cross in the depth of pain, suffering, and death. In this sense and in this sense only the resurrection is the sacrament of life not only for individual persons but for the world and for the entire creation. The truth of the matter, then, must be this:

> It is a simple fact that when Peter said to his friends up in Galilee, "You know, this Jesus whom they crucified and whom we loved so much is risen," the thoughts that went through these people's minds were not, "Oh, that means that there is eternal life for little me." That would be a rather odd way of making such a point. No, to them it meant that there was reason to believe that God's ultimate power of justice, vindicating the oppressed, the suppressed, and the martyred, had manifested itself.[32]

The resurrection is essentially the proclamation that the reign of God is here, that it is in the midst of us in the world. The resurrection life is life in the reign of God. To live that life is to live a life in all fullness in spite of the fact that it has to be lived in hardship, pain, and suffering. Jesus in what he said and did leaves no doubt that

> the kingdom [the reign of God] had taken a big step forward as one had been praying, hoping and dreaming for its coming. So that the issue of the most original Christian way of speaking about the end of life in the sign of the resurrection of Jesus was an issue that did not speak to the question of what is going to happen to my identity, but what is happening in and to the world. Is there reason to believe that justice will win out? It is a concern for where the world is going, not a concern for oneself.[33]

That is why the resurrection, to use our earlier expression, is a second act of creation. It is the transfiguration of life and the world not only at the end time but in the ongoing life and history of humankind.

Does this mean that the life of you and me has no significance in the resurrection? Is the risen Christ not related to us personally because he is related only to the world at large? The answer is of course no. But the

---

31. See "Who Were at the Last Supper?" in my *Jesus, the Crucified People*, 191–96.

32. Krister Stendahl, *Meanings: The Bible as Document and as Guide* (Philadelphia: Fortress Press, 1984), 198.

33. Ibid.

truth is that this "raising of the dead," this "faith's final and most daring utterance" is neither the result of our private search for the salvation of our souls nor the achievement of the ardent hope we cherish for eternal life after our death. Rather, the resurrection is "born of shared commitment and struggle"—our commitment to the common destiny of humanity in God's creation and our willingness to struggle for it within our own particular community. The resurrection must, then, be what is experienced as the epiphany of God's reign. That is why Jesus' life on earth, which is the supreme epiphany of God's reign, is already the resurrection life. That must also be why he, confronted with the death of Lazarus and surely the deaths of other men, women, and children who crossed his path, he is able to declare the resurrection and the life in the present tense. In short, "the life which the resurrection of Christ implies, and which will persuade the believer that his resurrection is true, is that which takes him beyond the individual and the private into the community which is committed to the offering of life to the world."[34]

The resurrection, in the statement of faith made by the Christian Workers Fellowship of Sri Lanka, cannot be separated from the experience of a community engaged in the construction of "a new society and a new humankind." What form does this new society have to take? How is it different from the old society? What makes humanity new? How is it distinct from the old humanity? The words recited by the members of the Christian Workers Fellowship at the common meal tell us what this new society and this new humanity must be like:

> We seek
> a revolution of mind and spirit,
> a revolution
> social, economic, political,
> an unceasing revolution
> in human relationships.
> Land to the tillers,
> factories to the workers
> leading to the realization
> of power
> by the working people
> in the interests of all.[35]

---

34. Peter Selby, *Look for the Living: The Corporate Nature of Resurrection Faith* (Philadelphia: Fortress Press, 1976), 177. The quotations cited in the same paragraph are also from the same source.

35. See Abayasekera, "Ecclesiological Issues Emerging from the Experience of Para-Church and Action Groups," 70f.

The word "revolution" occurs more than once in this eucharistic expression of faith. It does not mean taking up arms to fight the enemies. It does not refer to the overthrow of the oppressive powers by violent means.

Revolution does not always have to be bloody. There can be such a thing as a bloodless revolution. It is not for nothing that these words just cited are spoken at an *agape* meal, a love-feast, a fellowship dinner. What those who participate in the *agape* meal pray for is "a revolution of heart and mind," a radical repentance, a repentance that changes human beings and transforms human community. What can be a more urgent matter than radical repentance of this sort? When these words fall on deaf ears, when this prayer does not move the oppressors, and when this call to transfiguration of life and world goes unheeded, then a revolution, and a violent one at that, cannot be avoided. But do we human beings always have to be victims of the violence we commit against one another? History tells us that the answer, unfortunately, is often yes. But the reign of God Jesus taught and lived, the repentance of hearts and minds he made possible in not a small number of women and men through the centuries, and his cross that has transfigured a countless number of people, not only those inside the Christian church, but also some of those outside it, compel us also to answer no to the question.

The vision of Jesus' reign of God that becomes flesh in the epiphanies of God's reign in the hard realities of our world has to be the source of inspiration as we struggle for a new society and a new world. It empowers us to dare to dream of a new heaven and a new earth in the midst of the old heaven and the old earth. It enables us to perceive in the suffering Jesus the transfigured Christ and to encounter the risen Christ in the crucified Jesus. Is it not this vision we see, this dream we dream, and this faith we hold that is symbolized by the phoenix in a poem from Indian Malayalam literature that bears the name of that mythic creature?

> I will resurrect from the pyre
> Spreading my wings like petals
> Like the ember of a divine fire
> I reached the womb of the desert
> I sprouted forth like a pearly seed
> Flapping golden wings I flew high
> I shot forth like a golden plant
> Ripping open my womb of flames
> And I shot fiery arrows like a hunter
> As the summer thirsted for blood.

I fly singing shedding light
And shadow upon this revolving earth
And then green oases spring forth
And desert plants do flower
The desert becomes a golden song
That rises upward higher and higher
To the ebullient sun...

I turn myself a honey bee
I fly about, I sing my songs
As I with daring plumb the depth
Of music inexplicable, I burn
My burning feathers form a lighted lamp
At the altar of eternity
As I burn shedding light
I cease, gripped by nothingness.
But time bemourns my loss
And sheds its tears on my ashes
Tears on the ashes of my feathers, and then
Rising out of my ashes I will spread—
I will spread my rosy wings
And fly, singing as joyously as ever
In life human being may be defeated but never destroyed
Death does not have the final say.[36]

From desert to oases, from time to eternity, and from the ashes of death to a song of life! This is the resurrection of life. This is the transfiguration of the world.

This is the life and the world not only envisioned for the future but made possible in the present through justice won, freedom gained, and love fulfilled. What we have here is the operation called the reign of God against the forces of evil at work in human community to undermine what God intends for humanity and for creation. For this reason we can and we must pray with Jesus who taught us to pray saying: "Our God, your reign come, your will be done on earth as in heaven" (Luke 11:2 and Matt. 6:9-10). The whole life and ministry of Jesus is this prayer in action. In Jesus engaged in this prayer we are in the presence of him in the power of the Spirit—the Spirit who, as Jesus is said to have confided to his disciples in his farewell discourses, is the Spirit of truth that will guide us into all the

---

36. A poem by O. N. V. Kurup, quoted by K. M. Tharakan in "Images of Life and Death in Malayalam Literature," *Struggle against Death* (Kerala, India: Editorial Board for the Study Programme, 1982), 52–53.

truth (John 16:13). How this *Jesus in the Power of the Spirit* of the truth who will guide us into the truth and enlarge our vision of God's reign on earth as in heaven will be the subject of our continuing theological reflection in the third and final book of our series.

BIBLICAL INDEX

GENERAL INDEX